# Religion in America

# Religion in America

## Fifth Edition

## Julia Corbett Hemeyer

Professor of Religious Studies, Emerita
Ball State University

PEARSON

Prentice
Hall

Upper Saddle River, New Jersey 07458

Library of Congress Cataloging-in-Publication Data

Hemeyer, Julia Corbett
    Religion in America / Julia Corbett Hemeyer. — 5th ed.
      p. cm.
    Includes bibliographical references and index.
    ISBN 0-13-153914-0 (alk. paper)
    1. United States—Religion—1960- I. Title.
  BL2525.C67 2005
  200′.973—dc22                                         2004-060185
                                                          CIP

**VP, Editorial Director:** Charlyce Jones Owen
**Editorial Assistant:** Maureen Diana
**Marketing Manager:** Kara Kindstrom
**Marketing Assistant:** Jennifer Lang
**Production Liaison:** Marianne Peters Riordan
**Manufacturing Buyer:** Christina Helder
**Art Director:** Jayne Conte
**Cover Designer:** Bruce Kenselaar
**Cover Photo:** "Along the Mississinewa" by the author,
  copyright 2004 Julia Corbett Hemeyer.

**Director, Image Resource Center:** Melinda Reo
**Manager, Rights and Permission:** Zina Arabia
**Manager, Visual Research:** Beth Brenzel
**Manager, Cover Visual Research & Permission:**
  Karen Sanatar
**Image Permission Coordinator:** Craig A. Jones
**Composition/Full-Service Project Management:**
  Pietro Paolo Adinolfi/Preparé, Inc.
**Printer/Binder and Cover Printer:**
  Courier Companies, Inc.

Credits and aknowledgments borrowed from other sources and reproduced, with permission, in this textbook appear on appropriate page within text.

Pearson Education LTD.
Pearson Education Singapore, Pte. Ltd
Pearson Education, Canada, Ltd
Pearson Education — Japan
Pearson Education Australia PTY, Limited

Pearson Education North Asia Ltd
Pearson Educación de Mexico, S.A. de C.V.
Pearson Education Malaysia, Pte. Ltd
Pearson Education Upper Saddle River, New Jersey

**PEARSON**
Prentice
Hall

10 9 8 7 6 5 4 3 2 1

ISBN 0-13-153914-0

To my husband,
Tom,
with love and gratitude

and to Mike,
whose memory continues to bless my life

*For all that has been, thanks;*
*To all that shall be, yes.*

—Dag Hammarskjöld

# CONTENTS

# PREFACE

Far too often, when people discuss religion, the discussion becomes an unproductive and unpleasant argument about who is right and who is wrong. This does not have to be the case. The academic study of religion in the humanities offers a unique opportunity to learn about American communities of faith and practice in an atmosphere free of both judgment and partisan advocacy. It focuses on what each group does and believes and on what these practices and beliefs mean to those who participate in them. It does not evaluate whether those beliefs and practices are right or wrong nor does it make judgments about whether a religion is true or false. The academic study of religion does not judge and it does not advocate. It does not present religion as preferable to nonreligion nor does it favor secularity over religiousness. It does not attempt to make converts to or from any particular community of faith. Each community of faith is presented without its beliefs and practices being judged favorably or unfavorably.

Although religious beliefs and practices are presented impartially in this book, it is important that you know from the outset that this book is not value-free. I believe that religion is an important part of humanity's story. I also believe that nothing in the entire spectrum of human religiousness can be completely strange to any of us, because we are all human. I believe firmly in the freedom of religion that is guaranteed by the Constitution. In the climate of diversity that we have in the United States, respect for those who are different from ourselves is vitally important. I believe in the community of neighbors, not strangers. This is a community of dialogue, based on respect and the appreciation of differences. It is a community based on every individual's commitment to freedom of belief and freedom of religious practice within the boundaries of law.

You should be aware as you begin your study of religion in the United States that there is a vast distinction between religion as it is described in books—as I describe it in *this* book, for example—and religion as people actually live it. Many Jews and Christians do not attend corporate worship with any regularity, for example. Nor do they pray with the constancy their holy books instruct. Catholics do not necessarily follow their church's teachings about such personal matters as birth control and abortion. Some American Buddhists drink wine with dinner, in violation of a prohibition on intoxicants (which some read as a prohibition on intoxication). So do some Muslims, in the face of a similar prohibition. We choose from our religions' teachings those things that are personally meaningful to us and feel free to leave the rest alone. So when you meet actual Methodists or Hindus or Jews, they won't conform completely to what you have read. Their lives, however, *will* be informed at some level by their religious faith.

The fifth edition of *Religion in America* continues the emphasis on religious diversity in the United States that has always characterized this book. Correspondingly, there continues to be somewhat less emphasis on the religions of the majority. Attention is also given to responding to the religious diversity that surrounds us. Religious diversity makes the United States an ideal place to learn about religion, not only in books, but as it is embodied in the people with whom we come into contact every day.

This edition also continues the Web integration that began with the fourth edition. My Web site, *Perspectives on Faith*, can be accessed at *www.bsu.edu/web/jcorbett/relig*. All the Web references have been updated for this edition. Even so, the Web is a constantly changing medium, and sites that were available when I wrote this edition may no longer be current when you read it. So use the Perspectives site for more recently updated URLs.

There are several new features in this edition, as well. All the chapters on Christian communities of faith are together, with a new overview of Christian faith and practice. There is a completely new chapter (Chapter 3) on the conflicts and controversies in which religion has recently been involved, such as the sexual abuse scandal in the Catholic Church and the problem of religiously motivated violence. The material on the African-American religious experience in the United States has been thoroughly revised. You will find more about religion on college and university campuses, including new material on religious studies. Reading lists have been updated to reflect new scholarship in all areas of religious studies and religion in the United States.

I hope you will enjoy your study of religion in the United States. Religion, along with families and friends, work and creative endeavors, school and leisure time, helps to make life meaningful and good for most Americans. It is a fascinating and rewarding subject for study. Fundamentally, this is a book about people, because religion is about people. For most people in the United States, religion is also about something that transcends people, such as God or another higher reality. But it is always about people, what people believe and how they act in response to those beliefs. So this is a book about us, all of us, because even if we are not personally religious, our lives are influenced by the religiousness around us.

Books are always the product of far more people than just the author. Prentice Hall editor Ross Miller was responsible for getting this edition underway. Pietro Paolo Adinolfi supervised the details of the production process and was a true pleasure to work with. Many clergy and religious lay people provided information and encouragement. My former Department Chair, Dr. Juli Eflin, and former colleagues in the Department of Philosophy and Religious Studies at Ball State University have been, as always, unfailingly helpful and supportive. My colleagues at Ball Memorial Hospital have also supported my writing in many ways.

Our lives change continuously, often in ways we can neither imagine nor foresee. My husband of many years, Mike, died of cancer in 2001. Without the support of family, friends, colleagues, my religious community, and my faith, this edition would not have been possible. Ross Miller's willingness to extend me necessary extra time enabled me to finish this edition in spite of Mike's death, a subsequent relocation, and later remarriage. Special thanks also go to Chaplain Ken Nicola, for listening.

As I finish this edition, I am particularly thankful for Tom Hemeyer, whom I married in May of 2003. This edition is dedicated to him, as well as to Mike's memory.

# RELIGIOUS AMERICA:
# DIVERSITY AND FREEDOM

Before you begin to read this chapter, ask yourself what your attitude is toward those whose religion is different from your own. Do you feel curious? Interested to know more about them? Defensive? As if their religion is not "true" or "right"? Would you want to convince them of your own views? Do you think your own point of view might be enriched by dialogue with them?

Religious diversity in the United States and throughout the world is increasing. Today, all of us can expect to be part of communities, workplaces, and social groups that include people of many faiths and of none. The development and growth of this diversity is an important social phenomenon of our time and one that extends far beyond the confines of "religion":

> The radicalism of religious diversity is a fact of contemporary life and may well become the most significant feature in the development of society and culture in the twenty-first century. . . . A Muslim living in the United States today is not a Muslim only when he [or she] visits the mosque, recites *Allahu akbar*, or fasts during the sacred month of Ramadan. He is a Muslim when he votes in a local election, goes to market, visits a museum, or reads the newspaper. He is, indeed, a Muslim when he meets a Christian or a Jew in the local park.[1]

We encounter many other kinds of diversity also—racial, lifestyle, political, and sexual orientation, to name but a few. Thinking through our responses to religious diversity can help us be more conscious of how we respond to diversity of other kinds, as well. There is also a particular feature of religious diversity that should be noted. Most—although certainly not all—religions make claims to absolute truth. The existence of wide-ranging religious diversity coupled with absolute truth claims poses a particularly interesting challenge for thoughtful, reflective response.

[1]Richard Evans Wentz, *The Culture of Religious Pluralism* (Boulder, CO: Westview Press, 1998), p. 13.

## RESPONDING TO RELIGIOUS DIVERSITY

Each of the five responses described below stems from authentic human concerns. Many are grounded in the sacred writings of their proponents' religious tradition or in specific interpretations of those writings. Each has its adherents within most of the religions, as well as among the different religions. Different authors who write on responses to religious diversity may use the terms differently, as well.

We first need to distinguish all of these responses from *tolerance*, which may go along with any of them. Tolerance refers to the willingness to grant basic civil liberties to members of a faith other than one's own, regardless of how one feels about that other faith. Tolerance encompasses such things as willingness to grant the freedom to gather for religious meetings, to speak publicly in the hope of winning other people to one's viewpoint, and not to be discriminated against in matters of employment or housing, for example. A person who is tolerant may disagree, may be convinced that the other's position is simply wrong, but may still be willing to see the other person share these fundamental freedoms.

*Exclusivism* is the most clearly defined response. The exclusivist holds that, because religion deals with ultimate truth, there can be only one true or correct religion, and the rest are simply wrong. Exclusivism is found within most of humankind's religions. The following statement from *Evangelical Affirmations* provides a good example:

> Without Christ and the biblical gospel, sinful humanity is without salvation. . . . Any "gospel" without the Christ of the Bible cannot be the saving gospel, and leaves sinners estranged from God. . . . We affirm that only through the work of Christ can any person be saved and resurrected to live with God forever. Unbelievers will be separated eternally from God.[2]

Although exclusivism is a prominent response within the three monotheistic religions of Judaism, Christianity, and Islam, it is not wholly confined to them. Although mainstream Buddhism, for example, exhibits a great deal of openness toward other faiths, followers of Nichiren Shoshu Buddhism regard it as "the One True Way . . . whereby all the people are able to fundamentally overcome the basic universal sufferings of being born, of old age, sickness and death as well as doubts and disillusionments that plague mankind."[3]

At the opposite end of the response spectrum lies *relativism*. There are different forms of relativism, but all of them share the premise that all perspectives are limited, even those that lay claim to absolute truth. There is no

---

[2]Kenneth S. Kantzer and Carl F.H. Henry, eds., *Evangelical Affirmations* (Grand Rapids, MI: Zondervan Publishing House, 1990), pp. 30–31 and 36.
[3]Nichiren Shoshu United States Web site (www.nst.org/intro3.html).

unlimited viewpoint from which a truth that is relevant for all times, places, and persons could ever be known or expressed. This perception may lead the relativist in one of two directions: One approach is to maintain that, because religions claim absolute truth and absolute truth cannot be known, no religion is worthy of one's commitment. This approach leads to secularism or irreligiousness. Another kind of relativism, however, holds that, in the absence of knowable absolute truth, it is simply up to individuals to pick the religion that feels right for them.

A third approach is that of *inclusivism*. The inclusivist holds that there is one true or best religion, one that holds within itself the fullness of religious truth and human salvation. However, inclusivists believe there is something of this truth in some other religions, as well. Most Muslims believe, for example, that the revelation of God to the Jews and the Christians was true and brought salvation to its followers, but that it had been distorted by Muhammad's time. God's revelation to Muhammad is believed to confirm the truth of earlier revelations, while eliminating the distortions. The Second Vatican Council of the Catholic Church also affirmed an inclusivist view:

> From ancient times down to the present, there has existed among diverse peoples a certain perception of that hidden power which hovers over the course of things and over the events of human life; at times, indeed, recognition can be found of a Supreme Divinity and of a Supreme father too. Such a perception and such a recognition instills the lives of these peoples with a profound religious sense. . . . The Catholic church rejects nothing of what is true and holy in these [non-Christian] religions. . . . Yet she proclaims and is in duty bound to proclaim without fail, Christ who is the way, the truth, and the life (John 14:6). In him, in whom God reconciled all things to himself (2 Corinthians 5:18–19), men find the fullness of their religious life.[4]

The fourth position may be called *synthesis*. This view holds that all religions are essentially the same underneath a veneer of cultural particularity. The differences among the religions are downplayed in favor of the similarities among them. Thus, all will—or at least should—come together into a unity. This point of view is often associated with the New Age Movement:

> In the New Age, it is believed, people will recognize only one universal religion. While that one religion will assume many different forms. . . . the same mystical faith (i.e., the Truth) will underlie each grouping, no matter what label . . . it chooses.[5]

Hindu theologian and former president of India Sarvepalli Radhakrishnan takes a similar position, believing that what he calls *Sanatana Dharma* (the

---

[4]Walter Abbott, ed., *The Documents of Vatican II* (New York: Guild Press, 1966), pp. 661–663.
[5]"Introductory Essay: An Overview of the New Age Movement," *New Age Encyclopedia*, ed. J. Gordon Melton, Jerome Clark, and Aidan A. Kelly (Detroit, MI: Gale Research, Inc., 1990), p. xvi.

**Figure I-1**    The Baha'i House of Worship, located just north of Chicago on the shore of Lake Michigan at Wilmette, Illinois. The nine-sided building symbolizes the unity of all religions. It is listed in the National Register of Historic Places. *(Photo courtesy of Baha'i Publishing Trust.)*

"eternal religion," a name often used by Hindus to describe their faith) is the one religious reality that encompasses all others and toward which all others will eventually evolve. As human beings collectively mature religiously, the various manifestations of religion will converge on "the One Spirit which takes us beyond the historical formulations," which are only "imperfect halting expressions."[6]

The relatively recent world faith of Baha'i also holds a view that humankind is evolving toward one world religion. For Baha'is, one world religion is an aspect of a larger view that there will gradually come about a global civilization that includes a worldwide government, judicatory system, and currency. The authors of *The Baha'i Faith: The Emerging Global Religion* state that "in reality, there is only one religion, the religion of God."[7] Baha'u'llah, the founder of Baha'i, is quoted as saying that "all nations should become one in faith and all men as brothers; that the bonds of affection and unity between

---

[6]Sarvepalli Radhakrishnan, "Religion and Religions" in *Relations Among Religions Today*, ed. Moses Jung et al. (Leiden, 1963), pp. 131–132.
[7]William S. Hatcher and J. Douglas Martin, *The Baha'i Faith: The Emerging Global Religion* (New York: Harper & Row, Publishers, 1985), p. 82.

the sons of men should be strengthened; that diversity of religion should cease, and differences of race be annulled. . . ."[8]

The fifth response might be described as the *affirmation of religious diversity*. This view holds that the different religions are simply different, not headed toward a synthesis and not subsumable under the big umbrella of inclusivism. At the same time, each is ultimately true and must be honored as such. Affirmation has room for both commitment and openness. Describing this perspective, religious studies scholar Harold Coward writes:

> It is a recognition that deep religious commitment is necessarily felt as absolute and, as such, functions as the validating criteria for all of one's personal experience. This, however, does not impose it on others or rule out the recognition that in other persons there is a similar absolute commitment to a particular experience, which . . . will be different from one's own. . . . Thus, one is able to honor one's own commitment as absolute for oneself and at the same time respect the different absolute commitments of others. . . . In a dialogue this would mean the preservation of our differences in dignity and mutual respect.[9]

In discussing how such dialogue could go forward, Coward notes it requires that people have accurate information about one another's religions. In light of the fact that many persons are not well informed about their own religion, nor those of others, the academic study of religion has an important role to play. It facilitates dialogue informed throughout by accurate information and animated by a spirit of inquiry and respect for the commitments of others without compromising one's own commitments.

In her thorough discussion of this stance, which she labels "pluralism," Diana Eck, Director of Harvard University's Pluralism Project, notes these five points that help to clarify what an affirming stance is, as well as how it differs from some of the other views we have described:[10]

- It is not just the fact of religious diversity but "active positive engagement with it."
- It is not simply tolerance and a commitment to insure the rights of the followers of many faith traditions but "the active effort to understand difference and commonality through dialogue."
- While relativism does not allow for commitment, affirmation assumes that members of the different communities of faith are deeply committed to their chosen paths while practicing openness toward the chosen paths of others.
- It does not expect all religious to fuse together but looks for "ways to be distinctively ourselves and yet to be in relation to one another."

[8]Quoted in J.E. Esslemont, *Baha'u'llah and the New Era: An Introduction to the Baha'i Faith* (Wilmette, IL: Baha'i Publishing Trust, 1950), pp. 117–118.

[9]Harold Coward, *Pluralism: Challenge to World Religions* (Maryknoll, NY: Orbis Books, 1985), pp. 106–107.

[10]Diana Eck, *Encountering God: A Spiritual Journey from Bozeman to Benares* (Boston: Beacon Press, 1993), pp. 191–199. Professor Eck's book remains one of the best accounts of the perspective I take in this book.

- The foundation of affirmation is interreligious dialogue based on understanding rather than on agreement, holding that the understanding of difference is as important as agreement.

In his book on religious pluralism in the United States, scholar Richard Evans Wentz highlights three characteristics of the affirming attitude.

- It *respects* the religious "others" who share our space. Respect means being able to imagine their way of being religious as something that might have meaning for ourselves.
- It is *reverent*, a deepening of respect "to the point of honor and caring."
- Finally, it issues in *refinement*, the capacity to imagine "the kind of existence in which respect and reverence have exalted the human enterprise and lifted that enterprise to a new order of beauty and harmony."[11]

The attitude that we hold toward those whose religion differs from our own has pragmatic ramifications as well as philosophical ones. For example, it influences our willingness to grant freedom of religious expression to them. A Christian pluralist, for example, would be more likely to *willingly* give a Muslim employee time off from work during Ramadan, Islam's holy month, than would a Christian exclusivist. A college student whose approach was pluralistic would respond differently to a roommate of another faith than would a student who was an exclusivist. Our attitude toward religions other than our own also helps determine whether we try to "convert" others to our own viewpoint.

A recent event in Muncie, Indiana, where I live and work, illustrated the tensions that can arise from religious diversity. The organizers of the 2003 National Day of Prayer observance, which was held at City Hall in April, said that, while those of any faith could attend, only Christian prayers could be spoken. This led to an "alternative" observance, also at City Hall, in which Christians, a Jew, a Muslim, Hindus, a Buddhist, a Baha'i, a Unitarian Universalist, a Wiccan, and a nonbeliever, all participated. Both observances were well attended. There was newspaper coverage of the conflict and a flurry of letters to the editor that far exceeded anything I'd seen in the local paper before. On the one hand, this event called attention to the conflict and divisiveness of the religious issues involved. However, it also drew intense and sustained attention to religious diversity.

### QUESTIONS AND ACTIVITIES FOR REVIEW, DISCUSSION, AND WRITING

1. What two features make religious diversity in the United States an especially interesting issue for reflective thought?
2. Describe each of the five responses to religious diversity.
3. Describe the affirmative response in greater detail.

---

[11]Wentz, *The Culture of Religious Pluralism*, pp. 114–117.

4. Write an essay in which you describe your own attitude toward religious diversity. Be sure that you include any ideas you may have about *why* you feel as you do.
5. With several classmates, role-play different ways that members of one religion might approach members of another.
6. Visit the Ontario Consultants for Religious Tolerance Web site (www.religioustolerance.org), and read one of the essays. Write a response to what you have read. Be certain to include the title of the essay that you read.

### FOR FURTHER READING

In a book such as this, we look at world religions as they are found in the United States. Any of the following three books provides additional information on world religions.

ELLWOOD, ROBERT, and BARBARA MCGRAW, *Many Peoples, Many Faiths: An Introduction to the Religious Life of Humankind*, 7th ed. Upper Saddle River, NJ: Prentice Hall, 2001. This and the Fisher book that follows are good standard introductory texts.

FISHER, MARY PAT, *Living Religions: A Brief Introduction*. Upper Saddle River, NJ: Prentice Hall, 2001. This is an easily accessible, brief introduction that does not, however, oversimplify. I use it in my world religions classes.

SHARMA, ARVIND, ed., *Our Religions*. San Francisco: HarperSanFrancisco, 1993. Professor Sharma's book is especially valuable because it is a collection of essays written by people who are both religious studies scholars and adherents of the faiths they describe.

Three recent books that focus on religious diversity itself are worthy of attention.

ECK, DIANA L., *A New Religious America: How A "Christian Country" Has Become the World's Most Religiously Diverse Nation*. San Francisco: HarperSanFrancisco, 2001.

LIPPY, CHARLES H., *Pluralism Comes of Age: American Religious Culture in the Twentieth Century*. Armonk, NY: M.E. Sharpe, Inc., 2001. Lippy traces the development of pluralism through the twentieth century in this well-written and researched monograph.

PORTERFIELD, AMANDA, *The Transformation of American Religion: The Story of a Late-Twentieth-Century Awakening*. New York: Oxford University Press, 2001.

The following general works provide information about the range of religion and religions in the United States.

GAUSTAD, EDWIN, and LEIGH SCHMIDT, *The Religious History of America: The Heart of the American Story from Colonial Times to Today*. San Francisco: HarperSanFrancisco, 2002. A fully revised and updated edition of an historical approach first published in 1966. The authors have increased the emphasis on pluralism, religious practice, the interfaces of politics and religion, and religious seeking.

LEON, LUIS, and GARY LADERMAN, Eds., *Religion and American Cultures: An Encyclopedia of Traditions, Diversity, and Popular Expressions*. Santa Barbara, CA: ABC-CLIO, 2003. The editors are especially concerned to document diversity in religions and cultures in the United States. Good coverage of popular religion not found in the Melton work.

MELTON, J. GORDON, *The Encyclopedia of American Religions*, 7th ed. Detroit, MI: Gale Research, 2002. This book is a thorough and unbiased presentation of information about both consensus and alternative religions that is very carefully indexed.

NEUSNER, JACOB, Ed., *World Religions in America*, 3rd ed. Louisville, KY: Westminster John Knox Press, 2003. The authors of the chapters in Neusner's book focus on how each of the religions is present in the United States. There is new material on Scientology, nature religions, and Baha'i, and the chapter on Islam has been expanded.

### RELEVANT WORLD WIDE WEB SITES

The Interfaith Alliance: www.interfaithalliance.org

The Ontario Consultants for Religious Tolerance: www.religioustolerance.org

The Pluralism Project: www.fas.harvard.edu/~pluralsm

United Communities of Spirit: www.origin.org/ucs/home.cfm

These and other sites relevant to religious diversity can be accessed through the "Interfaith and Ecumenical Sites" Web page at the *Perspectives on Faith* Web site: www.bsu.edu/web/jcorbett/relig.

# STUDYING AND
# DESCRIBING RELIGION

---

Before you read this chapter, think about how and where you have learned about religion so far. What kinds of things did you study? What was the purpose of your study? Also, think about how *you* define religion. All of us have some idea of what religion is. What does the word *religion* mean to you?

---

## WHY STUDY RELIGION?

Many, perhaps most, of you reading this are studying religion to receive academic credit for a course. But there are other reasons for studying religion. Those of us who are religious study our own religion to learn more about a significant dimension of our lives. Our commitment to it matures as we base our devotion on greater knowledge and understanding.

Why study other people's religions? Doing so can help us to understand other people. Religion is an important, even essential, part of many people's lives, and by understanding and appreciating it, we come to know them better. Prejudice often results in part from a simple lack of knowledge and information. While knowledge and understanding do not guarantee freedom from prejudice, a lack of knowledge greatly increases the likelihood of prejudice.

It is also important that we understand religion because it has had an important role in history and continues to have a significant impact on contemporary events. Religion has had and continues to have an impact on cultural forms such as literature, art, and music. Finally, because all religions have deeply human roots, to understand anyone's religion helps us understand ourselves better. By understanding the similarities and differences between our own religion and those of other people, we also come to know our own better.

Statements by notable religious studies scholars highlight several important themes, including the practical applicability of religious studies, that help to relate the study of religion to the discussion of religious diversity:

Martin Marty points out that faith,

> both in individually packaged and communal forms, while it may not always be deep, is so widespread that it commends itself for study by anyone who wants to understand humans.

He continues that in our diverse culture, religion both defines and links subcultures. For example, a person may be identified primarily as an African American *Baptist* in one setting, while being more identified as an *African American* Baptist in another. Similarly, one can be both a *Catholic* feminist and a Catholic *feminist*.[1]

> By involving many young Americans in studying a variety of different religious traditions and at the same time relieving them of the requirement of loyalty to any particular tradition, religious studies contributed to the rise of eclectic forms of spirituality characteristic of American culture since the sixties.
>
> While contributing to a consumerist approach to religious life, . . . religious studies also had a stabilizing effect on religions's role in American public life. . . . [It] encouraged respect for religious difference along with increased self-consciousness about how religious symbols work and a general tendency to understand religion in humanistic terms. . . . [Religious] studies contributed to greater understanding of the ways in which religion functions to divide people from one another and the ways in which it could function to promote equality and build community. . . .
>
> Through its approach to religion as a universal human phenomenon manifest in a variety of different cultural forms, religious studies has contributed to the respect for religious difference that distinguishes the United States from countries where religious difference feeds violence and civil war.[2]

## STUDYING RELIGION AS A PART OF THE HUMANITIES

The study of religion has many dimensions. Studying religion as a part of a course of study in the humanities may involve attitudes and methods that are new to you.

Most of us who think about religion first learned to do so in a religious organization or a community of faith, or perhaps within our families. Maybe it was in preparation to become a member of a church or synagogue.[3] Perhaps it was learning about our own religion in Sunday school or Hebrew day school classes. For some, it was probably learning the prayers of our faith from our

---

[1] Martin E. Marty, "An Exuberant Adventure: The Academic Study and Teaching of Religion," in *Religious Studies News*, Vol. 12, No. 3 (September, 1997), p. 20.
[2] Amanda Porterfield, *The Transformation of American Religion: The Story of A Late-Twentieth-Century Awakening* (New York: Oxford University Press, 2001), p. 203–204.
[3] A *synagogue* is a Jewish place of worship and study.

parents. This way to study religion is sometimes called *theology*. This is study undertaken by members of a community of faith when they learn or study the practices and beliefs of their own religion. Therefore, we can call it an "inside" perspective. It usually involves the personal faith commitments of both teachers and students. It is, in Saint Anselm's classic definition, "faith seeking understanding."[4] Theology uses intellectual concepts to understand a particular religious tradition and to express its relevance for the present. It takes as its beginning point the faith of the community, the "givens" accepted as a part of their tradition. For Christians, for example, the uniqueness of Jesus and Jesus's special role in God's plan for the world is such a given. For Jews, the oneness of God has a similar role. Buddhists[5] take the early teachings of the Buddha as foundational. These starting points are often found in or derived from the group's sacred writings.

The goal of this kind of study is that those who engage in it will become more knowledgeable about and more committed to their faith. It does not have to involve assertions of the superiority of one's own faith, although it sometimes does. It is an important part of educating people in their faith and helping them to mature as religious persons. It is a significant aspect of the growth and development of any religion. A firm understanding of one's own faith is also one foundation for dialogue with others.

The **academic study of religion** differs from theology in that it makes no assumptions about the beliefs, or lack of beliefs, of the scholar. Religious studies teachers and students alike may be believers, nonbelievers, or agnostics (people who believe that we cannot be certain about religious matters) in their personal religious lives.

Rather than concentrating on one religion, the academic study of religion promotes a lively awareness of the diversity of religious beliefs, practices, and experiences that people have. It encourages open-minded investigation of that diversity. It investigates religions in their historical and cultural settings and examines a broad range of materials to provide the most balanced treatment possible. It distinguishes between things that most people accept as historical facts and other things that are taken as true only within the context of a particular community of faith. For example, most people in the United States would agree that the founder of Christianity was an historical person named Jesus who lived in the area of Nazareth. Non-Christians usually do not accept that Jesus was in a unique sense the Son of God.

In studying religion from an academic standpoint, we may try to *explain* religious behaviors and beliefs as well as simply *describe* them. You will see a number of examples of this in Chapter 13. However, such explanations should never become *reductionistic*. Reductionism is an oversimplification

---

[4]Saint Anselm was a Christian theologian who lived between 1033 and 1109 C.E. The abbreviations C.E. for Common Era and B.C.E. for Before the Common Era have replaced A.D. (*Anno Domini*, the year of our Lord) and B.C. (Before Christ) in most scholarly writing.

[5]You will learn more about Buddhism in Chapter 12.

**Figure 1-1**    The study of religion is an integral part of education in the humanities. *(Photo by the author.)*

that claims to exhaust the meaning of a phenomenon by explaining it in terms of some other, external factor. For example, saying that people are religious because economic deprivation in their earthly lives makes "pie in the sky by-and-by" attractive is a case of reductionism. While there may be some truth to this for some persons, it does not exhaust the meaning of religion.

When we study religion academically, the study takes place in an atmosphere that is free of advocacy. It promotes neither religion nor nonreligion. It educates about all religions and neither favors nor belittles any. It is loyal first of all to the guidelines of public scholarship. Its commitments are to knowledge and understanding for their own sake and to religion as a vigorous dimension of humanity's story (Figure 1–1). It does not involve the personal beliefs of its teachers and students. It is especially important to keep the distinction between theology and the academic study of religion clear in public, tax-supported schools, colleges, and universities. An institution supported by taxes paid by people of all faiths and by those who are not religious cannot favor one religion over others. Nor can it favor either religion or secularity. To do so clearly violates the disestablishment clause of the First Amendment to the Constitution. Our personal religious views *might* change when we study religion academically, but, if that happens, it is a personal by-product of the study and not its goal.

A recent study[6] looked at how religion was studied on four college campuses in the United States. One was a state university, two were religiously-supported schools, and the fourth was an historically black college that

[6]Conrad Cherry, Betty A. DeBerg, and Amanda Porterfield, *Religion on Campus: What Religion Really Means to Today's Undergraduates* (Chapel Hill: The University of North Carolina Press, 2000).

described itself as non-denominational. This study of four representative institutions found several common themes:

- Religious studies was a "vital and appealing" topic on all four campuses.
- In addition to religious studies classes, religion was a topic in many other classes, as well.
- General education and core curriculum classes, especially, exposed many students to the study of religion as a part of their educational experience.
- Even at the religiously-sponsored schools, teachers did not try to convert students to their own point of view. Students at all four schools felt free to express their own views in classes. Religious studies classes in the religiously-affiliated schools tended to promote religion more than did their secular counterparts. Religious diversity and pluralism were freely acknowledged, and critical inquiry into religion was encouraged.
- That having been said, faculty often tried to relate course content to students' own lives and spiritual journeys. Students made this connection even when faculty did not.

The 1963 United States Supreme Court decision in *Abington* v. *Schempp* ruled that public schools and school personnel could not mandate devotional activities in their schools and classrooms. People who favored activities such as prayer and Bible reading in the public schools charged that the Court had, in effect, supported the religion of secularism (nonreligion). Justice Clark, in replying to this charge, distinguished between the *practice* of religion, such as devotional exercises, and *study about* religion. He went on to say that study about religion as a part of human culture and the humanities is well within the guidelines established by the First Amendment to the Constitution. This Supreme Court decision allows for the academic study of religion at all levels of public education.

Religious groups cannot be barred from using public school facilities or other public buildings, however. If secular groups can use these facilities, then religious groups must have the same privilege The *Equal Access Act* was passed by the 98th Congress in 1984 and upheld by the Supreme Court in *Board of Education of Westside Community School District* v. *Mergens* (1990). For example, if a school board permits such noncurricular clubs as a chess club or Boy or Girl Scouts to use their facilities for meetings, then a Bible study club must have the same right. Usually, interpretation holds that teachers or other school personnel may not be officially involved in such groups. If a city or county building has a public meeting room, then religious groups must be allowed to use it on the same basis as secular groups. The combined effect of *Abington* v. *Schempp* and *Mergens* is that schools cannot actively promote religious activities, but neither can they prohibit them.

You may be wondering whether religious studies is defined by having a distinctive method or a distinctive subject matter. Religious studies scholars do not agree on the answer. In my opinion, religious studies is a distinct and identifiable academic discipline because it investigates the subject of religion in all its forms. Its *subject matter* is distinctive. In its investigation of its subject, it uses many methods. Human religious behavior is a very complex phenomenon and calls for many investigative tools. There is no single best way to study religion. A variety of methods is necessary, and no one of them can claim primary authority.

Within the academic study of religion, we can distinguish two interrelated types of inquiry. The **social-scientific study of religion** focuses on observation and on data that are quantifiable. Its goal is to be as objective as possible. The data that it provides makes a crucial contribution to our understanding of religion. Psychologists and sociologists who study human religious behavior often use social-scientific methods. The widespread use of computers for data processing and analysis has greatly enhanced this branch of the academic study of religion.

People **study religion as a part of the humanities** to understand a religious group, belief, or practice from the standpoint of what it is like for those who follow it. This approach encourages students and teachers to enter empathically into the life and experience of the religious "other." It seeks imaginative participation, developing what can be described as an "inside-outside" point of view. We can, with practice, become increasingly able to see religions other than our own *as if* from the inside, while remaining on the outside. We do not become followers, but we learn to value and appreciate the meaning that the religion has for those who are participants in it.

The academic study of religion may come under attack from either of two sides. On one side are traditional believers who are threatened by any viewpoint that refuses to judge the truth or falsity of religious beliefs. On the other side are those who refuse to take religion seriously and think that it must be explained away in terms of social, psychological, or economic factors. As a philosopher of religion Ninian Smart writes, in either case, people "forget that religions are what they are and have the power they have regardless of what we may think about their value, truth, or rationality. They also forget that . . . we have to listen to one another"[7] in a nation that is as religiously diverse as the United States.

Perhaps you have felt one of these two ways at times, or perhaps you do now. You might occasionally find yourself feeling threatened by some of the material studied, by the way it is studied, or by your classmates' comments. Remember that the study of religion from an academic viewpoint allows everyone ideological space in which to exist. All that is required is that you extend to the beliefs and practices of others the same respect that you wish for your own.

---

[7]Ninian Smart, *Worldviews: Crosscultural Explorations of Human Beliefs* (New York: Charles Scribner's Sons, 1983), p. 17.

## The World Wide Web: A Resource for Studying Religion

The World Wide Web is one of the most important—perhaps *the* most important—information resource to emerge in the twentieth century. Its eventual impact on human culture will rank with that of Gutenberg's invention of the printing press.

A recent survey by the Pew Internet and American Life Project found that slightly more than one-fourth of American adults who use the Internet have used it to find information about religion or spirituality. The greatest use was for educational or reference purposed, seeking knowledge and information.[8]

There is a great deal of information about religion and religions on the Web, and more appears daily. The Web is about communication—about people sharing information and gathering information. When information about religion, religious groups, and religious issues is presented on the Web, people of faith have the chance to speak for themselves, rather than an "outsider" speaking about them. When we visit Web sites, we have access to this information in whatever way suits us best. We can read and/or listen (many sites include sound) without feeling pressured to respond. We can read, reflect, come back and read again if we wish. The nature of the Web is such that we can always explore further along the same path, down a variety of side trails, or in another direction entirely.

### Evaluating Resources on the Web

One of the great strengths of the Web, in my opinion, is that anyone who has access to the appropriate hardware, software, and server, and even a modicum of skill, can create a Web page. It is, in other words, an extremely democratic, egalitarian environment. However, this characteristic brings with it a set of problems that concern evaluating what we find on the Web. When you go to a library to do research, or when you read a textbook, you make certain assumptions: the people who write articles for encyclopedias or for scholarly journals and the authors of textbooks are qualified to do what they've done. The material has been carefully reviewed by other scholars in the area. It probably has been reviewed by the library staff as a part of its collections development. *You simply cannot make these assumptions about any material on the World Wide Web.* Material on the Web is in this respect more similar to articles in popular magazines, although even there, editors exercise at least some control over the content of articles. No one owns the Internet or the Web; therefore, no one other than the consumer of its resources has a vested interest in

---

[8]"Internet Use and Spirituality," *AHP Perspective*, Association for Humanistic Psychology, April/May, 2003, p. 9.

the quality of what is published on it. Thus, an important part of becoming a savvy consumer of Web resources is carefully evaluating what you find there.

### Perspectives on Faith: A Web Site for Inquiry about Religion

I have developed and maintain a World Wide Web site specifically designed to help students locate Web resources that are relevant to religious studies courses. It provides numerous links to religion-related sites on the Web. The URL for this site is:

www.bsu.edu/web/jcorbett/relig

### DESCRIBING RELIGION

*Religion* is an ambiguous word. People use it to mean various things. Even scholars in religious studies cannot agree on its meaning. We do, nonetheless, have some idea of what religion is. If someone asks, for example, "What religion do you practice?" we know how to answer the question. If someone mentions a religious service, we have a general idea of what sort of activity is meant.

By itself, this everyday, unreflective approach is inadequate. It is probably limited to our own experiences with religion. Our understanding might be biased in some way, based on what we have been taught about religion. People's everyday definitions differ, and the same person may use different definitions at different times.

For purposes of study, we must have a good working description. A *working description* is one that is useful and adequate, but it is not the only possible one, nor even the only good one.

**1. A good working description of religion is broad enough to include all religions**. It should not define religion in a way that leaves out some manifestations of religion. Nor should it leave out any specific religion. For example, if we say that religion means belief in God (having in mind God as Jews and Christians think about God), we will leave out those people who worship many deities (a general word meaning "gods or goddesses") and those who worship none at all. This description also focuses on belief and excludes other important dimensions of religion.

**2.** At the same time, **it must be sufficiently specific to distinguish religion from other similar things**, such as a nonreligious philosophy of life or a deeply held and passionate commitment to a social or political cause.

**3. It also needs to be as free of prejudice or bias as we can make it**. Descriptions that state what true or genuine religion is often fall into the trap of imposing one person's or group's bias on the description of religion generally.

**Figure 1-2**

---

**WORKING DESCRIPTION OF RELIGION**

A *developed religion* is an integrated system of beliefs, lifestyle, ritual activities, and social institutions by which individuals give meaning to (or find meaning in) their lives by orienting themselves to what they take to be holy, sacred, or of the highest value.

---

We will use the working description given in Figure 1–2. It is important to know and understand this description, because it underlies everything that follows throughout the book.

Religions are also **communities of faith and practice**. They are groups of people knitted together by their shared commitment to a common worldview and their participation in shared experiences. The nature of religious commitment and experience means that it often claims its adherents' greatest, most intense loyalties. The ties within communities of faith are frequently among the strongest and most meaningful of human relationships.

Let's discuss this description of religion in greater detail. A developed religion is an *integrated system*. Ideally, all the dimensions in a religion hold together to make a comprehensive, coherent whole. Its various parts work together without conflict and with mutual support. The extent to which this is the case varies from one religion to another and from one person to another. But ideally, a religion does have coherence among its various dimensions. These dimensions include beliefs, a lifestyle, rituals, and institutions.

**Belief** takes many forms. Beliefs are the ideas of a religion. For example, most religions have an idea about what the purpose of human life is. Most have beliefs concerning how the world came into being and what happens to people after death. These beliefs are found in scripture, statements of faith, creeds (official written statements), hymns, stories, and theology books, to name but a few locations. The beliefs of a community of faith also exist in what its members actually affirm as truth for themselves.

Nearly all religions have guidelines for their members' daily **lifestyle**. These include codes of conduct and standards of behavior, as well as carefully worked out ethical systems. They involve both formal requirements and customs and less formal folkways and habits. Examples include dietary regulations followed by Jews and Seventh-day Adventists and dress codes followed by certain Christian groups and many Muslims.

Religions also include **ritual activities**. These are the ceremonial actions, usually repetitive in nature, that people perform as a part of their religious behavior. Religious rituals include worship, along with prayer, chanting, meditation, the lighting of candles, pilgrimages, and the devotional reading of religious books, to name but a few examples. There are religious rituals that are public and corporate, and there are those that individual people and families do privately. For many religious people, the rhythm of regular participation in the ritual life of their religion is more important than is reflection on religious beliefs.

Finally, although religion has to do with individual people, it also includes **social institutions**. Like-minded people join together for instruction, for rituals, and for fellowship. Structures for governance and decision making are necessary. Also in this category are arrangements for admitting members to the group and expelling them from it, educational functions, and arrangements for the selection, training, and support of leaders.

Religion is one way that **people give meaning to or find meaning in their lives**. A religion is a human creation or development. Its beliefs, lifestyle, rituals, and institutions are the products of human thought and activity. It is continuous with the many other ways that we either create or find meaning in our lives, such as through the personal relationships that are dear to us, the work that we do, and the values, ideals, and causes to which we give our loyalty. Religion is continuous with these other structures of meaning and shares their profoundly human roots.

Religion involves that which people take to be **sacred, holy, divine,** or **of the highest value**. Although religion is continuous with other structures of meaning, it is also unique. Most interpretations of religion hold that its uniqueness is in its reference to the sacred or to the highest value. It reaches beyond the individual and the ordinary concerns of day-to-day living. Religion puts us in touch with the sense of mystery that glimmers through the cracks of our common world. It has to do with the most comprehensive, fullest expression or embodiment of reality.

### QUESTIONS AND ACTIVITIES FOR REVIEW, DISCUSSION, AND WRITING

1. Write a paragraph in which you explain what you hope to gain from your study of religion in the United States. Are your goals academic, personal, or a combination of both? Compare your answer with those of other people.
2. Visit the American Academy of Religion Web site (www.aarweb.org) to learn how they answer the question, "Why study religion?" Look at the Overview and Mission Statement especially.
3. Take an issue in which religion has been involved, such as the abortion controversy or recent Middle Eastern wars, and analyze it from the perspective of theology, the social-scientific study of religion, and the humanities approach to the study of religion.
4. Ask several of your friends how they describe religion, and compare their answers. How are they alike? Different?
5. Look up the definition of religion in any standard dictionary, and write an essay in which you evaluate it based on what you have learned in this chapter.
6. If you are a part of a religious group, think about how the four dimensions of religion we discussed apply to it.

### FOR FURTHER READING

CAPPS, WALTER H., *Religious Studies: The Making of a Discipline*. Minneapolis, MN: Fortress Press, 1995. Capps's book is lucid and well-written, a very thorough introduction to the history and methods of the study of religion. Capps is a well-known scholar in the field. This is highly recommended.

CUNNINGHAM, LAWRENCE S., and JOHN KELSAY, et al. *The Sacred Quest: An Invitation to the Study of Religion*. 3<sup>rd</sup> ed. Upper Saddle River, NJ: Prentice Hall, 2001. This book, along with the Monk book, is a good introductory text that focuses on what religion is and how we can best begin to study and understand it.

MONK, ROBERT C., et al. *Exploring Religious Meaning*, 6th ed. Upper Saddle River, NJ: Prentice Hall, 2002.

A number of journals are relevant to the study of religion. Representative ones include the *Journal of the American Academy of Religion*, the *Journal of Biblical Literature*, *Sociology of Religion*, the *Journal for the Scientific Study of Religion*, and *Religion and American Culture: A Journal of Interpretation*.

## RELEVANT WORLD WIDE WEB SITES

The American Academy of Religion: www.aarweb.org

The Society for Biblical Literature: www.sbl-site.org

The Center for the Study of Religion and American Culture: www.iupui.edu/~raac

# RELIGION IN THE LIFE OF
# THE UNITED STATES

The United States has become known for its freedom of religion. People decide for themselves whether they will be a part of a religious group, and, if so, which one. Before reading this chapter, stop and think about what freedom of religion means to you personally. How important is it to you? In what specific ways does it affect your life? Do you think there should be limits on religious freedom? If so, what should they be, and why do you think they are necessary?

## DISESTABLISHMENT AND THE CONSTITUTION

Prior disillusionment with established religion and the existence of religious pluralism worked against the continued existence of established religion in the United States. The American experience with established churches was influenced by the experience of European settlers who were forced to flee from establishments of religion in their home countries. It was also influenced by the experiments with pluralism and freedom of religion that had been carried out in Rhode Island and Pennsylvania. Many people concluded that civil power and privilege for churches led to problems, while toleration and equality under the law was good for both the churches and society at large.[1] In addition, no single religious group had enough support throughout the original thirteen states to make its belief and practice the law of the land. Furthermore, the framers of the Constitution held several views of religion. Some were Protestant and Catholic Christians. Others were advocates of naturalistic religion based on rationality and morality and still others were nonbelievers or atheists. Freethinkers either questioned or rejected traditional Christianity, and their views helped to bring about the official separation of church and state that we have now. Still others came from those strands of Protestant Reformation thought that advocated strict separation of church and state.

---

[1]Henry Steele Commager, *The Empire of Reason* (Garden City, NY: Anchor Press, 1977), pp. 210–11.

Matters pertaining to religion are found in three places in the Constitution: Article 6, the First Amendment, and the Fourteenth Amendment.

**1.** Article 6 prohibits religious requirements for holding public office: ". . . no religious Test shall ever be required as a Qualification to any Office or public Trust under the United States." A person's religion or lack of religion cannot legally be a condition for holding public office in a pluralistic culture in which religion and government are separate functions.

**2.** The First Amendment to the Constitution contains some of the most important religious liberty legislation in our nation's history. It is part of the Bill of Rights, prepared under the leadership of James Madison: "*Congress shall make no law respecting an establishment of religion, or prohibiting the free exercise thereof,* or abridging the freedom of speech, or of the press; or the right of the people peaceably to assemble, and to petition the Government for a redress of grievances" [emphasis added].

The "establishment clause" says that the United States Congress cannot make any one religion the official religion of the United States. It cannot act in a way that gives preferential treatment or support to one religion above others. Nor can it support religion or nonreligion generally, one over the other. Insofar as possible, it must maintain a neutral stance toward religion.

The second clause is often called the "free exercise" clause. It states that the government cannot interfere with any person's religion. In *Reynolds* v. *United States* (1878), Reynolds held that a law against marriage to more than one person at the same time violated his religious freedom, because he was a member of the Latter-day Saints, who at that time advocated the practice. In a landmark opinion, the Court held that the free exercise clause applied to religious beliefs but not necessarily to the actions arising from those beliefs. It held that "actions which are in violation of social duties or subversive of good order" cannot be tolerated, even when they are done in the name of religion.

This is a dilemma that cannot be fully resolved. Because religion is an intimate joining of belief and action, it may seem odd to tell people that they may believe what they please but prevent them from acting on those beliefs. Yet clearly there are actions that cannot be condoned, such as the torture of people or animals, or random terror attacks on civilian populations. There are actions that, if permitted, would utterly disrupt the social order, such as the refusal to be bound by any laws. These sorts of actions cannot be tolerated, even in the hallowed name of religious freedom.

Freedom of speech, the press, and assembly also contributes to religious freedom. These freedoms mean that people may speak and write openly about their views on religious questions. They may gather peaceably to listen to speakers or to worship in whatever ways they choose.

The framers of the Bill of Rights could not possibly have known the range of circumstances these first ten amendments might be required to cover. The provisions of the bill are necessarily very broad, both allowing for and requiring constant reinterpretation by the courts:

ral principle deducible from the First Amendment and all that has
d by the Court is this: That we will not tolerate either governmentally
ned religion or governmental interference with religion. Short of those
ly proscribed governmental acts there is room for play in the joints prove of a benevolent neutrality which will permit religious exercise to exist
w. out sponsorship and without interference.[2]

**3.**   The Fourteenth Amendment is the final Constitutional reference to
religious liberty. The crucial point for religious liberty is in Section 1: "*No
State shall make or enforce any law which shall abridge the privileges or immuni-
ties of citizens of the United States*; nor shall any State deprive any person of life,
liberty, or property without due process of law; nor deny to any person within its jurisdiction the equal protection of the laws" [emphasis added].

Both Article 6 and the religion clauses in the First Amendment deal with
what the *federal* government may not do. The Fourteenth Amendment holds
that the *states* as well are not to "abridge the privileges" of their citizens, including the privilege of religious freedom.

The "play in the joints" of the Constitution has also led to additional legislation and executive actions concerning religion and the role it plays in the
public life of the United States. One example is the Religious Freedom Restoration Act signed into law in November 1993. In the early 1990s, freedom of religious practice for smaller and less popular religions appeared to have been
jeopardized by certain United States Supreme Court decisions. To cite a well-
known example, *Employment Division of the State of Oregon* v. *Smith* (1990)
overturned the principle that the government's interest had to be "compelling"
to justify restricting freedom of religion. In its majority opinion, the Court held
that the free exercise of religion deserves no special protection, as long as the law
applies to nonreligious groups also. This line of argument lays the groundwork
for the restriction of any unpopular religious practice.

In response to the perceived threats to religious liberty, a diverse coalition of religious leaders and groups came together to support the passage of
the Act. This bill sought to protect the free exercise of religion through a legislative act rather than by judicial means, enhancing protection especially for
the lesser-known and less-understood religions. The Religious Freedom
Restoration Act was later invalidated by the Supreme Court (*City of Bourne,
Texas* v. *Flores*, 1997) on the grounds that it violated the establishment clause.

This leaves religious freedom in question, especially for smaller and less-
understood groups. The government needs only demonstrate a *rational* basis
for curtailing freedom of religious practice; it does not have to show a
*compelling* interest in doing so.

Another example of a legislated provision for religious liberty is the No
Child Left Behind Act signed into law in 2001. The act mandates that in

---

[2] *Walz* v. *Tax Commission of the City of New York* (1970).

order to receive federal funds, school districts must show they do not limit student religious expression. To help clarify this, the federal Department of Education issued its *Guidance on Constitutionally Protected Prayer in Public Elementary and Secondary Schools.* This ruling allows for "student initiated" prayer at school functions and events such as assemblies and sports.

### By the Numbers: Data on Religious America at the Turn of the Century

Religion in the United States has been, by and large, a remarkably stable phenomenon, and analysis of the data at the turn of the century indicates this stability continues.[3] Slightly over half of adults are Protestant Christians, and about twenty-seven percent are Catholic Christians. Between two and three percent are Jewish, with sixteen percent saying they have no religious preference.

The Gallup Organization, a major academic polling organization, has identified the religion factors which have remained "remarkably constant over the years": belief in God, religious preference, membership in a religious organization, attendance at worship, and view on the importance of religion. The "confidence factors" are highly variable: confidence in the ability of religion to answer today's problems, in the church, and in the clergy.[4]

When asked about the strength of their religious preference, slightly more than one-third say it is strong, while just under half describe it as "somewhat strong." Fully three-fourths say that religion is an important part of their lives. Only one-fifth say they never attend religious services, but only slightly less than one-third claim weekly attendance or more. Where private prayer is concerned, over half say they pray daily. Over one-third believe the Bible is the actual, literal Word of God, and slightly under half believe it is inspired by God. Ninety percent express at least some confidence in organized religion, with slightly less than one-third expressing a "great deal" of confidence in it.

Several factors correlate positively with participation in religious organizations, as well as with private religious practice. These correlations have remained relatively stable over time. Women are more religious than are men, and African-Americans are more religious than are their white counterparts, at least when religiosity is measured in traditional terms. Religious practice increases with age. Protestant Christians are more observant than are Catholic Christians, and Jews as a group are less so than Christians as a whole.

Those who participate in a religious organization tend to do more than simply attend services. Almost 40 percent participate in small group activities and about one-third attend religious education programs and/or engage in

---

[3]Unless otherwise footnoted, the data in this section is based on the author's analysis of the National Opinion Research Center's General Social Survey and the National Election Study for the year 2000.
[4]"The Gallup Tuesday Briefing," The Gallup Organization, February 12, 2002.

volunteer work through their religious group. Those who volunteer through their religious group are also more likely to volunteer with other groups. Almost one-fifth are involved in music at their place of worship, and about a tenth participate in a sports league through their religious group.[5]

Participation in religious activities and groups ebbs and flows with stages in the life cycle, as we might expect. This ebb and flow has been documented since the 1930s. Children and teens are involved with religion in their early years, as part of their family of origin, and then become less involved as they move away from home to attend college or begin full time work. As they marry and perhaps begin their own families, they tend to return to religious practice. Religiosity continues to increase as people age, perhaps as they experience the deaths of their parents and become more reflective about the meaning of their own lives and deaths.[6]

Despite the increasingly visible diversity of religion in the United States, 16 percent say that the United States is a "Biblical nation" and another 29 percent call the U.S. a "Christian nation." Forty-five percent believe that we are a secular nation. On a related issue, survey respondents split about half and half over whether they would vote for an atheist for president if that person were otherwise well-qualified.[7]

The "2001 American Religious Identification Survey" (ARIS) conducted by the Graduate School of the City University of New York reveals some interesting shifts in American religiousness relative to their earlier 1990 National Survey of Religious Identification. While in 1990, 90 percent of adult Americans identified with a religious group, that figure had dropped to 81 percent in 2001. The percentage who identified with Christianity dropped from 86.2 in 1990 to 76.5 in 2001, a drop of about 0.9 percent annually. Were that rate of decline to continue—and there is no evidence to support a judgment either way—by 2042, non-Christians would outnumber Christians. In 2001, 14.1 percent said they followed no religion, nearly doubling the 8 percent figure from 1990. This was the greatest change, both in absolute and percentage terms. There was also a substantial increase in the number of respondents who refused to answer the religious preference question.[8]

## RELIGION IN PUBLIC LIFE: FAITH-BASED INITIATIVES

One of the major discussions about the role of religion in public life concerns what are sometimes called "faith-based initiatives," a plan proposed by President George W. Bush that would allow government funding for social pro-

---

[5]The Pew Forum on Religion and Public Life and The Pew Research Center for The People and The Press: *American Views on Religion, Politics, and Public Policy*, 2001, pp. 33–34.
[6]"Gallup Tuesday Briefing," The Gallup Organization, June 4, 2002, pp. 2–3.
[7]*Public Perspective, A Roper Center Review of Public Opinion and Polling*, January/February, 2003, pp. 19–20.
[8]Web site www.gc.cuny.edustudies/key_findings.htm

grams sponsored by religious organizations.[9] In general, it is clear that the public supports the idea of religious groups being eligible for federal funding for social service programs. However, a majority want to see that support limited to Judeo-Christian groups and many have reservations about funding for some of the less-understood Christian groups such as the Latter-day Saints.

There are a number of reasons given for federal support as well as against it. Belief that the power of religion can change people's lives is most strongly linked to support for this approach. The idea that faith-based programs can run more efficiently is cited by many who support funding for religious groups. Other reasons given by persons who back faith-based programs include the idea that people should have a variety of options in how to obtain needed services and the belief that religiously based service providers are more compassionate. On the other hand, opponents cite concern about recipients being forced to participate in religious services and erosion of the separation of church and state as primary concerns. Other reasons given for opposition include the fear that faith groups might be held to lower standards than secular groups, that funding would promote division among religions, and the feeling that faith-based funding would get the government too involved in religion.[10]

## RELIGION AFTER 9-11

As I write this, it is September 11, 2003, two years after the attack on the World Trade Center and the Pentagon. A quick look at the local newspaper reveals that there are several memorial and commemorative events planned for Muncie, Indiana, and the surrounding counties and towns. Most are sponsored by religious organizations or at least have strongly religious overtones. This is perhaps not surprising. But what long-term effect did 9-11 have on religion in the United States, if any?

Survey data from the weeks immediately following the attacks indicated that Americans had in fact attended religious services in higher numbers than usual, even discounting the special services in the aftermath of the attacks. There were thousands of such services, and the percentage of Americans who attended services on the weekend following the attacks rose by 6 percent.[11] Historical data indicate that a similar effect has followed other major crises.[12]

However, data from surveys done later indicate that there has been little, if any, long-term increase in religiosity. Increases in religious participation were of short duration, and mainly affected those who were very involved with religion before 9-11. Among those who were not particularly religious,

[9]This section draws on *American Views on Religion, Politics, and Public Policy*, The Pew Research Center for People and the Press, 2001.
[10]*American Views on Religion, Politics, and Public Policy*, pp. 15–18.
[11]Andrew Walsh, "Good for What Ails Us," *Religion in the News*, Fall, 2001, pp. 2–5, 26.
[12]*Public Perspective, A Roper Center Review of Public Opinion and Polling*, January/February, 2003, p. 25.

the events of 9-11 had little religious impact. Whatever effect there was had largely dissipated by the end of the year.[13]

While actual religious participation did not increase substantially, the public perception of religion's importance did. Polls since the 1990s indicated that a majority of people believed the influence of religion was lessening in the United States. Following the attacks, more than 75 percent said the influence of religion was rising. This was a broad perception, shared by the religious and the nonreligious alike, and distributed across racial, regional, and socioeconomic lines. However, this too was short-lived, and six months later, survey results returned to pre-attack levels.[14]

Although the attacks on the United States did not change the level of religious participation, those who are religious said their faith helped them deal with the attacks and their results. Even persons who are not deeply involved in organized religion indicated that their faith helped them cope.[15]

An examination of news coverage of events immediately following 9-11 describes another effect as well:

> American religious diversity received a new, and perhaps decisive, level of recognition. The cast of religious leaders summoned to the White House and to lead the memorial services organized and sanctioned by the government at the National Cathedral and at Yankee Stadium offered up a showcase of world religions. Henceforth, when religion is presented to the American public, the picture will include Hindus, Muslims, Buddhists, and Sikhs, as well as Protestants, Catholics, and Jews.[16]

It does appear that there *has* been a sustained determination to include Muslims alongside Jews and Christians at civic religious events such as National Day of Prayer services. There seems, to me at least, to be much less evidence that civic religious inclusiveness has continued to extend beyond the three major Abrahamic traditions, except in rare instances.

## RELIGION ON CAMPUS

Several studies of religion on college and university campuses in the 1990s focused on the ways in which religion and its influence have waned in higher education in the United States.[17] These accounts trace the change from a situa-

---

[13]*Public Perspective, A Roper Center Review of Public Opinion and Polling,* January/February, 2003, pp. 26–27.

[14]*Public Perspective, A Roper Center Review of Public Opinion and Polling,* September/October, 2002, pp. 30–31.

[15]*Religion and Ethics Newsweekly,* April 26, 2003.

[16]Walsh, "Good for What Ails Us," p. 3.

[17]See, for example, George M. Marsden and Bradley J. Longfield, eds., *The Secularization of the Academy* (New York: Oxford University Press, 1992); George M. Marsden, *The Soul of the American University: From Protestant Establishment to Established Nonbelief* (New York: Oxford University Press, 1994); and Douglas Sloan, Faith and Knowledge: *Mainline Protestantism and American Higher Education* (Louisville, KY, Westminster John Know Press, 1994).

tion in which religion and higher education were intimately intertwined, one in which religion, aside from the academic study of it, has been virtually evicted from campuses across the nation. Although the authors of these studies do not see this as an altogether bad thing, they do claim that important values have been lost in the process.

In 2001, three scholars in the area of American religion published a study in which they investigated what role religion actually does play in the lives of American college students.[18] They did ethnographic studies of four representative institutions: a state university in the West, an historically black university in the South, a Catholic university in the East, and a Lutheran liberal arts college in the North. The authors of the 2001 study wished to examine the role of religion empirically. We have already looked at their findings concerning the academic study of religion in Chapter 1.

While not claiming to provide "a comprehensive overview" of the state of religion on American campuses, the authors believe they have enough data to begin to draw certain generally applicable conclusions:

- Both in terms of organized religious groups and more individual spirituality, opportunities for student religious practice were widely available. Religion on campus is characterized "more by seeking, nomadic wandering and choosing among diverse options (spirituality) than by the more stable posture of dwelling in or inhabiting safe, sacred places (religion)."[19] I see this in the essays on their own religious stance that my own students write at the beginning of class. However, I also read a lot of essays from students who have found a religious "home" in one or another of the campus parachurch organizations such as Campus Crusade for Christ and The Revolution.
- Personal spirituality and volunteer social service appear to go hand in hand for students.
- Students are frequently involved in small group study and worship events such as residence hall Bible studies and prayer times.
- Students and faculty alike respected religious diversity and practiced tolerance, although none of the four campuses studied was free of tensions around religious issues. On the whole, religion was respected as an important aspect of life, yet, even in the religiously supported schools, students had the freedom to not be involved with religion. Openness to religious diversity existed side-by-side with missionary enthusiasm for promoting one's own viewpoint.

On the basis of the empirical data they collected, the authors of this study concluded that, rather than disappearing, the presence of religion in American higher education has become more pluralistic and participation more optional, but no less vibrant and engaging for students. "Indeed, we

---

[18]Conrad Cherry, Betty A. DeBerg, and Amanda Porterfield, *Religion on Campus: What Religion Really Means to Today's Undergraduates* (Chapel Hill: The University of North Carolina Press, 2000). See especially Chapter 6.

[19]Cherry et al., *Religion on Campus*, p. 276.

found religion on the four campuses sufficiently vital and inviting to make us wonder if it had ever been more so in the past. . . . [Our] study reveals that the ethos of decentered, diverse, religiously tolerant institutions of higher education is a breeding ground for vital religious practice and teaching."[20] This seems to reflect trends taking place in the population at large (see the discussion of the results of the ARIS study earlier). That the culture as a whole and the culture on college campuses is moving in the same direction suggests that these trends will continue and be magnified in American culture in the future.

## CIVIL RELIGION AND BEYOND

Sociologist Robert Bellah brought the concept of civil religion to scholarly attention and ultimately to the American popular mind. In a 1967 essay, Bellah wrote that in the United States there "exists alongside of and rather clearly differentiated from the churches an elaborate and well-institutionalized civil religion in America. . . . This public religious dimension is expressed in a set of beliefs, symbols, and rituals that I am calling the American civil religion."[21]

Bellah cited documents such as the Declaration of Independence and the Constitution, as well as the inaugural speeches of several presidents, along with holiday observances, in support of his thesis. He included belief in God, belief in America's role in God's plans for the world, commonly accepted standards of morality and civic virtue, and routinely observed holidays among the verities of civil religion.

Bellah's seminal essay gave religious studies scholars a new way of analyzing the roles that religion plays in the public life of the United States. It moved the study of religion beyond the study of ecclesiastical institutions and laid the groundwork for recognition of the importance of popular religion. The essay also provided great insight into the ways in which civic ideals and the legitimating principles of a culture are expressed powerfully in symbols that link them to divine realities.

How we view American religious culture has changed. Rather than a single voice, the United States has become a chorus of many voices. Any attempt to describe a single American voice inevitably seems sectarian and exclusive. It now seems better to focus on the diversity of religions and cultures that are present in the United States, rather than looking for a unity that many have come to doubt.

At the same time, there is a reality behind the civil religion thesis that cannot be overlooked in any discussion of the role of religion in the life of the nation. In a recent study of how sacred and secular have mingled throughout

---

[20]Cherry et al., *Religion on Campus*, pp. 294–95.
[21]Robert N. Bellah, "Civil Religion in America," *Daedalus*, 117, no. 3 (Winter, 1967), pp. 1, 4.

the history of the United States, R. Laurence Moore notes that making religion voluntary allowed it "to have an enormous influence on culture and public life."[22]

> Many Americans want to maintain religion as an important part of public, secular life because they believe that God blesses America. The Constitution posed a problem for them. In taking away an established church, it robbed them of a script for keeping religion in the public eye. They had to wing it.[23]

Moore also mentions that not all citizens agree that mixing the sacred and secular is a good idea, and this makes religion in public life a source of conflict.

## POPULAR RELIGION

I defined *religion* in Chapter 1 in a way that emphasizes religions as structured social systems, institutions, or organizations. This aspect of religion can be called **institutional religion**. The words *ecclesial* or *ecclesiastical* are sometimes used to describe this aspect of religion. There is another aspect of religion in the United States that is at least as significant: This is **popular religion**— religion that occurs outside the formal boundaries of religious institutions. These manifestations of religion is popular in two senses:

> On the one hand, they have "mass appeal," they "sell." On the other hand, they are "of the people": they are examples not of the kind of religion that is taught by theologians in seminaries, but rather of that which appeals to a wide variety of people of no special theological sophistication outside the context of formal "Sunday-morning" worship in the churches.[24]

The existence of widespread and flourishing popular religion in the United States indicates that, as one scholar puts it, the "determination of what counts as religion is not the sole preserve of academics."[25]

Most people in the United States belong to some sort of religious community—they are Protestants within particular denominations, Catholics, Jews, or Buddhists, for example. Many, however, supplement their formal membership and participation with a variety of other religious activities that do not come directly from their community of faith—revivals,

---

[22]R. Laurence Moore, *Touchdown Jesus: The Mixing of Sacred and Secular in American History* (Louisville: Westminster John Knox Press, 2003), p. 6.

[23]Moore, *Touchdown Jesus*, p. 13.

[24]Peter W. Williams, *Popular Religion in America: Symbolic Change and the Modernization Process in Historical Perspective* (Englewood Cliffs, NJ: Prentice Hall, 1980), pp. 3–4.

[25]David Chidester, "The Church of Baseball, the Fetish of Coca-Cola, and the Potlatch of Rock'n'Roll: Theoretical Models for the Study of Religion in American Popular Culture," *Journal of the American Academy of Religion* 59, No. 4 (Fall, 1996), p. 760.

watching religious television, various devotional activities such as private prayer and reading, chanting and meditation, wearing religious jewelry, or placing religious bumper stickers on their cars and trucks. For some, these activities and others similar to them become the primary focus of their religious life.

Popular religion is a "dimension of religious life that is elusive and difficult to describe," as one study of the phenomenon puts it.[26] There is no one agreed-upon definition of popular religion, but we can describe it.[27]

- Popular religion is the religious belief and practice of ordinary people rather than of theologians and religious leaders. It is transmitted through various channels outside of religious institutions.
- It exists alongside institutional religion as a complement to it. It is a supplement to participation in formal religion for some people and a substitute for it for others. People do not abandon formal religion for popular religiosity but use the latter to personalize their religion.
- It offers people more direct access to the sacred than they have through the mediation of formal religious groups. Formal religious organizations impose order and structure on religion. Popular religion is distinguished by a lively sense of the supernatural without the imposition of formal structure. It does not have the "conceptual coherence" of organized religion.
- It draws on the core religious institutions of the culture (in the United States, primarily Christianity) but blends this with other sources and traditions. It often reflects both mainstream and alternative values. It draws heavily on secular popular culture.

[For] the vast majority of Americans, a sense of the supernatural so lively that it cannot be contained in creed and doctrine permeates life. . . . [O]rdinary men and women have sought and continue to seek direct access to the realm of the supernatural in order to use its power to give them control over their lives and to endow their lives with meaning. . . . Sometimes they gain that access through religious traditions and institutions, but more often [they do so] through fusing together an array of beliefs and practices to construct personal and very private worlds of meaning. If we would understand the dynamics of being religious, American style, we must explore the phenomenon of popular religiosity.[28]

Examples of popular religion abound. Although angel popularity may have peaked, there continues to be considerable interest in them. Catalogs regularly offer angel-related articles, as do gift shops, evidence that the interest

---

[26]Charles H. Lippy, *Being Religious, American Style: A History of Popular Religiosity in the United States.* (Westport, CT: Greenwood Press, 1994), p. 1.
[27]This section draws loosely on Lippy, *Being Religious, American Style*, chap. 1.
[28]Lippy, *Being Religious*, pp. 18–19.

level remains at least fairly high. Near-death experiences provide what some people believe to be a glimpse into a world beyond this one. A series of billboards with snappy messages signed "God" dot the landscape. One example is "That love your neighbor business—I meant that."

The *Wall Street Journal* recently reported on what it termed "Do-It-Yourself Religion." Some Americans are participating in a variety of special interest religious groups to supplement or in some instances replace participation in a more traditional community of faith. These groups may be organized around worship, prayer, discussion, or other interests of the partici-pants. Not a new phenomenon, these groups are similar to the Christian "house churches" and Jewish *havurah* of the 1960s. Similar groups have come and gone at various times, and the *Journal* article notes that, although the movement is strong now, history indicates that its lifespan is limited.[29]

In the commercially oriented culture of the United States, the strength of popular religion is shown in part by how well it sells. Christian retail is a multibillion dollar industry. Some people place statues of Jesus, Mary, Saint Francis, or the Buddha in their yards, or cross or fish symbols on their cars or trucks. Many people wear religiously-themed tee shirts. There is religious music in any format people like. The musicals *Jesus Christ, Superstar* and *Godspell* continue to attract audiences. Gift items such as religiously oriented figurines, decorative items, and greeting cards sell well in religious book and supply stores and in secular stores as well. There are religious-theme comput-er games and educational software to help children learn about the Bible or the Qur'an.[30]

As noted earlier, most popular religion in the United States is in at least some sense Christian. However, it is not exclusively Christian. A number of cat-alogs offer a variety of items for people devising their own spirituality. One such catalog has an umbrella that features the eight major symbols of Tibetan Buddhism, as well as items reflecting Native American (and other) religions. In another catalog, those of Jewish faith can choose from a vast assortment of Jew-ish religious items such as prayer shawls, menorahs, Passover plates, and mez-zuzahs (which are described in Chapter 9). Several sources exist for Buddhists to obtain statues, meditation cushions and benches, and audiotapes or videotapes. *Hinduism Today*, a magazine for North American Hindus, routinely advertises Hindu religious articles such as deity statues, beads, and incense.

Although a lot of popular religion concerns material culture, it also in-volves religious practices, many of which are learned and practiced in people's homes. Countless parents pass on to their children the practice of saying bed-time and mealtime prayers, often using those they themselves learned as chil-dren. Parents read stories of faith to their children. College students pray for aid on exams. People wear cloth bracelets bearing the letters "WWJD?" The

---

[29]Elizabeth Bernstein, "Do-It-Yourself Religion," *Wall Street Journal* (June 11, 2004), pp. W1 and W5.
[30]The Muslim sacred scripture. See Chapter 11 for more discussion of Muslims and the Qur'an.

**Figure 2-1**    The conflict over abortion rights often includes a religious dimension. *(Paul Conklin/Monkmeyer Press.)*

acronym stands for "What Would Jesus Do?" a reminder to the wearer to ask that question when they cannot figure out the answer to a moral dilemma. Many people read devotional magazines, watch religious television, and listen to religious radio programming.

### QUESTIONS AND ACTIVITIES FOR REVIEW, DISCUSSION, AND WRITING

1. In your opinion, is government neutrality toward religion a good idea, or not? Why?
2. What are some classroom activities that would be prohibited by the *Abington* v. *Schempp* ruling? What kinds of activities are allowed?
3. Do you think that religious clubs (such as student Bible study clubs or prayer groups) should have the same opportunities to use classroom space before or after school hours as nonreligious groups do? Why or why not? You might want to organize a debate on this topic.
4. Is something like the Religious Freedom Restoration Act necessary in the United States? Why or why not?
5. Compare your experience of religion on your own campus with that described in this chapter.
6. Discuss with others in your class the manifestations of popular religion with which you are familiar. Organize a "popular religion scavenger hunt" in which people are alert for evidence of popular religion for a day or two and then report what they find.

### FOR FURTHER READING

CORBETT, MICHAEL, and JULIA CORBETT, *Politics and Religion in the United States*, New York: Garland Publishing, 1999. This book surveys the role of religion in American public life from colonial times through the present, with sections on history, the First Amendment, religion and public opinion, and religion in politics. Contemporary material is based on analysis of survey data.

McDANNELL, COLLEEN, *Material Christianity: Religion and Popular Culture in America*. New Haven, CT: Yale University Press, 1995. This book is a fascinating examination of the material objects that are a part of popular Christianity. Although it isn't a new book, it remains a valuable resource.

MOORE, R. LAURENCE, *Touchdown Jesus: The Mixing of Sacred and Secular in American History*. Louisville, KY: Westminster John Knox Press, 2003. Moore thoroughly describes the interplay of sacred and secular in the history of the United States.

SEGERS, MARY, and TED JELEN, *A Wall of Separation? Debating the Public Role of Religion*. Lanham, MD: Rowman & Littlefield Publishers, 1998. The authors examine the impact of organized religion on the political process and its significance in the creation of public policy. Seger and Jelen, both political science professors, do not overlook the complexity of these issues.

## RELEVANT WORLD WIDE WEB SITES

Remember that Web URLs change frequently. Check the *Perspectives on Faith* site (www.bsu.edu/web/jcorbett/relig) for updated URLs.

A number of excellent Web sites address issues of religion in public life from a variety of perspectives:

Americans United for the Separation of Church and State: www.au.org

The Christian Legal Society: www.clsnet.org

People for the American Way: www.pfaw.org

The Freedom Forum: www.freedomforum.org

The Interfaith Alliance: www.interfaithalliance.org

The Pew Forum on Religion in Public Life: www.pewforum.org

The Hartford Institute for Religion Research at the Hartford Seminary: www.hirr.hartsem.edu/: This site covers research in areas such as women and religion, church growth and decline, religion and the family, religion, and the Web, plus more.

These organizations maintain sites representative of how religion may be involved in public life.

Evangelicals for Social Action: www.esa-online.org/

Sojourners: www.sojourners.com

Call to Renewal: www.calltorenewal.com

Tikkun: www.tikkun.org

# chapter 3

# CONFLICT AND CONTROVERSY

If a pro-life advocate shoots an abortionist doctor, it is certain to hit the front page of every newspaper in the country. Meanwhile, millions of ordinary citizens will on that day have given some thought to their souls through prayer, meditation, Bible-reading and the like—activities that reach into the depths of the soul where the switches are thrown between kindness and cruelty, hope and despair. This passes without mention.[1]

I answered God's call to acknowledge myself as a gay man. Risking the loss of my children and the exercise of my ordained ministry in the Church was the biggest risk I've ever taken, but it left me with two unshakable things: my integrity and my God.[2]

Religion may lead to or enter into conflict and controversy in at least four ways: (1) Religion can come into conflict with itself when some of its members or leaders violate its own highest standards. (2) Controversy can also arise within communities of faith when different factions disagree sharply about what is right. (3) Religion can become a problem for individuals, or for society as a whole, when it leads to violence, terrorism, addiction, or other dysfunctional behaviors. Finally, (4) in the climate of pluralism and free religious expression that we enjoy in the United States, sometimes religious persons or groups express themselves in ways or in places that others deem inappropriate. This chapter illustrates each of these.

It is important to note two things at the outset. First, communities of faith are not the only organizations that are affected by these issues. Violations of norms, disagreements about conduct, violence and conflicting interests arise in many contexts. Second, the great majority of the time, religions do *not* lead to problems either for their adherents or for the larger society. Although opinions differ, I firmly believe that, on balance, religion contributes more good to humanity than it does ill.

---

[1]Huston Smith, *Why Religion Matters: The Fate of the Human Spirit in an Age of Disbelief.* San Francisco: HarperSanFrancisco, 2001, p. 115.

[2]The [Episcopal] Diocese of New Hampshire, The Rev. Canon V. Gene Robinson, www.nhepiscopal.org/BishopSearch/The_Rev_Canon_V_Gene_Robinson.htm.

Conflict and controversy centering on religion are not new in the United States. Our early history is replete with accounts of religious intolerance and people who have been looked down on and sometimes killed simply because they were of an unaccepted faith. In more recent history, countercultural movements in the 1960s gave rise to many new religious movements whose unusual practices and members' sometimes unquestioning loyalty to their leaders frightened those outside the groups. In the 1970s, opposition to nonconventional religions coalesced as the *anti-cult* movement. The 1980s saw the religious broadcasting industry and televangelism shaken to its core by financial scandals. Jonestown and the Peoples' Temple, and more recently, Heaven's Gate, still recall memories of men, women and children following their leaders to death by suicide. Mention of the Branch Davidians in Waco, Texas, recalls horrific news footage of their compound burning as federal officers closed in.

## SEXUAL MISCONDUCT BY THE CLERGY

Allegations of sexual misconduct and impropriety, whether substantiated or not, have frequently been directed at nonconventional religions. Until recently, however, people have usually not thought of these things as a problem with more common and better-understood religions. Since the mid-1980s, however, media reports of sexual abuse by mainline or mainstream clergy have become increasingly common. There is considerable agreement that the problem is extensive. Although news coverage has focused on abuse by Catholic priests, clergy sexual abuse is not a "Catholic problem." It affects virtually all Christian denominations, as well as Jewish, Hindu, and Buddhist faith communities, among others. The dynamics of abuse are similar whatever the faith community. Most reports of the problem in the United States comes from Christian churches, simply because they are such a majority. However, there have been sufficient reports from non-Christian communities of faith to support the view that this is truly an interfaith problem. In whatever context it happens, sexual abuse by clergy is a glaring example of religion's leaders acting in ways that violate the highest standards of their religion and the trust placed in them as religious leaders.

Accurate data on sexual abuse in general, and sexual abuse by clergy in particular, is hard to find. Underreporting is common. Psychiatrist Thomas Plante, author of *Bless Me Father for I Have Sinned: Perspectives on Sexual Abuse Committed by Roman Catholic Priests*, notes the "tremendous amount of media frenzy" and the "frantic, almost hysterical reaction" to reports of clergy sexual abuse. That notwithstanding, even *one* child or teen abused by a priest (or by anyone else) is too many. He also notes that the Catholic Church, especially early in the crisis, did not do a good job of being understanding and compassionate with survivors of abuse and their families, and in general mismanaged the crisis both locally and churchwide. Based on his own research as well as that of others, Dr. Plante estimates that between 2 and 5 percent of priests have had sexual contact with a minor under eighteen. That is consistent with the percentage of male clergy in other denominations having such contact, and less than the estimated 8 percent of males in the general population.[3] It is also consistent with other investigations that indicate about 4 percent of priests have had sexual abuse of minors allegations filed against them.[4]

He also makes a point that I believe to be very important in understanding this crisis, as well as indicating why it is resolving. Most cases of abuse, although being reported recently, go back two, three or even four decades. Survivors are just now coming forward to tell their stories. (This is not at all uncommon in these situations. The disclosure of abuse is threatening and painful for survivors.) The average age of accused priests is fifty-three. There was much less knowledge of the dynamics of abuse then than there is today, and the policy of allowing offenders to continue in their ministry after counseling appeared to make sense. In addition, at that time, most priests began their seminary training in high school, did not undergo any kind of psychological evaluation, and received no education in managing sexuality, maintaining professional boundaries, or impulse control. All those things have now changed. Men are more mature when they begin seminary, they undergo comprehensive psychological testing that includes specific evaluation for sexual problem risk factors, and they are extensively trained in how to manage sexual issues.[5]

Other investigations show similar findings. The report of the lay National Review Board, established as an independent agency by the church to review and report on the crisis, indicates the problem was most severe from the 1960s through the very early 1980s. About 80 percent of those who have filed charges are male, and the largest proportion was between eleven and fourteen years old at the time of the assault. The two crucial factors in how the church dealt with the problem were found to be the failure of seminaries to screen out seminarians who were potential abusers, and the failure of bishops to deal forthrightly and swiftly with those charged with abuse.[6]

The element of psychological evaluation is especially important. Plante's research indicates that 70 percent of the accused priests are themselves survivors of abuse. "Almost all" have serious psychological problems such as substance abuse and/or mood and personality disorders. While this in no way excuses their behavior, it may help us to understand it. Research also indicates that neither the requirement of priestly celibacy nor the presence of gay priests is a contributing factor.[7]

The church's approach has also changed. The comprehensive Charter for the Protection of Children and Young People, drawn up by the United States

[3]Thomas Plante, "A Perspective on Clergy Sexual Abuse," www.psywww.com/psyrelig/plante.html.
[4]Andrew Walsh, "Godawful Numbers," *Religion in the News*, Vol. 7, No. 1 (Spring, 2004), p. 19.
[5]Plante, "A Perspective on Clergy Sexual Abuse," www.psywww.com/psyrelig/plante.html.
[6]Walsh, "Godawful Numbers," *Religion in the News*, Vol. 7, No. 1 (Spring, 2004), p. 19.
[7]Plante, "A Perspective on Clergy Sexual Abuse," www.psywww.com/psyrelig/plante.html.

Conference of Catholic Bishops, notes that this is "a crisis without precedent in our time":

> The sexual abuse of children and young people by some priests and bishops, and the ways in which we bishops addressed these crimes and sins, have caused enormous pain, anger, and confusion. Innocent victims and their families have suffered terribly. In the past, secrecy has created an atmosphere that has inhibited the healing process and, in some cases, enabled sexually abusive behavior to be repeated.[8]

The lengthy document contains sections that address the need for healing and reconciliation with victim/survivors and their families, guarantees rapid and effective response to all allegations of sexual abuse including the offender's permanent removal from active priesthood, a checks-and-balances system to ensure that procedures are followed and that there is full accountability, and careful safeguards to protect children and young people in the future. One specific action was the establishment of the lay National Review Board with independent authority to investigate and report on the church's handling of abuse allegations. Another is on-site audits of all dioceses to determine the extent of their compliance with child protection standards. An initial audit in 2003 was followed by a second in 2004. At least 90 percent of United States dioceses are in full compliance.

It may help to put the crisis in the Catholic Church in perspective to realize that, unfortunately, we live in a culture in which the sexual abuse of children is not uncommon. A draft report on educator misconduct in the public schools, which came out at about the same time as the bishops began addressing the issue in their church, notes that between 6 and 10 percent of public school children are sexually abused or molested by school staff or employees.[9] Research also indicates that a far greater percentage of children are abused by family members than by priests.

The publicity surrounding sexual abuse by Catholic priests has raised consciousness in other communities of faith, and many have established stringent and detailed policies for ensuring the safety of children and young people. These often include such things as never having a child alone in a room with an adult, an open door policy in classrooms, extensive screening and background checks on all personnel who come into contact with children, and detailed procedures for reporting suspected abuse and dealing with offenders.[10]

This publicity has also led to survivors of abuse in other denominations coming forward, and to the creation of support groups for survivors. One example is Silent Lambs, a support and advocacy organization for survivors of

---

[8]United States Conference of Catholic Bishops, "Charter for the Protection of Children and Young People, Revised Edition," available at www.usccb.org/bishops/charter.htm.

[9]Patrick Novacosky, "100 Times Worse: America's Other Abuse Crisis," www.catholic.net/ (4-9-04).

[10]See, for example, The United Synagogue of Conservative Judaism's "Model Guidelines for Congregational Policy Against Harassment," www.uscj.org/images/mgcph.PDF.

abuse by Jehovah's Witnesses leaders.[11] The founder of this group, William Bowen, a former congregational leader, says that the Witnesses are "where the Catholics were on the abuse issue about 20 years ago."[12] Mr. Bowen resigned as an elder in a Kentucky congregation after the organization refused to take action against an accused molester. As with the Catholic Church, Witness survivors point to structural or systemic practices within the church that make it easy for abusers to go unpunished and for victims to be revictimized by the process itself. Witnesses policy requires that any accusations first be brought before the congregation's elders. If the accused person denies the charge, two credible eyewitnesses to the crime are required. The nature of sexual abuse makes this virtually impossible. In the absence of these witnesses, the person is deemed innocent. Those who speak about the situation have frequently been disfellowshipped, "an extreme penalty that means a total cutoff of relationships by family members, friends, and business associates who are Witnesses."[13]

Charges also were filed against the Evangelical Lutheran Church in America and one of its seminaries after a man was ordained as a pastor who was found to have molested fourteen young boys. A missionary for the Presbyterian Church (USA) was alleged to have molested nineteen girls.[14]

One of the larger organizational attempts to address the problem of sexual abuse by religious leaders is the Interfaith Sexual Trauma Institute, a project of Saint John's Abbey and Saint John's University in Minnesota. They publish a newsletter and journal, maintain a resource center, and sponsor conferences and other educational programs, as well as other activities. Unlike secular agencies, the Institute specifically addresses the religious and spiritual ramifications of sexual abuse by clergy. Their vision is to build "safe, healthy, and trustworthy communities of faith," and promote "the prevention of sexual abuse, exploitation, and harassment through research, education, and publication," and "is committed to achieving long term systemic change." Their goals include working actively to:

1. educate clergy and seminary students about sexual misconduct;
2. develop models in which survivors, religious leaders, helping professionals and even offenders can work together to promote healing and restitution;
3. support the theological study of healthy sexuality and appropriate use of power;
4. publish relevant materials;
5. advance research;

---

[11]www.silentlambs.org.
[12]"Catholics, Jehovah's Witnesses Sheltering Sexual Abusers?" *Religion Watch*, Vol. 17, No. 5 (March, 2002), p. 2.
[13]Richard N. Ostling for The Associated Press, "Group: Jehovah's Witnesses protect child abusers," Salt Lake Tribune, April 3, 2004, pp. C1 and C3.
[14]Ostling, "Group: Jehovah's Witnesses protect child abusers," p. C3.

6. provide accurate information about sexual misconduct;
7. work with other organizations dealing with this problem.[15]

## SAME-SEX MARRIAGE AND THE ROLE OF GAYS AND LESBIANS IN COMMUNITIES OF FAITH

Issues around human sexuality have also been front and center in communities of faith in two other ways. Increasing discussion of same-sex marriage has forced religious organizations to reconsider their stance. The appointment of an openly gay Anglican bishop has heightened the debate over the role of gays and lesbians throughout the Christian church. Both illustrate the conflicts that can come about when people in faith communities differ in their interpretation of what course of conduct is most consonant with their religious traditions.

In 2004, the state of Massachusetts began granting marriage licenses to gay and lesbian couples. While many, both gay and straight, applauded the move toward full equality under the law, others heard it as the death knell of the traditional marriage and family structure on which society is based. In religious terms, the response is often depicted as a conservative versus liberal issue, and to some extent, it is. But, as is often the case, the reality is more complex than such a simple division suggests. There are religious liberals who favor legalizing same sex civil unions, for example, but who do not want the term *marriage* used to describe them. And there are religious conservatives who use pro-family arguments to support same-sex marriages. Neither is it simply a debate between those who favor religion and those who do not.

Statistically, people who are "very committed" religiously are more strongly opposed to gay marriage than is any other group of Americans. According to a survey by the Pew Research Center, almost 80 percent of those who attend religious services at least weekly (one measure of religious commitment, albeit an imperfect one) oppose gay marriage, and nearly 60 percent of them are against same-sex civil unions. On the other hand, under half of those who never attend religious services oppose same-sex marriage, and less than a third oppose legalizing same-sex civil unions.[16]

Certainly opposition is more common among religious conservatives. Data from one survey, for example, indicate that only 13 percent of evangelical Protestants favor gay marriage, while 37 percent of mainline Protestants and 35 percent of Catholics do so.[17] Although the divide over same-sex marriage is not simply a liberal-conservative issue, there is clear preliminary indication that the issue has revitalized conservative Christian political activism,

---

[15]Interfaith Sexual Trauma Institute, www.csbsju.edu/isti/mission.html.

[16]"The Ties That Divide: A Conversation on Gay Marriage with Andrew Sullivan and Gerard Bradley," The Pew Forum on Religion and Public Life, http://pewforum.org/events/.

[17]"Religious Beliefs Underpin Opposition to Homosexuality," http://pewforum.org/docs/index.php?DocID=37.

which had grown somewhat listless in recent years. Conservative activists see the defense of traditional marriage as a "lightning rod for fresh energy" and a way to "rally new troops" in the movement.[18] The Christian Coalition Web site, for example, gives a lot of attention to its goal of getting a marriage amendment added to the Constitution. The Coalition has long supported Congresswoman Marilyn Musgrave's (R, CO) Federal Marriage Amendment which states:

> Marriage in the United States shall consist only of the union of a man and a woman. Neither this Constitution or the constitution of any state, nor state or federal law, shall be construed to require that marital status or the legal incidents thereof be conferred upon unmarried couples or groups.The Coalition also supports the Federal Marriage Amendment sponsored by Senators Wayne Allard, Sam Brownback, and Jeff Sessions introduced in Dec. 2003.[19]

In response to the legalization of same-sex marriage in Massachusetts, supportive clergy formed a coalition, the Religious Coalition for Freedom to Marry.[20] Their Web site has contact information for clergy who perform same-sex marriages and a declaration of their support, along with other resources. All of the clergy whose contact information is listed would reasonably be described as liberal. The list of those who signed the declaration itself is a bit broader, but still overwhelmingly liberal. The site states their view in terms of civic justice and freedom of conscience. They state their opposition to the use of religion to deny the legal right of marriage to same sex couples and affirm the right of all adults to marry and affirm complete freedom of conscience on this question. When they examine the faith traditions they share, they

> are resolved that the State should not interfere with same-gender couples who choose to marry and share fully and equally in the rights, responsibilities, and commitments of civil marriage.[21]

Most often, those who oppose gay marriage believe extending the right to marry to gays and lesbians is an attack on religion and the traditional values it historically has supported. Opponents see the Massachusetts decision as one more item in a more general trend in American culture that allows and even celebrates individual sexual license over responsibility. Proponents, on the other hand, tend to see it as a civil rights issue and the right to marry as a vic-

---

[18]Avery Johnson, "Christian Coalition Working for a Revival," *The Wall Street Journal* (June 21, 2004), p. A4.
[19]Christian Coalition of America, www.cc.org.
[20]Religious Coalition for Freedom to Marry, www.ftmmass.org/rcfm/.
[21]Massachusetts Declaration of Religious Support for the Freedom of Same-Gender Couples to Marry, http://www.ftmmass.org/rcfm/declare.htm.

tory for individual civil rights. The Massachusetts "decision recognizes and codifies, social changes that have been evolving over decades. For proponents, this was why same-sex marriages should be legally recognized; for opponents, precisely why they shouldn't be."[22]

Opponents of same-sex marriage see it as part and parcel of the same attitude that has eroded marital commitment and sexual responsibility across the board. This, they say, has brought with it an increase in the divorce rate, in cohabitation, in infidelity, in the number of children born to single mothers, in sexually-transmitted diseases, and pornography, among other things. Proponents, while hardly celebrating results such as the increased incidence of sexually transmitted diseases and infidelity, nonetheless herald the underlying attitude as a positive increase in individual freedoms and a beneficial lessening of social and governmental control over what consenting adults do with each other behind closed doors.

Speaking from a self-identified conservative viewpoint, Andrew Sullivan, a participant in the Pew Forum on the issue, described his position as "at root a very pro-family argument." Essentially, his point is that all persons should be permitted to enter into marriage and family ties, for the sake of the entire society.[23]

Referring specifically to the desire for an amendment to the Constitution to ban same-sex marriage, Sullivan stated his belief that since all persons are made in God's image, all deserve the same treatment under the law. The Constitution should not forbid to one group the rights it grants to another.[24]

Most religious conservatives do not agree with this position. James Dobson's Focus on the Family organization has been outspoken in its opposition, citing reasons ranging from negative changes in the public schools, adoption and foster care plans to stresses on health care delivery systems and the Social Security system to the threat that children in same-sex families will not be taught the Christian faith and the world will become "as it was in the days of Noah" (that is, destroyed by God for its sins).[25]

The Southern Baptist Convention, a large conservative/fundamentalist Protestant denomination, passed a resolution in support of a constitutional amendment banning same-sex marriage. It cites marriage as "the foundation of the God-ordained institution of the family" and states that the "union of one man and one woman is the only form of marriage prescribed in the Bible as God's perfect design for the family." It further defines marriage as "the uniting of one man and one woman in covenant commitment." The document

---

[22]David W. Machacek, "Same-Sex Culture War," *Religion in the News*, Vol. 7, No. 1 (Spring, 2004), p. 6.

[23]"The Ties That Divide: A Conversation on Gay Marriage with Andrew Sullivan and Gerard Bradley," The Pew Forum on Religion and Public Life, http://pewforum.org/events/.

[24]"The Ties That Divide: A Conversation on Gay Marriage with Andrew Sullivan and Gerard Bradley," The Pew Forum on Religion and Public Life, http://pewforum.org/events/.

[25]Focus on the Family Web site, www.family.org. This site contains a wealth of good material on the conservative Christian opposition to same-sex marriages and civil unions.

calls on both the House and Senate to pass such an amendment and upon all Southern Baptists to work actively for its passage.[26]

In sharp contrast, the Reverend William G. Sinkford, President of the liberal Unitarian Universalist Association, officiated the wedding of Julie and Hillary Goodridge, lead plaintiffs in the case that led to the legalization of same-sex marriage in Massachusetts. It was the first wedding Mr. Sinkford had performed since he signed a pledge not to officiate any weddings until same-sex marriages were legal. He commented that it "was great privilege to participate in the marriage of this loving and committed couple. It is a great and happy day for Unitarian Universalism and for all of the citizens of the Commonwealth." And on May 20, 2003, fifty same-sex couples were married in the Unitarian Universalist Arlington Street Church in Boston. The Association's Web site also provides an extensive *Same-Sex Wedding Guide* for persons who are called upon to officiate such ceremonies.[27]

Although there is nothing in the Massachusetts decision that requires the leaders of churches or synagogues to perform same-sex marriages, the legalization of it puts the question before communities of faith collectively and individually in a way that is new and promises to intensify both discussion and debate.

In 2003, an openly-gay Episcopal clergyman was elected bishop in the Episcopal Diocese of New Hampshire. Bishop Robinson, previously married and the father of two adult daughters, now lives in a committed relationship with a male partner. One source described the result as "the culmination of a three-month story that has precipitated the biggest crisis in the Anglican Communion since 1534, when Henry VIII declared that he and not the Pope would be the Supreme Head of the Church of England."[28] Interestingly enough, the 1534 crisis also concerned human sexual arrangements. Henry VIII declared himself head of the Church of England because he wanted to be able to divorce his wife and remarry without censure from his church.

Communities of faith have discussed, debated, and sometimes fought over the issue of what roles homosexual persons could have in their faith communities for many years. The Episcopal Church has been no exception. This faith tradition has ordained gays to the priesthood for several years, and has elevated them to the status of bishop as well. What made the consecration of Bishop Gene Robinson and his election to the New Hampshire office different is that he is *openly* gay.

Reaction from those not in favor was strong and swift. Bishop Robert Duncan of Pittsburgh, Pennsylvania, spoke on behalf of those opposed, noting that they were "filled with sorrow" and felt a "grief too deep for words." He voiced concern that the assembly had "denied the plain teaching of Scripture and the moral consensus of the church throughout the ages," and had

[26]Available on the Southern Baptist Convention Web site, www.sbc.net.
[27]The Unitarian Universalist Association, www.uua.org.
[28]Frank Fitzpatrick, "The Anglican Crackup," *Religion in the News*, Vol. 6, No. 3 (Fall, 2003), p. 2.

"divided itself from millions of Anglican Christians throughout the world."[29] Some Episcopalians began talking about schism and leaving the historic church, while others counseled caution and forbearance.

At this time, the debate within the Episcopal Church in the United States, as well as in the worldwide Anglican Communion, continues. The American Anglican Council, a conservative movement within the American church, has issued "A Place To Stand: A Call To Action." It repudiates the consecration of Bishop Robinson and the church's acceptance of same-sex union blessing ceremonies. It calls on the church's leaders to repent and withdraws financial support as far as possible from any church structures that support them.

Despite these initiatives in response to Bishop Robinson's election, the widely-predicted schism has not happened, neither between the Episcopal Church in the United States and the worldwide Anglican Communion, nor between factions within the United States, at least not as of this writing. Meanwhile, the American church continues to serve its parishioners and the larger world while continuing the discussion and debate. Further, the traditional Episcopal approach of being able to contain within itself dramatic variations of opinion seems to be holding. Even the most distressed, angry, and vocal dissenters have not wanted to make the radical move to actual disunion. Despite very deep and heartfelt differences of opinion on homosexuality and on the consecration of Gene Robinson as a Bishop, the prevailing desire seems to be to avoid schism. There is even a (as yet, informal) movement referred to by the term *Via Media* or "Middle Way," whose purpose is to prevent schism from happening by encouraging individual dioceses not to pursue disunion.

## RELIGION AND VIOLENCE: AFTER 9-11

Prior to September 11, 2001, concern about religion's potential for violence had focused largely on those religions that people often label *cults*. Satanists were often accused of acts of particularly gruesome violence. Krishna Consciousness devotees and The Way were accused of weapons stockpiling. The image of the Branch Davidian compound in Texas engulfed in flames was fresh in many peoples' minds. Christian Identity, a militantly racist and anti-Semitic movement, raised fears that their radical talk about being "soldiers in God's army," responsible for helping bring about Armageddon, might translate into violence.

By the turn of the century, popular concern about religion's potentially dangerous underside had already come to focus largely on the Catholic Church, a firmly established part of mainstream religion in most peoples' minds, as it dealt with the scandal of sexual abuse by priests. Then the planes tore into the World Trade Center and the Pentagon, and life for most people in the United States changed forever. Fear about religion's potential for violence

---

[29]CNN.com http://www.cnn.com/2003/US/08/05/bishop/.

shifted abruptly to the interface of religion and nationalism, and especially to the relationship between religion and violence in Islam.

A recent study of religion and violence focuses on the three closely related religions, Judaism, Christianity, and Islam, that are predominant in the United States. The study's author notes that all three exhibit a profoundly ambiguous attitude about violence:

> We look to our sacred scriptures for words of consolation and hope and we find them there pervasive, but many of the words in sacred scriptures express threat and violence. Western cultures have been shaped by religions that, at best, have sounded uncertain trumpets. Judaism, Christianity, and Islam are all forms of spirituality and religious practice that derive directly from ancient Israelite religion, and that religious tradition speaks with remarkable and disappointing ambiguity.[30]

In the current situation, there are no clear-cut "good guys" and "bad guys." Although many persons and groups both here and abroad seek to give simple answers and point fingers of unambiguous blame, doing so is dishonest and further exacerbates the problem.

## The Muslim Response

Muslims, of course, lived in the United States for many decades before 9-11; the first Muslim mosque (place for prayer and worship) was built in Cedar Rapids, Iowa, in 1934. Throughout the years, their presence had become increasingly visible, especially as the numbers of Muslims in the professions—law, teaching, medicine—grew.

In the days immediately following the attacks, law enforcement agencies received hundreds of reports of incidents of harassment, discrimination, and attacks on Muslim people and places. Mosques were defaced and threatening messages left on their voice mail. Religiously-based slurs and epithets were directed at Muslims and anyone who "looked Muslim." I have a number of female Muslim friends who wear the traditional Muslim head covering. Many of them were afraid to leave the safety of their homes for fear of reprisals. Muslim children stayed home from schools, and Middle-Easterners who are not Muslim feared for their safety as well.

A study by The Council on American Islamic Relations (CAIR) showed a 15 percent increase in the number of incidents and experiences of anti-Muslim violence, discrimination, and harassment during 2002. Further, there was an increase in "negative results produced by government policies that target

---

[30]J. Harold Ellens, "Introduction: The Destructive Power of Religion," in *The Destructive Power of Religion: Violence in Judaism, Christianity, and Islam*, ed. J. Harold Ellens, Vol. 1, *Sacred Scriptures, Ideology, and Violence* (Westport, CT: Praeger, 2004), p. 2.

ordinary Americans based on religion, ethnicity, or national origin."[31] Hardened attitudes could be seen in the publication of books detailing the "Islamic menace" and portraying Islam as a blood-thirsty and evil religion.

Most American Muslims moved quickly to condemn the actions of the terrorists and acquaint non-Muslims with the peaceful aspects of Islam. Heightened public scrutiny following the attacks, while uncomfortable for most Muslims, also gave Muslims the opportunity to provide more accurate information about mainstream Islam and to counter the actions of the few. Many pushed aside their fear of persecution in order to interact with their non-Muslim counterparts, speaking publicly, answering questions, writing newspaper pieces, and addressing church groups and interfaith associations. This was certainly the case in the city in which I live. Our small Muslim community became much more vocal and visible in the wake of 9-11. The mosque sponsored events, and Muslims as individuals reached out to those of us who are not Muslim in the attempt to build bridges of understanding and peace.

At the same time, although some non-Muslim Americans reacted with hatred, most responded differently, realizing that the terrorists did not represent mainstream Islam. At a local hospital, non-Islamic staff reached out to Muslim physicians and non-Muslim Middle Eastern staff members with concern and compassion. Students and staffs of universities and colleges made a point of reassuring Muslim students and staff members that the university was a safe place where they would be respected. There were interfaith gatherings across the country in which people of all faiths and of none pledged to stand together with Muslims and against violence in the name of religion.

In the wake of continuing incidents, those of Muslim faith still experience the hatred of their fellow Americans. A CAIR document from July 4, 2004, reported that an American Muslim convert who wears a head covering was attacked at a stop sign in Illinois. A man and two women began kicking her car and screaming anti-Muslim epithets after asking her for a light for a cigarette. When she got out of her car, she was beaten and her head scarf torn off. In California, a Middle Eastern Muslim was attacked and beaten outside a grocery store. Anti-Islamic threats and vandalism struck several Islamic centers in Florida, with similar incidents occurring in New Jersey and Missouri, as well as in other states.

At the same time, Muslims themselves continue to reach out. Writing in the May 16, 2004, Muncie *StarPress* newspaper, my friend and former colleague Faiz Rahman responded to the beheading of prisoner Nick Berg:

> I express my deepest disgust of the killers. They are nothing but subhuman, barbaric creatures. My disgust is amplified by the fact that these criminals claimed their affiliation to Islam—my religion. They are, in fact, an affront to Islam. . . . Prophet Muhammad instructed Muslims to treat prisoners with

---

[31]CAIR Web site, www.cair-net.org/asp/crr2003.asp.

compassion, not to kill them, and not to mutilate any dead bodies. Yet these thugs did exactly that and claimed they were doing it in the name of Islam. . . . The fanatics and zealots represent only themselves, whatever religion or country they may come from.[32]

## Why Religious Violence?

It is important to remember that, worldwide, the last decade has seen violence perpetrated by people who claimed affiliation with religions other than Islam. Religious studies scholars Mark Juergensmeyer and Catherine Wessinger call to mind the shooting of doctors who perform abortions, the bombing of abortion clinics, and the destruction of the Murrah Federal Building in Oklahoma by right-wing Christians. There was the standoff at Ruby Ridge, and the suicidal events in the Solar Temple and Heaven's Gate. Violence has erupted between various Jewish groups, and has been perpetrated by Jews against Palestinians as well as Palestinians against Jews. Sikhs in India have been involved in assassinations, most notably that of Indira Ghandi, and Japanese radicals who claimed affiliation with both Hinduism and Buddhism left deadly nerve gas in a Tokyo subway.[33] It is also important that we keep in mind that all religious violence has not been directed at persons and groups outside the perpetrator's own faith. There has also been violence between Muslim groups, for example, and between Jewish groups, as well as between Christians.

Recent incidents of religious violence, no matter where they have occurred, have become a part of nearly everyone's lives as they have been reported and shown in graphic detail on international television. The attacks on the World Trade Center and the Pentagon brought religious violence home to Americans in a way that we had not known before. Foreign embassies had been attacked previously, but attackers from outside the United States had not attacked on American soil. Scholars began to search for answers to the pressing question, "*Why?*" To be able to answer that question offers some comfort, making the violence seem less random and chaotic. It may also lead to better informed efforts to minimize future violence. As Mark Juergensmeyer notes:

> If the answer is no, these cases may suggest a worldwide loosening of social control that makes inexplicable acts of violence possible. If it is yes, and if we can find convincing explanations for these patterns, we may shed some light on why

---

[32]Faiz Rahman, "Acts of Fanatics Don't Show Real Islam," Muncie, Indiana, *StarPress*, May 16, 2004, pp. D1 and D6.

[33]Mark Juergensmeyer, *Terror in the Mind of God: The Global Rise of Religious Violence* (Berkeley, CA: The University of California Press, 2000), chapters 2–6, and Catherine Wessinger, *How the Millennium Comes Violently: From Jonestown to Heaven's Gate* (New York: Seven Bridges Press, 2000), chapters 3 through 7.

violence and religion have reemerged so dramatically at this moment in history, and why they have so frequently been found in combination.[34]

Given the clear diversity of religious violence, can we discern any common factors? Several authors have responded to that question. One thing that seems to predispose to violent tactics in the name of religion is a sharply dualistic worldview. This view divides the world sharply and clearly into us and them, good and evil, often put in terms of God and Satan. It makes the other the enemy. Most religious persons who hold such a view—and there are many who do—engage the conflict through prayer, faith, and worship. A small minority turn to physical, armed conflict. A belief in outside persecution and a sense that the group will be unable to achieve its goals increase the likelihood of overt violence.[35]

Dualism can lead directly into the concept of *divine or cosmic warfare*, another predisposing factor. This image is a persistent one in many religions. Again, most who believe that they are called to engage in cosmic warfare do so through nonviolent methods, while a very few take up arms in what they perceive to be the cause of God. Sometimes this imagery is linked with real-world political confrontations in which nationalism or tribalism plays a large role. In these instances, the divine warfare imagery places the worldly encounter in a much larger context, giving it even greater importance than it would otherwise have. It becomes not just earthly warfare, but an earthly embodiment of a transcendent battle whose beginnings may reach back to the creation of the world.[36]

This divine warfare has become what one author calls the "Master Story of Western culture." He states his thesis provocatively:

> This violent metaphor . . . has settled into the center of the psyche of the communities of faith we know as Judaism, Christianity, and Islam. Through them it has shaped the unconscious psychosocial assumptions of our cultures. This set of unconscious apocalyptic assumptions forms the sources and stage set for what we find meaningful in our cultures, from the violent game machines in the arcades our teenagers frequent to the actions of the Islamic Fundamentalists who flew airplanes into the World Trade Center and the Pentagon. It is a short psychospiritual step from the vicarious forms of wishful mythic violence in the arcade machine to the mythic wishes that hurled gasoline-laden flying machines into the workplace of twenty thousand New Yorkers.[37]

Whether we agree or not with his assertion that the distance between arcade game violence and terrorist attacks is a short step, there is little doubt

---

[34]Juergensmeyer, *Terror in the Mind of God*, p. 119.
[35]Wessinger, *How the Millennium Comes Violently*, pp. 17–18.
[36]Juergensmeyer, *Terror in the Mind of God*, Chapter 9.
[37]Ellens, "Introduction: The Destructive Power of Religion," p. 4.

that much of the world lives, as do we in the United States, in cultures in which powerful images of violence abound.

The religiously motivated acts of violence that have occurred in the last decade have been what Juergensmeyer calls *performance violence*. They have been not only acts of violence, destruction, murder, and bloodshed, but acts "executed in a deliberately intense and vivid way. It is as if these acts were designed to maximize the savage nature of their violence and meant to purposely elicit anger."[38] Performance violence is symbolic in that it refers to something beyond itself. It refers to the "master story" cited earlier. These "explosive scenarios are not *tactics* directed toward an immediate, earthly, or strategic goal, but *dramatic events* [that is, performances] intended to impress for their symbolic significance."[39] This feature of religious violence made the World Trade Center an especially apt target for the 1993 bombing, and later for the 2001 attack. The tallest buildings in New York City, the twin towers stood as a fitting symbol of all that the radical Muslim world had come to define as the enemy other, the tool of Satan. They also symbolized the radical secularity of American public life, and to the terrorists' minds, destroying that symbol was a gain for religion, if only for a moment. They seemed to many Americans invulnerable living monuments to American economic power and international position, and for that reason, an important part of the "performance" was to show them in their greatest vulnerability. The attack on the Pentagon was similar in that it was designed to showcase the vulnerability of the American military, the agency of what the terrorists believed to be American international domination. The attempted attack on Washington, D.C. targeted the American governmental system.

The performance and symbolic nature of religiously motivated violence is also served by the extent to which these events compel unceasing media attention. Mahmud Abouhalima, convicted in the WTC bombing in 1993, once remarked that the news media is completely controlled by secular forces and Islam was thus not able to have its side of the story presented in the media. To have focused worldwide media attention virtually nonstop on the attacks was seen as a victory of radical religion over the pervasive forces of secularism.[40]

Religiously motivated warfare is portrayed as being a conflict between divine forces and the forces of Satan. Thus, it demonizes the enemy. It also produces *martyrs*, sacrificial victims, another very long-standing and powerful religious image. Especially in the context of the intense religious-political commitment many have called fanaticism, martyrs sacrifice their lives for both their religion and their political agenda, gaining as it were a "double blessing." Juergensmeyer points out that sacrifice is ritual destruction that has

---

[38]Juergensmeyer, *Terror in the Mind of God*, p. 119.

[39]Juergensmeyer, *Terror in the Mind of God*, p. 123.

[40]Juergensmeyer, *Terror in the Mind of God*, chapter 7. Juergensmeyer develops his thesis in response to the bombing of the World Trade Center in 1993, but its usefulness in understanding the events of 9-11 is even clearer, in my opinion, and I have applied it accordingly.

been found in every religious tradition at some time. The word *sacrifice* itself comes from the Latin *sacrificium, to make holy,* suggesting that the act of destroying, or in the case of martyrs, volunteering to be destroyed, is sanctifying. The struggle itself, and giving one's life for it, regardless of whether there is any realistic hope of worldly success, becomes ennobling and sanctifying.

Yet another partial explanation for religious violence lies in the fact that all of the groups that have sanctioned violence in the form of terrorism have been marginal—in varying degrees—within their own religious societies.[41] Their violence has been in part a counterbalance to their marginality, a way of empowering them within their own religious communities.

Their marginality comes from three aspects of their religious style: They reject any compromise with liberal religious or secular values, compromise which characterizes the mainstream of most religions. Second, they do not believe religion should be a private matter, but rather should direct and perhaps dictate what goes on in the public square. Finally, they espouse a demanding form of the religious tradition that often characterized its earliest days. Because this is decisively not the style of mainstream religion, these groups become marginalized within their communities of faith.[42] They see themselves as embattled defenders of "pure faith" against the compromises of the less pure and rigorous.

## Violence and Islam

When religiously motivated violence arises in the context of Islam, the word *jihad* inevitably arises alongside it. Although many, perhaps most, non-Muslims routinely take it to mean aggressive holy war, it is a word with complex layers of meaning in the Qur'an (Muslim sacred scripture), in Muslim tradition, and in the understanding of ordinary Muslims. There is no single interpretation that all Muslims everywhere have ever agreed upon. It changes over time and with circumstances, and different individuals and groups give it their own interpretation. Its use and misuse by politicized extremist elements within Islam to garner support and justify their actions has encouraged its interpretation as violent holy war among non-Muslims.

Islam is a religion of action. It encourages its followers "to struggle (*jihad*) to implement their belief, to lead a good life, to defend religion, to contribute to the development of a just Islamic society throughout the world."[43] This is the larger context of the term jihad, the propensity of Muslims to understand their religion as active struggle, as striving, in all ways, following the model provided by the earliest traditions about the life of Prophet Muhammad and his followers.

---

[41]Juergensmeyer, *Terror in the Mind of God,* p. 218.
[42]Juergensmeyer, *Terror in the Mind of God,* p. 221.
[43]John L. Esposito, *Unholy War: Terror in the Name of Islam* (New York: Oxford University Press, 2002), p. 5.

American scholar of Islam John L. Esposito calls jihad "a defining concept or belief in Islam, a key element in what it means to be a believer and follower of God's Will."[44] Although it does not have to mean violence, the concept is ready at hand for those who wish to use it in that way. Muslims often distinguish between the greater and lesser jihads. The greater jihad is the daily struggle of individual Muslims to submit their wills to Allah (God). The lesser jihad is related to doing battle for the faith.

There are a number of other meanings and nuances of meaning, as well. Jihad as literal, armed warfare may be defensive, fighting against attack and oppression from without, or offensive, a more general struggle against all unbelievers and responsibility to spread the message of Islam. There are sharp differences of opinion about the extent to which it is permissible to use jihad as a tactic for conversion, as well. Most Muslims cite Qur'anic verses that speak against the use of any force in conversion, but others cite a Muslim obligation to convert everyone by whatever means necessary. Sometimes the word is used to refer to the struggle obligatory on any Muslim society to establish a just and righteous social order based on Islamic principles.

Today, the term jihad has become nearly all things to all Muslims, and the traditional criteria for what constitutes valid jihad—carefully spelled out in Islamic just war theory—are ignored by many of those who use the term to inflame hearts and minds against the United States and support their own use of violence:

> Today the term jihad has become comprehensive; resistance and liberation struggles and militant jihads, holy and unholy wars, are all declared to be jihads. Jihad is waged at home not only against unjust rulers in the Muslim world but also against a broad spectrum of civilians. Jihad's scope abroad became chillingly clear in the September 11 attacks against both the World Trade Center and the Pentagon, targeting not only governments but also civilians.
>
> Terrorists such as bin Laden and others go beyond classical Islam's criteria for a just jihad and recognize no limits but their own, employing any weapon or means. They reject Islamic law's regulations regarding the goals and means of a valid jihad (that violence must be proportional and that only the necessary amount of force should be used to repel the enemy), that innocent civilians should not be targeted, and that jihad must be declared by the ruler or head of state. Today, individuals and groups, religious and lay, seize the right to declare and legitimate unholy wars in the name of Islam.[45]

In 1967, the combined force of Egypt, Syria, and Jordan suffered a particularly devastating defeat at the hands of Israel in the Six-Day Arab-Israeli War. This defeat was a decisive turning point for Islam. The once-powerful

[44]Esposito, *Unholy War*, p. 26.
[45]Esposito, *Unholy War*, p. 157.

Muslim world was humiliated and angered. It called for jihad against Israel, fought in 1973. An Arab oil embargo, the results of which were felt around the globe, helped restore shattered Arab pride. Internal reform and opposition movements also increased within the House of Islam. All of these things contributed to an increased potential for violence within Islam.

Internal problems in many Muslim countries also have contributed to the establishment of politicized Muslim groups:

> During the past two decades, many Muslim countries have faced a large, restless younger generation; unemployment; housing shortages; maldistribution of wealth; and corruption. At the same time, globalization and increasing Western influence are seen by many as a threat to Islamic traditions. These elements have combined to create powerful Islamic political (fundamentalist) movements. . . . [Religious] extremist organizations and movements . . . "hijack" their religion, using it to justify violence and terrorism and calling for a jihad against their own societies, America and Europe.[46]

The extremists are a small minority, but they are a volatile and dangerous one.

Like many conservative members of other religions, notably Judaism and Christianity, conservative and fundamentalist Muslims believe that the values of the highly secularized Western world are fundamentally at odds with those of Muslim faith and culture. With the globalization of Western culture, many Muslims have developed a siege mentality, feeling constantly under attack. Under these circumstances, some individuals and groups will choose to fight back violently, as do those Christians in the United States who attack abortion clinics and stockpile weapons to fight in the coming "God's war."

Many Muslims also view the United States as supportive only of democratic forms of government (unless doing otherwise is in the political-economic interest of America). The difference between authoritarian and democratic governing structures may well be the "most glaring difference between the Muslim world and the West. . . ." Muslim nations typically remain "security states" in which rulers focus "on retaining their power and privilege at any cost through strong military and security forces." Those in which there is some semblance of democracy are very limited democracies at most. Even as the debate within Islam regarding the compatibility of Islam and democratic government has intensified, "modern Muslim experience supports the impression that Islam and democracy are incompatible."[47] In this situation, some Muslims feel United States support of democratic regimes to the exclusion of others as an attack on Islamic values and an attempt by American military and economic might to bring the Muslim world to heel. Even those Muslims who support liberalization and democratization of their governments emphasize that it should not be modeled on Western-style democracy. They believe that

---

[46]John L. Esposito, "Islam in the World and in America," in *World Religions in America, Third Edition*, Ed. Jacob Neusner (Louisville, KY: Westminster John Knox Press, 2003), p. 183.
[47]Esposito, *Unholy War*, pp. 142–43.

"Islam can provide the framework for combining democracy with spirituality and religious government."[48] Again, there is a small minority who calls for jihad against what they perceive to be oppression.

Yet another factor that makes the relationship between the United States and the Muslim world problematic for Muslims is their perception that the United States supports Israel uncritically while being unduly tough-handed in dealing with Islamic governments. This is a lightning rod issue because there are points of contention between Israel/Judaism and Islam that go back literally to biblical times and conflict over control of Jerusalem, a holy city for both faith traditions. Ironically, *Jerusalem* means "city of peace." The conflict between Israel and Palestine over land and sovereignty is but the most recent embodiment of a seemingly endless conflict.

Whether the United States dominates and exploits Muslim nations and the rest of the world, or seeks to do so, is a matter of spirited intellectual and popular debate in the United States and overseas. What *is* certain is that a substantial segment of the world's people, including those in traditionally Muslim nations, *believe* that it does. Within the Muslim world, as well, some groups perceive themselves deeply oppressed by other groups or individuals. This situation sets off a "virtually inevitable spiral of violence," according to one author. This spiral can be described in four stages: First, structural violence in the form of injustice and abuse of persons arises from the social order imposed by exploitive and predatory domineering forces. Second, protest and resistance to injustice arises. Third, the domineering group or individual uses whatever additional repression they deem necessary to put down the rebellion. The destruction continues, fourth, in an ever-increasing spiral of rebellion and repression.[49]

The prevalence of both the theme and the occurrence of violence throughout many of humankind's religions, including Christianity and Judaism as well as Islam, and extending to the Asian religious paths as well, strongly suggests to me that both the reaction "Islam is a bloody and militaristic religion" and the counterreaction, "Islam is all about peace" are both far too simple. Most of our religious traditions and faith communities have elements of both in their history, and most have been involved in overt violence, either in the past or currently. This may indeed be one of the rare instances in which saying *all*, rather than *most* is not specious overgeneralization.

### RELIGIOUS EXPRESSION IN A RELIGIOUSLY PLURAL CULTURE

The United States is one of the most religiously diverse, if not *the* most religiously diverse, country in the world. In such a setting, it is perhaps inevitable that the ways in which some religious organizations and individuals choose to

---

[48]Esposito, *Unholy War*, p. 146.
[49]R.A. Horsley, *Jesus and Empire: The Kingdom of God and the New World Disorder* (Minneapolis, MN: Fortress Press, 2003).

express their religiousness will offend others. As a result, those who have taken offense may attempt to curtail that expression. What ties the following otherwise disparate items together is that they all center conflicts over religious expression in our religiously diverse culture. All of them also have to do with the principles of disestablishment and the free exercise of religion that are guaranteed in the Constitution of the United States (see Chapter 2).

## The Ten Commandments in Alabama

One of the highest-profile incidents in recent years has been the furor ignited by the installation in the rotunda of the building that houses the Alabama Supreme Court of a 5280 pound granite monument with the Ten Commandments inscribed on it. The stone also contains quotations supporting the Decalogue, a part of both Jewish and Christian moral teaching, as the foundation of the American system of justice. Alabama Chief Justice Roy Moore had the monument placed in the rotunda late in the summer of 2001. It was placed at night, and no one had been notified that it would be installed. Justice Moore had earlier had a wooden Ten Commandments plaque in his circuit court courtroom. His fight against a lawsuit seeking the removal of that plaque led to his campaign and election as Alabama's Chief Justice, running as the "Ten Commandments Judge."[50]

In fall, 2001, the American Civil Liberties Union and Americans United for the Separation of Church and State filed suit to have the monument removed on the grounds that its presence in the Supreme Court Building sent a clear message of government support for the Judeo-Christian religious tradition and thus violated the disestablishment clause of the First Amendment. The initial ruling was in favor of the plaintiffs. Demonstrations both for and against the monument followed in short order.

Justice Moore, as would be expected, appealed the ruling. In the summer of 2003, the Eleventh Circuit Court of Appeals again ruled in favor of the plaintiffs. They ordered the monument removed. Justice Moore refused and appealed to the United States Supreme Court to intervene. The Court rejected his appeal. The Appeals court had ordered removal by midnight August 20. On August 22, Justice Moore was suspended as Chief Justice for refusing to obey a court order. Workers removed the monument from its place in the rotunda several days later, placing it in a locked closet in another part of the building. That fall, the United States Supreme Court rejected an appeal by Justice Moore that the monument be allowed to be displayed in another part of the building. Moore, for his part, rejected a proposal that the Ten Commandments be displayed alongside other, secular historical documents that form the foundation of American law. Such displays have been judged constitutional in the past. In November, 2003, Justice Moore was permanently removed from his office.

---

[50]www.CNN.com, November 14, 2003.

A poll carried out by CNN, *USA Today*, and the Gallup polling organization following the removal of the monument found that slightly over three-fourths of Americans in its sample disapproved of the order to remove the monument.[51]

Moore, as expected, fought to have himself reinstated. In Spring, 2004, however, a seven-member special review court upheld his removal from office. In a unanimous ruling, the review court held that Moore's removal from office was "proper" on the grounds that he had violated state ethics codes when he refused to comply with the federal court order requiring removal of the monument. Although this ruling appeared to be his last opportunity for an appeal, Moore has indicated he may appeal again to the United States Supreme Court.

More often than not, disestablishment issues and free exercise of religion issues are two sides of the same coin, or seem so in the protagonists' minds. Moore and his supporters, including several conservative Christian organizations, see the courts' decision as a violation of the free exercise of religion. The Reverend Barry Lynn, executive director of Americans United for Separation of Church and State, however, called it "a tremendous victory for the rule of law and respect for religious diversity."[52]

## "Under God" in the Pledge of Allegiance

Cases involving the Pledge of Allegiance have been heard in the Supreme Court a number of times. The most recent case dealt with the inclusion of the phrase "under God" in the Pledge. *Elk Grove Unified School District* v. *Newdow* was brought by a California atheist who challenged the inclusion of the Pledge as part of the daily ritual in his daughter's public school classroom. As an atheist, he believed that his daughter's reciting "under God" in the Pledge amounted to government coercion of religion. Children are not required to participate in reciting the Pledge, but Dr. Newdow believed that his daughter's presence while it was being recited violated his religious convictions. Although the government did not rule on the church-state issue posed by Dr. Newdow's suit, its ruling leaves the words "under God" in the Pledge.

The Court ruled that Dr. Newdow did not have legal standing to speak for his daughter since he is the noncustodial parent. Although in agreement that Newdow did not have legal standing to bring the case, Justices William Rhenquist, Sandra Day O'Connor, and Clarence Thomas wrote separately to note that the recitation of the Pledge with "under God" included does not violate the separation of religion and government. In this case, the Supreme Court's ruling overturned a two-year-old ruling that had deemed it unconstitutional for teachers to lead students in the Pledge.

[51]www.CNN.com, November 14, 2003.
[52]www.CNN.com, November 14, 2003.

Response from both sides of the issue again indicates the close relationship between establishment and free exercise. Barry Lynn of Americans United commented "The justices ducked this issue today, but it is likely to come back in the future. Students should not feel compelled by school officials to subscribe to a particular religious belief in order to show love of country." On the other side, a representative of the American Center for Law and Justice, a conservative Christian organization, noted that "[while] the court did not address the merits of the case, it is clear that the Pledge of Allegiance and the words 'under God' can continue to be recited by students across America." Not originally a part of the Pledge, the phrase "under God" was added in 1954. Those who supported the addition of the phrase stated that the words distinguished the United States from "godless communism."[53]

## No Government Financial Aid for Students Studying for Ministry

According to a recent United States Supreme Court ruling, states may refuse financial aid to students studying for professional ministry. Joshua Davey was a student at an Assemblies of God-affiliated college in Washington state. A scholarship he had been awarded earlier was rescinded when he chose to major in business administration *and theology*. Attorneys for Mr. Davey had argued that banning aid to a student because he was studying for professional ministry was a violation of the religious freedoms guaranteed in the First Amendment because it discriminated on the basis of religion.

The Court disagreed. Chief Justice William H. Rehnquist wrote for the Court: "Training someone to lead a congregation is essentially a religious endeavor. Indeed, majoring in devotional theology is akin to a religious calling as well as an academic pursuit." Thus, to allow state aid to such students would constitute a government establishment of religion. Washington state's attorney general, Christine Gregoire, agreed: "The framers of Washington's Constitution believed that religious freedom was best protected by ensuring that public money would not be used to support religious activity with which others may disagree."[54]

The 2004 ruling echoes previous rulings that have not permitted the use of government funds for sectarian religious education at any level. Two things should be noted. (1) The ruling does not affect students who attend religiously-affiliated colleges and universities to study other subjects. Scholarship aid is available to those students as it is to those who choose to attend schools not sponsored by religious organizations. (2) The ruling also does not affect students who major or minor in religious studies from an academic perspective.

[53]Anne Gearen for the Associated Press, "Supreme Court Preserves 'God' in Pledge," www.comcast.net/news, 6/14/04.
[54]Reported in *The Chronicle of Higher Education*, February 26, 2004, www.chronicle.com.

The ruling affects only those students studying for professional ministry in communities of faith, involved in a course of study of theology from a devotional perspective.

The Court's decision was a 7–2 vote, with Justices Antonin Scalia and Clarence Thomas dissenting sharply. Justice Scalia wrote, "Let there be no doubt: This case is about discrimination against a religious minority." This interpretation echoes that of Mr. Davey's attorney, Jay Sekulow, who said the ruling "clearly sanctions religious discrimination" and that the Court had "missed an important opportunity to protect the constitutional rights of all students."

This is yet another situation in which perspective is hugely important. From one angle of vision, not allowing government funding for students who wish to prepare for ministry rather than, for example, teaching English or chemistry, appears to discriminate against those students on the basis of their choice of a religious vocation. But looked at from the opposite perspective, funding their education would appear to be government support of religion. Adjudicating First Amendment cases has been a delicate balancing act from the outset. As religious diversity continues to increase and religious groups and individuals become more outspoken in their views and expectations of equal treatment under the law, negotiating their competing interests will, it seems, only become more complex.

### Religion Exemptions and Hiring for Tax-Funded Positions

The question of whether religious organizations may choose to hire only those of their own faith for programs for which they receive tax funding raises issues similar to those in the *Davey* case. The House of Representatives recently rejected by a 232 to 183 vote an attempt to prevent religious organizations from doing so. The importance of this issue has increased with the initiative toward faith-based initiatives for social services (see Chapter 2).

The Community Services Block Grant Act (H.R. 3030) contains a provision which permits religious groups that receive funds under the program to hire only those of their own faith. This differs from hiring by other employers, who are forbidden by law to discriminate based on religion (as well as on the basis of several other things):

> Federal civil rights laws from the 1960s prevent employers from discriminating on the basis of religion but contain special exemptions that allow churches and similar religious organizations to hire only adherents of their own faith. However, several federal programs deny government contracts and funding to groups that practice job discrimination, including on religious grounds.[55]

Language is important here. The connotations of exemption and discrimination are rather different. The Act simply provides an exemption that allows

---

[55]"House approves another bill allowing religious discrimination," Baptist Joint Committee, *Report from the Capital*, Vol. 59, No. 2 (February, 2004), p. 1.

religious organizations to hire based on the religious affiliation of the applicant. It becomes discrimination in the eyes of those who see it as a negative thing.

This matter concerns jobs that are not directly related to religion, and jobs for which there is at least some federal funding. There has never been any attempt to restrict the hiring practices of communities of faith for religiously sensitive positions or for which they were not receiving tax money. Presbyterians for example, are quite free to hire only Presbyterians as ministers of congregations, choir directors, or church educators. Jewish pre-schools and day-care centers may hire only Jewish teachers, so long as they are not government-funded. The concern comes in when religious organizations receive part of their funding from tax monies for social services programs. The following two comments illustrate the dilemma:

> Why should it be legal for a group to accept a $5 million Head Start or job-training grant from the taxpayers and say we are not going to hire Jews or Catholics? [Representative Chet Edwards, a Democrat from Texas]

> Why should a faith-based organization that is providing tremendous community services give up the protections granted to them under the 1964 Civil Rights Act just because they accept federal dollars in their mission to help low-income people? [Representative John Boehner, an Ohio Republican][56]

These types of questions can be expected to continue and to increase as religious organizations participate in faith-based initiatives to provide social services. The interface of funding and hiring is one of the ongoing concerns of people who oppose faith-based initiatives.

### No Hats, No Caps . . . No *Hijab?*

*Hijab* is the Arabic term for the head covering worn by many Muslim girls and women. Technically, hijab is a scarf that covers the head and neck and extends down around the shoulders. Many choose to wear it in obedience to scripture and tradition, and as a symbol of their identification with Islam. Other Muslim women and girls choose to wear a scarf wound around the head and knotted at the nape of the neck.

Nashala Hearn, an eleven-year-old school girl in Oklahoma, was suspended from school twice for wearing her hijab. School officials said that her head covering violated the school policy against students wearing "hats, caps, bandannas, plastic caps or hoods on jackets" in the building. She and her family sued for her right to cover her head. The Department of Justice intervened in support of the family. Nashala was granted the right to wear her hijab to

---

[56]Cited in "House approves another bill allowing religious discrimination," Baptist Joint Committee, *Report from the Capital*, Vol. 59, No. 2 (February, 2004), p. 1.

school, and the school district was required to rewrite its dress code to allow for religious exemptions.[57]

Similar questions have arisen in employment settings, not only about Muslim hijabs but about Jewish males, for example, who wear a *kippah* or head covering, or female members of some Christian groups who may not want to wear a uniform with slacks or short sleeves rather than a skirt and long sleeves. As a general rule, the courts have held that employers and school officials need to accommodate religiously-based requests for exemptions to dress codes, and that employees and students must be allowed to wear religiously symbolic items such as hijabs, crosses, or wrist malas (a bracelet of prayer beads worn by some Hindus and Buddhists). They may, however, require modifications based on safety or other considerations. For example, if a Muslim woman wearing hijab will be operating machinery, the loose ends of her scarf need to be tucked in. An employer may tell a Jewish man that the color of his kippah may not clash with the color of his uniform.

It appears that controversy around religious issues, both within communities of faith and between faith groups and the larger culture, will continue, and perhaps even intensify in coming years. Both culture and religion in the United States are dynamic and evolving, and in that situation, conflicts are bound to occur. It also appears that religiously motivated violence will remain a factor both here and abroad.

### QUESTIONS AND ACTIVITIES FOR REVIEW, DISCUSSION, AND WRITING

1. In a paragraph each, respond to each of the quotations with which this chapter begins.
2. Read the Charter for the Protection of Children and Young People (www.usccb.org/bishops/charter.htm). Write an essay in which you respond to its provisions.
3. Similarly, write an essay in which you respond to the work of the Interfaith Sexual Trauma Institute.
4. In your own opinion, should communities of faith bless or recognize in some other way marriages or commitments between partners of the same sex? What reasons can you give for your position?
5. If possible, have a representative of the Muslim faith come and speak to your class about the Muslim response to the events of September 11, 2001.
6. Summarize each of the reasons given in this chapter for religiously motivated violence.
7. What restrictions, if any, do you believe should apply to religious expression in our culture?
8. Should religious organizations be able to hire only those of their own faith for programs for which they receive government funding? Why or why not?

---

[57]Reported in Baptist Joint Committee, *Report from the Capital*, Vol. 59, No. 5 (May, 2004).

## *For Further Reading*

J. Harold Ellens, Ed. *The Destructive Power of Religion: Violence in Judaism, Christianity, and Islam.* Westport, CT: Praeger, 2004. This four-volume set draws on the expertise of theologians, social scientists, and psychologists to analyze both recent and historical religiously motivated violence. This is an important study.

John L. Esposito. *Unholy War: Terror in the Name of Islam.* New York: Oxford University Press, 2002. This analysis of how terrorists and terrorist actions come to be is focused on Osama bin Laden and al-Qaeda, but the insights it offers are applicable beyond them.

Mark Juergensmeyer: *Terror in the Mind of God: The Global Rise of Religious Violence.* Berkeley: University of California Press, 2002. After a survey of religiously motivated violence both here and abroad, Juergensmeyer offers a careful analysis of the internal logic of religious violence. This is a thought-provoking study of the ideology and culture of violence.

Thomas G. Plante: *Sins Against the Innocents: Sexual Abuse by Priests and the Role of the Catholic Church.* Westport, CT: Praeger, 2004. As in the Ellens books, a team of scholars from a variety of disciplines give a very thorough analysis.

## *Relevant World Wide Web Sites*

United States Conference of Catholic Bishops: www.usccb.org.

Ontarion Consultants on Religious Tolerance: www.religioustolerance.org.

# PROTESTANT CHRISTIANS AND DENOMINATIONAL PROTESTANTISM: A DECREASING MAJORITY

What do you think of when you think of "ordinary" religion in the United States? It is probably at least similar to the style of religion described below. It is the religion of the majority of the population of the United States, and has been so for nearly all of the nation's history.

As you learned in Chapter 2, Christians are the majority religion in the United States, accounting for about three-fourths of the population. In this section, we investigate the many forms Christianity takes in the United States. After describing Christian faith and practice in broad strokes, we will focus first on Protestants, who make up the majority of Christians in America. In later chapters, we will look in turn at Catholic Christianity, African-American and Eastern Orthodox Christianity, and several forms of Christianity that began in the United States. Because they share a common heritage of Christian practices and beliefs, they are more alike than they are different. At the same time, each gives this common heritage its own distinctive stamp.

## CHRISTIAN FAITH AND PRACTICE: AN OVERVIEW

In introducing Christianity, we'll follow the description of religion introduced in Chapter 1. Thus, we begin with basic Christian **beliefs**. Christian beliefs are based on the Bible—both the Old Testament and the New Testament—and on the tradition of the church. The emphasis given to either varies from group to group.

Like Jews and Muslims, Christians are *monotheists*, people who believe in one God. The religious life of Christians—Protestants, Catholic, Eastern Orthodox, and others as well—centers on the person, life, death, and resurrection

**Figure 4-1**

---

**THE APOSTLES CREED**

I believe in God, the Father Almighty,
Creator of heaven and earth.

And in Jesus Christ, his only son, our Lord,
Who was conceived of the Holy Ghost,
And born of the Virgin Mary.
He suffered under Pontius Pilate,
Was crucified, dead, and buried.
He descended into Hell.
[Alt: "He descended to the dead." Some omit completely.]
On the third day he rose again from the dead.
He ascended into Heaven
And sits at the right hand of God the Father almighty,
From whence he will come
To judge the living and the dead.

I believe in the Holy Spirit, the holy catholic church,
The communion of saints, the forgiveness of sins,
The resurrection of the body, and the life everlasting.

---

of Jesus. **Christians are those people who are defined by their faith in Jesus as their Lord and Savior.**

Two classical creeds[1] of the early Christian church form the basis for our discussion of the beliefs and practices that are shared by most Christians. There are certainly variations in interpretation, but, with a few exceptions, most members of this largest community of faith in the United States could affirm what is contained in the Apostles and Nicene creeds.

The *Apostles Creed* (Figure 4–1) is so named because it is a summary of essential Christian beliefs as held by the Church at the time of the Apostles. It was not written by the Apostles, as legend has it, but goes back to the very old Roman Creed. In its current form, it probably dates from the seventh century, C.E.

The *Nicene Creed* (Figure 4–2) was written at the Council of Nicaea in 325 C.E. and revised at the Council of Constantinople in 381 C.E. It is somewhat longer than the Apostles Creed. Both, however, contain much the same material.

Both the Apostles and the Nicene creeds cover four basic topics: God the Father, Jesus Christ, the Holy Spirit, and a paragraph of miscellaneous affirmations. Christians, following Jesus' example, believe that God is a loving parent who cares deeply for humankind and for the rest of creation, as well.

---

[1] A *creed* is an official, written statement of the beliefs of a particular religious group.

**Figure 4-2**

---

**THE NICENE CREED**

We believe in one God, the Father, the Almighty, maker of heaven and earth, of all that is, seen and unseen.

We believe in one Lord, Jesus Christ, the only Son of God, eternally begotten of the Father, God from God, Light from Light, true God from true God, begotten, not made, of one Being with the Father. Through him all things were made. For us and for our salvation he came down from heaven: by the power of the Holy Spirit he became incarnate from the Virgin Mary, and was made man. For our sake he was crucified under Pontius Pilate; he suffered death and was buried. On the third day he rose again according to the Scriptures; he ascended into heaven and is seated at the right hand of the Father. He will come again in glory to judge the living and the dead, and his kingdom will have no end.

We believe in the Holy Spirit, the Lord, the giver of life, who proceeds from the Father [some add, "and the Son"]. With the Father and the Son he is worshiped and glorified. He has spoken through the prophets.

We believe in one holy catholic and apostolic Church. We acknowledge one baptism for the forgiveness of sins. We look for the resurrection of the dead, and the life of the world to come.

---

God is also the creator who brings everything "seen and unseen" into being. Nothing, in other words, came or comes into being except by God's will and power, which also sustains all things.

Of Jesus Christ, it is stated that he is the only Son of God, who came into being through the power of the Holy Spirit and was born to a virgin. Whether these affirmations are taken literally or not, the intent is clear. Jesus was not simply a human being, although Christians believe that he was fully human. He is somehow special, related to God in a way that makes him unique. According to most Christians, Jesus was God incarnate. The church's belief about the most relevant points of Jesus's career are summarized: his birth, his suffering and death, his resurrection, and his future return to Earth. According to the Nicene Creed, all of this was for the salvation of humanity. One of the most striking elements of Christian belief is the affirmation that the one God became fully human (i.e., *incarnate*) in order to save human beings from the results of sin. Because Christians believe that the God of Abraham, Isaac, and Jacob became fully human in Jesus, they are drawn into an especially intimate *relationship* with him. It is stated also that Jesus will return to earth to judge both the living and the dead. When he returns, Christians believe, those who have put their faith and trust in him will live eternally with him.

These and other classic creeds of Christianity reflect the teachings that are found in the Christian Bible. Although Protestant and Catholic versions of the Bible are very similar, the Catholic Church had not until recently given its approval to any of the translations of the Bible commonly used by Protestant Christians. In late 1991, the United States Council of Catholic Bishops gave their Church's official approval to the *New Revised Standard Version* of the Christian Bible. This means that Catholic and Protestant Christians (as well as Eastern Orthodox Christians, whose leadership had approved the new translation earlier) now have a translation of the Christian Bible that all can use.

Along with the Father and the Son, Christians believe in the Holy Spirit or Holy Ghost as the third person of the *Trinity*. To say that God is a Trinity means that most, though not all, Christians believe that God is best understood as three persons who are one and yet distinguishable. This doctrine itself is not found in the Bible (although it is supported by certain passages in the New Testament such as Matthew 28:19 and 2 Corinthians 13:14), but it was defined very early in the history of the Christian church, especially in these two creeds. Most Christians believe that this is something about God that people could not have known on their own but that can be known because God revealed it. The doctrine points to the centrality of relationship, not just in how God relates to human beings but within God as well.

Finally, most Christians do not believe that earthly death is the end of life. The faithful will be resurrected at the end of time and will live eternally with God. Some Christians believe that heaven is an actual place. Others describe eternal life as simply life with God.

The worship of God is the principal **ritual** act of Christians. Christian *worship* has a dual focus, Word and Sacrament. *Word* refers not only to the Word of God in the Bible, which is always read as a part of the service, but to other aspects of worship as well: responsive readings, hymns and prayers, repeating a creed, and the sermon given by the pastor, minister, or priest. *Sacraments* are special ritual acts performed in worship. Different Christians understand their meaning in differing ways, and recognize different numbers of sacraments, but in any case, they help enact and make present the grace of God.

*Communion*, also known as Holy Communion, the Last Supper, or the Eucharist (thanksgiving) is a central sacrament. Bread and wine or unfermented grape juice are shared among believers with appropriate and often very solemn ritual. It is a ritual that brings the faithful into intimate contact with the central truths of their faith. Interpretations of the exact meaning of Communion vary among Christians. Some believe that the bread and wine actually become the body and blood of Christ. Others teach that Jesus is present symbolically in the elements, while some understand Communion simply as a way of remembering Jesus's death and resurrection.

The ritual of *baptism* is the rite of incorporation into the Christian community of faith. It is also a public witness of commitment to Christ. Some Christians believe that it is necessary for the forgiveness of sin, as well. Water is nearly always used. Specific practices vary from full immersion into water to a sprinkle of water on the head of the person being baptized. Some churches baptize people of all ages, including infants. Others believe that people who are being baptized must be old enough to understand its meaning. Most

Christians are baptized in the name of the Father, Son, and Holy Spirit, although some churches baptize in Jesus's name only.

Some Christian churches also recognize marriage, the ordination of people for professional service in the church, confirmation, confession of sin, and the anointing of the sick as sacraments. Other denominations consider them important rites of the church without sacramental significance.

There is variation in **lifestyle** among different Christians. The majority live quite similarly to others in their culture. Most believe that the material, physical world, created by God, is good, and can be affirmed and enjoyed within the boundaries of morality. God's love is seen as completely altruistic, without self-interest, and Christians believe they are called to embody that type of love in their lives. Some express their understanding of the moral life in terms of doing what Jesus would do were he alive now.

When the creeds refer to "one holy catholic church," the word *catholic* is being used to mean "universal," rather than "Catholic" as a distinct branch of Christianity. In spite of the many divisions within Christianity, it is understood to be *one Church*, having one Lord, and continuing back to the time of the twelve apostles whom the Christian New Testament says that Jesus gathered around himself during his earthly life. The followers of Jesus the Christ are called into a community, the church. The church is not simply a human community, although it is that. It is a community called into being by God and sustained in its life by its relationship with God.

Organizationally, the Christian church has three major branches. Protestant Christianity and several of the major Protestant denomination are described in this chapter. The Catholic Church and the Eastern Orthodox churches are described in Chapters 6 and 7. All its branches have their roots in the Christian community of faith that came together following Jesus's death and resurrection. Eastern Orthodox and Catholic Christianity divided over religious, social, and political issues in 1054. The Protestant Reformation of 1517 led to the formation of the many Protestant denominations. In addition to these three groups, there are other Christians who do not trace their heritage to any of these three branches. Some of these are described in Chapter 8.

## PROTESTANT CHRISTIANITY

The term **Protestant** in most people's minds calls up the image of German reformer Martin Luther protesting against certain practices of the Catholic Church in his time. But the word also goes back to an earlier meaning of the term *protest*: it means to testify to what one believes. Protestants are those Christians who affirm an interpretation of Christianity that goes back more than half a millennium. Its beginnings are usually linked with the life and work of Martin Luther in Germany, but the forces that led to reform had been at work centuries before him.

Belief and practice vary somewhat among Protestant denominations, and even among congregations within a denomination. There are features of Protestantism that make it distinct, however, and that transcend denominational differences. Despite the diversity, there were, and still are, certain beliefs and practices that, although with modifications, have been a part of Protestantism since Reformation times. We will use the now-familiar four elements of religion to organize our thinking about what most Protestants hold in common.

We can identify a core of **beliefs** that most Protestants share. We have already touched on some of these as we discussed the beliefs that most Christians have in common. First, **the Bible plays an absolutely central role for Protestants**. Protestants, along with other Christians, Jews, and Muslims are a "people of the Book," and this theme is highly developed in Protestantism. Martin Luther's classic phrase was *Sola Scriptura*, the authority of the Bible only. With this, he pointed out the sharp contrast between the new faith and Catholicism.[2] Catholics recognize two sources of religious authority: the Bible and the long record of the Church's teaching and interpretation. The Church is, in effect, the guardian and official interpreter of the Bible. Protestants, on the other hand, go directly to the Bible, using the church's interpretations of its meaning only in an advisory capacity. John Calvin, for example, emphasized the need to check one's own private interpretation against that of the community of faith in the interest of preserving good order.

It was this need for some statement of the church's belief to counterbalance a too-individualistic view that led some of the Reformation churches to formulate creeds. For Protestants, the authority of any creed or confession of faith is subordinate to that of the Bible, and any such document is valid only insofar as it is an accurate representation of what the Bible teaches. Creedal groups use written creeds or statements of faith to express the essence of their beliefs. The Presbyterians developed the Westminster Confession of Faith and the Episcopalians retained much of the Church of England's theology in their Thirty-Nine Articles of Religion. Lutherans use the Augsburg Confession as one standard statement of faith. There are also more recent statements, such as the Presbyterian Confession developed following the 1985 merger and the Barmen Declaration. Some groups require that candidates for membership affirm that a particular creed or confession of faith embodies biblical teaching. Congregational repetition of a creed is usually a regular feature of worship, and the study of the creed is an important part of religious education.

Other communities of faith do not have a formal creed as such, although some of them may make occasional use of creeds, especially of the early ones. Adherence to a creed is not a prerequisite to membership in these groups. Communities of faith that do not have a formal creed take this position for a variety of reasons. Some believe that formal creeds are too restrictive and

---

[2]The Catholicism of Luther and Calvin's time was vastly different from Catholicism in the United States now. Significant changes came about with the Second Vatican Council in the early 1960s. In particular, the differences between the two types of Christianity were much larger than they now are. Chapter 6 provides more information on contemporary American Catholicism.

violate the right of individual conscience in religious matters. Others fear that acceptance of a creed can too easily become a substitute for faith in Jesus.

What is important for Protestants is not the Bible itself, but the Word of God contained in it. This has two meanings. First, the Bible is the direct access to the Word made flesh in Jesus: "In the beginning," writes the author of the Gospel according to John, "the Word that was with God, that was in fact God, became flesh and came to live on the earth, where people could see God's glory made visible" (John 1:1–2). The only mediator between God and humankind, according to Protestants, is revealed to be the eternal Word made flesh, and this all-important story is told in the pages of the Bible. The term **Word of God** also has a second layer of meaning in Protestant thought. Through the action and influence of the Holy Spirit, the words of the Bible become the Word of God for the believer, God's direct and personal communication to each and every individual.

It was the prominence given to the Word contained in the Bible that led to the Protestant enthusiasm for translating the Bible into the language of the people. Having only Latin Bibles reinforced the Church's position as the only interpreter and official custodian of biblical truth, because only the priests and higher officials of the Church could read and understand Latin. Even though illiteracy was high—few people could read even in their own language—having Bibles available in the common language of a people meant that people could hear the Bible read in the language they understood and could come to their own interpretation. It is perhaps difficult to imagine the thrill some of these people must have felt upon hearing the Bible read in their own language for the first time. It was as if God were speaking directly to them, rather than addressing them through a translator or interpreter.

Protestants believe that **salvation is a gift from God**, an effect of grace and grace alone. There is nothing that people can do to earn salvation. All are equally guilty, equally subject to death due to sin. People cannot possibly make themselves worthy before God. At the same time, there is nothing that people need to do to earn salvation, because God has made it a gift of his grace in and through Jesus, who for this reason is known by Christians as Savior (see, for example, Ephesians 2:8–9).

Protestants believe that **the church is the gathered fellowship of believers**. It is the people meeting together to hear the Word preached, to participate in the sacraments of baptism and communion, and to encourage and help each other. It is the people, rather than the institution or the hierarchy. In a very real sense for Protestants, the church is not a *something* that *is* as much as it is an *event* that *happens* each time and place that believers gather. Prior to the Reformation, the church had functioned as a complex system of two-way mediation between God and people. Through the Church's teaching (including but not limited to the Bible), hierarchy, and sacraments, God's will and grace became available to people. People reached God by following those teachings and participating in the means of grace the Church made available. The reformers simplified this structure of mediation, teaching instead that

God relates to people through their trust and faith, on a model analogous to human relationships. This relationship then calls people into the church, the community of the faithful.

This gathered fellowship, Protestants say, is a **priesthood of all believers**. Protestants find support for this belief in the New Testament and in the writings of the Reformers. In the first letter to Peter, the faithful are called a "chosen people, a royal priesthood" (1 Peter 2:9).

The priesthood of all believers means shared responsibility, shared worship, and shared authority. Each Christian has the responsibility to pray for, teach, and encourage every other Christian and to tell God's story to nonbelievers. The responsibility for a shared ministry belongs to all equally; it is not reserved for those who are ordained as priests or ministers. Each person offers his or her own worship to God and is a priest in that sense also. Corporate worship is the collectivity of the worship of each and every individual, not a common act of the church's worship in which individual worshipers are overshadowed. And each Christian shares with all others the same authority. No one has an inside track and no one is relegated to outsider status in matters of religious authority. All are equal, because all have equal access to the Word.

Protestants, in other words, distinguish between priesthood and ministry. Baptism makes all Christians priests, some of whom are then called out of the congregations to preach, administer the sacraments, and govern as ministers. The minister is one who is chosen to serve a congregation, rather than one given special powers by God or special honor by the institution.

What of **Protestant lifestyle**? This is not as easy to identify as are the specific beliefs, and we must make some distinctions. Most Protestants feel that their faith directs them squarely into the middle of the world. Martin Luther entered a monastery early in his life, believing that to be the surest way to salvation. He later left the monastery. Christian faith, say most followers of its Protestant branch, must be lived out in the midst of the world, not in retreat from it. God provides all the various arenas of human activity, such as marriage and family, vocation and work, civil government and politics, leisure and play. Each in its place is equally good, equally capable of being transformed by grace. One is not to turn one's back on the world, but to live in it, glorifying and obeying God in all things.

For Luther and his followers and for those who were a part of the English reformation, enjoying life and one another and the good things the earth had to offer was a way of praising God, although moderation was important. The Calvinists, on the other hand, were more strict. Restraint and sobriety were the hallmarks of their way of life. Too much enjoyment might lead one away from the proper path, and a certain sternness pervaded all they did. Some Protestants who believe that the world is saturated with evil and temptation separate themselves from it insofar as possible. Contact with the world and its pleasures brings with it the danger of spiritual contamination and should be avoided. This attitude remains today in some of the holiness churches.

For all Protestants, living decently, charity toward others, upholding the law, and being faithful in one's commitment to God and to the community of God's people are important virtues. Freed from its role in bringing about salvation, morality became a central feature of Protestants' lifestyle, as a joyful (Luther and the English reformers) and obedient (Calvin) response to God's freely given gift of salvation.

Two things stand out when we look at the **specific religious acts** of Protestants. Whereas the earlier church had observed seven sacraments (a practice which continues in the Catholic, Episcopal, and Orthodox Churches today), most Protestants have only two. **Baptism** and the **Lord's Supper,** or **Communion,** are the only two acts that Jesus specifically commanded his followers to carry on after his death, according to the Protestant reading of the New Testament. The age for baptism varies; many Protestants baptize babies, but not all do. Immersion, pouring, and sprinkling each have their advocates within the Protestant community. Likewise, the exact understanding of the Lord's Supper varies, but Protestants are united in their denial of its sacrificial character. Architecturally, its context is that of a table that echoes the one around which Jesus and the disciples are said to have gathered, rather than the altar of sacrifice. Some congregations pass the elements through the pews and some come to the front of the church. The roles played by the minister and lay people vary somewhat. All use bread, leavened or unleavened; some use wine, and some use unfermented grape juice.

Here again, we can note both Protestantism's uniformity and its diversity. On the one hand, the Episcopal Church celebrates all seven of the traditional sacramental rituals. On the other, Baptists, although they observe the Lord's Supper and baptize believers, do not consider these acts to be sacraments. They are ordinances, important rites of the church with no sacramental character.

The second thing that stands out is the **importance of preaching**. The pulpit occupies a prominent place in Protestant churches, and the sermon is considered the focal point of worship. Ministers usually receive extensive training in biblical preaching, and a potential minister's skill as a preacher plays a large role in the selection process when it is time to call a new pastor. Because of the centrality of the Word made flesh, words become very significant in Protestantism.

Finally, what can we say about Protestant **organization** or structure, its institutional arrangements? In the first place, there is no central authority. Each Protestant denomination is self-governing. There is no worldwide organization. Individual denominations have various organizational patterns, as we have seen. We have also seen that all, in one way or another, allow for and encourage active participation of the laity in the life of the church.

Another institutional feature is that most ministers are married rather than celibate. The rejection of monasticism goes together with a rejection of celibacy as the proper lifestyle for ministers. Some denominations, although not all, ordain women as well as men to the ministry.

**Figure 4-3**

---

### DISTINCTIVE PROTESTANT BELIEFS AND PRACTICES

Beliefs
1. The centrality and sole authority of the Bible in matters of religious truth
2. Salvation by grace through faith
3. The church as the gathering of believers
4. The priesthood of all believers

Lifestyle
1. For most, religion lived out in the midst of world
2. For some, separation from the world
3. Morality is of central importance

Ritual
1. Two sacraments: Baptism and the Lord's Supper/Holy Communion
2. Preaching is an important aspect of worship

Organization
1. No central authority
2. Clergy usually marry; women ordained in some denominations
3. Variety of organizational styles

---

## DENOMINATIONAL PROTESTANTISM

Denominational Protestantism reflects the religious sensibilities of many people in our culture. It has been an important aspect of American religious culture for a long time. These are the groups that historically have tried to relate religion to the larger culture in positive ways. For example, they have lobbyists in Washington and speak out on the important moral and ethical issues of the day. According to sociologist Robert Bellah, these communities of faith

> . . . have tried to develop a larger picture of what it might mean to live a biblical life in America. They have sought to be communities of memory, to keep in touch with biblical sources and historical traditions not with literalist obedience but through an intelligent reappropriation illuminated by historical and theological reflection.[3]

---

[3]Robert N. Bellah, Richard Madsen, William M. Sullivan, Ann Swidler, and Steven M. Tipton, *Habits of the Heart: Individualism and Commitment in American Life* (New York: Harper & Row, Publishers, 1985), p. 237.

Denominations recognize themselves as one religion among many. Even as they claim their own authenticity and recognize themselves as clearly bounded, they acknowledge the authenticity of other, competing religions.[4] They also understand religion as a part of the culture and one among many aspects of life with a legitimate claim on people's time and attention. They share most of the characteristics that sociologists identify with denominational religion, including

- friendly or at least tolerant relationships with other religions and with secular groups as well
- reliance on births within the congregation to increase membership, or, if they try to make converts, they focus on people with no religious affiliation, rather than on those who are members of another group
- acceptance of at least some change in teaching and practice as circumstances change, and tolerance of diversity of interpretation within the denomination
- relatively routinized worship without a strong emphasis on innovation and spontaneity
- a professional clergy who must meet specific educational and certification requirements for ordination.[5]

There is an important link between this form of religious organization and the religious pluralism described in the Introduction. In a situation of religious pluralism, religion becomes a matter of voluntary participation, and the dominant religious traditions take on a new form:

> The denomination is thus marked perhaps most significantly by this voluntarism of support coupled to mutual respect and forbearance of all other competing religious groups. It is, indeed, this quality of *competition* that is the unique hallmark of the pluralistic religious situation; acceptance of the "free market" situation in religious ideas is the critical operating principle of denominationalism. Denominations are the structural—functional forms that dominant religious traditions assume in a pluralistic culture.[6]

Especially among denominational Protestants, ecumenical organizations provide a forum and a method for working together to achieve commonly shared goals. The **National Council of Churches of Christ in the U.S.A.** came into being in 1950 when a group of churches agreed to try to demonstrate in their organization the unity they believed the Christian church should have. It was the successor to the Federal Council of Churches, which had begun in

---

[4]Russell E. Richey, "Denominations and Denominationalism: An American Morphology," in *Reimagining Denominationalism: Interpretive Essays*, ed. Robert Bruce Mullin and Russell E. Richey (New York: Oxford University Press, 1994), p. 76.

[5]Ronald L. Johnstone, *Religion in Society: A Sociology of Religion*, 5th ed. (Upper Saddle River, NJ: Prentice Hall, 1997), p. 91.

[6]Swatos, William H., Jr., ed., *Encyclopedia of Religion and Society* (Walnut Creek, CA: AltaMira Press, 1998), p. 134.

1908. It has become known as an organization of liberal Protestant denominations and includes many Eastern Orthodox and other Christian churches as well. Its position statements characteristically have affirmed social action and justice while downplaying evangelism and doctrinal precision. The magazine *Christian Century* is an important national voice for this perspective.

Since the early 1960s, an ecumenical organization called The Consultation on Church Union (COCU) had worked to further ecumenical dialogue and participation among denominational Protestants. That organization disbanded in 2002 in order to form a new organization, **Churches Uniting in Christ (CUIC)**. Within the structure of CUIC, each

> . . . communion retains its own identity and decision-making structures, but they also have pledged before God to draw closer in sacred things—including regular sharing of the Lord's Supper and common mission, especially a mission to combat racism together. Each church also committed itself to undertake an intensive dialogue toward the day when ministers are authorized to serve and lead worship, when invited, in each of its communions.

> Churches Uniting in Christ is not a new structure. It is an officially recognized invitation to live with one another differently. Christians in the pews know that we belong together because we all belong to the same Lord. Churches Uniting in Christ is a framework for showing to the world what we truly are—the one Body of Jesus Christ.[7]

## WOMEN IN DENOMINATIONAL RELIGION

Before you read this section, take a moment to reflect on your own experience. Have you thought about the role and status of women in religious organizations? What is your impression? If you attend or have attended worship services, what roles did women play? Have you heard a female minister or pastor preach? If so, how did you feel about that? If you had a personal problem that you wanted to discuss with a religious counselor, would it matter to you if that person were a woman or a man? Why or why not? How much do you think your answers to these questions are influenced by your own gender?

### Tradition and Change

A lot of attention has been paid to the role and status of women in American religious organizations. Religion has often limited women to traditional female roles. It has often supported and encouraged the belief that women's proper roles were those of wives and mothers. The home was often believed to be women's only proper sphere of action. Until the last half of the twentieth

---

[7]What Is CUIC? www.eden.edu/cuic/whatiscuic/whatiscuic.htm.

century, women usually were unable to be ministers, pastors, rabbis, or priests in most of America's communities of faith. Nor have they been able to be deacons, elders, or other lay officers of their congregations. Religion has also offered encouragement and comfort to those women who themselves support traditional female roles in the face of cultural demands for change.

But this is only one side of the story, because religion has also been a catalyst for change. Women have found encouragement in the scriptures of both Judaism and Christianity to work toward full equality and rights. Churches and synagogues have supported movements for women's rights. Although many communities of faith denied official roles to women, in others, men and women functioned as equals. It is very important to evaluate the role that religion has played in the context of its own time. Feminist theologian Rosemary Radford Ruether cautions us that if we approach history from the viewpoint of the twentieth century, religion's tendency to support traditional roles will loom larger than it actually was, and we will be in danger of missing the extent to which religion has encouraged change.[8]

## Women's Responses

Women, and men who share their concerns about continuing male predominance in denominational Protestantism, respond in a number of ways. The tradition-supporting response remains common, whether in an active or passive mode. People remain in their religious institutions and do not challenge practices and policies. For example, women continue to worship in services that use gender-exclusive language, either actively affirming that tradition or simply not challenging it.

Others remain in their religious traditions and work actively for change. One approach entails renewed examination of the scriptures and traditions of a group from the standpoint of women's experience to reconstruct beliefs, rituals, and history that have been obscured and neglected by male history and interpretation having been taken as universal. For example, while parts of the Christian New Testament have been used to justify "keeping women in their place," other passages can be shown to challenge that view in favor of greater equality. Other men and women in those groups that do not ordain women to the clergy work actively to change that policy. Still others remain active in their community of faith but supplement that involvement with participation in a variety of distinctively women's spirituality groups in which clearly feminist ideas and rituals are embraced. For most people within a community of faith, its scriptures and history have to be taken into account. They may have to be reinterpreted, parts may simply have to be discarded, but scripture and history set the boundaries and must be dealt with.

---

[8]Rosemary Radford Ruether and Rosemary Skinner Keller, eds., *Women and Religion in America, Volume I: The Nineteenth Century* (San Francisco: Harper and Row Publishers, 1989), p. x.

It is especially important to note that *most* of the women (and men) who feel alienated from their communities of faith are not leaving but are "defecting in place," choosing the difficult path of working actively for change within their local, regional, and national organizations.[9]

However, there are those for whom their traditions seem so alienating and bankrupt that they do make the equally difficult decision to abandon them altogether. Some become secular persons, without religious affiliation or participation. Others develop their own spirituality essentially in solitude, working out values, ideas, and sometimes rituals that provide spiritual sustenance without a group context. Still others find their way to, or form, women's spirituality groups that focus on goddess worship or espouse a non-gendered view of the sacred.

## Continuing Issues

While great strides have been made to redress the grievances that feminists have with their communities of faith and the institutions that undergird them, for many feminists, a lot more needs to be done. For many consensus Protestants ordination and participation in the higher ranks of church leadership are a reality, but there are still limits. Writing on the basis of interviews with clergy women in several Protestant denominations, one author concludes the following:

> Women are permitted to discuss women's issues, forge professional identity, and nurture the growth of a few struggling parishes. Occasionally, they are admitted to the second or third tier in larger churches.
>
> Less frequently, they are granted the opportunity to make the choices that shape some small part of the "performance." By and by, however, they are forced to live on the fringes of a church where men discuss the church's theology and its ministry, shape their professional identity in close proximity with the centers of ecclesiastical power, and govern the affairs of the largest churches.[10]

### DENOMINATIONAL DISTINCTIVENESS

Denominational differences play a much smaller role in religion in the United States than they did a few decades ago. American religion has been "restructured" along a different set of lines. As sociologist Robert Wuthnow points out, the "symbolic boundaries have changed."

---

[9]Miriam Therese Winter, Adair Lummis, and Allison Stokes, *Defecting in Place: Women Claiming Responsibility for Their Own Spiritual Lives* (New York: Crossroad, 1994).

[10]Frederick W. Schmidt, Jr., *A Still, Small Voice: Women, Ordination, and the Church* (Syracuse, NY: Syracuse University Press, 1996), pp. 169–170.

These changes . . . involve new modes of religious identification, new distinctions in the web of religious interaction, alterations in the lines of moral obligation that define religious communities, changes in the categories that are taken for granted in religious discourse.[11]

At least in a sense, we are a postdenominational religious culture. Nonetheless, there remain distinguishing features of denominations that are important to those who are a part of them. It is to those that we now turn.

I found support for Wuthnow's "postdenominational" thesis as I worked on this chapter. When I was working on the manuscript for the previous (2000) edition, it was quite easy to find denominational distinctives; a quick visit to a denomination's Web site usually revealed a concise paragraph or two on "how we're distinctive." If such information is available at all currently, it isn't featured. At least in the United States, Protestant denominations are significantly downplaying their distinctiveness.

About 60 percent of adults in the United States are Protestant. About one-third of these are Baptists. Methodists account for about 15 percent and Lutherans about 12 percent. About 6 percent are Presbyterians, and 5 percent are Episcopalians. The last three groups described in this section each account for less than 1 percent.

## Baptists

About three-fourths of Baptists in the United States are members of either the Southern Baptist Convention or the American Baptist Convention. The rest are part of one of many smaller Baptist groups or are independent Baptists. Baptists are the largest Protestant denominational family in the United States and second only to the Roman Catholic population in size.

A recent sermon on the Cooperative Baptist Fellowship Web site expressed the essence of Baptist faith in the form of four related affirmations.[12] **Bible freedom** is central for Baptists. Christians have the freedom and the responsibility to read, study, and interpret the Bible for themselves. "For a Baptist, only the Bible as understood under the Lordship of Christ and the leadership of the Holy Spirit is our authority." Neither creeds nor leaders can demand conformity, leaving the Bible as the sole authority. Baptists also regard all creeds as inadequate because they believe that no creed can adequately express the fullness of the Christian gospel and that the full significance of vital, living faith cannot be bound by any statement.

Baptists also affirm **soul freedom**. Also called *soul competency*, this means "the inalienable right and responsibility of every person to deal with

---

[11]Robert Wuthnow, *The Restructuring of American Religion: Society and Faith Since World War II* (Princeton, NJ: Princeton University Press, 1988), p. 10.
[12]David W. Hull, "What Is a Baptist?" (www.cbfonline.org/about/quickfacts.cfm), July, 2003. All quotations are from this sermon.

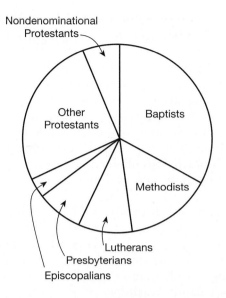

**Figure 4-4**    Among those who are Protestants, about 38 percent are Baptists, 15 percent Methodists, 12 percent Lutherans, 6 percent Presbyterians, 5 percent Episcopalians, and 6 percent nondenominational Protestants; 18 percent identify with some other Protestant group. *(Data from the 1996 National Opinion Research Center General Social Survey.)*

God without the imposition of creed, the interference of clergy, or the intervention of civil government." Each individual relates to God and to Christ directly, personally. This is why Baptists practice *believer's baptism*, often regarded as a main distinguishing characteristic of the Baptist denominational family. Baptists believe baptism must be a free and knowledgeable act of the one participating in it, not something done on behalf of a child too young to understand. Church members are people who have been baptized upon their profession of faith in Jesus Christ as Lord and Savior. Many Baptists say that people are not Baptist by birth, but by *re*birth.

For Baptists, **church freedom** means that each local congregation is self-governing. In the Baptist tradition, "local churches are free, under the Lordship of Christ, to determine their membership and leadership, to order their worship and work, to ordain whom they perceive to be gifted for ministry, male or female, and to participate in the larger Body of Christ, of whose unity and mission Baptists are proudly a part."

Although Baptists cherish their congregational independence, they are also interdependent, and these larger denominational organizations (frequently called *conventions*) are important for the whole fellowship of Baptists. The conventions also perform activities that cannot be maintained efficiently by local congregations alone, such as higher education, missionary, and social service work and retirement programs for church employees. Some local congregations, however, do refuse to join any larger group, maintaining a strict independence.

Also strongly related to the dominant themes of freedom and choice, **religious freedom** means freedom of, for, and from religion. Baptists are passionate supporters of religious liberty. Freedom of religion is an inherent right of the human soul, say the Baptists, because human beings are created to be both free and responsible. For freedom of religion to be a reality, religion and the civil government must be kept strictly apart. Baptists certainly are not alone in their support of religious liberty and the official separation of church and state. However, these concepts play an especially significant role in both Baptist history and present-day concern.

Baptists are the most likely of any of the Protestants to be fundamentalist in their religious outlook. Some, particularly in the South, in rural areas of the country, and in the smaller, more conservative Baptist groups, also advocate a stricter personal morality than is the prevailing custom in the culture. Some of these groups also advocate a close alliance of church and state that is different from historic Baptist teaching.

In worship, many Baptists emphasize openness to the leading of the Holy Spirit over the use of set format and ceremony. Their worship tends to be somewhat more emotional and evangelistic than that of the other denominational Protestants, although this is not always the case. Each congregation develops its own patterns of ritual activity, blending repeated common elements with innovation. The Lord's Supper is believed to be a remembrance of Jesus's last supper with the disciples and a memorial of his sacrificial death. Baptists do not believe that Jesus is present spiritually or symbolically in the elements.

Many denominations in the Baptist family of churches joined together in 1936 to sponsor the Baptist Joint Committee on Public Affairs in Washington. This committee reflects the Baptists' commitment to religious liberty. It is the only church office of any faith that works full time on religious liberty and church-state issues.

The Southern Baptists are distinguished by being considerably more conservative theologically than their American Baptist counterparts. For example, they affirm the importance of converting Jews to Christianity and of traditional roles for women and men.

### Methodists

In their beliefs, Methodists are distinguished by a great latitude and variety in what is acceptable. They affirm the central beliefs of Protestant Christianity while continuing Wesley's emphasis on experience over the details of doctrine. Their focus has always been more on how life is lived than on what is believed. Wesley taught that religion should be **of the heart**, and that believers should trust in God's love, and accept Christ's redemption in faith. It should be **of the will**, manifested in personal piety and devotion and steadfast love and concern for one's neighbor. Belief in the inner experience of religion and its social application in love and charity toward other people are still hallmarks of Methodism.

Methodist interpretation of the Bible, as might be supposed from what has been said previously, ranges widely from literalism to more liberal, figurative styles of interpreting its message. The overall tendency is toward flexibility. Most Methodists believe that the main message of the Bible is the love and mercy of God toward all of creation.

Methodists cite four sources of religious truth. It is unique in its spelling out of these four, although other denominations also use similar sources. The first and primary source is the **Bible**, primarily—but not exclusively—the New Testament. Second, Methodists recognize their roots in the **tradition** of the theology and worship of the church. The third is **experience**, a pragmatic taking into account of what works for people in particular circumstances. The last is **reason**; faith must be in accord with what the mind says is rational and true.

Methodists teach a threefold order of salvation that is based very closely on Wesley's teaching. *Justification* is the individual's acceptance of salvation as the free gift of God's grace. *Conversion* is regeneration and cleansing through the action of God. Finally, *sanctification* is the ongoing and increasing expression of holiness through a life of prayer and works that attempts to do something positive in the face of the ethical and social problems that prevail in one's time and place.

Although there are doctrinal standards set out by the denomination as a whole, each congregation and each individual is free to use them as they see fit. There is thus no precise answer to the question: What do Methodists believe? Their use of the four guidelines and the threefold order of salvation to interpret the basic Christian teachings, with the accent on the love and mercy of God, are emphases that began with John Wesley himself.

Methodists have also highlighted the social dimension of the Christian life. As with most Methodist teachings, this is a particular emphasis on a theme widely shared among Christians, as well as among many non-Christians. "We insist that personal salvation always involves Christian mission and service to the world. By joining heart and hand, we assert that personal religion, evangelical witness, and Christian social action are reciprocal and mutually reinforcing."[13]

John Wesley formulated three guidelines for members of his religious societies:

- Do no harm and avoid evil of all sorts.
- Do good of every possible sort, and insofar as possible to all people.
- Observe the ordinances of God, including public worship, the ministry of the Word both read from Scripture and explained in preaching, participation in the

---

[13]"Doctrinal Standards and Our Theological Task," The United Methodist Church Web site www.umc.org. The United Methodist Social Creed can be found on this site.

Lord's Supper, family and private prayer and Bible reading, and fasting and abstinence.

With the exception of fasting and, in some instances, abstinence from alcohol, many Methodists' lives today can be described in the same way.

Like their beliefs, Methodists' patterns of worship vary widely. There is no required form of worship, although the *Book of Worship* gives suggested forms for Sunday services as well as for several special services, including those for the special occasions of the church year, the significant passages of human life, and a service of healing. Local congregations make use of it and modify it as they adapt it to their particular needs.

Methodists baptize people of all ages. Water is usually sprinkled on the head of the person being baptized. It is a rite of incorporation into the community of faith. Most Methodists believe that Christ is symbolically present to the faithful in the elements of bread and grape juice in the communion service in a "heavenly and spiritual manner." It is a solemn yet joyful service, taken with great seriousness by most members of this diverse group of Protestants.

Like the Baptists, though to a somewhat lesser extent, Methodist organization is marked by its being a large family of related church groups. There are more than twenty separate religious bodies that claim the Methodist heritage. The United Methodist Church came into being in 1968 with the merger of the Methodist Church and the Evangelical United Brethren, both of which were themselves products of earlier mergers. The United Methodist Church includes approximately 80 percent of the Methodist population.

Besides the United Methodist Church, there are three large, predominantly black churches in the Methodist group: the African Methodist Episcopal Church, the African Methodist Episcopal Zion Church, and the Christian Methodist Episcopal Church. In addition, there are several smaller groups, the names of which often point to either their geographic region or a particular point of view, such as the Free Methodist Church of North America, the Southern Methodist Church, and the Evangelical Methodist Church. Others use the name *Wesleyan* to refer to their link with John Wesley and his teachings.

## Lutherans

The Lutheran family of churches, including the large Evangelical Lutheran Church in America (ELCA) and the more conservative Lutheran Church–Missouri Synod, embrace the basic teachings and practices of Protestant Christianity as interpreted by the founder, Martin Luther, the German "Father of the Protestant Reformation." Some of the things that help to distinguish Lutherans from other Protestants include:

> You don't hear Lutherans say, "It doesn't matter what you believe, just so you live right." Lutherans think that a way of living is a by-product of a way of believing. Since Lutheranism developed from Luther's intense experience of salvation through faith, it has been marked by a concern for faith as the essential part of

religion. So Lutherans, more than most other Protestants, emphasize doctrine. They insist on unusually thorough education of their pastors and require young people to engage in a long period of study of the Lutheran Catechism before being admitted to full church membership. . . .

Since Luther had been an ardent Roman Catholic before his excommunication, he was less drastic than some later reformers in abandoning Catholic forms of worship. These are retained among Lutherans in a simplified form.

Lutherans observe the festivals and seasons of the historic church year. In their churches, they have the altar, cross, candles, vestments, and other equipment of worship that most other Protestants discarded as "too Catholic." Lutherans believe that these forms of liturgy . . . are valuable because of their beauty and because, through them, we share in the experiences of the family of Christian worshipers of all ages.[14]

Unlike Baptist and Methodist Christians, Lutherans are a creedal denomination. For Lutherans, the Bible is the inspired Word of God, containing God's full revelation to humankind. It is the only source of true Christian teaching and the only rule and norm of Christian faith and life. The creeds have no authority in themselves but are of value only as they reveal the true Word of God. The three **ecumenical creeds** of the whole church are among them: the Apostles, Nicene, and Athanasian creeds. The **Augsburg Confession**, written in 1530, is a central statement of Lutheran essentials. Many of the important creeds of Lutheranism are drawn together in the *Book of Concord*, first published in 1580.

Lutherans teach that both the law and the gospel are necessary. The law is necessary to awaken sinners to their sinful condition and to arouse them to repentance and a longing for redemption. The gospel assures the repentant sinner of God's forgiveness in Christ. Thus, both must be held together. Like so much in Lutheranism, this belief follows Luther's own teaching closely.

One of the more conservative branches of the Lutheran family, the Missouri Synod Lutheran Church, sponsors a church-related school system in the United States that is second in size only to the Catholic school system. Like the Baptists, who are involved in the Christian school movement, these Lutherans want the education their children receive at school to reinforce and complement that which they receive at home and at church.

Worship is very important to Lutherans. Lutheran worship follows a precise liturgical format. Worship is orderly, using an adaptation of the worship of the early church as interpreted through Luther's modifications. Many hymns are used. Prominence is given to hymns written by Luther, who is

---

[14]G. Elson Ruff, "What Is a Lutheran?" in *Religions of America: Ferment and Faith in an Age of Crisis*, ed. Leo Rosten (New York: Simon and Schuster, 1975), p. 159. This older statement is still accurate.

often regarded as one of the greatest hymn writers the Christian church has ever known. He is probably best known for "A Mighty Fortress Is Our God," which became a key hymn of the Reformation.

Preaching and the sacrament of Communion are both very important elements in Lutheran worship. The altar, a symbol of Christ's presence in the sacrament, and the pulpit, symbolizing God's presence through the Word, are equally important in their church architecture. This contrasts with many Protestant churches, in which the pulpit (perhaps along with a lectern from which the Bible is read) vastly overshadows the altar, which is frequently a simple table.

Communion is an important part of Lutheran worship. Lutheran congregations are encouraged to include Communion as a part of each Sunday's worship. The distinctive Lutheran view holds that the risen Christ is truly present in the bread and wine. The bread and wine continue to exist as bread and wine, but along with this, Christ is actually present. This teaching is sometimes referred to as the **Real Presence**. Lutherans believe this is what Christ promised at the Last Supper.

The Evangelical Lutheran Church in America, the largest Lutheran body, is firmly within the sphere of denominational Protestantism. As the religious consensus in the United States has become more conservative, religious groups that would have been outside the consensus a decade or two ago are now within it. The Missouri Synod Lutheran Church is one of two major evangelical and conservative Protestant groups in the United States that is now a part of the broad consensus, along with the Southern Baptist Convention. Neither completely fits the description of denominational Protestant churches. For example, both have remained outside the National Council of Churches. However, their size and the increased conservatism of the consensus warrants their inclusion here.

### Presbyterians

Presbyterian churches are distinguished by their theology, which is usually called "reformed," and their form of church government, which is strongly connectional, so much so that this type of church organization is sometimes called *presbyterian* (lowercase *p* to distinguish it from the denomination). The Presbyterian Church (U.S.A.) is the largest embodiment of reformed theology among churches in the United States. Another consensus denomination in the reformed theological tradition is the United Church of Christ, discussed later in this chapter.

A recent statement about the uniqueness of the Presbyterian Church describes its theology and organization:

> Presbyterians are distinctive in two major ways: they adhere to a pattern of religious thought known as Reformed theology and a form of government that stresses the active, representational leadership of both ministers and church

members. . . . Reformed theology . . . emphasizes God's supremacy over everything and humanity's chief purpose as being to glorify and enjoy God forever. . . . The *presbyterian* pattern of church government . . . vests governing authority primarily in elected lay persons known as elders. The word *presbyterian* comes from the Greek word for elder. Elders are chosen by the people. Together with ministers of the Word and Sacrament, they exercise leadership, government, and discipline and have responsibilities for the life of a particular church as well as the church at large, including ecumenical relationships. Presbyterian elders are both elected and *ordained*. Through ordination they are officially set apart for service. They retain their ordination beyond their term in office.[15]

Like Lutheranism, Presbyterianism is a creedal faith. A group of religious leaders gathered at Westminster Abbey from 1643 to 1648 to write the Westminster Confession of Faith, as well as the Larger and Shorter Catechisms that are based on it. A later *Book of Confessions* (1967) contains the creeds and confessions. Following a merger in 1983, a new statement of faith was written for the newly formed Presbyterian Church (USA). It is not intended to stand apart from the other confessions of faith included in the *Book of Confessions* but to continue them.

In general, biblical and theological interpretation among Presbyterians ranges from fairly conservative and literal to more liberal and figurative. The larger denominations within the Presbyterian family of denominations tend toward the liberal, while the smaller ones, many of which grew out of doctrinal disputes, tend to be more conservative.

Presbyterian worship is usually carried out with great dignity and order. It is stately, as befits the worship of a sovereign God. Presbyterian worship is usually more intellectual than emotional and gives the worshiper an experience of logical thoughts, ordered behavior, and a restrained atmosphere. According to Presbyterians, worship is not something done for God, who does not need to be worshiped, nor is it something done for the people themselves. It is preeminently a part of God's work in the world, one of the means whereby God interacts with the created order. It is centered on the sermon, including the exposition of the Scriptures and the ordered presentation of the great truths of the Christian faith as Presbyterians understand them. The sermon has mainly a teaching function. Presbyterian ministers are formally called *teaching elders* to distinguish them from the *ruling elders*, whose function is church governance.

Presbyterians believe very strongly that children, along with their parents, are members of the "household of faith," and they baptize people of all ages. While baptism is not thought to be necessary for salvation, it is considered a sacrament and is important as the rite of incorporation into the church. It is usually performed by sprinkling.

Presbyterians reject the Lutheran view of the real presence of Christ in the elements of Communion. They also reject the view that the Communion

---

[15]Presbyterian Church (USA), www.pcusa.org/101/101-distinct.htm.

is only a memorial. In the elements of bread and (usually) unfermented grape juice, Christ is spiritually present and is known by faith. Being in a proper frame of mind and spirit to receive Communion is important to Presbyterians, for whom this is a very solemn service of worship.

The Presbyterian Church in the United States of America (PCUSA) was formed in 1983 by a merger of the Presbyterian Church in the United States (PCUS, the southern branch) and the United Presbyterian Church in the U.S.A. (the northern branch). In addition, there are several smaller groups that are part of this denominational family, such as the Cumberland Presbyterian Church, the Orthodox Presbyterian Church, and the Reformed Presbyterian Church. Most of these smaller branches are more conservative to fundamentalist in their thinking and are not regarded as part of the consensus.

## Episcopalians

The Episcopal Church is regarded as a bridge between Protestantism and Catholicism and is sometimes said to be **Protestant in belief** while being **Catholic in worship**. Some interpreters describe it as "a different way of being Christian than Protestantism, Roman Catholicism, or Eastern Orthodoxy."[16] It accepts the Apostles and Nicene creeds as accurate reflections of the teachings of the Bible. *The Thirty-Nine Articles of Religion* is a distinctive statement of Episcopal belief in the United States. The Episcopal Church accepts a wide range of opinion in matters of theology and doctrine. It stresses the importance of "loyalty in essentials and liberty in nonessentials," and the smaller points of theological difference fall into the nonessential category.

The *Book of Common Prayer* is the product of the service books used in the church throughout the centuries and contains orders for Sunday worship and for many other services of worship. A contemporary American revision that was approved in 1980 was the first major revision since 1928. The use of the *Book of Common Prayer* for worship is generally regarded as more important to defining what Episcopalianism is than is doctrine.

Most Episcopal priests are married, and whether to marry or not is left up to the individual. Women also can be priests. The Episcopal Church does have a few groups of nuns and monks who take the traditional three vows of poverty, chastity, and obedience.

The sacraments are at the center of Episcopal worship. Episcopalians believe that the sacraments are "visible signs and effectual means" of God's acting in people. The understanding of the sacraments as "effectual means," having power in and of themselves to convey God's grace, sets Episcopalians apart from other Protestants.

---

[16]David L. Holmes, "The Anglican Tradition and the Episcopal Church," in *Encyclopedia of the American Religious Experience*, Vol. 1, ed. Lippy and Williams, p. 392.

The principal act of Christian worship on Sundays and on other significant church festivals is the Holy Eucharist, which is similar to the Catholic mass. The Eucharistic service is frequently called a mass. The Eucharist is the most frequently used term for holy communion among Episcopalians. **They believe that Christ is actually present within the elements of bread and wine**, although they refrain from trying to express or explain what they consider to be a holy mystery. In this, they are similar to Lutherans, while differing from those Protestants who regard the presence of Christ as symbolic only.

Infants, as well as children and adults, are baptized, usually by sprinkling. Baptism is believed to cleanse from sin, unite the person with Christ in Christ's death and resurrection, bring about rebirth by the action of the Holy Spirit, and make people adopted children of God the Divine Parent. These two sacraments are understood to have been instituted by Jesus as the chief sacraments of the church.

Episcopalians also believe that other traditionally important rites, including confirmation, reconciliation of a penitent (also called confession and forgiveness), marriage, ordination to the priesthood, and the anointing of the sick, have sacramental significance. The importance placed on the seven traditional sacraments is distinctive for this group of Christians.

The word *episcopal* in the name of the church refers to the importance of bishops in its governing structure. Bishops' authority is believed to have been handed down across the centuries in an unbroken line of succession. They trace this back to an account in Matthew 16, in which Jesus is said to have given Saint Peter the keys to the kingdom of heaven. Usually, the clergy person is called a priest. In recent years, the Episcopal church has involved lay people more at all levels. Each congregation elects a *vestry* to govern the local church. The spiritual head of the Episcopal church worldwide is the Archbishop of Canterbury, England. Although the American church is self-governing, its members honor the head of the whole Church of England.

In the 1970s, the Episcopal Church voted to ordain women to the priesthood and also revised the *Book of Common Prayer*. These two actions gave rise to the Anglican Church of North America (or Anglican Catholic Church; both names are used), dedicated to upholding traditional Episcopalianism. There are also several other small Episcopal denominations.

**The Episcopal Church is the Church of England in the United States**. Although it has spiritual ties to England, it is independent. Its churches combine wide latitude and tolerance in matters of belief, with uniformity in dramatic, liturgical worship that is centered on the seven sacraments.

## Other Denominational Protestants

We now turn to a consideration of three more Protestant denominations that are not as large as the major five but which clearly fit into the category of denominational Protestantism. These include the United Church of Christ, the

Christian Church (Disciples of Christ), and the Friends Yearly Meeting, also known as the Quakers.

## The United Church of Christ

The UCC was founded in 1957 as a union of several different Christian traditions:

> from the beginning of our history, we were a church that affirmed the ideal that Christians did not always have to agree to live together in communion. Our motto—"that they may all be one"—is Jesus' prayer for the church.[17]

This self-understanding has made the United Church of Christ one of the most diverse of America's Protestant denominations.

The beliefs and practices of the United Church of Christ are very similar to those of other consensus Protestants. A statement of faith adopted in 1959 loosely follows the format of the Apostles Creed, with sections on God the Father, Jesus Christ the Son, and the Holy Spirit. Concluding paragraphs discuss the nature of the church and the role of Christians and affirm the two Protestant sacraments and eternal life in the Kingdom of God. The statement of faith is not binding on any local congregation, nor is it used as a test of faith for individual members. It is regarded as a *testimony* of faith, never as a *test* of faith.[18]

This denomination is a strong supporter of ecumenism, and, with other consensus Protestants, is a member of both the World and National Councils of Churches. The United Church of Christ is one of the most socially liberal and activist churches in the United States.

## The Christian Church (Disciples of Christ)

The Christian Church (Disciples of Christ) is one of the communities of faith that grew out of what we now call the **Restoration Movement** in American Christianity. It is the only one of the denominations in this chapter that began in America.

Prior to the Civil War, religious thinkers in many parts of the country were dismayed over the divisions within the Christian churches. They believed that the Bible taught that there was to be but one Christianity, yet there were many churches. As often as not, the relationships between these churches were not friendly, marred by arguments over creeds and church structures. The Restoration Movement sought to end these divisions.

A passionate desire for Christian unity lay behind the Restoration Movement. Everyone in the movement believed that the multitude of divisions in

---

[17]About the UCC, www.ucc.org/aboutus/index.html.
[18]This statement can be read at www.ucc.org/faith/faith.htm.

the Christian Church was offensive to Jesus's intentions for his followers. They believed that the unity that they sought could be achieved by a return to the New Testament as the only guide to faith and practice, down to the smallest detail of church government. An early slogan, "No creed but Christ," highlights their belief in the importance of avoiding humanly invented creeds.

Congregational worship is dignified and rather formal, with both instrumental and vocal music. Disciples emphasize both communion and the Lord's Supper:

> Two really important things to Disciples are communion and baptism. We celebrate communion, or the Lord's Supper, each time we get together to praise God. We like it when there are a lot of different people at communion. We believe that Christ heals the pain of human separation around the communion table.

> People who become Christians in a Disciples congregation do a couple of things. First, they say "I believe that Jesus is the Christ, the Son of the Living God, and I accept him as my personal Savior." Then, usually on another day, they are baptized—that is, they are dunked fully under water in a small pool right in the church. When they come up they are new people in Christ and their congregation pledges to support them and help them grow into a deeper relationship with God through Jesus Christ. People who have been baptized in another way in another Christian tradition are welcome.[19]

The Restorationists believed that each local congregation should be autonomous or self-governing. They held that each local gathering of believers was, in fact, the church. There should be no structures that took over things that were properly the responsibility of the local church (such as mission boards), nor any that limited the authority of each local fellowship of believers (such as presbyteries). A strong national structure has been developed, beginning in 1968, but the local congregation remains the basic unit.

### The Friends

The Religious Society of Friends, also known as the **Quakers**, is the last community of faith we will consider in this chapter. The name "Friends" comes from John 15:15 in the Christian New Testament, in which Jesus says to his followers, "I have called you friends." The Friends began in England in the 1600s. The cofounders, George Fox and his wife, Margaret Fell, were sincere seekers who had failed to find religious peace in any of the churches of their time. They did find it in a quiet, personal relationship with God, and this trait has been a part of the Quaker heritage ever since.

The Quakers or Society of Friends are distinctive in a number of ways:[20] They do not regard the Bible as the final, complete revelation of God. Revelation continues as the Holy Spirit speaks to persons and groups through the

---

[19]Christian Church (Disciples of Christ), www.disciples.org/general/whoare.htm
[20]Based on information found on The Religious Society of Friends Web site at www.quaker.org/friends.html.

words of scripture. Each individual is endowed with the *Inner Light*, a measure of Christ's own light and truth. For this reason, individual conscience is inviolable. People receive guidance and direction from God by listening for God's voice within in contemplative silence. Everyone—both genders, all races, nationalities, sexual orientations, economic classes, ages—is equal before God and thus ought to be dealt with as equals by human beings as well. All of life is sacramental; outward sacraments are not necessary and are not observed in Quaker meetings for worship. While some Quaker "meetings" worship in ways that resemble other Protestant services, many have unprogrammed worship in which worshipers sit in silence and anyone may speak as led by the Spirit to do so. Friends also follow the practice of waiting in silence when making decisions in meetings, seeking the "sense of the meeting." This is not just a search for consensus; rather, it is seeking for God's will to be expressed through the meeting.

One of the most distinctive emphases of the Friends is their **peace testimony**, their opposition to all war, and their commitment to nonviolence in every aspect of life. A late colleague of mine, for example, whose outlook was strongly influenced by Quaker teachings, helped make us all more aware of the violence implied in certain expressions that are very common in our language, such as "I could have killed him!" or even "That was a killer exam!" The Friends' commitment to the sanctity of individual conscience, however, leaves room for participation in the military for those to whom it seems right, and there are Quaker chaplains in military service.

The American Friends Service Committee (often known by its initials, AFSC) has an outstanding record of relief work in both wartime and peace. Wherever there is a disaster, at home or abroad, AFSC volunteers can usually be found helping people pick up the pieces and begin to put shattered lives back together again. The committee was awarded the Nobel Peace Prize in 1947.

The Friends have never actively sought converts. They are content to be a quiet presence in the culture, seeking to worship and live in their own way, free from interference, and granting the same privileges to others. Although the "thee" and "thou" of plain speech and the simplicity of traditional Quaker dress have largely disappeared, the Friends remain distinctive in their emphasis on the Inner Light and their witness to peace.

## WOMEN IN DENOMINATIONAL PROTESTANTISM

Denominational Protestantism usually has been receptive to the cultural and social changes that have brought about new opportunities for women. Most denominational Protestant churches ordain women to the ministry. Examples include many Baptist congregations, the United Methodists, the Presbyterian Church, (U.S.A.), many of the Lutheran churches, the Episcopal Church, the United Church of Christ, the Disciples, and the Friends. Women are entering the ministry in increasing numbers. By and large, the opportunities have never been better for women who want to enter the professional ministry.

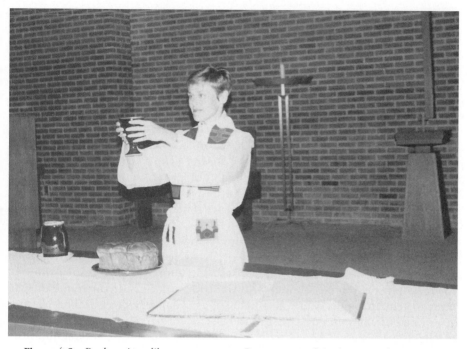

**Figure 4-5**    Presbyterians, like most consensus Protestants, ordain women to the ministry. *(Courtesy of Pastor Jean Holmes, Nauraushaun Presbyterian Church, Pearl River, NY.)*

"Women in the late twentieth century are experiencing their day in the sun in many areas of institutional church work. More positions of greater responsibility and authority are being opened to them than ever before. For the first time in history, a woman often receives preferential treatment for posts of leadership in volunteer and professional capacities."[21]

Women are also successful in gaining placements in churches, although a disproportionate number are still employed in smaller churches that pay less than their larger counterparts. Most of the churches that have called a woman as minister or pastor are well satisfied with that choice. Women have also moved into the ranks of church officials in larger numbers than before.[22]

Lay positions that historically had been closed to women, such as usher, communion server, and membership on the board of trustees or board of elders, usually are open to both sexes equally. Some local churches have made it a policy to have equal numbers of women and men in such capacities.

---

[21]Rosemary Skinner Keller, "Patterns of Laywomen's Leadership in Twentieth-Century Protestantism," in *Women and Religion in America, Vol. III: 1900–1968*, eds. Rosemary Radford Ruether and Rosemary Skinner Keller (San Francisco: Harper & Row, Publishers, 1986), p. 276.

[22]Edward C. Lehman, Jr., *Women Clergy: Breaking through Gender Barriers* (New Brunswick, NJ: Transaction Books, 1985).

The communities of faith described in this chapter attempt to use gender-inclusive language in worship and in publications. They have supported publication of revisions of the biblical books of Psalms, the Gospels, and the Pauline Letters in which inclusive language is used. They have also supported publication of inclusive language lectionaries.[23]

The following examples are representative of the ways in which these churches address the need for gender-inclusive language. In United Church of Christ publications, it is no longer permissible to use language that refers to God as "Father, Son, and Holy Spirit." An acceptable alternative is God as "Creator, Redeemer, and Sanctifier." A *Book of Worship* endorsed by the United Methodist General Conference includes prayers addressed to God as "Mother and Father." The United Church of Christ revised its statement of faith to eliminate gender-specific language. The language of the new Presbyterian statement is inclusive as well.

Denominational Protestant churches have been instrumental in supporting women's rights in general. Most have national boards that focus on women's issues, both within and outside the church. For example, most of them do not discourage women who want to work outside the home or who want to remain single. Many also help sponsor day-care centers. The National Council of Churches of Christ in the U.S.A. formally supported the passage of the Equal Rights Amendment to the U.S. Constitution, unanimously passing a resolution urging its passage.

## CONCLUSION

Denominational Protestants were the backbone of American religion, and certainly of American Protestant Christianity, for many decades. More recently, their numbers and influence have waned. Catholic Christians, African-American Christians, Eastern Orthodox Christians, conservative and fundamentalist Protestants and variant Christian communities of faith that began in the United States have all taken their rightful places at the expanding table of American religion. It is early yet to analyze what effect this shift will have on religion in the United States. It has already made the dialogue around the table more interesting, varied, and more noisy.

### QUESTIONS AND ACTIVITIES FOR REVIEW, DISCUSSION, AND WRITING

1. Describe what is distinctive about Christian faith and practice.
2. Do the same for Protestant faith and practice.
3. Describe denominational religion in your own words. How is it related to religious pluralism and diversity?
4. What is the National Council of Churches?

---

[23]A *lectionary* is a book of biblical readings arranged for use in worship.

5. Describe the variety of responses to male predominance in religion.
6. What roles do you think women should be able to play in their communities of faith? Why do you feel as you do? You might want to organize a discussion of this issue as a class project.
7. If you had a problem that you wanted to discuss with a pastor, minister, priest, or rabbi, would it make a difference to you if this person were female or male? Why?
8. With your professor, invite a female minister, priest, or rabbi to discuss with your class how she perceives the situation of women in denominational religion. Or organize a panel discussion on this topic.
9. Why are denominational differences less important in American religion than they were formerly?
10. What is unique and distinctive about each of the Protestant denominations described in this chapter?
11. Attend a worship service at both a Baptist church and an Episcopal one, and write an essay in which you compare and contrast them.
12. Visit the Web site of the National Council of Churches and write a paragraph in which you describe what its self-understanding appears to be.
13. Visit the Web sites of each of the denominations described in the chapter. From each, discover something about each denomination that you had not learned from the book.

### FOR FURTHER READING

BALMER, RANDALL, *Grant Us Courage: Travels along the Mainline of American Protestantism.* New York: Oxford University Press, 1996. An ethnographic study of twelve Protestant churches, focusing on how they have changed and stayed the same in the last half of the twentieth century. An older work, but still recommended for its ethnographic approach.

BALMER, RANDALL and LAUREN F. WINNER, *Protestantism in America.* New York: Columbia University Press, 2002. A cogent exploration of how key issues such as feminism, homosexuality, and social justice affect both liberal and conservative Protestantism. This is a nicely done analysis which recognizes the complexity of Protestantism in the United States.

BRAUDE, ANN, *Women and American Religion* (*Religion in American Life Series*). New York: Oxford University Press, 2000. Although intended for a high school audience, this book, which covers more than just Christianity, is an excellent starting point. It covers both history and the contemporary situation and has good reading lists.

MELTON, J. GORDON, *The Churches Speak On: Women's Ordination: Official Statements from Religious Bodies and Ecumenical Organizations.* Detroit: Gale Research, Inc., 1991. Like most of Melton's encyclopedic works, this is a thorough collection that includes Protestant, Catholic, Mormon, and Eastern Orthodox Christian statements, as well as several Jewish ones.

ROBERT BRUCE MULLIN and RUSSELL E. RICHEY, eds., *Reimagining Denominationalism: Interpretive Essays.* New York: Oxford University Press, 1994. The editors include a variety of essays dealing with both Christian and Jewish themes that examine the role and interpretation of the denomination as a distinctively America form of religious organization.

PAULA D. NESBITT. *Feminization of the Clergy in America: Occupational and Organizational Perspectives.* New York: Oxford University Press, 1997. Nesbitt presents a 70 year study of women's ordination, primarily in the Episcopal and Unitarian Universalist churches, that compares the patterns before and following the large influx of female clergy in the 1970s.

FREDERICK W. SCHMIDT, JR., *A Still Small Voice: Women, Ordination, and the Church.* Syracuse, NY: Syracuse University Press, 1996. The value of this particular study of the women's ordination issue in several Protestant denominations and the Catholic Church is twofold: It relies heavily on first-person interview material, and it expands the discussion to include the impact of this "women's issue" on men.

### RELEVANT WORLD WIDE WEB SITES

Basic Christian Beliefs: www.beswick.info/basicch.htm
Ontario Consultants for Religious Tolerance: www.religioustolerance.org/christ.htm
National Council of Churches: www.ncccusa.org
American Baptist Churches: www.abc-usa.org
Disciples of Christ: www.disciples.org
Episcopal Church: www.ecusa.anglican.org
Evangelical Lutheran Church: www.elca.org
Friends: www.quaker.org
Lutheran Church–Missouri Synod: www.lcms.org
Presbyterian Church in the U.S.A.: www.pcusa.org
Southern Baptist Convention: www.sbcnet.org
United Methodist Church: www.umc.org
United Church of Christ: www.ucc.org

# DIVERSE THEMES
# IN AMERICAN CHRISTIANITY

My dad was very "God and rule," and my mom sort of took it all with a grain of salt. But they were very strict about everything. They kept the sabbath on Sunday. You couldn't watch any TV or listen to the radio, or even just read a book that wasn't a religious book or listen to music that wasn't religious.[1]

After one year of disappointing results Demos [Demos Shakarian, founder of Full Gospel Businessmen's Fellowship International] decided to give up the Fellowship. While pouring out his heart in prayer the Friday night before the final meeting, he was lifted by the Spirit high into the air. In this vision, as the earth revolved each continent came into view.

"I could see people around the world—their race and color of skin," he said. "As a zoom camera can show minute details from a distance, I could see people close together but no real contact between them. Every face rigid, wretched, locked in his own private death." Billions of lost souls from every nation. Demos cried out, "Lord, help them!" Suddenly God showed him these same men, faces radiant, their hands raised to heaven, praising the Lord. At that moment, Demos' wife, Rose, gave the prophetic utterance, "My son, the very thing you see before you will soon come to pass."[2]

This chapter brings together a number of themes that are not confined to one denomination within Christianity. Neither are they specific groups, by and large, but movements and sensibilities that cut across groups. Most occur largely or exclusively within Protestantism. Some, such as the charismatic renewal movement, have affected Catholic Christianity as well.

---

[1]Penny Edgell Becker and Nancy L. Eiesland, *Contemporary America Religion: An Ethnographic Reader* (Walnut Creek, CA: AltaMira Press, 1997), pp. 106–107.
[2]Full Gospel Businessmen's Fellowship International (www.fgbmfi.org).

## FUNDAMENTALIST AND VERY CONSERVATIVE CHRISTIANS

The word *fundamentalism* derives from a series of pamphlets called "The Fundamentals," written in the early 1900s as a reference point for conservative Protestants. Some Protestant churches whose members have fundamentalist religious attitudes are part of the religious consensus. The increase in religious conservatism in the last several decades has brought many fundamentalists into the consensus. The type of fundamentalism with which this chapter deals is different. It is characterized by a strong desire to remain separate from other groups and individuals who do not believe as they do. Many of these churches are members of the **American Council of Christian Churches**, founded in 1941 by Dr. Carl McIntire.

The self-understanding of this group and why its supporters believe it to be necessary are clearly described on its Web site:

> The American Council of Christian Churches is a Fundamentalist multi-denominational organization whose purposes are to **provide** information, encouragement, and assistance to Bible-believing churches, fellowship to individuals; to **preserve** our Christian heritage through exposure of, and separation from, doctrinal impurity and compromise in current-day trends and movements; to **protect** churches from religious and political restrictions, subtle or obvious, that would hinder their ministries for God; to **promote** obedience to the inerrant Word of God.[3]

Its Doctrinal Statement is a summary of traditional Christian beliefs. The first and the last of these are especially useful in defining the group's identity:

- The plenary Divine inspiration of the Scriptures in the original languages, their consequent inerrancy and infallibility, and as the Word of God, the supreme and final authority in faith and life.
- The necessity of maintaining according to the Word of God, the purity of the Church in doctrine and life.[4]

Separatist fundamentalists firmly believe that biblical Christianity is completely incompatible with Christian modernism or liberalism, as well as with anything secular. They try to keep the boundaries between themselves and the secular world drawn sharply. Nonfundamentalist Christians are regarded as part of the unsaved world, so fundamentalists remain separate from them, as well.

Fundamentalism is not only a matter of religious belief in certain doctrines regarded as absolutely true and fundamental to faith and salvation. Scholar Karen Armstrong notes that separatist fundamentalists believe that

---

[3]The American Council of Christian Churches, www.amcouncilcc.org, emphasis in original.
[4]The American Council of Christian Churches, www.amcouncilcc.org.

religion is under attack in contemporary culture and experience a "profound fear of annihilation":

> It is a defensive, embattled religiosity that is fighting for its life. . . . Most [fundamentalists] are simply trying to live what they regard as a true religious life in a world that seems increasingly hostile to faith, and all have developed in symbiotic relationship with a secularism that is felt as invasive and destructive. Every single fundamentalist movement that I have studied is convinced that modern secular society is trying to wipe out religion. And besides religious fundamentalists, there are secular fundamentalists who often have as bigoted and inaccurate an idea of religion as fundamentalists have of secularism.[5]

Fundamentalism reflects the reality that a substantial and significant part of the population of the United States feel themselves as cultural "outsiders" in contemporary American culture. Secularization, the privatization of religion, and the dramatic changes in moral standards that followed the turbulent decade of the 1960s helped to create a culture in which some people could not feel at home. "Fundamentalists would not be fundamentalists without deep-seated feelings of dispossession, resentment, and alienation, and it is important to understand . . . these emotions."[6]

Relatively more women than men are fundamentalists, by a ratio of about four to three. Fundamentalism as an outlook reflects the kind of passivity that our culture has traditionally associated with women. The fundamentalist emphasis on God rather than on human potential encourages that passivity and gives it divine support. Fundamentalism often encourages women to be submissive to their husbands, remain at home, and accept a limited and traditional (although significant) role in the life of their church. While this seems restrictive to some women, for others it means the security of clearly defined roles that relieve the murkiness that cultural change has brought to women's lives in the last several decades.

Separatist fundamentalists have also been among the strongest supporters of the private **Christian school movement**, as well as of the home-schooling movement. Private Christian schools provide a way for parents to shield their children from the secular and humanistic influence of the public school system. They also offer greater control over the curriculum. In most private Christian schools, children do not learn the Darwinian theory of evolution, nor do they study sex education and other subjects deemed inappropriate by fundamentalists. Their textbooks support traditional values and attitudes. More important, all subjects are taught from a Christian perspective. The school day begins with worship. The teachers are committed Christians, most of whom understand their work as a religious calling.

---

[5]Andrew Cooper, "The Freelance Monotheist: An Interview with Karen Armstrong." *Tricycle: The Buddhist Review*, XII/4 (Summer, 2003), p. 110.

[6]Joel A. Carpenter, *Revive Us Again: The Reawakening of American Fundamentalism* (New York: Oxford University Press, 1997), p. 242.

Perhaps most important in understanding why fundamentalist Christians view the Christian school movement as so important, Christian schools are a primary element in the advancement of fundamentalism's sociocultural goals. "By reuniting the three major socializing institutions of family, church, and school, [fundamentalists] hope to achieve a greater coherence in their own lives, bring their children up in the faith, and bring morality back to the United States."[7]

The private Christian school movement continues to grow, but not as rapidly as the home-schooling movement. **Home schooling** means that parents teach their children at home, often using materials provided by Christian organizations. Individual parents have even more control with home schooling than with private schools. Both methods help to guarantee that children during their younger, most formative years will be socialized into the values that are central to fundamentalist Christians and into those values only.

Fundamentalist Christians also support a number of colleges in which higher education is carried out within the framework of their values and concerns. Among the best known of these schools is **Bob Jones University**. Students take required religion classes, and there is a dress code and careful control of dating behavior among students. The University's mission statement expresses very well the spirit that animates fundamentalist Christian higher education:

> Within the cultural and academic soil of liberal arts education, Bob Jones University exists to grow Christlike character that is Scripturally disciplined; others-serving; God-loving; Christ-proclaiming; and focused above.[8]

Many of the churches that fit this profile are independent, with no ties outside the local congregation. They believe that this most closely resembles the way in which the church was organized in New Testament times. It also affords each congregation the greatest opportunity to set its own standards of correct belief. Two groups of churches, however, do fit in here. In Chapter 4, you read about the Restoration Movement and the Christian Church/Disciples of Christ that is a part of it. Two other churches whose roots go back to the Restoration Movement reflect the separatist fundamental approach to Christianity.

The **Christian Churches/Churches of Christ** have no organization beyond the local congregation. There is less variation in belief among members of these independent churches than among the Disciples. Most are strongly conservative to fundamentalist. As in the other Restoration churches, the Lord's supper is served weekly. Like that of the Disciples, their worship includes instrumental music as well as the singing of hymns. The Christian

[7]Susan D. Rose, "Gender, Education, and the New Christian Right," in *In Gods We Trust*, Eds. Thomas Robbins and Dick Anthony (New Brunswick, NJ: Transaction Books, 1981), p. 100.
[8]Bob Jones University, www.bju.edu/.

Churches do not participate in ecumenical discussions or organizations, and the network of schools, colleges, and benevolent organizations they sponsor is supported entirely by local churches. They are located primarily in the lower Midwest and in Kentucky.

The **Churches of Christ** is the largest group within the Restoration churches. They are centered in the South and Southwest, although there are congregations throughout the United States. Like the Christian Churches, there is no organizational structure beyond the local church and no participation in ecumenical boards or groups. These churches seek "to speak where the Bible speaks and to be silent where the Bible is silent" in matters of faith and morality. They believe that this is the biblical pathway to Christian unity. As in the other Restoration congregations, the Lord's supper is a weekly celebration and believers are baptized by full immersion. Unlike the Disciples and the Christian Churches, the Churches of Christ use no instrumental music in their worship. Instrumental music, these Christians believe, is not biblical but is instead one of the ways the church accommodated itself to the demands of more wealthy members.

## EVANGELICAL CHRISTIANS

**Evangelicalism** is not new in the United States. Both evangelicals and pentecostals trace their heritage back to revivals that began in the eighteenth century. By the early 1700s, Puritan religion in the northeast had experienced a dramatic decline. In the mid-1700s, the northeastern and the mid-Atlantic colonies were the site of the first of a number of religious revivals that swept through America. Scholars have named this first outpouring of revival enthusiasm the **Great Awakening**.

The revivalists' messages were simple and straightforward. They concentrated on the outlines of the Christian message as Puritanism interpreted it: People are lost, trapped in sin, without any hope of saving themselves. God's free offer of salvation through grace and faith in Jesus must be accepted, because there is no other hope. Acceptance of God's gracious offer brings release from the terrible anxiety of the sin-stricken soul. The preaching style of Jonathan Edwards, George Whitefield, and other Great Awakening preachers assured that their hearers would be moved both intellectually and emotionally. Intense, abrupt experiences that people interpreted as conversion from their old lives to new lives in grace became the standard by which people's response was judged.

The **Second Awakening** occurred on the frontier in the 1800s. The basic theology and the simplicity of the message remained the same. The frontier population, however, was less educated and much less stable geographically; these factors brought about a change in revival preaching. The Second Awakening revivalists developed a style that was more emotional and less intellectual than that of their predecessors. A strong appeal to people's emotions, and equally emotional responses, were very common. Preachers pressed their hearers for immediate conversion, because many in the audience might well move on in a matter of hours. Conversion was often accompanied by emotional and physical manifestations, such as running and jumping about, unintelligible vocalizations, and fainting. Some preachers spoke out against these phenomena, believing that they were unseemly and excessive, but others encouraged them as signs of true conversion and the experience of God.

The simple message and the emotional style of the Awakenings continue in modern-day revivals. Testifying to one's faith and the centrality of the conversion experience are still important aspects of the evangelical way of being religious.

Consensus religion in the United States has usually been a relatively private matter. Who has not been reminded that it is "not polite" to discuss politics or religion? People's religion, like their political preferences, has been considered too personal to be discussed very much. Whatever may have been the fate of politics in recent years, religion has come front and center for many Americans. It has gone public. The upsurge of interest in evangelical religion, and its very public presence, has been one of the most noticeable features of American religion in the last two decades. Survey data indicate that, among Christians, over 80 percent have talked with someone about their faith with the goal of converting the other person to Christianity.

Recent surveys have helped to establish the criteria of the "minimal essence" of evangelicalism in the United States. They include the following characteristics:

> (a) salvation only through faith in Jesus Christ (the mechanism of the evangel); (b) an experience of personal conversion, commonly called being "born again" (the mechanics of the evangel); (c) the importance of missions and evangelism (sharing the message of the evangel); and (d) the truth or inerrancy of Scripture (the source of the evangel).[9]

It is very important to evangelicals to share their faith with other people. The word itself comes from the Greek and means "messenger of good news." Telling other people about the joy, peace, and happiness they have found in their relationship with Jesus is a top priority in the lives of most evangelicals. One campus evangelical organization, for example, is called Top Priority Outreach. In many ways, **witnessing**, or talking about their faith with other people with the intention of leading them to put their faith in Jesus also, defines evangelicalism. Evangelicals believe that the responsibility for missionary work rests on each and every Christian. They believe that Jesus's command to go into the whole world and preach (Mark 16:15) is directed to all Christians.

Most evangelical Christians also say they have been born again, and they emphasize the importance of this particular religious event. Being born again refers to a person's being able to point to a very specific event, a time, and place

---

[9]Swatos, William H., Jr., ed., *Encyclopedia of Religion and Society* (Walnut Creek, CA: AltaMira Press, 1998), p. 176.

in which they accepted Jesus Christ as their personal Lord and Savior. Being born again and asking Jesus to come into their lives establishes a warmly personal relationship with God that far exceeds anything they might have experienced prior to their conversion. It is this relationship that evangelical Christians want to share with those who have yet to experience it. Even those who had been active church members say that they became a Christian at that point in time. They distinguish sharply between being a member of a church and being a Christian. Usually, it is understood that virtually all Christians are church members, but not all church members are Christians. The emphasis on a datable, identifiable conversion experience goes back to Puritanism. The Puritans required testimony of such an experience as a condition of full church membership. Among all Christians, about half can identify such an experience in their religious lives.

Evangelicalism is very public in America in other ways as well. On college campuses, evangelical groups like Navigators, Campus Crusade for Christ, and Intervarsity Christian Fellowship draw many students, many of whom have participated in Young Life in high school. Members of these groups often witness to other students in the library or student center. There are evangelical groups within professional fields, such as Christian Nurses and the Society of Christian Philosophers. Christian bookstores can be found in most cities. They offer a wide selection of books, music, videotapes, and jewelry that reflects the evangelical viewpoint. Christian music has become the music of choice for many listeners, and hymns such as "Amazing Grace" and "Morning Has Broken" have become easy-listening standards.

Christian music has its own awards program, the Dove Awards. Jewelry featuring crosses, fish symbols, and "One Way" and "Jesus First" slogans are silent witnesses to all who see it being worn. Many cars have bumper stickers

**Figure 5-1**    Christian music is an important part of evangelical Christianity. *(Photo by the author.)*

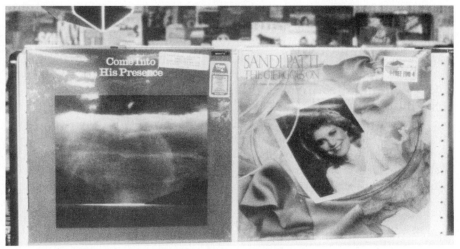

stating the driver's religious position. *Christianity Today*, a major weekly religious periodical, was founded to promote the evangelical viewpoint. Finally, public testimonies by leading figures in the sports, entertainment, and business communities have increased the public visibility of evangelicals.

**Billy Graham** (b. 1918) is the foremost contemporary exemplar of the evangelical and revivalist tradition in American religion and is the most public symbol of the style of evangelicalism that began in the 1950s and continues today. His radio program, *The Hour of Decision*, began in 1950, and he was soon familiar to television viewers as well. The core of Graham's message is traditional: Repent and surrender to Jesus as Lord and Savior. However, his preaching also addresses social problems and national sins. He has spoken out strongly against racism and classism in the United States and supports nuclear disarmament. His style of presentation is restrained and theologically informed. He established a close working relationship with the White House in the 1950s during the Eisenhower administration, a relationship that has continued with Eisenhower's successors. Graham has since passed the responsibility for his ministry to his son, Franklin Graham.

Evangelicals usually distinguish themselves from fundamentalists, who are their closest ideological neighbors. Most evangelicals regard fundamentalists as too militant, too exclusive, and as having too low an opinion of modern scholarship. Evangelicals, although certainly conservative in both theology and ethics, do accept some compromise. The new style of evangelicalism is characterized by a cautious acceptance of some of the insights of biblical scholarship, while maintaining that the Bible is inspired by God. Evangelicals affirm the generally agreed-upon doctrines of Christianity in their traditional forms. Historically, evangelicals have emphasized personal morality, and this emphasis remains. There is a new spirit of sociopolitical involvement, too, that replaces the tendency of earlier evangelicals to remain outside the rough-and-tumble of political action.

Evangelicals preach a relatively simple message that emphasizes human sinfulness and the need for rebirth, the need for and joys of a personal relationship with Jesus, and the necessity of making a definite decision for Christ. Evangelicals certainly believe that conversion is a result of the action of God's grace upon a person. They also teach the important role of human free will in the process. Evangelicalism is more concerned with the quality of religious experience than with belief in particular doctrines. It is pietistic, emphasizing personal prayer, devotion, and Bible reading.

Most evangelicals believe in a supernatural God who constantly intervenes in the affairs of the world through miracles. For example, an evangelical who recovered from a serious illness would probably explain that recovery by referring to God's role in the healing process. A religious liberal or humanist would be more likely to attribute healing to the skill of medical personnel and the effect of medication.

Most evangelical churches are not members of the National Council of Churches, because they believe that the strong desire for cooperation that led to the formation of the National Council also led to a compromise of biblical faith. Many, however, are members of the National Association of Evangelicals.

One contemporary manifestation of the evangelical spirit is **Promise Keepers**, a men's organization founded in 1990 by Bill McCartney, former University of Colorado football coach. Unlike women, who have historically come together for spiritual support, men have lacked such groups. Promise Keepers was founded in order to provide such fellowship and to provide specific structure for men seeking to live an evangelical Christian life. Men in the organization commit to seven promises that are understood as guidelines for Christian growth. Promise Keepers are committed to:

1. honoring Jesus Christ through worship, prayer and obedience to God's Word in the power of the Holy Spirit.
2. pursuing vital relationships with a few other men, understanding that he needs brothers to help him keep his promises.
3. practicing spiritual, moral, ethical, and sexual purity.
4. building strong marriages and families through love, protection, and biblical values.
5. supporting the mission of his church by honoring and praying for his pastor, and by actively giving his time and resources.
6. reaching beyond any racial and denominational barriers to demonstrate the power of biblical unity.
7. influencing his world, being obedient to the Great Commandment (see Mark 12:30–31) and the Great Commission (see Matthew 28:19–20 ).[10]

The numbers of men drawn to this movement indicate that it meets a need that many feel keenly. Although Promise Keepers is a men's organization, women make up almost 40 percent of the national staff and 50 percent of the volunteers at the large stadium conferences and have been described as "indispensable" to the Promise Keepers ministry.

Evangelicalism is not limited to any one Christian church or denomination. Evangelical Christians are people who believe that their lives have been decisively changed for the better by a vibrant experience that they attribute to God's love, the saving grace of Jesus, and the working of the Holy Spirit. In their enthusiasm for their experience, they seek to share it with others (Figure 5–2).

## MEGACHURCHES

From the standpoint of the sociology of religion, the sudden growth and expansion of megachurches is one of the most notable phenomena in American religion in the past two to three decades. There were only ten megachurches in

---

[10]Promise Keepers, www.promisekeepers.org.

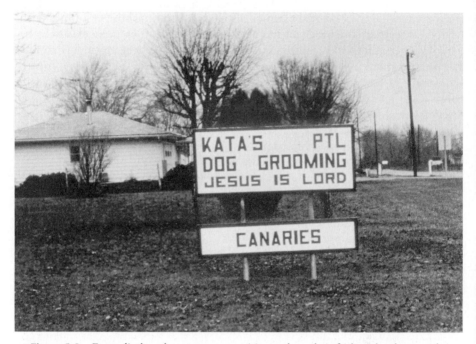

**Figure 5-2** Evangelicals seek many opportunities to share their faith with other people. On this business sign, PTL stands for "Praise the Lord." *(Photo by the author.)*

1970; now there are approximately 740.[11] Sociologists define megachurches as "non-Catholic churches with at least 2000 members."[12] Most are nondenominational, or maintain only very loose ties to their parent denomination. The majority are theologically conservative/evangelical or fundamentalist, and some are charismatic. While size and extraordinarily rapid growth are important criteria for what counts as a megachurch, and have given the movement its name, they are not by far the only important features of this distinctively American religious phenomenon. Research shows that the growth of these congregations is a response to features of the American cultural landscape that affect nearly everything we do.

Scott Thumma of the Hartford Institute for Religious Research has studied the megachurch phenomenon extensively. He points out that their size alone draws people to these churches, thus increasing their size even more.[13] Many of these churches have reached their distinctive size very

[11]Luisa Kroll, "Megachurches, Megabusiness," Forbes.com (www.forbes.com/2003/09/17/cz_lk_0917 megachurch.html).

[12]Luisa Kroll, "Megachurches, Megabusiness," Forbes.com (www.forbes.com/2003/09/17/cz_lk_0917 megachurch.html).

[13]Scott Thumma, "Exploring the Magachurch Phenomenon: their characteristics and cultural context." Hartford Institute for Religious Research (hirr.hartsem.edu/bookshelf/thumma_article2.html). This section relies primarily on Dr. Thumma's analysis.

quickly and this in itself helps define them. It leads to the public perception that something religiously significant is happening at these churches, and helps to generate publicity.

The majority of megachurches are located in the sunbelt region of the south, in the suburbs of its major cities such as Houston, Phoenix, Atlanta, and Dallas/Fort Worth. While the availability of land and less restrictive zoning in the suburbs provide incentives to locate there, even more important is the fact that the type of people likely to be attracted to a megachurch are also likely to live in the suburbs. They are upwardly mobile, well educated, and middle class.

Megachurches demonstrate several pervasive features beyond their explicit distinctiveness. Their leaders and congregations have a consciously chosen identity with a distinctive vision of their God-given mission to the world. Unlike congregations with a clear denominational identity, these churches have to construct their own.

They emphasize programming. Their large size makes it both possible and necessary to support a range of programs that offers something—many things, in fact—for everyone. Programming is typically anchored by worship services that are productions whose quality and approach rival the secular productions the congregants are used to. They are well produced and not at all amateur. Like programming in general, several worship services throughout the week offer different approaches. Although commonly focused on preaching, they usually make use of the arts, too, including choral and instrumental music, dance, and drama.

Megachurches also offer a very wide range of ministries and groups within the congregation. These may be focused on religious and spiritual issues (for example Bible study groups for all ages and interests), strengthening ties and ministering to specific needs of persons in the congregation (new members groups, discipleship groups, singles groups, parents' groups, or grief groups, for example), and groups to train the large numbers of volunteers their programs require. Many support elementary and secondary schools. Many offer literally hundreds of social and religious activities from which congregants may choose. Intense involvement is strongly encouraged and supported by how congregational life is structured. However, their large size allows for anonymity for those who seek it.

Their preachers, most usually the founders of the congregations, are in effect religious stars, whose churches reflect their charisma and personality. Although the organization and size of megachurches calls for a large cadre of subordinate staff, they frequently are *quite* subordinate to the guiding vision of the founding minister/executive. The centrality of the founding minister raises serious questions about what will happen when that person retires, leaves to found another church, or dies.

Megachurches typically attract people with identifiable characteristics: They are mainly young, with a median age of 38 or less. They are predominantly female, white, and married with children. They are both mobile and transient. Interestingly, most come to megachurches from other Christian churches rather than from the ranks of the unchurched. Although these are the generalizations, there is considerable diversity in some megachurches, and some emphasize their diversity as a selling point. Although the majority of members are upper middle class, membership includes all socioeconomic levels. Members tend to be highly involved in church activities, a trait which these congregations carefully nurture. But in addition, one of the emphases of the megachurches is usually that religion has to be lived 24/7.

Megachurches typically rely heavily on modern communications technology to stay in touch with their vast and scattered congregations. Web sites are the norm, and written, audiotape, and video communication is also commonly used. Staff make extensive use of modern electronic communication tools such as e-mail, pagers, and cell phones to be always and instantly accessible.

Although the large megachurch itself stands out, they frequently draw a constellation of smaller, loosely associated churches into their sphere of influence. These constellations of smaller churches around the larger one is itself an innovation in American religious organization. These affiliations tend to be looser than denominations and the member churches choose to belong.

Thumma has identified three distinct ways in which megachurches embody these general traits. Many are what he labels as "nontraditional." They try to attract persons without religious affiliation or who are put off by ordinary Christianity. Their message is "this is not your parents' church." "Conventional" congregations retain the tradition, but reinterpret it significantly. "This is your parents' religion," they preach, "but bigger and better." A third, "composite" approach blends these two styles.

American culture at the beginning of the twenty-first century provides a cultural context for megachurches. Many of us deal with mega-institutions on a daily basis. Many of you attend universities and colleges that might be described this way, and some of you work in such institutions or are preparing for such a career, if not both. We are accustomed to going to malls and selecting from a truly amazing array of options. We are at home in such settings, and we've come to expect and value the range of choices such settings provide. We are consumers, whether of raisins or religion.

Finally, megachurches have a symbolic function. It is frequently lamented, and sometimes celebrated, that religion's influence is declining sharply in our secular society. The rise of the megachurch symbolizes religion's continued strenght and vitality.

## THE RELIGIOUS-POLITICAL RIGHT

Evangelical religion was a strong force in American politics until the second decade of the 1900s. During the period between the end of World War I and the early 1970s, its influence on American government lessened dramatically. The early 1970s saw a renewal of evangelical and fundamentalist involvement in the political life of the nation, a trend that continued into the new century.

The **religious-political right** is a loose coalition of groups and individuals who are united by their conviction that the United States is in the midst of a severe spiritual and moral decline, a decline that could well snowball into a landslide that would lead to downfall of the United States and the defeat of democracy in the world. They believe that a **return to the traditional values of American life**, best safeguarded by fundamentalist Christianity, will prevent this landslide and again make America the strong and righteous nation that they believe existed in an earlier time. They are also united in their desire to **use the legislative process to make their goals into the law of the land**.

There are several groups whose alignment with the goals and concerns of the religious-political right is fairly constant. The most reliable support, in terms of both programs and finances, comes from **those whose religious outlook is very conservative or fundamentalist**, some of whom are evangelicals and some of whom are not. Some are pentecostals, while some are not.

**Protestants are clearly the backbone of this group**. On certain issues, such as the movement to limit legal abortions, support also comes from Catholics, Eastern Orthodox Christians, and even some Orthodox Jews. On others, such as the campaign against ratification of the Equal Rights Amendment (ERA), the coalition has included support from the **Latter-day Saints**, who value traditional male and female social roles. **A second major segment of support comes from political conservatives**. They desire to see the balance of government power shifted from the federal to the state government and hope to return the responsibility for welfare programs to the private sector of American life. This leads them to support the religious right on these types of issues. A third group is related to the second. **Social and economic conservatives** share many of the same concerns that motivate the political conservatives' involvement with the religious-political right. Economic conservatives especially favor the modifications in the welfare program it encourages, as well as its support for private business interests. We can also cite a fourth group—those who, without any clearly defined religious motivation, subscribe to the **belief that America has a special role to play in the history of the world**. They describe this role using the biblical metaphors of a light to the nations and a city set on a hill. A final group is more difficult to define but just as important. We can call them the **social traditionalists**—those whose motivations are not clearly religious, political, or economic but who believe that a return to older values would be a beneficial course for America to follow. They comprise a loose back-to-the-basics interest.

The goals of the religious-political right are stated in various ways. However they are described, they revolve around the **intention to bring about major changes in American government and American life**. They seek to make the United States a moral and righteous nation, defining morality and righteousness in terms of the authority of the Christian Bible as the only legitimate guide.

The religious-political right also describes its goals as an all-out war on an enemy that they have identified as being at the root of America's moral problems: secular humanism (see Chapter 10 for a discussion of humanism). Secular humanism stands for nearly everything that the new right believes is wrong. Most supporters subscribe to an interpretation of recent history that holds that secular humanists in high government positions are conspiring to make secular humanism the official religion of the land. A significant part of this conspiracy centers on what is being taught and what is permissible in the public schools.

Not all the groups involved in this coalition fully agree about what its specific agenda should be. Nor do they agree on the relative importance of the various items. There are, however, certain planks that can be found in nearly all statements of their platform.

The religious-political right regards the family as the mainstay of American culture. They approve of only one form of family structure, which they identify as the **traditional form of family organization** in the United States. The traditional family is the family that consists of a man and a woman, married for life, with children. Premarital chastity and marital monogamy are the only acceptable forms of sexuality. Both the Old and New Testaments of the Christian scriptures are cited in support of the position that homosexuality is a heinous sin and a prime contributor to America's spiritual degeneracy. Sex education should be taught only by Christians to ensure that proper values will be taught along with factual information. The Equal Rights Amendment and the "feminist revolution" appear in every list of national errors that are said to threaten America. Opposition to abortion, especially government support for abortion in the form of Medicaid payments and federal funding for abortion clinics, is another important part of their family policy.

They also support a thorough cleanup of commercial television, not only to eliminate violence and the use of sexually suggestive advertising but also to eliminate the portrayal of alternative lifestyles. They oppose pornography in all its forms and want to have laws enacted that would mandate stiff penalties for those who create and distribute pornographic literature, films, videotapes, and so forth. Another priority is support for programs that will help to solve the problem of illegal drug use.

These concerns are shared by people who do not identify with the religious-political right explicitly. Survey data indicate that approximately 90 percent of Americans believe that extramarital sex is always or nearly always wrong. About 80 percent feel that way about active homosexuality. Over half support at least some restrictions on the availability of legal abortion. Over half the population favors laws prohibiting the sale of pornography to people under the age of eighteen, and almost half oppose the sale of pornography to anyone, regardless of age. Many Americans are concerned about illegal drugs, as they are about sex and violence (and the frequent close association of the two) on commercial television.

The large role the federal government has assumed in administering welfare programs is another concern. The religious-political right does recognize that there will always be people who cannot care for themselves because of age or physical or mental infirmity. They want to shift the responsibility for the care of such people from the government to the private sector, including churches, businesses, and, above all, the families of the people themselves. For example, they support tax credits for those families who have a dependent elderly parent living with them.

Government regulation of business and industry is yet another concern. Free enterprise, ambitious management, and competition unfettered by government regulation are held to be biblical values that are a part of God's plan for humanity.

The religious-political right wants the nation to return to the values of an earlier, much less complicated period in history, when the population was much smaller. The members of this movement believe that the values that worked in that setting are what America needs now. Although not all Americans agree with them, their vision of a renewed America based on traditional values has captured the hearts and minds of a significant number of people. The religious-political right is one of the most significant religious and political movements of recent history.

The religious-political right believes the schools, both public and private, bear the responsibility, alongside the family and the churches, for rearing children who have a strong sense of and commitment to these values. Their approach to education has two main facets. The first is what they want to see happen within the public school system. The second is their goals concerning the establishment of a system of private Christian schools and support for home schooling to supplement the public schools.

The **public schools, according to this analysis, have been taken over by secular humanists** and are being used as the main tool for indoctrinating youngsters with the values held dear by humanists. The U.S. Supreme Court decision that made mandated prayer and other school-sponsored devotional exercises in the public schools illegal is of particular concern. They want voluntary prayer and other devotional exercises returned to the public school classroom. They also want any academic study of religion eliminated, because it maintains a position of neutrality concerning the truth of specific religions. This conflicts sharply with their belief that Christianity is the one true faith. To help accomplish these goals, they have increasingly focused on getting supporters elected to local school boards.

A related concern is that the public schools do not teach one absolute truth in any area. For example, in dealing with families in a high-school sociology class, a classroom discussion of many styles of relationships between adults and many approaches to parenting takes the place of the promotion of the traditional family as the only acceptable family. Rather than advocating that women remain at home as wives, mothers, and homemakers, the public schools attempt to prepare their students to assess the strengths and weaknesses of various arrangements. Rather than teaching the immorality of premarital sex, health teachers encourage their students to explore their own values and attitudes and introduce the cautions deemed necessary in the face of disease and the possibility of unwanted pregnancy. Government classes, instead of promoting democracy and condemning other forms of government, have students evaluate various forms of government.

You might want to pause a moment here and think back over the textbooks from which you learned as a child. How was religion portrayed, if at all? What messages were being presented in the pictures of boys and girls, men and women? When you took the required (in most school systems, at any rate) government or civics course, were different types of government portrayed equally, or was democracy held up as an ideal?

The teaching of evolution is another focal point for the critique of public school education. Some want the theory of evolution dropped from the curriculum completely in favor of teaching an account of the beginning of the world and humankind that is compatible with the creation stories in Genesis. Others want to see evolution and creationism or creation science taught alongside each other as theories. Again, think back to your high-school (perhaps junior-high or middle-school) biology, botany, or life-science classes. Were you taught about evolution? Were you taught the creation stories in Genesis? Was the entire subject ignored? Some textbook publishers and some schools have taken this last approach to avoid a confrontation over this explosive issue.

A final point of contention with the public schools has to do with the teaching of sex education. In the first place, many supporters of the religious-political right want all sex education removed from the schools and left in the hands of parents and the churches. If sex education is to be taught in the public schools at all, the values of premarital chastity, marital fidelity, and lifelong monogamy should be the only things taught. Sex education cannot be separated from family life education, and the traditional family style must be upheld in the public schools.

An editorial reflection is in order here. The values of traditional Christianity have been a major influence in American life for many centuries. The Genesis accounts of how the world began have guided the thinking of uncounted millions of people and continue to do so. Sexual morality based on the teachings of the Christian Bible is the framework that has made family life meaningful and good for generations of Americans. These values deserve a place in public school education because they are a significant part of the story of humanity and of the history and present culture of the United States. However, in a pluralistic culture, they must be presented as one set of values alongside others from which people have chosen. They must not be taught as the only right values, to the exclusion of others. A similar point can be made concerning the omission of religion in descriptions of the history and present culture of the United States. Religion has been and continues to be an important factor in American life. To omit it is to present an inaccurate picture of both past and present. The distinction between teaching religion and teaching about religion must be scrupulously maintained, however, and the approach must always be descriptive rather than normative.

Every bit as important in the religious-political right's approach to public education is its **support for a network of private Christian schools**. When we discuss Catholicism in Chapter 6, you will learn that the Catholic Church sponsors the largest private school system in the United States. It is usually called the parochial school system. Among Protestants, the Lutherans sponsor a number of schools. The network of Christian schools has grown steadily in the United States. Those who support Christian schools do so largely because they believe that home, church, and school should reinforce each other by presenting the same values and truths. Supporters of Christian schools want to see the development of a system that exists apart from the teacher training and licensing requirements enforced by the states. They do not want to be subject to the same curriculum requirements that guide the public schools.

There is more at stake, according to the supporters of private Christian schools, than simply being able to begin and end the school day with prayer and Bible reading or to say grace before lunch. Christian school advocates are asking for the right to control their children's education with minimal interference from the government. Government regulation is looked upon as harassment and as infringement on freedom of religion. For those whose values and home life are guided by the views and principles of fundamentalist Christianity, public school attendance is a very real threat to their children's spiritual welfare. It threatens both their earthly happiness and their eternal life. As we noted earlier, home schooling allows for even more parental control than do private schools.

Catholics earlier had pressed for and won the right to their own schools because they believed that there was a clear Protestant bias in the public schools. **Fundamentalist Christians believe there is a clear humanistic bias in the public schools**. They seek the right to take decisive action to protect their youngsters. It is for this reason that education has become such a pressing issue.

The **military strength of the United States** and its position in relation to the other nations of the world are also important to the religious-political right. They believe that the United States must always be the first and foremost world military and economic power. They believe this is necessary mainly to protect the values of democracy and capitalism both in the United States itself and in the world. They believe the strongest possible national defense is not only a political necessity but a religious obligation. The United States has been chosen by God for a special destiny in the history of God's interaction with the world, and defending that destiny militarily is part of carrying out the divine plan.

The religious-political right works through **direct political action** as well as through its efforts to educate people and persuade them to support their point of view. It seeks to elect public officials who are sympathetic to its programs and views. Those who think along these lines describe government as the provision of "godly leadership."

Followers of this perspective believe that only by governing according to the Bible can a leader govern rightly. A direct practical implementation of this point of view came from the Christian Voice organization when it developed the Congressional Score Card to track the way that members of Congress voted on certain critical moral issues such as abortion support and the ERA. Voter registration drives have been another important focus, and voter registration has been done after Sunday morning worship in some fundamentalist churches.

## The Christian Coalition

The Christian Coalition exemplifies the organizational embodiment of the religious-political right. It describes itself as "every Christian's instrument for affecting a spiritual response to our nation's domestic and international challenges." It takes an approach that is "distinctively and exclusively Christian" to work on the following goals, which mirror closely the emphases of the religious-political right generally:

> Strengthening the family
> Protecting innocent human life
> Returning education to local and parental control
> Easing the tax burden on families
> Punishing criminals and defending victims' rights
> Protecting young people and our communities from the pollution of pornography
> Defending the institution of marriage
> Protecting religious freedom[14]

It employs methods that have a long history in political activism both secular and religious, such as conferences and training seminars for activists, federal and state lobbying, telephone and e-mail alerts for members on important issues and upcoming votes, and attempts to get out the vote on issues of concern.

## The Christian Reconstruction Movement

The Christian Reconstruction movement is a variation on the religious-political right theme. Its Chalcedon Foundation is a nonprofit organization established in 1964 by R. J. Rushdoony. It seeks to educate people about the "Biblical standards for life, both individual and social." It supports the view that the only answers to individual and social problems can be found in the Christian Bible. Biblical standards as the Chalcedon Foundation interprets them apply to all people, not just to Bible believers, and the Bible gives God's blueprint for government as well as for individual and church life. The group's Mission Statement provides a clear articulation of the movement's perspective: They propose explicitly Christian and biblical solutions to what they under-

---

[14]The Christian Coalition, www.cc.org/

stand as the problems of the modern world. They seek to build a distinctively Christian civilization in which all of life is regulated by Christian norms as they understand them.

They employ two basic methods for doing so. First, they attempt to show the "bankruptcy" of all philosophies and systems of ethics other than their own interpretation of Christianity. Second, Chalcedon offers its own understanding of biblical Christianity as the only sound alternative for rebuilding all areas of private and public life.[15]

### CHRISTIAN TELEVISION

Do you watch the television programs on any of the major Christian networks, such as TBN or FAM? If you do, why do you enjoy them? If you do not watch them, why not? What kinds of thoughts come to mind when someone uses the phrase "television preacher" or "television evangelist"?

The religious message that is broadcast on Christian television is not new. Nor is religious broadcasting itself new. It began with radio and continued with commercial television. What *is* new is the medium. High-tech communications technologies, such as cable television and communications satellites, have revolutionized the religious broadcasting industry. Christian networks, satellite connections, super high-tech studios, and computers have transformed Christian broadcasting from a small segment of broadcasting over all to a major component in the field. Major Christian networks such as the Family Network (FAM), Trinity Broadcasting Network (TBN), and the Christian Television Network (CTN) provide most of the programs that make up Christian television today.

The electronic church, as it is often called, has been hailed by those favorable to it as the greatest tool the church has ever had for telling "the greatest story ever told." It has also been the most harshly criticized method of outreach the church has ever used. Whatever one's opinion of religious television, it now has a firm place in the overall landscape of the American love affair with both television and religion.

You have already been learning about Christian television, because most of the programming on Christian television reflects the views of evangelical Christianity, fundamentalism, and the religious-political right. It is primarily an extension of the revivalist and evangelical tradition that has characterized American religion at least since the Awakenings.

This particular form of religious broadcasting has often been referred to as **televangelism**. That word is somewhat inaccurate, because its main audience is composed of those who already share its point of view and religious beliefs. **Christian television** is a more accurate term. It is an outgrowth and an

---

[15]The Chalcedon Foundation, www.chalcedon.edu.

integral part of the conservative/evangelical/fundamentalist point of view in American Christianity. It provides alternative television for those who find it difficult to locate acceptable programs on the commercial channels. It reflects the same religious worldview that supports contemporary Christian music.

This designation also helps us to understand the importance of the resurgence in evangelical and fundamentalist Christianity in the United States for Christian television. There is now a group of consumers available who have clearly defined tastes in entertainment. It is this group of consumers that makes up the viewing audience for Christian television. It is also important to note that persons who do not identify themselves as conservative evangelical Christians are also part of the viewing audience.

Who watches Christian television? Several studies have been done in the attempt to answer this question, and they all agree on the main points. Holding evangelical and fundamentalist or very conservative religious beliefs is the factor most strongly correlated with watching Christian television. Most viewers live in the South and the Midwest, with a disproportionate number in the South. The majority of viewers are female, and viewers are older than the general population. Between two-thirds and three-fourths are age fifty or over. Another important fact that emerges from these studies is that watching religion on television does not substitute for church attendance and participation. Most viewers are regular churchgoers and contribute to the financial support of their local congregation as well. The early predictions that Christian television would be the downfall of many a local congregation have not proven accurate. Christian television is used as a substitute for attendance by only one category of people—those who, for whatever reason, find it difficult to get out to attend church. Ratings indicate, finally, that there are fewer viewers by far than the massive audiences claimed by the broadcasters themselves. There are, especially, fewer regular viewers.

The fund-raising techniques used by Christian television have been widely criticized. Several methods are popular. Seeking donations is a common method. In return for a specified donation, donors may be memorialized in some fashion, such as by having their names inscribed in Oral Roberts' Prayer Tower or on chairs in Schuller's Crystal Cathedral. It should be noted here that donors' names have often been inscribed on pews or stained glass windows as local churches sought to raise money, too. Clubs such as the 700 Club or Faith Partners offer privileges and benefits in return for a specified sum per month. Besides a magazine or newsletter, participants gain a sense of being a part of something important, of being related in a personal way to the work being carried out by their favorite Christian television personality. Money is also raised by the sale of pens, bumper stickers, lapel pins, Bibles, records or audiotapes, and books. Frequently these items are not "sold" but offered in return for a donation. Most Christian television personalities are quite skilled at the personal-appeal style of fund-raising, in which they simply ask for donations. The "going off the air" appeal is a variant of this method, in which the personality makes a highly emotional appeal, in which it is said that only contributions over and above the usual will keep the program from having to go off the air. Again, contributors gain a feeling that they have helped to accomplish the work that the preacher set out to do.

For most of its founders, the initial goal of Christian television was evangelism. They wanted to bring their version of the Gospel message to millions of viewers and win additional souls for Christ. The great majority of its viewers now count themselves among those who already agree with the viewpoint being presented. It does help to reinforce existing beliefs and behaviors. For the largely convinced viewing audience, what they see and hear models the behavior and beliefs they themselves are trying to live. It reinforces and supports, and many come away from its programs with renewed conviction and determination.

We can best think of Christian television as viewer-supported alternative television. A significant number of people cannot find many programs on commercial television that do not run afoul of their values and tastes in entertainment. They want something more from television. One segment of the population turns to public television for what they want. A larger segment turns to Christian television. It is, in other words, a response to a need for viewing options other than those provided by commercial networks, most cable and satellite channels, and public television. As the percentage of conservative, fundamentalist, and evangelical Christians in the population has increased, so has the need for and the popularity of Christian television. The increasing conservatism and evangelicalism of American Christianity indicates that Christian television will continue to be an important element in the entertainment industry and in religion.

The 1980s was a decade of crisis for Christian television. Federal Communications Commission testimony demonstrated that funds collected by the several television ministries had been seriously misused. Allegations of sexual misconduct, actions that go to the very heart of the fundamentalist definition of sin, were hurled in several directions and later substantiated. The National Religious Broadcasters organization enacted new, tougher standards for its 1300-plus members.

Three things seems clear in the wake of that crisis. The problems of the 1980s and 1990s hurt Christian television. It appears unlikely that it will rebound to the level of financial support from viewers that it enjoyed prior to the 1980s. It is equally clear that the injuries were not fatal. Christian television has continued to be a significant aspect of our entertainment-oriented culture, providing programming for a segment of the population who cannot find acceptable television elsewhere. In the process, it has moved closer to the mainstream of American life and culture, or perhaps the mainstream has moved closer to it.

Religious television is not limited to Christian television, although that is clearly its largest component. The National Council of Churches of Christ in the U.S.A. is involved in two ecumenical and interfaith-oriented broadcasting ventures. Two interfaith committees within the NCC facilitate religious television programming on network television and the Hallmark cable channel:

> The *Interfaith Broadcasting Commission* is a working alliance of the National Council of Churches, the U.S. Catholic Conference, the Southern Baptist Convention, and the Jewish Theological Seminary. Through this alliance, the NCC's 36-member communions participate in the production of an annual series of faith-based television presentations on the three major broadcast networks, ABC, CBS, and NBC.

> The *National Interfaith Cable Coalition* is another cooperative venture founded by the NCC and other religious organizations to create the VISN cable network in 1988. After it merged with the Southern Baptist-sponsored ACTS channel, VISN was renamed the Odyssey network. Today, the coalition is known as Faith and Values Media and serves as a gateway for faith-based programming carried on the Hallmark cable channel.[16]

## HOLINESS CHRISTIANS

Holiness is a movement that involves several groups of Christian believers, rather than being a group in and of itself. It is rooted in Jesus's admonition that his followers be perfect, even as God is perfect (Matthew 5:48). To follow this directive means to work toward ever-increasing holiness and perfection of life in this world. Sin and the evidences of sin are to be progressively rooted out. The search for perfection usually has been accompanied by a sense of separation from those who are not engaged in a similar search. Holiness is a matter of both belief and lifestyle. Its adherents believe in the possibility and the necessity of sanctification, understood as a work of the Holy Spirit distinct from justification. By **justification**, a person is forgiven for past sin and placed in a new relationship with God. By **sanctification**, that new relationship becomes more and more evident in the person's life as the Holy Spirit continues to bring about growth in grace. Other people are likely to be made aware of someone's membership in a holiness church by their lifestyle, which reflects, in ways that vary somewhat from church to church, their understanding of how a sanctified life is to be lived.

When it began, the **holiness movement** in the United States took many of its cues from John Wesley's teaching about Christian perfection. Wesley, you remember, was the founder of Methodism in England. When Methodism came to the United States, it brought Wesley's emphasis on sanctification and perfection with it. Originally, Methodists had many of the characteristics that

---

[16]The National Council of Churches of Christ in the U.S.A., www.ncccusa.org/about/partners/html.

have come to be associated with the holiness movement. As Methodism grew in numbers and wealth and became more a religion of the middle class, outward holiness was downplayed. Groups that disagreed with this lessening of outward holiness broke away. They often referred to themselves as Wesleyans, in order to distinguish themselves from the Methodists and to express their loyalty to the original intention of John Wesley.

The rejection of that which is "of the world" in order to attain holiness brought with it disagreements over precisely what was to be rejected. Over time, these disagreements led to there being many divisions within the movement. There are now several holiness groups made up of many churches as well as many independent communities of believers without ties outside their own group.

What, then, are some of the things that holiness Christians reject as being too much of the world? The use of alcohol, tobacco, and illicit drugs are universally banned among such groups. They are very careful in their language, avoiding not only obvious swearing and blasphemy but much of the common slang used in our culture. Gambling, too, is universally forbidden. Attending movie theaters and sometimes watching television are not permitted. Dancing is avoided by most. Swimming, or swimming in mixed groups of males and females, is sometimes disallowed. Children often do not participate in physical education classes that violate their standards, such as those involving folk dancing or those that require girls to wear slacks or shorts. Some holiness students also ask to be excused from participating in regular classroom work that conflicts with their beliefs. Examples include the teaching of evolution in biology or botany classes, sex education in health classes, or when movies are shown in class.

It is especially important, according to holiness teaching, that women follow a virtuous lifestyle. Women's role in the home and in the rearing of children makes them the primary transmitters of holiness. Frequently, women are discouraged from cutting their hair or at least from wearing it shorter than shoulder length. The use of cosmetics and the wearing of much jewelry is frowned upon. A simple wristwatch and a wedding band are often the only permissible jewelry. High-cut necklines and at least elbow-length sleeves are the norm, and women wear dresses or skirts rather than slacks or shorts.

Those in search of holiness tend to socialize with like-minded people who reinforce their values and way of life and who support them in their difference from the world. Marriages usually take place within the group, and children are encouraged to find their playmates among church members' children. Families are often large, and divorce is strongly discouraged if not forbidden. This pattern of socialization has the twofold effect of reinforcing the sense of community within the group and maintaining the separation between those who are "of the world" and those who are not.

There are many independent churches within this movement. There are also some groupings of churches. Some of the better-known groups include several in the Church of God family, the Churches of Christ in Christian

Union, and some conservative Mennonite groups. Two of the largest are the Church of the Nazarene and the Wesleyan Church, both of which are especially strong in the Midwest. Several statements included in the Wesleyan statement of faith and practice, "This We Believe," illustrate the holiness perspective. Members are called on to abstain completely from gambling and from the "production, sale, or purchase" from alcohol, tobacco, and non-medical drugs. They are to participate in "public worship, the ministry of the Word of God, the Lord's Supper, family and personal devotions, and fasting." The church "vigorously opposes public acceptance of sexual promiscuity and all factors and practices which promote it." They also protest "the inclusion of such questionable items as social dancing in the public school curriculum" and uphold the rights of their members to be excused from participating in any school activities that are contrary to their beliefs. Families are called upon to be diligent in the "regulation of the use in the home of mass media, such as current literature, radio, and television, guarding the home against the encroachment of evil," and to not participate in social dancing, attending movie theaters and other commercial ventures that "feature the cheap, the violent or the sensual and pornographic." Games that might be addictive or promote gambling are also forbidden. Modesty and "Christian simplicity" in clothing are encouraged as well.[17]

Perhaps the best known of all the holiness organizations, because it maintains the highest public profile, is the *Salvation Army*. While most people probably associate the Salvation Army with thrift shops and Christmas bell ringers, it is also a fully functioning church. In addition to the social programs for which it is best known, Army Citadels hold Sunday and midweek services for a membership of about 500,000. Their wholehearted identification with the poorest of the poor and the outcasts of society make them able to reach out to people who are likely to be overlooked by other churches. The United Pentecostal Church is a major holiness denomination that is also pentecostal.

Some of you may feel that the restrictions that holiness imposes amount to a program for avoiding life in the real world. It certainly is true that there are fewer worldly temptations for people who conscientiously follow this path. Consider, however, the burden of difference that these people take upon themselves for the sake of the higher goals they seek. Students who are not a part of the ordinary round of school activities, and whose dress and behavior set them apart from other students, may be ridiculed, or at least misunderstood and socially isolated. Acceptance by others comes slowly or not at all under these circumstances. Those of all ages voluntarily limit social contacts and activities taken for granted by the majority culture. It is a life of difficult choices, the final validation of which must of necessity wait until an unspecified time in the future.

---

[17]The Wesleyan Church, www.wesleyan.org.

## PENTECOSTAL CHRISTIANITY

Part of the variety in American religion stems from variations in the way that different communities of faith balance out their appeal to the intellect, the will, and the emotions. Some services of worship are calm and dignified and offer stimulation primarily to the intellect. Those that emphasize ethical behavior and social service appeal to the will. Some offer more in terms of emotional satisfaction.

The experience of highly emotional worship and religious ecstasy is the foundation of pentecostalism. It has been a part of American religion for many years in the form of traditional pentecostalism and has gained in acceptance and visibility in the charismatic renewal movement. Pentecostalism is also one of the fastest-growing forms of Christianity, both in the United States and around the world. Two of the American denominations showing the most rapid recent growth—the mostly white Assemblies of God and the mostly black Church of God in Christ—are pentecostal.

The word **pentecostalism** refers to an event recorded in the Christian New Testament, in the Book of Acts. The disciples were gathered together following the devastating events of Jesus's crucifixion and death. They must have been a discouraged and disheveled band of men. As the biblical account goes, the Holy Spirit came to the disciples in a new and powerful way, described as "tongues like flames of fire, dispersed among them and resting on each one" (Acts 2:3, New English translation). They began to speak in languages other than those they usually used, and all present heard in their own languages. In the confusion that followed, Peter is said to have spoken, quoting the Hebrew prophet Joel (God is said to be speaking here): "This will happen in the last days: I will pour out upon everyone a portion of my spirit; and your sons and daughters shall prophesy; your young men shall see visions, and your old men shall dream dreams" (Joel 2:28, New English translation). Most Christian churches celebrate this event annually in the spring, on Pentecost Sunday, as the anniversary of the founding of the church. For some Christians, however, it has meant much more. Pentecostal Christians (whether traditional pentecostal or charismatic Christians[18]) believe that what God did at Pentecost continues to happen today. People can receive the Holy Spirit in the same way as did the disciples, according to the Book of Acts.

Pentecostals believe that certain phenomena accompany and give evidence of the work of the Holy Spirit. The principal evidence of this gift is usually said to be the ability to **speak in tongues**. This phenomenon is also called *glossolalia*. Speaking in tongues takes two forms. People may speak in a recognizable human language. On the other hand, some pentecostals say that their tongues are not recognizable human languages, but a private language given

---

[18]The *charismatic renewal movement* is discussed in the next section.

**Figure 5-3** Pentecostal worship is emotional and enthusiastic. *(Guy Gillette/Photo Researchers, Inc.)*

by God. Linguists who have studied this type of glossolalia have found that, although it is not a known human language, it has the characteristics that identify it as distinctly human speech. Pentecostal Christians are urged to expect and actively seek this gift: An Assemblies of God statement expresses it this way: "All believers are entitled to and should ardently expect and earnestly seek the promise of the Father, the baptism in the Holy Ghost and fire, according to the command of our Lord Jesus Christ. This was the normal experience of all in the early Christian Church. With it comes the enduement of power for life and service, the bestowment of the gifts and their uses in the work of the ministry."[19]

Pentecostals make another distinction as well. For some, tongues are a prayer language between the individual and God and do not call for interpretation. Others believe that tongues are a way that God uses to communicate with an entire congregation. In these instances, an interpreter is required to "translate" the message. Interpretation also is thought to be a gift of the Spirit. Usually, the speaker and the interpreter are two different people.

Speaking in tongues is regarded as the primary manifestation of the action of the Holy Spirit. The United Pentecostal Church International considers it "the initial sign of receiving the Holy Ghost," and "an immediate,

[19]Assemblies of God, www.ag.org.

external evidence" of the Holy Ghost's indwelling. Other gifts of the Spirit are mentioned in the New Testament. Examples of such lists can be found in 1 Corinthians 12:8–10, 28, and 29–30. The healing of physical and psychological illnesses is considered second only to tongues by most pentecostals. Prophecy and the interpretation of tongues receive considerable attention. Preaching and administration in the church are considered gifts. Exorcism, or the removal of unclean spirits, is practiced by some. Wisdom and knowledge are gifts, as is the ability to distinguish good from evil spirits. A very few pentecostals handle venomous snakes and drink poison in response to a statement attributed to Jesus in the Gospel of Mark, which says that believers can do these things without harm (Mark 16:17–18).

Some of the divisions that occurred within the holiness-pentecostal movement came about as churches began to differ about the role of glossolalia. The Wesleyan Church's statement on this topic illustrates the position that some churches take:

> The Wesleyan Church believes in the miraculous use of languages and the interpretation of languages in its biblical and historical setting. But it is contrary to the Word of God to teach that speaking in an unknown tongue or the gift of tongues is the evidence of the baptism of the Holy Spirit or of that entire sanctification which the baptism accomplishes; therefore, only a language readily understood by the congregation is to be used in public worship.[20]

Traditional pentecostalism began in America in the late nineteenth and early twentieth centuries. It was an outgrowth of the holiness movement. Like holiness, traditional pentecostalism usually emphasizes the necessity of outward holiness. More important, pentecostals focus on what they call the baptism of the Holy Spirit (often referred to in these churches as the Holy Ghost). This is said to be an encounter with God that may precede or follow water baptism. The specific religious experiences believed to be associated with the gift of the Holy Ghost became more important than the lifestyle associated with the holiness movement.

Two people are especially associated with the early history of pentecostalism in the United States. Charles Fox Parham was a traveling ex-Methodist preacher who settled in Topeka, Kansas, and founded a Bible school called the College of Bethel. In December 1900, some thirty or forty of Parham's students received the gift of tongues after studying Acts 2. The key person behind the development of pentecostalism as a movement, however, was William Joseph Seymour, a former slave who was at one time a student of Parham's. After receiving the gift of tongues himself in 1906, Seymour rented a run-down building on Azuza Street in Los Angeles, which became the site of the well-known Azuza Street Mission. Seymour held very enthusiastic religious revivals at Azuza Street, and many people received the various spiritual

---

[20]Wesleyan Church, www.wesleyan.org.

gifts under his leadership. The mission was eventually renamed the Apostolic Faith Gospel Mission, developed a missionary program both at home and overseas, and published a monthly newsletter plus several other publications. A movement had been born.

Several of the early pentecostal churches still exist in the United States, including the Assemblies of God (the largest), the Church of God (Cleveland, Tennessee), the Church of God in Christ, the Pentecostal Holiness Church, the Foursquare Gospel Church, and the United Pentecostal Church. Many still retain at least some emphasis on holiness, as well. There are also numerous independent churches in the pentecostal category, which are more likely to require a holiness lifestyle in addition to clear-cut evidence of the spiritual gifts. Their membership tends to come from the lower socioeconomic classes. Many congregations, although certainly not all, are predominantly black. Although they are not limited to any one geographical area, their greatest strength is in the Midwest, the lower Midwest, and the South.

Although linked by their pentecostal experiences, the various pentecostal denominations also have differences. As noted above, some, such as members of the United Pentecostal Church, affirm a holiness lifestyle, while others, such as members of the large Assemblies of God, do not. The United Pentecostal Church is also the largest of the "Oneness Pentecostal" churches, affirming the oneness of God rather than belief that God is a trinity of three persons in one God. People are baptized in the name of Jesus only, rather than with the more usual "in the name of the Father, the Son, and the Holy Spirit." Father, Son, and Holy Spirit are believed to be different manifestations of the one God rather than distinct persons united into a single God. By contrast, the Assemblies of God is trinitarian.

Although pentecostalism began as an interracial movement, segregated congregations and denominations became the norm. At present, new efforts toward racial unity are occurring. The predominantly white Pentecostal Fellowship of America, which includes several pentecostal churches, is reorganizing to include black churches, including the rapidly growing Church of God in Christ. Interest in unity has come about in part due to the necessity to work together in inner-city ministries.[21]

Pentecostal worship is emotional and enthusiastic, marked by frequent outbursts of pentecostal phenomena and shouts of "Amen!" and "Praise Jesus!" from the congregation. It addresses the human need for religious experience very directly. Traditional pentecostalism is, in its own right, a significant aspect of American religion. It also forms the background against which we can better understand the modern-day charismatic renewal movement. This movement shares important characteristics with traditional pentecostalism and at the same time has significant differences. An Assemblies of God college professor and former president of the Society for Pentecostal Studies

[21]*Christianity Today*, April 25, 1994.

summarizes his tradition this way: "This is the experiential religion par excellence. It fills a vacuum for meaning in life and does so at the deepest levels of one's experience. But it also incorporates one into a movement and community larger than oneself." [22]

## THE CHARISMATIC RENEWAL MOVEMENT

The intense emotional involvement that characterizes pentecostal worship was not a part of mainstream religion prior to the charismatic renewal movement. Since the revivals of America's early history, there have been sharp differences of opinion about the appropriateness of such "manifestations of the Spirit." Most of the consensus churches either ignored the pentecostals or criticized their worship as undignified and excessively emotional. **The charismatic renewal movement** refers to a group of Christians who have had pentecostal experiences but who are not members of traditional pentecostal churches. The word **charismatic** is derived from a Greek word that means "gift" and refers to the gifts of the Holy Spirit enumerated in the Christian New Testament. The charismatic renewal movement began in the United States, as far as we know, in 1960. The reverend Dennis Bennett of Saint Mark's Episcopal Church in Van Nuys, California, his wife, and about seventy other members of his congregation received the gift of tongues during a prayer meeting. The phenomenon spread very rapidly and soon had appeared in every major Protestant denomination as well as in the Roman Catholic Church.

Richard Quebedeaux, in his classic study of the charismatic renewal movement titled *The New Charismatics, II*, explains its importance this way: The consensus Christian churches typically teach that God is present with the faithful, that new life in Christ is possible now, and that the Holy Spirit is present in the church, but they fail to make this message believable. There is no experiential evidence that would enable people to know beyond doubt that the message was true and that God was present to them personally. The charismatic renewal movement rejects both the "liberal, nonsupernatural god who really isn't there anyhow," and the "rational evangelical god of the intellect," whose specialty is propositional truth. It embraces a "God you can feel, respond to, and *love*." He continues, "It is the knowledge of this God, given through the experience of his Holy Spirit, that has bound charismatics together." [23] Modern-day charismatics are not content to be told about the presence of God in their churches and the presence of the Holy Spirit in their hearts. They seek knowledge and certainty, the certainty provided by the religious experience of the charismatic renewal movement.

There are several characteristics of the charismatic renewal movement that set it apart from traditional pentecostalism. For the most part, there has

---

[22]Quoted in Don Lattin, "Touched by the Fire," *Common Boundary*, July/August 1995, p. 34.
[23]Richard Quebedeaux, *The New Charismatics, II* (New York: Harper & Row, 1983), pp. xiii–xv.

been no large-scale exodus of charismatics from noncharismatic churches. Usually they meet together in small prayer groups in addition to remaining involved in other church activities. In addition, however, the movement has given rise to charismatic groups that include charismatics from all sorts of church backgrounds. The movement emphasizes experience rather than doctrine and has become thoroughly ecumenical, with people of different backgrounds and theologies united in a common bond of experience.

The largest of these ecumenical organizations is the **Full Gospel Businessmen's Fellowship, International**, founded in 1951. Although founded before the rise of the new charismatic movement, it attracts people who count themselves among the new charismatics. The organization has grown rapidly and now has male and female members from all walks of life, a women's group (Women's Aglow Fellowship), and teen and youth groups. Members usually meet for a meal and to share experiences and testimony. Groups of charismatic students meet regularly on most college campuses in the United States. The charismatic renewal movement also holds nationwide conferences yearly, one of the largest of which is at the Catholic Notre Dame University in north-central Indiana.

In contrast to the highly emotional outpourings of early pentecostalism, the charismatic renewal movement is quieter. This toning down clearly reflects the middle-class and upper-middle-class nature of the charismatic renewal movement, another feature in which it differs from traditional pentecostalism. Most charismatics say that they receive the Holy Spirit in quiet prayer with a small group of other Christians. Those who have already had such experiences gather around people who are seeking the experience, pray with them, and place their hands on the seekers' heads. There is an incident recorded in the Book of Acts in which Paul is said to have laid his hands on some of the disciples. When he did, "the Holy Spirit came on them, and they spoke in tongues and prophesied" (Acts 19:6, New International Version). The initial experience of tongues is usually followed by continuing to speak in tongues and receiving other spiritual gifts. Because it is ecumenical and experiential, it is theologically diverse as well, with very little commonly held theology. Charismatics (who are also called *neopentecostals* or *new pentecostals*) are bound together by their experience and by their belief in that experience.

The lifestyles of contemporary charismatic Christians differ little from the lifestyles of other people in their culture. The requirements of outward holiness that often mark traditional pentecostalism are absent. Charismatics share with evangelicals the desire to share the faith and joy they have found, and many actively witness to their experiences. For all their differences, though, modern-day charismatics are one with traditional pentecostals in their belief that God works experientially in the lives of believers now.

Both traditional pentecostalism and charismatic renewal offer people who participate in them the assurance that their God is present with them.

Belief is superseded by experiential evidence. Those outside the movement often wonder how those inside it can be sure that what they experience is in fact the work of the Holy Spirit. Nonparticipants often believe that phenomena such as speaking in tongues are the result of self-induced hysteria. There is a middle ground between the uncritical acceptance of the believer and the skepticism of the nonbeliever. When viewed from the empathic perspective of the academic study of religion, the heart of pentecostal religion, old or new, is seen to be both the experience itself and the meaning that it has for those who are a part of it. Whatever the explanation for the experience, it is clear that its meaning to those who are the recipients of it is religious and provides the certainty that they seek.

### QUESTIONS AND ACTIVITIES FOR REVIEW, DISCUSSION, AND WRITING

1. What might be the advantages and disadvantages of the separatist position taken by the fundamentalists described in this chapter?
2. Has anyone ever witnessed to you? How did you feel, and why? If you yourself witness to other people, reflect on what doing so means to you.
3. Write a brief essay in which you describe and then respond to the megachurch phenomenon as a distinctive expression of American culture.
4. What is your response to the views of the religious-political right? Be sure that you can state the reasons for your response.
5. Do you think that the Christian Reconstruction Movement is a good thing or a bad thing for the United States? Why?
6. If you are able to get cable television, or if you can get religious television on a commercial channel, watch two different programs and write an essay in which you reflect on what you observe.
7. If you are not a holiness Christian yourself, how would your life be different if you were? Try to see both positive and negative possibilities. If you are, reflect on what being a holiness Christian means to you.
8. If you are not a pentecostal or charismatic Christian yourself, discuss with friends or classmates who are what that experience means to them. If you are, reflect on what it means to you.
9. If possible, attend a pentecostal or charismatic worship service and write an essay in which you reflect on what you observed and experienced. Women: If you attend a traditional pentecostal service, remember that many of these churches do have a dress code for women. You may want to call first and inquire.
10. Web sites for some denominations relevant to this chapter are listed at the end of the chapter. Visit several of them to locate specific examples of the viewpoints and practices described in the chapter.

### FOR FURTHER READING

COWAN, DOUGLAS E.: *The Remnant Spirit: Conservative Reform in Mainline Protestantism.* Westport, CT: Praeger Publishers, 2003. Cowan describes and analyzes the growth of conservative sentiment within mainline Protestantism, especially in response to denominational involvement with controversial social and moral issues.

HARDING, SUSAN FRIEND: *The Book of Jerry Falwell: Fundamentalist Language and Politics.* Princeton, NJ: Princeton University Press, 2000. Harding's is an excellent anthropological analysis of the culture of fundamentalism as embodied in speeches, direct mail, videos, and television broadcasts. It provides a good portrait, not only of Mr. Falwell but of fundamentalist/evangelical religion and its relationship to politics more generally.

LOVELAND, ANNE C. and OTIS B. WHEELER: *From Meetinghouse to Megachurch: A Material and Cultural History.* Columbia, MO: University of Missouri Press, 2003. This is an excellent historical study that clearly documents how megachurches have arisen out of a complex matrix of historical and sociocultural factors.

McCLYMOND, MICHAEL JAMES: *Embodying the Spirit: New Perspectives on North American Revivalism.* Baltimore: Johns Hopkins University Press, 2004.

SYNAN, VINCENT: *The Holiness-Pentecostal Tradition: Charismatic Movements in the Twentieth Century. Second Edition.* Grand Rapids, MI: William B. Eerdmans Publishing Co., 1999. This is a comprehensive account of the history of these interwoven movements in the past century, updated to take Synan's analysis to the end of the century.

SHERRILL, JOHN L., *They Speak with Other Tongues.* New York: Pyramid Books, 1964. Although this is an older book, it can be highly recommended. Sherrill is a reporter who was assigned to do a story on the charismatic renewal movement and became a part of it as a result. His account is fascinating and provides a unique look at his journey from skeptical outsider to convinced insider.

### *RELEVANT WORLD WIDE WEB SITES*

Promise Keepers: www.promisekeepers.org

American Council of Christian Churches: www.amcouncilcc.org

Trinity Broadcasting Network: www.tbn.org

Christian Broadcasting Network: www.cbn.org

Full Gospel Businessmen's Fellowship International: www.fgbmfi.org

Aglow International: www.aglow.org

United Pentecostal Church International: www.upci.org

Church of the Nazarene: www.nazarene.org

Wesleyan Church: www.wesleyan.org

Assemblies of God: www.ag.org

Church of God in Christ: www.cogic.org

Foursquare Gospel: www.foursquare.org

Christian Churches/Churches of Christ: www.christian-church.org

Christian Coalition: www.cc.org

Eagle Forum: www.eagleforum.org

National Association of Evangelicals: www.nae.net

# Catholic Christians: Similar, Yet Distinctive

---

If you are not a Catholic Christian, ask yourself what your attitudes and feelings about Catholic people are. If you are a Catholic, are you aware of any anti-Catholic prejudice? You might want to discuss these questions with friends who are and are not Catholic.

---

Catholics make up approximately one-fourth of the population of the United States, making this group the largest single community of faith in the nation. It is these people's story, or rather, stories, to which we now turn in our exploration of the Christian majority in the United States. In Chapter 4, we looked at the distinctiveness of Christianity, and then of Protestant Christianity. Now we turn to Catholicism, its similarities to Protestantism and its distinctiveness.

## THE DISTINCTIVENESS OF CATHOLIC CHRISTIANITY

Before examining the distinctiveness of Catholicism, it is important to locate Catholicism within the larger environment of which it is one aspect. American Catholic theologian Richard P. McBrien helps us to do that: "Catholicism is not a reality that stands by itself. The word *Catholic* is not only a noun but an adjective. As an adjective it is a qualification of *Christian*, just as Christian is a qualification of *religious*, and religious is a qualification of *human*."[1] To be a Catholic, then, is to be a religious human being whose faith and life are guided by the Catholic interpretation of Christianity.

Catholicism shares most characteristics with the whole Christian family of faiths. There are, however, characteristics that distinguish Catholicism, "a particular *configuration* of characteristics within Catholicism that is not

---

[1]Richard P. McBrien, *Catholicism*, 3rd ed. (San Francisco: HarperSanFrancisco, 1994), p. 6. Emphasis in the original.

duplicated anywhere else in the community of Christian churches."[2] These characteristics include sacramentality, mediation, and communion.[3] In a finely nuanced explanation, McBrien highlights the distinctiveness of Catholicism while showing how Catholicism and Protestantism *together* describe a balanced approach to Christian faith.

**Sacramentality** points to the understanding that all of reality is sacred, infused throughout with the sacred. God can be seen in all things. As God became human, and very visible, in Jesus, whom Christians call the Christ, so too that which is visible, tangible, finite, and historical reveals the God who is invisible, intangible, infinite, and eternal. The transcendent God is also the indwelling God. There is, for Catholics, no dichotomy between nature and grace because the two interpenetrate each other. McBrien notes the importance of the Protestant warning that sacramentality, with its insistence on the presence of the sacred in the ordinary, must never cross the fine line into idolatry, must never fully identify God with the ways in which God is visible in the world.

**Mediation** further develops the principle of sacramentality. Protestants believe that the sacraments signify or represent sacred realities. Catholics experience the sacraments as actually bringing about what they signify. They make the spirit of God effectively present for the faithful. This is quite similar to how Episcopalians understand sacraments. Here, too, Protestantism sounds a warning note for Catholics. The principle of mediation can lead to a magical view in which, for example, people believe that a certain number of repetitions of a prayer will guarantee a certain result.

**Communion** highlights the importance of the community of faith in the Catholic tradition. Even in its most individualistic aspects, people's relationship with God is mediated through a community of faithful persons. The fellowship of the church, clergy, and sacraments of the Church are the mediator, the primary means by which people experience God. This, according to McBrien, is the heart of Catholic distinctiveness, because in the Church, the three principles of sacramentality, mediation, and communion converge. Here too, Protestantism insists on caution. Sacramentality can become idolatry, mediation can lead into magic, and communion can stifle individuality and impose an authoritarian view that impinges on the freedom of the individual's relationship with Jesus and God.

Catholicism is distinctive among American denominational forms of Christianity, as well, in that it considers itself the only complete instance of the Church as the Body of Christ on Earth. In particular, the Catholic understanding of the Eucharist and tracing the papacy back to Peter (see Other Important Catholic Beliefs) demarcate its self-understanding as the true Church. As much as the Second Vatican Council opened the Church to ecumenical[4] understandings and endeavors, it did not change this basic teaching.

---

[2]Richard P. McBrien, *Catholicism*, p. 9.
[3]Richard P. McBrien, *Catholicism*, pp. 11–14.
[4]*Ecumenical* refers to dialogue and cooperation among various Christian churches and organizations.

## The Second Vatican Council, 1962–1965

Prior to Vatican II, the boundaries that marked Catholicism off from other Christian communities of faith were drawn quite clearly, or at least so it seemed. Those boundaries became much less distinctive after the Council. There is continuity between the pre-Vatican II church and the post-Vatican II church, but they are also quite different, and the differences make the post-conciliar church less distinctive.

The council "solved some of the lingering problems of being a Catholic in the United States." Catholics no longer felt as "different," nor did their non-Catholic neighbors regard them as such:

> Most important, the Council reversed earlier Catholic teaching by affirming the separation of church and state and religious liberty for all. In one stroke a major sore point for American Catholics was removed. Also, the Council redefined the Church as the "People of God" and advocated increased democratization of church structures, a more participative liturgy [worship], use of the vernacular in worship, reduction of rules of abstinence [here, from meat], ecumenical goodwill with other Christians, an open door to biblical scholarship, and greater self-determination for men's and women's orders. . . . The siege mentality of the early twentieth century was gone. Ever since, the dominant mood of Catholics has been to embrace American society with little reservation . . . and to feel like full participants in American life.[5]

## Other Important Catholic Beliefs

Catholics share with Protestants the belief that **salvation comes to people by the grace of God. However, a great deal more emphasis is placed on the role of the Church as the official agent and mediator of God's grace**. The Church mediates by its official teaching and interpretation of the Bible, and it mediates through its administration of the sacraments. The sacraments as administered by the Church are believed to be channels through which the grace of God flows to people.

Catholics, although they regard the Bible as the original revelation, also teach that the tradition of the Church is equal with the Bible in authority. They believe that the Church is the official interpreter of the Bible. Tradition and Scripture together are accorded the same respect and veneration. The writings of the Church Fathers, the decisions of Church councils, and the pronouncements of the Popes from Peter onward are all regarded as genuine sources of religious truth and as a part of the whole revelation of God to the Church. The Second Vatican Council placed greater emphasis on the Bible. For example, it said that the Liturgy of the Word, in which the Bible is read,

---

[5]William V., James D. Davidson, Dean R. Hoge, and Ruth A. Wallace, D'Antonio et al., *Laity American and Catholic: Transforming the Church (Kansas City: Sheed and Ward, 1966)*, pp. 9–10.

is not just preparation for the Liturgy of the Eucharist in the Mass, but is an integral part of a single act of worship. It also urged people to seek renewed spiritual vitality through increasing attention to the word of God in the Bible, as well as through continued participation in the Eucharist. The sharing of authority between the Bible and the Church and the Church's role as the official interpreter of the Bible are distinctive Catholic beliefs.

The doctrine of papal infallibility is unique to the Catholic Church. Many non-Catholic people misunderstand this teaching of the Church. It does not mean that the Pope never makes a mistake or never sins. In reality, this doctrine applies in only a very few circumstances. When the Pope speaks officially on matters of faith and morals that are absolutely central to the life of the Church, it is believed that God prevents him from making errors. The current *Catechism of the Catholic Church* describes infallibility in a way that relates it to the whole church and its founding:

> In order to preserve the Church in the purity of the faith handed on by the apostles, Christ who is the Truth willed to confer on her a share in his own infallibility. . . . The Roman Pontiff, head of the college of bishops, enjoys this infallibility in virtue of his office, when, as supreme pastor and teacher of all the faithful—who confirms his brethren in the faith—he proclaims by a definitive act a doctrine pertaining to faith or morals. . . . The infallibility promised to the Church is also present in the body of bishops when, together with Peter's successor [the Pope], they exercise the supreme Magisterium [authority].[6]

Catholics also believe that authority in the Church has come down in a direct line from Peter, and hence from Christ himself. This view is called apostolic succession. This doctrine, operative through the sacrament of Holy Orders by which men are ordained to the priesthood, is the temporal foundation of the Church. The principal biblical support for apostolic succession comes from a passage in the Gospel of Saint Matthew. In these verses, Jesus is speaking to one of the apostles: "You are Peter, and on this rock I will build my church, and the powers of death shall not prevail against it. I will give you the keys of the kingdom of Heaven; and whatever you bind on earth shall be bound in heaven, and whatever you loose on earth shall be loosed in heaven" (Matthew 16:17–19). "The Lord made Saint Peter the visible foundation of his Church. He entrusted the keys of the Church to him. The bishop of the Church of Rome [the Pope], successor to Saint Peter, is head of the college of bishops, the Vicar of Christ and Pastor of the universal Church on Earth."[7]

There are other mediators as well. Any discussion of Catholic belief and practice would be incomplete if the Catholic **devotion to Mary**, the mother of Jesus, **and to the other saints** were not mentioned. Unlike Jesus, who, the

---

[6]*Catechism of the Catholic Church,* ¶¶889 and 891. This document itself is an excellent example of the official nature of the Magisterium of the Church, in that it is the English version of the official teaching of the Church.

[7]*Catechism of the Catholic Church,* ¶936.

Church teaches, was both divine and human, the saints and Mary were fully human and no more while alive on Earth. A good deal of Catholic private devotion centers on these figures, who are in a sense "closer" to the believer because of having shared their human condition without benefit of simultaneous divinity. Catholics teach that Mary and the other saints pray to God on the believers' behalf and watch over the needs and concerns of the faithful. As the author of a study of Catholic women states,

> For Catholics . . . Mary the mother of Jesus has been the feminine face of God. To be sure, Mary is not God, according to orthodox Christian theology. . . . Nevertheless, people pray to Mary. She may not be God in their spoken creed, but in the language of the heart, she functions as God.[8]

The unique Catholic doctrine of **purgatory** illustrates the mediating role of the church, as well. Catholics believe with other Christians that the faithful will have life after physical death. Purgatory is believed to be **a place or condition of further purification after death in which some must exist before they attain the beatific vision of God**. Upon death, individuals without any taint of sin may enter heaven directly. However, few people are this pure. In purgatory, people make amends for less serious sins that were not forgiven or for more serious sins that had been forgiven prior to death. Freed from guilt and punishment, the soul can enter into heaven, not only beholding God directly but being of the same mind and heart with God. The justice of God that requires that sin be punished and the mercy of God that seeks the salvation of all are thus reconciled. The doctrine of purgatory also provides a means by which the living may assist the souls of the dead through prayers and good works, because it is taught that such prayers and works may shorten the length of time a soul spends in purgatory. In this way, the belief in purgatory can help those who grieve for a loved one to work out their grief. It is important to note here that Catholics believe that God is an infinitely loving parent who will not reject anyone who does not reject God. God creates people with free will and the freedom to sin or to obey, and God goes to great lengths to see to it that disobedience does not result in condemnation unless there are no other alternatives.

## CATHOLIC WORSHIP: WORD AND SACRAMENT

The central act of Catholic worship is called the **Mass**. The Mass is an integrated experience of worship that is made up of two parts that work together. The **Liturgy of the Word** includes those parts of the Mass that focus on verbal communication, such as Bible readings, prayers, responsive readings, and a

---

[8]Jane Redmont, *Generous Lives: American Catholic Women Today* (Liguori, MO: Triumph Books, 1992), p. 102.

sermon, often called a *homily* by Catholics. The Bible readings always include a reading from one of the four Gospels and another reading from either the New Testament or the Old Testament. The **Liturgy of the Eucharist** reenacts, in words and actions, Jesus' sharing bread and wine with the disciples at the Last Supper. Catholic worship is highly liturgical, with ornate symbolism; the use of incense and chanting, symbolic colors, and vestments worn by the priest; and an air of high solemnity. Since the Second Vatican Council, many Catholic Churches have experimented with more casual masses that often include folk songs and liturgical dance, but the twin elements of the Liturgy of the Word and the Liturgy of the Eucharist are always present.

Catholics believe that in the **sacrament of the Eucharist**, the bread and wine actually become the body and blood of Jesus Christ when the priest speaks the words of consecration ("This is my body. . . . This is my blood"— words that the Gospel records Jesus as saying to his disciples at the Last Supper). This belief in **transubstantiation** is based on a philosophical distinction between what something actually is (its substance) and what it appears to be. In transubstantiation, the substance of the bread and wine become the body and blood of Christ, who is fully present under the appearances of bread and wine. This sacrament, received often throughout a Catholic's life, is ordinarily received at Mass, but it may also be received privately when circumstances such as illness call for doing so.

> The Eucharist is the heart and summit of the Church's life, for in it Christ associates his Church and all her members with his sacrifice of praise and thanksgiving offered once for all on the cross to his Father; by this sacrifice he pours out the graces of salvation on his Body which is the Church.

> As sacrifice, the Eucharist is also offered in reparation for the sins of the living and the dead and to obtain spiritual or temporal benefits from God.[9]

## Other Sacraments

The first sacrament in which Catholics participate is **baptism**. "Baptism is birth into the new life in Christ. In accordance with the Lord's will, it is necessary for salvation, as is the Church herself, which we enter by baptism."[10] Catholics believe that baptism is necessary for the removal of the inborn sin that is a part of all persons simply because they are human. Most Catholics are baptized when they are babies. When the sacrament is performed for an adult, it is often called the *Rite of Christian Initiation*, a name that points to its other function as the ritual of incorporation into the Church.

The sacrament of **confirmation** completes what is begun in baptism. It signifies that the person has become an adult in the eyes of the Church and

---

[9]*Catechism of the Catholic Church*, ¶¶1407 and 1414.
[10]*Catechism of the Catholic Church*, ¶1277.

confirms the promises made by others at baptism. The one who is being confirmed is anointed on the forehead with oil that has been blessed to signify the seal of the Holy Spirit. This sacrament is believed to give the grace necessary to live a mature Christian life in the Church:

> Confirmation perfects Baptismal grace; it is the sacrament which gives the Holy Spirit in order to root us more deeply in the divine filiation, incorporate us more firmly into Christ, strengthen our bond with the Church, associate us more closely with her mission, and help us bear witness to the Christian faith in words accompanied by deeds.[11]

The sacrament of **reconciliation,** or **confession**, nourishes and supports Catholics throughout their lives. Penitents confess their sins to God through the priest, who, in the name of God and with the authority of the Church, pronounces forgiveness. Special prayers or other activities (sometimes called *penance*) may be assigned to assist people in recovering from the effects of their sins. Catholics are expected to confess through a priest at least annually, but many find that the practice helps them be aware of God's forgiving grace and confess more frequently. Non-Catholics often stereotype Catholics by saying that Catholics can confess to a priest and then go out and sin all over again. Catholic Christians, however, believe that the rite of reconciliation must be accompanied by genuine sorrow for having sinned and by a clear intention to avoid it in the future.

The Second Vatican Council revised the Church's understanding of this sacrament somewhat, lessening the emphasis given to the penance performed and emphasizing the rite as one of reconciliation, which is the spiritual reuniting of the penitent with God, other persons, and the Church.

A fifth sacrament is now commonly known as the sacrament of **anointing the sick**; formerly, it was called extreme unction or, simply, the last rites. This sacrament, in which a priest uses oil to anoint a person who is ill or in danger of dying from accident or old age, is a way of mediating the concern of Christ and the Church for the suffering person. Catholics believe that the sacrament gives grace for healing, if that is God's will, or to assist a person in the passage from life to death and beyond if that is to be the final outcome. The understanding of this rite was broadened by Vatican II to include its use for those who are seriously ill but not in immediate danger of death.

The sacrament of **marriage** is one to which most Catholics look forward. The majority of Catholics, like the majority of all Americans, marry at some time in their lives. Although the stereotype of Catholics having larger-than-average families no longer holds true, marriage and family continue to be very important, because marriage is a sacrament. Blessed by a priest, authorized by the Church, and entered into only after a period of required counseling, Catholics believe that the sacrament of marriage gives the couple the special

---

[11]*Catechism of the Catholic Church,* ¶1316.

grace necessary to carry out the promises they make to each other. Because marriage is a sacrament in which two people are believed to be joined by God, the Catholic Church teaches that it is a lifelong commitment:

> The sacrament of Matrimony signifies the union of Christ and the Church. It gives spouses the grace to love each other with the love with which Christ has loved his Church; the grace of the sacrament thus perfects the human love of the spouses, strengthens their indissoluble unity, and sanctifies them on the way to eternal life.[12]

The Church does not recognize divorce and teaches that persons who divorce and remarry are held to be living in sin and are barred from receiving the sacraments. There is a process through which a couple can obtain an *annulment* of their marriage. If an annulment is granted, it is as if the marriage had never happened. People whose marriages have been annulled can remarry in the Church. Because the marriage bond is sacred, however, such annulments are difficult to obtain. Statistical data indicate that, in actual practice, American Catholics divorce and remarry in about the same proportions as do non-Catholics. In this matter, American Catholics are influenced more by the culture of which they are a part than they are by the teachings of their Church.

The sacrament of orders, or **ordination to the priesthood**, sets a man apart for the official sacramental ministry of the Church. Catholics believe that it gives the priest the grace required to carry out the demands of his priesthood. Only men are ordained to the Catholic priesthood.

> Holy Orders is the sacrament through which the mission entrusted by Christ to his apostles continues to be exercised in the Church until the end of time; thus it is the sacrament of apostolic ministry.

> Through the ordained ministry, especially that of bishops and priests, the presence of Christ as head of the Church is made visible in the midst of the community of believers.[13]

## NOTES ON CATHOLIC LIFESTYLES

In the main, the moral views of Catholic people in the United States differ little from those of their non-Catholic counterparts. This is true even in those areas in which the Church speaks the most forcefully: artificial conception control, abortion, premarital sexual activity, and homosexuality. For example, recent survey data show Catholic teens are more likely, and in some cases far more likely, than their Protestant counterparts to approve of marriage between homosexual persons, as well as to approve of premarital sex and premarital

---

[12]*Catechism of the Catholic Church,* ¶1661.
[13]*Catechism of the Catholic Church,* ¶¶1536 and 1549.

cohabitation. These views closely reflect those of Catholic adults. Neither group, however, condones extra-marital affairs.[14]

The context in which these issues are set for Catholics is distinctive, however. The Church's opposition to abortion is a useful case in point. In Protestant fundamentalism, opposition to abortion is usually linked with support for capital punishment, welfare conservatism, support for nuclear arms and for defense spending. In the Catholic Church's *consistent life ethic*, opposition to abortion is linked with support for both private and government-funded services for pregnant women and for the children of single mothers and with opposition to capital punishment, nuclear weapons, and excessive funding for the military. Except for questions of personal sexual morality, the positions that United States bishops take are usually to the liberal end of the continuum of American views, particularly on economic and defense issues.

Another example is the noteworthy range of things covered under the discussion of the fifth commandment ("you shall not kill") in the contemporary *Catechism*: The core point is that no one can claim the right to end a life because God alone is Lord of life from beginning to end. Killing when necessary in self-defense or in defense of another is upheld. The death penalty is held not to violate the commandment "in cases of extreme gravity" to protect society, but "if bloodless means are sufficient" then "public authority should limit itself to such means." Refusing assistance to people in danger violates the commandment. Societal acceptance of widespread famine is given as an example. Direct abortion is of course included among violations, as is direct euthanasia. Discontinuing heroic medical measures and the use of painkillers to alleviate suffering even when such use may shorten life is, however, acceptable. Suicide also goes against the commandment. Society is charged with the responsibility to help all of its citizens to attain "living conditions that allow them to grow and reach maturity: food and clothing, housing, health care, basic education, and social assistance." Temperance and the avoidance of excess is mentioned, and it is noted that people "who, by drunkenness or a love of speed, endanger their own and others' safety on the road, at sea, or in the air" are said to "incur grave guilt." Kidnapping, hostage taking, and other terrorist acts are forbidden by the commandment, as are any but therapeutic amputations, mutilations, and sterilizations performed on innocent people. Autopsy and organ donation are acceptable. Safeguarding peace and avoiding war is encouraged. In conjunction with this, acts of war that destroy entire cities or vast areas and the people in them are condemned, and the specific danger of weapons of mass destruction is addressed.[15]

A key feature of life for a minority of Catholic youngsters is that they attend parochial schools sponsored by their church. Parochial schools provide education within the context of Catholic values. Education about their faith and regular participation in Mass are included in their school experience. So is

---

[14]The Gallup Organization, "Gallup Tuesday Briefing," April 9, 2002, p. 5.
[15]*Catechism of the Catholic Church*, ¶¶2258 through 2317.

learning about religions other than Catholicism. They may be taught by nuns or brothers or by lay teachers. A flourishing parochial school is a focal point of the parish and a center for its social life as well as an educational institution.

Fewer Catholic youngsters attend parochial schools now than in the past, a part of the loss of distinctiveness of Catholic life in the United States. Slightly over one-fourth of Catholic elementary- and middle-school children and under one-fifth of Catholic high-school students attend parochial schools. Among Catholic college students, only 10 percent attend colleges sponsored by the Church.[16]

Catholic education is not limited to parochial schools. About 600,000 students are enrolled in 236 Catholic institutions of higher education. These include one of the historically black universities and 49 women's colleges, which account for half of the women's colleges in the country.[17] Although the question of what exactly is *Catholic* about education in these institutions is difficult to answer, their place in the overall picture of American higher education remains very important.

In addition, the Catholic Church maintains an active ministry to Catholic students on both Catholic and non-Catholic campuses. In the late 1800s, a society where Catholic students could meet regularly for fellowship and support was organized. Cardinal Newman was a well-known name in Catholic circles, and was associated with university education, having been involved in the founding of the Catholic University of Ireland in Dublin, and his name was picked for the organization. By 1920, there were "Newman Clubs" on many campuses. Following the Second Vatican Council, the name was changed to the *Catholic Student Ministry*; many local groups still retain a reference to Cardinal Newman in their name.[18]

## THE CHURCH AS A SOCIAL INSTITUTION

Protestant Christians strongly emphasize the individual's personal relationship with Jesus, unmediated by the organization of the church or by its priesthood and its sacraments. Catholics, on the other hand, emphasize equally strongly the communal nature of the encounter between God and humankind. There can be no relationship with God, with Christ, that exists entirely without the church.[19]

---

[16]Dean R. Hoge, "Catholics in the U.S.: The Next Generation," in *The Public Perspective: A Roper Center Review of Public Opinion and Polling*, vol. 2, no.1 (November/December 1990), p. 11.

[17]David J. O'Brien, *From the Heart of the American Church: Catholic Higher Education and American Culture* (Maryknoll, NY: Orbis Books, 1994), p. 70.

[18]Thanks to Rev. James R. Bates, former Director of Ball State University's Newman Center, for information on the Catholic Student Ministry.

[19]McBrien, *Catholicism*, p. 13.

**Figure 6-1**    The Pope is the leader of worldwide Catholicism. Pope John Paul II led the Church from 1978 through early 2005. *(Orbis-Bettman.)*

The Catholic Church is hierarchical in its organization. The **Pope** is the worldwide leader and is revered by Catholics as the **Vicar**[20] **of Christ on Earth** (Figure 6–1). He is also **Bishop of Rome**. The Pope is assisted by the College of Cardinals and by the Roman Curia. The College of Cardinals advises the Pope and is responsible for electing a new Pope upon the death of the previous one. The Curia has a more administrative function. Archbishops and bishops are appointed by the Pope, taking into account the recommendations of local leaders. Archbishops are in charge of large geographical or population units and bishops have authority over smaller areas. Local priests have jurisdiction to the extent that it is delegated to them by their bishops. In the Catholic Church in America, local councils of priests and bishops meet in an advisory capacity, and lay parish councils in the local church advise the priest and serve as a link between the ordained leadership and the lay people who make up the broad base of the organizational pyramid.

The Catholic Church has many male monastic orders and many orders of nuns for women. Nuns and monks serve as full-time religious workers in parochial schools, in Church-sponsored hospitals and other agencies, as teachers in Catholic colleges and universities, and in a variety of other tasks. Much of the outreach work of the Church is done by these dedicated men and women who, while not priests, have a ministry that is of equal importance in

---

[20] *Vicar* means "official representative."

the life of the Church. The requirement that priests remain unmarried is an important part of Catholic practice. Although this practice has not always been a part of the Church's teaching, and its historical development is somewhat confusing, its present-day practice seems to have two main functions: The priest is understood to be in the likeness of Christ, and, as far as we can know from the biblical accounts, Jesus never married. Not having the responsibility for a family also frees the priest to devote his full attention to his priesthood.

There are many laymen and laywomen who work professionally in Catholic churches, as well. They often have seminary training, as do the ordained. They serve as chaplains in hospitals, schools, and prisons; as parish outreach workers; as counselors; as teachers of theology in colleges and seminaries; and as leaders of retreat centers and other organizations.

For American Catholics, as for Catholics elsewhere, their local parish is the heart of their experience of their church.

> The parish is the central structure through which Catholics experience, nurture, and act out their faith. It is a community of particular people living in a particular society as part of an international church. . . . It is a vehicle for both experiencing the faith and for motivating Catholics to relate to the broader community and to shape it according to Gospel values.[21]

## WHO ARE AMERICAN CATHOLICS?

There is very wide diversity within Catholicism in the United States, as there is within most Christian denominations and other religions as well. One source of this diversity is the presence of three distinctively different Catholic generations of Catholic laity and clergy, each of which had a distinctive religious upbringing:

- Pre-Vatican II Catholics who matured before the council tend to prefer the older model of the Church with which they are familiar, hierarchical and traditional in its ways of doing things and having a great deal of authority in the lives of believers. Being Catholic and being Christian are the same thing, and God's law and the Church's law are one. They tend to take their Church's teachings "whole," without distinguishing among them.
- Vatican II Catholics, those who came of age during the council, have one foot in each Church, so to speak, and their views tend to lie between those of the younger and the older generations.
- Post-Vatican II Catholics have experienced only the postconciliar Church, prefer the more democratic and less institutional Church of their formative years, and are much more individualistic in their interpretation of what it means to be

---

[21]Jim Castillo and Joseph Gremillion, The Emerging Parish: *The Notre Dame Study of Catholic Life Since Vatican II* (San Francisco: Harper and Row, 1987), pp. 194–195.

Catholic. They distinguish between being Catholic and being Christian, and between God's law and the laws of the Church.[22]

Another source of diversity, somewhat related to the first, is the variety of styles of being Catholic practiced by individual Catholics. A recent study identifies five categories.[23]

1. "By the Rules Catholics" fit the profile of what would traditionally have been described as a "good Catholic." They attend Mass at least weekly, obey the church's teachings in matters of faith and morals, and in general look to their church as their primary guide through life.
2. "Bend and Break the Rules Catholics" identify with the Church and participate in its worship and programs regularly, but disagree with the Church on certain points. They might, for example, practice artificial birth control or believe that premarital sex is acceptable under certain circumstances.
3. "Ignore the Rules Catholics" go to Mass irregularly and pick and choose which teachings and practices they will follow. In making these decisions, their own point of view and conscience clearly take precedence over official Church teaching and practice. They are within the Church yet operate to a large extent independently of it.
4. "Rules Don't Pertain to Me Catholics" claim Catholicism as their faith but have little contact with the Church except at times of crisis and major Christian festivals such as Christmas and Easter.
5. "Don't Know the Rules Catholics" were baptized into the Catholic Church but this is their only connection with it. They do not participate and do not look to the Church for guidance and support. They may still, however, wish to marry in the Church, have their children baptized, and be buried with its blessing.

## CATHOLIC AND *AMERICAN*, AMERICAN AND *CATHOLIC*

The relationship between official Catholicism—its doctrines, *Catechism*, dogmas, conciliar documents, papal encyclicals and bishops' pastoral letters, and official ritual life—and Catholicism as it is interpreted and lived out by the diverse American Catholic population is a complex one. Jay P. Dolan, an emeritus professor of history at Notre Dame University, a prominent Catholic university, writes, "I believe American and Catholic represent two souls, two strivings. . . . These two fundamental strivings, to be both Catholic and American, have animated me throughout my life, and they are not unreconcilable."[24]

---

[22]D'Antonio et al., *Laity American and Catholic*, Chapters 4 and 5.
[23]Chester Gillis, *Roman Catholicism in America* (New York: Columbia University Press, 1999), Chapter 1. Although Gillis's study concerns Catholics, these types can be found throughout the religious world.
[24]Jay P. Dolan, *In Search of an American Catholicism: A History of Religion and Culture in Tension* (New York: Oxford University Press, 2002), pp. 3–4.

Although the major Protestant denominations were also imported into the United States, they had been shaped from birth by the democratizing tendencies of the Protestant Reformation itself, which was in part a struggle to make religion of the people and for the people, to shift its focus away from the institutional church. Catholicism did not have that prior democratizing influence. In coming to the United States, the Catholic Church came to a country whose ways of doing things challenged it and invited, sometimes necessitated, adaptation. That process continues to this day.

Dolan identifies five themes or issues in the challenge of being both Catholic and American.

**1.**   The first is the democratization of local parish life. How much say should lay people have in how their local churches are run? How much authority should the hierarchy exercise over local church affairs? Increasing involvement of lay people has meant correspondingly less control in the hands of their priests. American Catholics have faced a dilemma brought about by the interface of America's long heritage of democracy with the structure of their church, which has not been at all democratic.[25]

**2.**   Immigrant American Catholics, coming as they did from various parts of Europe, brought with them styles of devotional Catholicism that were part of their home cultures. The liturgy, although standardized in structure, was nevertheless strongly influenced by the piety of national origins, as were the styles of private devotion. As time went on, immigrant Catholics, and especially their descendants, became less identified with their countries of origin and more American. Change and adaptation occurred as they sought to develop a style of worship and devotion that was more suited to their new environment. Two very visible results were a decline in the observance of pietistic devotions such as praying the rosary, and the presence of fewer religious artifacts such as statues and crucifixes, in Catholic homes.

**3.**   The question of national identity itself became a source of debate. The Catholic Church encompassed a great deal of diversity in national and ethnic parishes in which people could continue not only their familiar style of Catholicism but their larger cultural identity as well. As American nativism burgeoned in the final decades of the nineteenth century, Catholics came under attack. Prejudice flared against the persistent national identities of immigrant Catholics. In addition, Protestant America interpreted Catholics' loyalty to Rome as a threat. Could the Catholic Church become a truly American church?[26]

The tension between religion and nationality continues, stimulated by the arrival of Catholic immigrants from places such as Mexico and the Caribbean.

---

[25]Dolan, *In Search of an American Catholicism*, p. 84. This discussion draws on Chapter 3 of Dolan's excellent study.

[26]Dolan, *In Search of an American Catholicism*, pp. 92–93.

**4.**   A fourth debate was over the development of a distinctive American Catholic doctrine. How distinctive should the American church be? How different from the "faith of the fathers" in Rome? And if it were to develop distinctively, then what of its relation to the worldwide Church? The forces that tended toward "Americanization" and the proponents of American Catholic distinctiveness called for change in a church in which unity and tradition were paramount.

**5.**   Finally, changes in the roles of women in the United States challenged Catholics' thinking about the roles of women in society and in the Church itself. The traditional idea of women primarily as mothers was embraced by most Americans, Catholic or not. Tensions developed as women sought to redefine women's roles and place in society. These tensions affected Catholic women acutely. Catholic women felt and continue to feel that they receive mixed messages about women's proper roles from their church.[27]

The situation in which the American church found itself—pluralism, disestablishment, and freedom of religion in a democratic state—differed greatly from that which has prevailed throughout most of its worldwide history. This led directly to the questions of adaptation or inculturation described earlier. Inculturation, according to one Catholic author, is "the process of deep, sympathetic adaptation and appropriation of a local cultural setting in which the Church finds itself in a way that does not compromise its basic faith in Christ."[28] Inculturation, then, is something the Catholic Church has done worldwide. In the United States, it has taken place almost from the beginning of the Church's presence here. However, the pace of change in the United States, especially since the 1960s, and the wide divergence between American and traditional ideas and ideals, has made these issues particularly intense here.

These issues have also led to liberal and conservative disagreement within the Church. While most American Catholics find themselves somewhere in the middle between these two extremes, there are vocal proponents of both extremes. The heart of the divide seems to be the question of authority: To what extent must Catholics accept their church's authority over their lives and to what extent may they rely on their individual conscience in making religious and moral decisions? Additional issues include the democratization of the church and appropriate roles for laypeople, differences related to ordination, and disagreements on specific moral issues.

Typically, for example, **Catholic conservatives**

- believe Catholics are duty-bound to follow the directives of the Church on all matters of faith and morals and believe that obedience to the Church is obedience to God;

---

[27]Dolan, *In Search of an American Catholicism*, p. 124.
[28]William Reiser, "Inculturation and Doctrinal Development," *Heythrop Journal*, No. 22 (1981), p. 135.

- support papal infallibility
- believe that the values of the secular world are unalterably opposed to those of the Church
- believe the government of the Church must remain in the hands of the hierarchy
- accept the decisions of the Second Vatican Council, but cautiously, and believe their implementation by the Church in the United States has been too extreme
- are concerned that changes in the liturgy of the Mass imperil its holiness are erode the sense of mystery and divinity it should have
- support the Church's ban on artificial birth control, homosexual activity, pre-marital sex, abortion, the ordination of women, and the marriage of priests.

On the other hand, **liberal or progressive Catholics** more often

- believe Catholics may follow their individual conscience on matters of faith and morals and distinguish between obedience to the Church and obedience to God
- have reservations about the doctrine of papal infallibility
- believe that the values of the secular world are not inherently dangerous and that some may be incorporated into the life of the Church, using appropriate caution
- support the democratization of church government at all levels
- affirm the decisions of the Second Vatican Council and encourage their full implementation
- believe that changes in the liturgy of the mass make it more alive and accessible to lay people
- challenge the Church's ban on artificial birth control, homosexual activity, pre-marital sex, abortion, the ordination of women, and the marriage of priests.

## WOMEN IN THE CATHOLIC CHURCH

The Catholic Church's attitude toward women has always been complex. Mary, as the mother of Jesus, has been given great respect and honor and is looked upon as the first among women. Her status comes from her mother-hood. She fulfilled in a very special way the role traditionally held up as the most important one for women. Traditional Catholic teaching also empha-sizes Eve, the temptress, as the key figure in the drama of original sin and the human fall from grace, partially offsetting the effect of the veneration of Mary.

Catholic orders of nuns are another example of this complexity. These orders were the first institutional opportunity for the involvement of women in religion in America. They provided a setting in which women could carry out specific duties within the context of a close-knit community of women. Especially for those who did not have the desire or the opportunity to marry, these orders were a means to security and respectability. Negatively, the female orders were closely governed by male superiors in the Church and had little, if any, autonomy in their early years.

In the nineteenth century, many nuns taught in public and private schools, as well as in parochial schools. Others worked as nurses in hospitals and other institutions and in private homes. They served heroically as nurses during the Civil and Spanish-American Wars. They played a major role in overcoming American suspicion and hostility toward Catholicism and Catholic people because of their dedicated work in these areas.[29]

During the nineteenth century, nuns in America sought ways to adapt to democracy. They often broke with their European motherhouses (the American nuns were branches of European orders and responsible to them) in order to adopt regulations that were better suited to their new environment.[30] They also founded American orders. **Mother Elizabeth Bayley Seton** was the first American to be officially declared a saint by the Catholic Church. Seton established the **Sisters of Charity**, the first religious order founded in the United States, in 1809. She is also remembered as the founder of the American Catholic parochial school system.

In the twentieth century, nuns have demonstrated continued commitment and service in the areas of nursing, education, and social work. They have also broadened their participation in the cause of international peace and in addressing the plight of the Third World nations. They are in the forefront of a more general Catholic concern for personal spiritual formation, developing and practicing new ways of personal and community devotion that are compatible with life in the modern era.

The Second Vatican Council brought about new opportunities for nuns. It permitted greater self-government in religious orders. It allowed nuns to increase their contact with the world outside their convents. They no longer had to live in communities with groups of nuns but could live much more on their own in the society. They could find employment in agencies that were not related to the Church. Nuns began attending graduate schools in significant numbers and went on to teach in colleges, universities, and seminaries. In many orders, being a nun no longer meant wearing the distinctive clothing that set them apart from other women in the population.

A cluster of reproductive issues has been at the forefront of much of the discussion about the Catholic Church's attitude toward women. The U.S. Catholic Conference (USCC), the official Washington lobby of U.S. Catholic bishops, has consistently worked to have **abortion** and abortion funding banned. It has voted to work to eliminate clinics that make contraceptive information available in public high schools. The Church continues to restate its well-known teaching that the use of **artificial birth control** is sinful. The Church teaches that the natural result of sexual intercourse is the procreation of children and that any method of contraception that interferes with this end is against the laws of God and the Church. The Church also teaches that the

---

[29]Mary Ewens, "The Leadership of Nuns in Immigrant Catholicism," in *Women and Religion in America, Volume I: The Nineteenth Century*, ed. Rosemary Radford Ruether and Rosemary Skinner Keller (San Francisco: Harper & Row, Publishers, 1981), pp. 101–102.
[30]Ewens, "The Leadership of Nuns," p. 105.

fetus has a soul and is a human being from the moment of conception. Therefore, abortion is murder. Feminists see the Church's position on all these issues as a violation of women's rights to control over their own bodies.

Many women view traditional Catholic teaching about marriage and divorce as yet another unwarranted intrusion of the Church into areas that are best left up to individual morality. The Church's teachings limit women's (and men's) options to lifelong marriage or celibacy. The presence and at least partial acceptance of other options in the larger culture has caused many Catholics to question and sometimes openly challenge their Church's official teachings.

Ordination to the priesthood is a particularly troublesome issue. As it is now, only men can be ordained priests. The Church's teaching on the ordination of women to the priesthood, repeatedly restated throughout Pope John Paul II's papacy (1978–2005), is unequivocal: Jesus chose men to be his apostles, and they did likewise when they chose their successors. The sacrament of ordination links the priests with the twelve apostles, making the apostles, in effect, present today. "For this reason, the ordination of women is not possible." [31]

Many women are particularly distressed that full priesthood is denied to them. The Second Vatican Council allowed women to serve in many important lay ministries such as assisting with the Eucharist and reading the Bible during Mass. As a result, many, if not most, Catholic churches in the United States permit this. Girls as well as boys can now be altar servers. In most instances, any lay position available to men is now also available to women. Progress? Yes, say the women who want full ordination as priests in the Church—but not enough. For many, the only way for their church to make good on its pronouncements about the equality and full personhood of all people is to grant women full ordination to the priesthood and accept women as equals for ordination to the higher ranks of bishop, archbishop, and cardinal. According to these women, the necessary changes will not have been made until it is possible for a woman to be elected Pope.

Many Catholic women also think that the ordination of women would help to solve the severe shortage of priests that the Church faces. Fewer and fewer men have entered the priesthood in recent years, leading to shortages that are nearing crisis proportions. These women claim that the Church can ill afford not to use the additional resource that their ordination would make available. Often, people who urge the ordination of women also urge that priests be allowed to marry, another move that many feel would help to increase the number of candidates for ordination.

One current manifestation of women's desire for ordination concerns ordination to the diaconate. Deacons (male) are ordained to service ministries as well as it being a transitional ordination on the way to priesthood. Many Catholics in the United States feel that, because women serve in recognizably diaconal ministries already (in hospitals, prisons, and religious education, for

---

[31] *Catechism of the Catholic Church,* ¶1577.

example), they should be able to be ordained as permanent deacons (deacons for whom diaconal ordination is not a stepping stone to ordination to the priesthood). It is unclear at this point what the final outcome of this discussion will be.

For some Catholic women, the quest for ordination has transformed into a quest for an entirely new approach to worship and liturgy, one that does away with the need for priests altogether. The *Woman-Church* movement understands all Christians to be engaged in equal ministry to each other, with no hierarchy. While it is difficult to say exactly how many women are involved, such communities are being formed nationwide, and national Woman-Church conferences draw thousands of attendees.[32]

All this having been said, two things bear noting. While some Catholic women are dissatisfied with how their Church deals with their specific concerns as women, most are not talking about leaving the Church. Second, the conservative/traditionalist movement, discussed earlier, includes women among its strong supporters. Specifically, Women for Faith and Family organized in 1984 as a voice for such women. One point in their "Affirmation for Catholic Women" document reads, "We affirm and accept the teaching of the Catholic Church on all matters dealing with human reproduction, marriage, family life, and roles for men and women in the Church and in society."[33]

The Church's position on these issues is not likely to change in the foreseeable future. Someone once remarked that people would know that the Catholic Church had made progress when bishops were permitted to bring their wives to Church conferences. They would know that even more progress had occurred when bishops brought their husbands to these conferences.

All in all, it would seem that the Pope's stated goals of "discipline, order, commitment, and obedience" for the Catholic Church will not meet with easy acceptance in the United States. On the other hand, it must be noted that American Catholics, as they have always been, are loyal to the Church. They are a people of two clear loyalties, to their nation and to their church. Neither has wavered over the course of Catholic presence in America.

We have seen that American Catholics share a great deal with Catholics around the world, as members of the one Catholic Church. They are also unique, and in many ways this uniqueness has come about as a direct result of the conditions under which American Catholicism has developed.

Historian Jay P. Dolan writes:

> A new Catholicism is taking shape in the United States. Once again, people are asking what it means to be Catholic in modern America. Catholics have asked this question time and time again over the past two hundred years. This time the questioning is much more widespread, much more revolutionary. . . . In the United States, Catholics have accepted the challenge of fashioning a new

---

[32]Rose Solari, "In Her Own Image," *Common Boundary*, July/August 1995, pp. 18–27.
[33]Mary Jo Weaver and R. Scott Appleby, *Being Right: Conservative Catholics in America*, pp. 177–178.

Catholicism. . . . that is faithful to the Catholic tradition and at the same time is rooted in American culture.[34]

### QUESTIONS AND ACTIVITIES FOR REVIEW, DISCUSSION, AND WRITING

1. If you are not Catholic, try to attend a Catholic Mass. If you are Catholic, try to attend a Protestant service. Notice both the similarities and the differences.
2. If you are not Catholic, talk with friends who are about what being Catholic means to them. If you are Catholic, talk with someone about what being a Protestant Christian means.
3. Look at a good road atlas of the United States. Note the prevalence of place names that reflect the Spanish and French Catholic influence in the Southwest, Florida, Louisiana, and the upper Midwest.
4. Are you aware of any anti-Catholic prejudice in your community? Elsewhere? Among other students? What forms does it take? Is it organized or informal? What might be done to end it?
5. In what ways is the Catholic Church distinctive?
6. Describe the Catholic sacramental system. In what way is it a "sacred materialism"?
7. Think about the issue of how much authority a community of faith ought to have over the lives of its members. Should it have a little or a lot? Are there things that you believe should be left up to the individual? What are the advantages and the disadvantages of a community of faith having great authority? Little authority? You might also discuss this issue with other people in your class.
8. In your opinion, should women be able to be ordained as priests in the Catholic Church? As permanent deacons? Why do you think the way you do on this issue?

### FOR FURTHER READING

CUNEO, MICHAEL W., *The Smoke of Satan: Conservative and Traditionalist Dissent in Contemporary American Catholicism.* New York: Oxford University Press, 1997. Cuneo's thorough treatment makes careful distinctions between different types of dissent and their impact.

DOLAN, JAY, *In Search of an American Catholicism: A History of Religion and Culture in Tension.* New York: Oxford University Press, 2002. Dolan investigates the long-standing and still-present tension among Catholics in the United States between democratization and traditionalism in the Church. He gives thorough attention to popular devotionalism, a topic often obscured in other treatments.

GILLIS, CHESTER, *Roman Catholicism in America (The Columbia Contemporary American Religion Series).* New York: Columbia University Press, 2000. Gillis describes the distinctiveness of American Catholicism, the variety of viewpoints in today's church, and Catholic views on contemporary social issues, as well as the influence of Catholicism on the larger culture of the United States.

HELLWIG, MONIKA, *Understanding Catholicism, Second Edition.* Mahwah, NJ: Paulist Press, 2002. Dr. Hellwig's book has been a standard work in basic Catholic theology for years. This is a completely updated edition that is sensitive to the present situation within Catholicism in the United States.

---

[34]Jay P. Dolan, *In Search of an American Catholicism*, p. 197.

REDMONT, JANE, *Generous Lives: American Catholic Women Today*. Liguori, MO: Triumph Books, 1992. In this excellent study of American Catholic women, discursive chapters alternate with first-person accounts by women of all ages, nationalities, and economic backgrounds, both lay and ordained.

### RELEVANT WORLD WIDE WEB SITES

Catholic Information Center on the Net: www.catholic.net

Catholic On-Line: www.catholic.org

Official Vatican Home page: www.vatican.va

Call To Action: www.cta-usa.org

National Conference of Catholic Bishops: www.usccb.org

Spring Hill College Theological Library: www.shc.edu/theolibrary

# ETHNIC DIVERSITY IN CHRISTIANITY:
# TWO EXAMPLES

Since the late 1970s, Chicago's black inner city has become a harsher place to live. In the same period, storefront churches have flourished. . . .

In the storefront church, low-income blacks create ways of thinking about the world and acting in the world that reverse degrading public assumptions about inner-city blacks. . . .

Racist stereotypes about lazy, ineffective, immoral, and unresourceful blacks are contradicted by rigorous church protocols, steadfast commitment to work for the church, and creativity and skill on the part of the community of believers to maintain the storefront mission. . . . [Members] meaningfully address the problems they have securing work; the violence and crime they endure in their neighborhoods; the deprivation they see on the ghetto streets; and the hostility, indifference, and humiliation they suffer because they are poor and black.[1]

## ETHNIC CHRISTIANITY

**Ethnic Christian communities of faith** are groups of people whose religion and ethnic, racial, or national identities are inextricably linked together. Eastern Orthodox Christians and black Christians in traditional black churches and black independent congregations are the two major representatives of ethnic Christianity in the United States. Although both of these groups include converts whose ethnic heritage differs from that most closely identified with the group—Eastern Orthodox of non-Eastern European descent and whites who are members of black churches—the ethnic identity of the group as a whole remains clear and important in its self-understanding.

[1]Frances Kostarelos, *Feeling the Spirit: Faith and Hope in an Evangelical Black Storefront Church* (Columbia, SC: University of South Carolina Press, 1995), pp. 123–126.

These religious groups are important carriers of ethnic and cultural identity. For Eastern Orthodox Christians, the church often provides not only a place for worship, but a place in which native dress, language, food, and other cultural customs are preserved, understood, and appreciated. The church and its members become the primary social center for the group. Churches may also sponsor cultural festivals that help to bring the native culture of their members to the larger community. The church helps provide a link to "the old country," allowing its members to be both American and distinctively ethnic. By doing so, it plays an important role in easing the transition for new immigrants and in helping to keep the ethnic heritage from becoming lost in succeeding generations.

As you will learn, the black church played a central role in helping blacks become an integral part of American culture. At the same time, it helped to keep alive the traditions of distinctively black worship and religious life. It continues to do so today. The black churches provide a place in which black heritage and pride in blackness can be nurtured in an otherwise oppressively racist society. They also provide resources to help blacks advance in the predominantly white culture.

The ways in which religion and ethnicity are interrelated are too complex for full exploration here. Three important points can be noted, however, in addition to what has already been said. Religion is an important source of stability and comfort among immigrants and others who are not fully at home in American culture. Immigration—whether forced or undertaken by choice—means the loss of the familiar. Often it entails separation from not only friends but family as well. Although for many, coming to the United States has meant the hope of a new beginning, it has brought with it grief and a sense of loss. In the midst of such feelings, religion offers something of "home" that can come with the immigrant.

Another point at which religion and ethnicity intersect is in the role of religious leaders. The religious leaders are usually among the better-educated members of the ethnic community and are usually respected in this country simply because they are religious leaders. This puts them in an excellent position to serve as spokespersons for the ethnic, national, or racial group in question. This has been particularly evident in the role of articulate black ministers in the civil rights movement.

As the recent American Religious Identification Survey notes, social identity in the United States is "multilayered, an amalgam of religious, ethnic and cultural elements."[2] These elements have declined in social significance as diversity and pluralism have increased, although some individuals continue to assign great importance to them. Inherited identities often mean less socially than they have in the past. Intermarriage frequently weakens these ties even more. Religion is becoming more and more a matter of personal choice, and thus ethnicity is becoming less important as a factor in religious identity. This

[2]The American Religious Identification Survey, www.gc.cuny.edu/studies/religion_identity.htm.

continuing trend will likely increase the cultural diversity of America's congregations. Becoming genuinely multicultural and multiethnic communities of faith will bring with it both new opportunities and new challenges.

## EASTERN ORTHODOX CHRISTIANITY

Some of you reading this book are undoubtedly Eastern Orthodox Christians. The majority of you are not. For those of you who are, this chapter is an invitation to see your church in a new way, from the point of view of the academic study of religion. For those of you who are not, I invite you to imagine yourselves in the world of an Eastern Orthodox service of worship. Bearded priests dressed in ornate vestments (Figure 7–1) lead an impressive procession to the front of the church. The air is heavy with the smell of incense. Around the church are many icons—paintings of Jesus, Mary, and the saints done in glowing colors, embellished with gold. The priest and the people chant responsively in Greek, its measured cadences seeming to belong to the time that the Christian New Testament was written. An air of mystery makes you catch your breath.

The **Eastern Orthodox churches** are a group of churches whose members follow the teachings and practices of Christianity as it was practiced in the major cities of the Eastern Roman Empire in the first centuries of the Common Era. They include the Greek and Russian Orthodox Churches and churches with national ties to the former Yugoslavia, Ukraine, Serbia, Croatia, Armenia, Bulgaria, and Romania.

**Figure 7-1**   The vestments of Orthodox Christian priests are ornately symbolic. *(Audrey Gottlieb/Monkmeyer Press)*

## History

For the first ten centuries of its existence, the Christian church was essentially one and undivided, although there were certainly differences between churches in various geographical locations. Within a few years of the beginning of Christianity, there were communities of believers in all the major cities of the Roman Empire, one body of Christians with a diversity of beliefs and practices. There was as yet no central leadership, with the responsibility for guidance shared among the leaders in the different cities.

It is not necessary to trace the intricate political and religious differences that led up to the final division between Christianity in the West and in the East in order to understand American Orthodoxy. The political and economic factors were at least as important in bringing about the final division as were the religious ones. In 1054 C.E., an emissary of the Bishop of Rome excommunicated the Bishop of Constantinople, who, in turn, excommunicated the Bishop of Rome, making formal and official a division that had been growing for centuries.

The first Orthodox church in the United States was a Greek Orthodox church in New Orleans in 1864, although there had been a colony of Greek Orthodox people at New Smyrna, Florida, a century earlier. Orthodox immigration into the United States came relatively late. The first significantly large numbers were not present until the nineteenth and twentieth centuries. The first archdiocese[3] in the United States was the Orthodox Archdiocese of North and South America, incorporated in New York in 1921. Large numbers of Greek immigrants arrived in the United States at the turn of the century, bringing their Orthodox faith with them. Large numbers of Russians arrived after 1917, when the Bolshevik Revolution began in Russia.

Two other events played significant roles in Orthodox history in the United States. First, missionaries from the Russian Orthodox Church established missions in Alaska as early as 1794, providing a base from which Orthodoxy could enter the United States. The large number of Orthodox Christians in Alaska meant that when Alaska became a state in 1959, the number of Russian Orthodox in this country rose dramatically. Second, thousands of Orthodox immigrants came from Greece, Asia Minor, Russia, and Eastern Europe between the Civil War and World War I.

In spite of the close national connections of the Orthodox churches, early archdioceses often included all the national churches, because the total numbers were small. Such archdioceses were incorporated in New Orleans in 1864, in San Francisco in 1867, and in New York City in 1870. As the numbers increased, national churches were organized. A Serbian Orthodox church was incorporated in 1926, a Romanian church in 1935, Antiochene and Ukrainian churches in 1937, and a Bulgarian church in 1938. These churches still have a strong national consciousness that plays a major role in keeping them apart organizationally.

---

[3]An *archdiocese* is a church governmental unit, usually a metropolitan center, headed by an archbishop.

## EASTERN ORTHODOX CHRISTIANITY IN THE UNITED STATES

About 1 percent of Americans are members of Orthodox churches. Most are members of either the Greek or Russian churches. There are several monasteries, two schools of theology, a college, and several other institutions.

### Belief

People of Orthodox Christian faith believe and practice in ways that are both like and unlike those of their Protestant and Catholic neighbors. Orthodox belief is based on the Bible and on the official teachings of the **seven ecumenical ("of the whole church") councils** of the Christian church, which took place during the first 1000 years of its history. Like Catholics but unlike Protestants, Orthodox Christians accept both the Bible and the church's tradition as genuine sources of revelation. Tradition is not found in a single document, but in many. The Nicene Creed is the principal creed. The creeds of the other councils are also believed to be true expressions of God's revelation. The Divine Liturgy (the principal act of worship) itself is an authoritative part of the tradition, as are the teachings of the early church Fathers. So is the Orthodox Churches' long history of **iconography**, the depiction of religious figures in special paintings. The veneration of icons will be discussed in the section on ritual.

The Christian belief that **God is a trinity** is very important to Orthodox Christians. They also give **great honor to Mary as the Mother of God**. Although she is not God, Orthodoxy teaches that at one time she contained God in the person of Jesus. She is called **Theotokos**, the bearer of God. With other Christians, the Orthodox affirm Jesus's full divinity and humanity, and hold that he plays the essential role in the drama of human sin and redemption.

**God**, according to Orthodox thought, **remains shrouded in holy mystery** and cannot be comprehended by human beings. Orthodox Christians believe that, because God is "absolutely incomprehensible and unknowable" (Saint John of Damascus, c. 675–749 C.E.), all that people can say about God is what God is not. Thus, God is *in*corporeal, *in*visible, and *in*tangible.

Like those of Catholic faith, Orthodox Christians believe that the grace of God is a divine, saving power available to persons through the sacraments of the church. **Divine grace requires human cooperation**. Salvation is not based on grace alone, as most Protestants affirm, but on both grace and human cooperation, another belief that the Orthodox share with their Catholic counterparts.

Orthodox Christians believe that the image of God in humanity is distorted and tarnished as a result of the disobedience of Adam and Eve that is recorded in Genesis. This ancestral sin continues to be transmitted to all people. Although the image of God is in each person, sin distorts it and makes it unclear. Orthodox Christians believe that by means of the cooperation between divine grace and human effort, the image of God can become clearer and clearer. By participating in the church as a worshiping community, human beings can become more and more like God. Although this process stops short of a full deification of humanity, the accent on the divine potential of human beings certainly tends in that direction in Orthodox thought and is an image of hope for all who follow it. God did not become human to satisfy the demands of divine justice, according to Orthodoxy, but to enable other human beings to become like God. **As people grow in God's grace, the image of God shines ever more brightly**.

Death means the separation of the soul or spirit from the body. Orthodox Christians believe that people immediately begin to experience something of heaven or hell—of being in communion with God or not. They also believe that there will be a final judgment. Based on the character of people's lives, their "resurrected existence will then live eternally in heaven in communion with God, or eternally in hell, out of communion with God."[4]

## Ritual

While the Catholic Church emphasizes correct teaching and belief, Eastern Orthodox Christianity puts its greatest emphasis on worship and other ritual. Proper worship defines what it means to be Orthodox and links the various national churches together in close communion. The central act of worship is called the **Divine Liturgy**. It is a solemn yet joyful act that is stylized and highly liturgical. Originally, the language of the Divine Liturgy was Greek. In most churches now, the custom is to use the language of the people for most of the service or to use a combination of the two. In some churches, a choir chants most of the congregational responses. The Sunday morning liturgy is usually based on an order of worship developed by Saint John Chrysostom (347–407 C.E.), or on one developed by St. Basil the Great (c. 330–379 C.E.). It expresses the holy mystery of God without compromising it. In worship, the mysterious holiness of God is not so much to be understood as to be experienced and adored. The liturgy takes place in a church that is usually designed in the form of a cross, the arms of which project equally from the center, over which a dome is built (Figure 7–2). The Eastern arm of the cross is set apart by a richly decorated screen, the *iconostasis*, behind which the priest enacts the holy mysteries, shielded from the view of the congregation.

There are **three parts of the Orthodox liturgy**. The first, sometimes called the **morning service**, includes the preparation of the communion elements and recalls Jesus's birth and God's incarnation. The second, the **processions**, consists of responsive prayers, Bible readings, the sermon, and the Great Procession, in which the prepared communion elements are brought out. This symbolizes Jesus's coming to humankind to teach and to

[4]Stanley S. Harakas, *The Orthodox Church: 455 Questions and Answers* (Minneapolis, MN: Light and Life Publishing Company, 1988), p. 97.

**Figure 7-2**  This Greek Orthodox Church near Chicago incorporates the traditional domed roof over the sanctuary into distinctively modern architecture. *(Photo by the author.)*

heal. The third part is the **communion** service itself. The priest goes behind the iconostasis, consecrates the elements, and places the bread into the chalice[5] of wine. The chalice is carried among the people, and all those who are prepared to do so partake. This third part of the liturgy symbolizes Christ's sacrifice for humankind. As do Catholic Christians, the Eastern Orthodox believe that the bread and wine actually become the body and blood of Christ. The entire service may last up to three hours. Not everyone attends for the full service, and it is not uncommon for people to leave the church and return during the service. It is customary for families to worship together, with even the youngest children present for much of the service. Orthodox Christians believe that it is beneficial even for children who are too young to grasp its meaning to be present for the Divine Liturgy.

In addition to the majestic Divine Liturgy on Sunday morning, there are various services throughout the day, marking out the passage of time into a holy cycle. Most people, of course, do not participate in all these services, but in the monasteries, these rites pace the monks throughout the day and night.

The Orthodox Churches celebrate the **seven traditional sacraments,** which are often called the **Holy Mysteries**. The sacraments are believed to convey grace by the presence of the Holy Spirit within them. "God touches, purifies, illumines, sanctifies and deifies human life through the mysteries. . . . In them, we encounter Christ in order to be Christ."[6] **People are bap-**

---

[5]A *chalice* is a special cup or glass, usually with a stem, used for the wine in the Eucharist.
[6]Alciviadis C. Calivas, "Orthodox Worship," in *A Companion to the Greek Orthodox Church,* ed. Fotios K. Litsas (New York: Department of Communication, Greek Orthodox Archdiocese of North and South America, 1984), pp. 31–32.

**tized by triple immersion**, symbolizing both the three persons of the Trinity and the three days Jesus is said to have lain in the tomb. Infant baptism is the usual practice, in which case baptism may involve only partial immersion. Confirmation, or chrismation, in which the person is anointed with oil that has been blessed for that purpose, follows immediately. Newly baptized people, infants or adults, then receive their first communion.

Leavened bread and wine are used as the communion elements. As noted above, Orthodox Christians believe that the elements become the body and blood of Christ. It is expected that all Orthodox Christians who are baptized and confirmed will partake regularly, and participants often fast from the evening meal prior to the service. Only Orthodox Christians who are in good standing with the Church may receive communion. The laity usually receive the bread and the wine together in a small spoon made for that purpose; priests receive the elements separately. In some churches, Orthodox Christians who did not receive the communion elements, and non-Orthodox people as well, are offered the "bread of fellowship" after the communion as a way of sharing in the service more fully.

The rite of penance as practiced in Orthodoxy reflects a number of themes that have already been mentioned. Baptism is only the beginning of a lifelong process of healing and restoring the damaged image of God within each person. This process is carried out in part through the sacrament of penance. The priest stands with the penitent, approaching God on the penitent's behalf and pronouncing God's forgiveness. Penance, writes one Greek Orthodox scholar, "is essentially a healing mystery, since sin is viewed primarily as a disease that needs to be healed, rather than a crime that needs to be punished."[7] The Orthodox are not altogether different from their Protestant and Catholic neighbors in this interpretation, although non-Orthodox Christians (and especially some Protestants) are more likely to emphasize a juridical interpretation of sin and forgiveness. The Orthodox focus on healing the separation between people and God and the restoration of the divine image in people.

The sacrament of **ordination** sets men apart for the Orthodox priesthood. Married men may be ordained as priests, but priests are not permitted to marry after they are ordained. Bishops and other leaders in the hierarchy are always drawn from the ranks of the celibate monks. Priesthood is limited to men, because the ministry of Christ is carried out in the Church by the priests who are in Christ's image. Through the priest, Christ is present in and to the Church.

**Marriage** reflects the union of Christ with the faithful, of Christ and the Church. It is believed to be for life. However, because marriage involves human free will, there is always the possibility that a mistake will be made. When divorce happens, the Church usually holds that a true marriage did not occur. The marriage did not show its necessarily eternal character. The laity

---

[7]Calivas, "Orthodox Worship," p. 48.

may have up to three attempts to establish a true and valid marriage. A fourth marriage is absolutely forbidden. The rites for marriages other than the first are subdued and have a penitential character. Clergy may marry only once, because they are expected to set a good example for the laity.

Customs surrounding Orthodox weddings vary from group to group, but two are widespread. At one point in the ceremony, crowns are placed on the heads of the bride and groom. The crowns are sometimes linked together with a ribbon. Although there are several meanings associated with the crowns, primarily they signify the new status of the couple as the king and queen of a new Christian household. Orthodox Christians traditionally wear their wedding rings on their right, rather than their left, hands. The rings signify the couple's solemn pledge to each other, and the right hand is associated with strength and authority.[8]

Ill persons are anointed with blessed oil. Like the Catholic sacrament for the sick, this special service is intended to assist in recovery if that be God's will or to ease the passage from earthly to eternal life.

Because the Orthodox churches follow the Julian rather than the Gregorian calendar, the dates of the major festivals differ from those celebrated by other Christians. For example, Holy Week (Palm Sunday through Easter) may be a week earlier or later than it is for Western Christians.

Orthodox ritual life, both in the church and in the home, is marked by the use of **icons**. Icons are special paintings that function as windows through which the sacred, without compromising its mystery, becomes visible. The painting of an icon is a devotional act carried out by a monk whose commitment to his work is not only artistic, but spiritual. According to Orthodox belief, icons are not to be worshiped; to do so is idolatry. Orthodox Christians worship only God, as do other Christians. But Orthodox Christians affirm the *veneration* of icons. In becoming human in Jesus, God accepted everything pertaining to humanity, including "being depictable." Thus, "to refuse to venerate an icon is . . . to deny the reality of the Incarnation."[9] Icons are carried in procession and venerated by bowing in front of them, kissing them, and lighting candles before them.

## Lifestyle

The lifestyles of Eastern Orthodox Christians are determined as much by their national heritage and the extent of their accommodation to American culture as by their faith. Except for the celibate priests and monks, Eastern Orthodox Christians do not separate themselves from life in the secular world.

---

[8]Harakas, *The Orthodox Church*, pp. 198–199.

[9]Paul D. Garrett, "Eastern Christianity," in *Encyclopedia of the American Religious Experience: Studies of Traditions and Movements*, eds. Charles Lippy and Peter Williams (New York: Charles Scribner's Sons, 1988), vol. I, p. 328.

Marriage and family life are highly honored and respected. Deviations from this pattern, such as premarital or extramarital sex or active homosexuality, are regarded as inconsistent with a Christian life. Sexually abusive behavior is explicitly condemned.

Orthodox Christians may not marry non-Christians in the Church, but they may marry baptized non-Orthodox Christians. If married outside the Church, they may not participate in the Eucharist, nor may they serve as a godparent for an Orthodox infant or as a sponsor at an Orthodox wedding.

Abortion is not permissible except in cases in which the pregnancy or birth of the baby would gravely endanger the life of the mother. Although children are valued and seen as an important part of marriage, conception and birth are not regarded as the only reason for physical intimacy. Therefore, birth control is left up to the conscience of the couple.

Eastern Orthodox Christians are encouraged by their church to uphold all just laws. They may in good conscience break an unjust law. Orthodox Christians, for example, participated in nonviolent civil disobedience during the civil rights marches of the 1960s. Involvement in public life is encouraged. Orthodox Christians support full human rights for all persons. Most churches officially supported the Equal Rights Amendment while simultaneously emphasizing the importance of the family. They remain, however, adamantly opposed to women being ordained to the priesthood, for the reasons noted in our discussion of ordination.

## Organization

Organizationally, each of the nationally associated Orthodox churches is independent (the preferred word for this among the Orthodox is *autocephalous*, "self-headed"). Patriarchs lead the churches in each of the four ancient centers of Orthodoxy: Constantinople, Antioch, Alexandria, and Jerusalem. Among these four, the Patriarch of Constantinople is said to have primacy of honor and spiritual leadership. He is called first among equals but has no more authority than the rest. He is often referred to by the honorific title of His All Holiness Ecumenical Patriarch. The current Ecumenical Patriarch is Bartholomew I.

In addition to these four patriarchates, each of which has divisions within it, there are other major autonomous bodies of believers, such as those of Russia, Greece, and Serbia. Although they are independent in their organizational structure, they are united on important liturgical and theological points.

Orthodox Christians believe that the original Christian church was governed by bishops who presided over limited geographic areas. There was no one central authority. The Orthodox interpret the "rock" referred to in Matthew 16:18 ("upon this rock I will build my church") as Peter's faith rather than Peter himself, thus undercutting the primacy that the Catholic Church ascribes to the Bishop of Rome. This style of government has been maintained to the present time. Within each autonomous Church, government is hierarchical.

In practice, the American Orthodox churches operate with considerable autonomy. National consciousness notwithstanding, there is a degree of unity among Orthodox Christians in the United States. Particularly in the United States, most Orthodox Christians long for even greater unity:

> The more deeply the Orthodox strike roots in North America, the more they lament the ethnic foliage that conceals a united confession of faith. Immigration history, not theology, separates the Orthodox people. And in general they long for and anticipate their union in one organically Orthodox fellowship.[10]

The **Standing Conference of Canonical Orthodox Bishops in the Americas** is one voice for American Orthodoxy. There are two views of how Orthodox unity in North America might come about. The **Orthodox Church in America** was formed in 1970 by the merger of several Russian churches. Its goal is to unite the Orthodox churches of the United States into a single body. It is headed by an archbishop who has the title, "Archbishop of Washington [D.C.], Metropolitan of All America and Canada." The fact that Russians were the first Orthodox Christians in the United States leads the Russian Orthodox Church to the belief that they have precedence in the United States. Greek Orthodox Christians, who far outnumber the Russians, however, have been reluctant to accept the Russian-founded group as representative. The **Greek Orthodox Archdiocese of North and South America** has become the center of the point of view that holds that all Orthodox Christians owe allegiance to the Patriarch of Constantinople (the Ecumenical Patriarch). In 1999, Archbishop Demetrios Trakatellis, born in Greece and educated at Harvard, was enthroned as Archbishop of America. In his inaugural speech, Archbishop Demetrios announced a "threefold plan" for Orthodoxy in the United States:

> "a) cultivating, nurturing, and sustaining of a vibrant and dynamic Orthodox faith in the Unites States, b) teaching and practicing limitless love and philanthropy, and c) emphasizing, pursuing, and enhancing the establishment of a strong and unbreakable unity within the Church and the human community in general."[11]

Saint Vladimir's Seminary (Russian) in New York state has become a training center for Orthodox clergy of many national backgrounds. There is also a Greek Orthodox seminary in the United States, the Holy Cross Greek Orthodox School of Theology in Boston. There is also an Orthodox Theolog-

---

[10]Anthony Ugolnik, "An Ecumenical Estrangement: Orthodoxy in America," *The Christian Century*, 109, no. 20 (June 17–24, 1992), p. 611.

[11]Athanasios Antonopoulos, "Biographical Sketch of His Eminence Professor Demetrios Trakatellis, Archbishop of America," www.goarch.org/en/archbishop/demetrios/biography/.

ical Society of America, which includes members of all groups, and an Ortho-dox Inter-Seminary Movement. In worship, pan-Orthodox liturgies on the first Sunday of Lent have become an American tradition.

Eastern Orthodoxy is an embodiment of Christian faith centered in a rich liturgical life that vibrates with the resonances of a tradition as old as the Christian Church itself. For a significant number of American citizens, it is the faith that provides the sacred meanings that make life good. It relates the passage of time throughout the year and the passage of life through its various stages to God, providing a context of holy mystery that transfigures the mundane world.

## AFRICAN-AMERICAN CHRISTIANITY

If you worship or have worshiped in a predominantly black congregation, you have an idea about what black Christianity is.[12] If you have not experienced it directly, you may not know much about it. In that case, have you seen black Christianity depicted in the movies or on television? How is it portrayed? In either case, what comes to mind when you think of African-American Christianity and worship?

Whether they participate in a community of faith or not (although the vast majority do), spirituality is a "core value" for African-Americans, and most are well aware of the spiritual influences that have come to them from previous generations. African-American churches are extended families for their members, and the values and mores of church and family are deeply connected.[13] Religion has been "the one ongoing positive force" in their lives throughout their history, in large measure because "no other institution primarily served the good of the African-American community."[14] Approximately 90 percent of all African-Americans who participate in a community of faith do so in black-controlled churches.[15]

Data from surveys that include questions about frequency of attendance at worship, private prayer and Bible reading, strength of religious preference, and religious commitment typically show that blacks participate in both public worship and private religious acts more frequently than their white counterparts. Their religious preference and commitment are stronger. They are

---

[12]Both the term "black Christianity" and "African-American Christianity" are current in literature written by African-American Christians themselves. I will use the two interchangeably.

[13]Donelda A. Cook and Christine Y. Wiley, "Psychotherapy with Members of African American Churches and Spiritual Traditions," in *Handbook of Psychotherapy and Religious Diversity*, eds. P. Scott Richards and Allen E. Bergin (Washington, D.C.: American Psychological Association, 2000), pp. 369–370, 377.

[14]Peter J. Paris, "African American Religion," in *World Religions in America: An Introduction, Revised and Expanded*, ed. Jacob Neusner (Louisville, KY: Westminster John Knox Press, 2000), pp. 54 and 58.

[15]Hans A. Baer and Merrill Singer, *African American Religion: Varieties of Protest and Accommodation, Second Edition* (Knoxville, TN: University of Tennessee Press, 2002), p. 101.

more likely to consider religion a very important part of life and are more likely to believe that it can solve most or all of today's problems. Blacks are much more likely to be fundamentalist in their religious outlook, by about three to two, and are half as likely to be liberal.

### The "Lost Third Theme" of the Religious History of the United States

One study of African-American religion in the United States[16] advances the thesis that there have been two themes that have guided the interpretation of American religious history. One is pluralism—the existence of religious diversity and the extent to which it has been affirmed or at least tolerated. The other theme is Puritanism and the necessity that America have a collective purpose, a theme that appears to be fundamentally at odds with the first. These two, however can be seen as an evolving dialectic. As Puritanism and the sense of collective purpose and mission have lost ground, the affirmation of diversity has gained. When diversity has lessened, the sense of collective mission has gained.

There is, however, a third theme that cannot be subsumed under either of the other two: A major aspect of the religious history of the United States is the encounter between black and white. The Puritan theme has its primary locus in New England, and the pluralism and toleration theme begins in the middle colonies such as Pennsylvania, Delaware, and Rhode Island. The southern colonies and later southern states do not fit comfortably in with either of these.

> It is this problematic encounter of black and white—which tests the limits of all our views of pluralism and undermines every attempt to formulate a sense of collective purpose—that is the Southern theme in American religious history. . . . [And] it is not only a Southern theme.[17]

Although the religious history of the United States demonstrates a relatively steady increase in diversity and toleration, the black-white encounter is "the story of a persistent and seemingly intractable gap." In spite of efforts to overcome it, some of which will be described below, the gap endures and remains "one of the foundational realities of our national religious life."[18]

### The Ambiguity of Christianity for African-Americans

Christianity has always been ambiguous for the descendants of the African slaves brought to this country in the holds of ships. They were first introduced to Christianity by those who enslaved them, and it was usually used to under-

---

[16]David W. Wills, "The Central Themes of American Religious History: Pluralism, Puritanism, and the Encounter of Black and White," in *African American Religion: Interpretive Essays in History and Culture*, ed. Timothy E. Fulop and Albert J. Raboteau (New York: Routledge, 1997), pp. 9–10.
[17]Wills, "The Central Themes of American Religious History," p. 15.
[18]Wills, "The Central Themes of American Religious History," pp. 15 and 20.

gird obedience to the slave masters. One author describes the beginning of this ambivalence dramatically:

> This ambivalence is not new. It was ours from the beginning. For we first met the American Christ on slave ships. We heard his name sung in hymns of praise while we died in our thousands, chained in stinking holds beneath the decks, locked in with terror and disease and sad memories of our families and homes. When we leaped from the decks to be seized by sharks we saw his name carved on the ships' solid sides. When our women were raped in the cabins they must have noticed the great and holy books on the shelves.[19]

On the other hand, Christianity provided benefits for the slaves. Some of the slaveholders allowed their slaves at least a measure of control over their religious expression, and patterns of worship developed that the slaves could claim as their own. Even being taken into town to the "white" church provided a social outing and some relief from the burdens of work. Later, especially as slaves and former slaves embraced the Exodus story of the Hebrews' escape from Egyptian slavery, Christianity provided a context for liberating action.

## The Christian Churches and the Civil War

Religion figured prominently in the events that led up to the Civil War, in the war itself, and in the various attempts at interpreting its meaning that followed it. Both North and South looked to their faith, their churches, and their religious leaders to justify their position on the matter of slavery and to sustain them in the terrible bloodshed that pitted American against American and kin against kin. Both were certain that God was on their side, that theirs was the righteous cause, and that God would help them to prevail over their opposition. Both attempted to demonstrate support from the Christian scriptures. And, in both South and North, religious people sought to minister to those caught up in the war. There were chaplains with both armies, and aid societies assisted them in their work by providing reading materials, visitation, and facilitating communication between soldiers and the families they had left behind. It fell to these volunteers to deal as best they could with the grief of those from whom the war had taken family members, friends, and neighbors. The accounts of their work, along with that of the chaplains and medical personnel, are a stirring record of humanity amidst the inhumanity of war.

Religious perspectives gave rise to some of the most memorable literary and artistic responses to slavery and to the Civil War. Harriet Beecher Stowe's staunch and thoughtful Congregationalism led to her writing of *Uncle Tom's Cabin*. James Russell Lowell's stirring "Once to Every Man and Nation," familiar to most Protestant churchgoers, reminds us of the prophets of the Hebrews

---

[19]Vincent Harding, "Black Power and the American Christ," in *Black Theology: A Documentary History, 1966–1979*, ed. Gayraud S. Wilmore and James H. Cone (Maryknoll, NY: Orbis Books, 1979), p. 36.

when they called on their people to make a decisive, once-and-for-all choice between good and evil. And Julia Ward Howe's "The Battle Hymn of the Republic," although it became an anthem of the North, spoke eloquently of God's judgment on any people who made the wrong choice in that decision.

After the guns of battle were silenced, the religious categories of divine wrath and punishment and the religious overtones of sacrifice were brought into play by both sides to interpret the meaning of the war and of victory gained or defeat suffered. Others, keenly aware of the ambiguous nature of the entire situation, called for repentance on both sides and reconciliation of hearts as well as governments.

## The Free Black Church

Emancipation led to the development of black religion in the context of official freedom coupled with social repression and oppression that continued long after the Emancipation Proclamation was signed.[20] This complex dialectic continues to influence African-American Christianity.

The Baptist and Methodist churches carried out the most vigorous work among the blacks after emancipation. The vast majority of freed blacks were a part of one of these two communities of faith. A smaller, yet significant, number, especially in Maryland and Louisiana, were Catholic. Following the war years, the black church grew rapidly. Rejection or segregation of black members by historically white denominations (such as the Baptists' and Methodists' insistence on separate seating) led to the growth of all-black congregations within these denominations as well as to the formation of a number of black denominations. It was in these black denominations and in the all-black congregations within predominantly white denominations that black religion continued to evolve its distinctive style and message.

The black churches played a unique role in the developing black community, in the North and South, in rural areas, and in cities, to which increasingly large numbers of blacks were moving in search of work. The black churches were much, much more than simply religious institutions, although their primary identification as religious institutions influenced everything else in which they were involved. As a landmark study of the black church in the United States describes it:

> The black church has no challenger as the cultural womb of the black community. Not only did it give birth to new institutions such as schools, banks, insurance companies, and low income housing, it also provided an academy and an arena for political activities, and it nurtured young talent for musical, dramatic, and artistic development . . . in addition to the traditional concerns of worship, moral nurture, education, and social control. Much of black culture is

---

[20]The *Emancipation Proclamation* was a statement issued by President Abraham Lincoln on New Year's Day, 1863, that ended slavery throughout most of the South.

heavily indebted to the black religious tradition, including most forms of black music, drama, literature, storytelling, and even humor.[21]

As historian Sydney Ahlstrom points out, black churches also served as a "surrogate for nationality" that substituted religious identification for the tribal identity that had been left behind.[22]

The Christian ministry was the only profession open to blacks, and the black churches were the only institution controlled by blacks. As such, they served as schools for leadership training and development. Most of the black political leaders in the United States trace their roots back to the church and many to the ministry itself. Frequently in the history of the black church, the minister, who was the most highly educated member of the black community, served as the liaison between the black community and that of the dominant whites. This function remains important, even though blacks have joined the ranks of the educated and the professionals in increasing numbers.

### The Black Church and Civil Rights

**Black religion was at the heart of the civil rights movement**. It had helped the slaves maintain some sense of humanity and peoplehood. It had provided structure and organization in the years following emancipation. And it provided a framework in which hopes for civil rights could become political realities.

Too, **the civil rights movement became an integral part of black religion**. Most of the significant events of the civil rights movement occurred in the period that is centered on the turbulent decade of the 1960s and extends for a few years on either side of it. The black churches, their people, and their leaders were intimately involved.

**Dr. Martin Luther King, Jr.**, pastor of the Dexter Avenue Baptist Church in Montgomery, Alabama, was the undisputed leader of the civil rights movement. He brought to the task his lifelong experience of the black church, the moving preaching style of the black minister, and a social conscience informed by the liberal Protestantism he had learned while obtaining his doctorate at Boston University. Dr. King advocated **nonviolent protest**. His reading of the lives and teachings of Jesus and of Mohandas Gandhi, the Indian Hindu political leader, convinced him that nonviolence was the morally right way to deal with the situation in which blacks found themselves. Nonviolence meant **civil disobedience** in the spirit of Christian love rather than hatred and revenge against whites. Civil disobedience meant deliberately breaking laws that were unjust but being willing to endure verbal and even

---

[21]C. Eric Lincoln and Lawrence H. Mamiya, *The Black Church in the African American Experience* (Durham, NC: Duke University Press, 1991), p. 8.

[22]Sydney E. Ahlstrom, *A Religious History of the American People* (New Haven, CT: Yale University Press, 1973), p. 710.

physical abuse without fighting back and to go to jail if necessary for one's actions. It meant working for reconciliation, not encouraging separatism.

Within a few years, many blacks, especially students, had used King's nonviolent methods in sit-ins at segregated lunch counters throughout the South. Freedom rides began to protest segregation in interstate commerce facilities. Many blacks rode interstate buses and entered facilities, such as eating areas and restrooms that were reserved for whites. Such segregation was by that time illegal, but the laws were not enforced.

In January 1957, the **Southern Christian Leadership Conference** (popularly, SCLC) was formed, with Martin Luther King, Jr., as its founder. It proved to be one of the most effective black organizations throughout the 1960s and early 1970s. Protests in Birmingham, Alabama, were among the largest organized by the SCLC. King's "**Letter from Birmingham Jail**," a classic of the movement, was written while he was jailed in Birmingham as a result of his participation in these efforts. In it, King distinguished between a just law and an unjust law. A just law is one that squares with the moral law or the law of God. An unjust law does not. Unjust laws also legalize inequality and difference and are inflicted upon a minority who, by reason of not being allowed to vote, had nothing to say about their passage. People should obey just laws. Unjust laws, on the other hand, should be broken, but in the spirit of nonviolence and love already indicated.[23]

In the late summer of 1963, a massive demonstration in Washington, D.C., focused on segregation in accommodations. The following summer, the **Civil Rights Act** was passed. This piece of legislation received strong support in Congress from leaders of Protestantism, Catholicism, Eastern Orthodoxy, and Judaism, and from blacks and whites alike.

March 1965 saw the well-known march from Selma to Montgomery, Alabama. With King's able leadership, clergy and laity from all the major branches of Christendom and Judaism, along with humanists and free thinkers, marched and sang together in protest. Many went to jail. In August of the same year, the **Voting Rights Act** was passed. When Martin Luther King, Jr., was assassinated in the spring of 1968, many of the goals of the early civil rights movement had been met. But there was much more to do.

### Black Christian Militancy and Black Power

Gradually, the mood of the civil rights movement changed. Leaders arose who felt that these methods worked too slowly. They believed King was too willing to compromise, too moderate, too willing to work with whites. Why the change in mood? Black Presbyterian theologian Gayraud S. Wilmore puts it

---

[23]Martin Luther King, Jr., "Letter from Birmingham Jail," in *Why We Can't Wait* (New York: Harper & Row, Publishers, 1963).

this way: By the mid-1960s, "many believed that following King meant to give more attention to loving the enemy than to doing something about the suffering of brothers and sisters."[24] In most respects, King was a moderate among Christian ministers. For many blacks, patience with moderation had worn thin. When it had been formed, the Student Nonviolent Coordinating Committee (SNCC) had been committed to King's nonviolent methods, but its early commitment to nonviolence had lessened. Its leaders and rank-and-file members alike were willing to accept and condone violence in the service of righting the wrongs of previous centuries. The passage of the Voting Rights Act in the summer of 1965 sparked an incident that drew national attention, and, in some quarters, outrage. There was a week of bloody and destructive race riots in several major American cities. The week of uprisings highlighted the great frustration of the black community and showed both whites and more moderate blacks how far the militants were willing to go to meet their goals.

In the summer of 1966, **James Meredith** was shot and wounded while leading a 220-mile voting rights walk from Memphis, Tennessee, to Jackson, Mississippi. **Stokely Carmichael** and others who took over leadership on that march led the marchers in chants of "black power!" with clenched fists raised in what would become a nationally recognized symbol. The chants of "black power" were often led by church people, and they were accompanied by talk of God's judgment upon America for the injustices done to blacks and of coming retribution for oppression.

In 1967, the National Committee of Negro Churchmen became the National Committee of Black Churchmen. In 1969, the committee sponsored a conference on black economic development. Most of the key leaders of the black religious community had long since come to recognize that economic freedom was one of the main keys to ending oppression, a key without which no amount of good intention was enough. At that conference, James Forman read the "**Black Manifesto**." It is a document that "burns with anger and despair,"[25] as Forman said his brothers and sisters did. It made demands—demands that white Christian churches and Jewish synagogues pay reparations that would begin to offset the damage done by economic oppression. It explicitly accused these communities of faith of conscious and willing participation in the processes of slavery and oppression and of not moving nearly rapidly enough to bring about change. Specifically, it demanded $500 million. The money was to be spent in a variety of ways. Loans for land and homes were a main goal. Publishing, printing, and television networks were to be established. Training and skills centers were to be built. A National Black

---

[24]Gayraud S. Wilmore and James H. Cone, eds., *Black Theology: A Documentary History, 1966–1979* (Maryknoll, NY: Orbis Books, 1979), p. 16.

[25]James Forman, *Black Manifesto*.

Labor Strike and Defense Fund was to be established. A black university was to be established in the South.

On May 4, 1969, Forman read the Manifesto, uninvited, to the congregation of New York's prestigious Riverside Church. The white churches and synagogues strongly resisted paying any money for reparations. Those that did discuss it seriously often found their congregations split. The Manifesto was an effective tool for drawing national attention to the economic problems that had not been solved. It also illustrated the distance that the civil rights movement had moved from King's style of leadership. No longer willing to work with white religious groups, the supporters of the Manifesto drew clear battle lines.

Not all black churches supported the black power movement, and the movement itself drew support from people and groups not associated with the churches. Nevertheless, the growing consciousness of Jesus as Liberator that would highlight black religious thought gave support and religious legitimation to a powerful new thrust in the ongoing struggle of the black community.

### The Character of African-American Spirituality and Christianity Today

We can identify at least three sources of African-American Christianity. There are continuing influences from the tribal religions of Africa. It also has been influenced by patterns borrowed from white European-American Christianity. Finally, it has developed a unique character as African-Americans responded, first to slavery and then to their ongoing history of living in an oppressive and racist society.[26]

From its beginning, black religion in America has been affected by its context of "white racism and capitalist exploitation."[27] For this reason, the theme of freedom has been a paramount one:

> Throughout black history, the term "freedom" has found a deep religious resonance in the lives and hopes of African-Americans. . . . During slavery it meant release from bondage; after emancipation it meant the right to be educated, to be employed, and to move about freely from place to place. [Now], freedom means social, political, and economic justice. From the very beginning of the black experience in America, one critical denotation of freedom has remained constant: Freedom has always meant the absence of any restraint that might compromise one's responsibility to God. The notion has persisted that if God calls you to discipleship, God calls you to freedom. And that God wants you free because God made you for Himself and in His image.[28]

> Furthermore, there is a crucial difference in the connotations of freedom for black and for white Americans. While whites have characteristically interpreted

---

[26]Baer and Singer, *African American Religion,* p. 1.
[27]Baer and Singer, *African American Religion*, p. xxi.
[28]C. Eric Lincoln and Lawrence H. Mamiya, "The Religious Dimension: The Black Sacred Cosmos," in *Down by the Riverside: Readings in African American Religion,* ed. Larry G. Murphy (New York: New York University Press, 2000), pp. 33–34.

freedom through the lens of individualism, African-Americans have seen it as communal in nature. No one is truly free until all are free.[29]

African-American religion is Exodus religion. In coming to the New World, whites had drawn on the Exodus narrative in the Christian Old Testament. They saw themselves as the New Israel, the New World as the Promised Land, and their former life in Europe as bondage in Egypt. African-Americans have of necessity given the Exodus story a different interpretation. They are the Old Israel, suffering in bondage to the new Pharoah of racism, in an American Egypt far short of the Promised Land. This American Egypt stands under God's judgment.[30]

The biblical Exodus remains a powerful metaphor. Exodus is not only an event that occurred long ago in Hebrew history. It occurs now, as well, every time God raises up a "new Moses" and rescues the captives from the new Egypt. It is not only the deliverance of the Hebrews, but the deliverance of American blacks. It calls contemporary African-Americans to cooperate with the God of the Exodus to bring racial bondage to an end.

Along with the Exodus theme, Jesus is understood primarily as the Liberator, God as a human being who stands in solidarity with all those who are poor and oppressed. This is the Jesus of Luke's Gospel, who identifies himself as one sent to proclaim release to all in captivity of any sort and liberty to all who are oppressed (Luke 4:18–19). Jesus is the bringer of the age of liberation (Luke 7:22). Jesus, and hence God, is clearly and unambiguously on the side of the downtrodden and oppressed, and firmly against the oppressors, whomever they may be. The suffering of black people throughout their history finds "immediate resonance with the incarnational view of the suffering, humiliation, death, and eventual triumph of Jesus in the resurrection."[31]

Jesus as the liberator means liberation now, in this world, in terms of voting rights, jobs, equal access to good education, and adequate housing. The liberation that Jesus offers certainly includes freedom from the eternal punishment of unforgiven sin. It certainly includes a hoped-for future in which oppression and pain of every kind shall cease for all persons, and indeed for all creation. But first and foremost, Jesus means liberation now, sociopolitical and economic liberation. He means full humanity for people who have never had full humanity.

For some African-Americans, Jesus the Liberator is also Jesus the black man. They point out that in a literal sense, Jesus "was a Palestinian Jew whose racial ancestry may have been partly African but definitely not European."[32]

---

[29]Lincoln and Mamiya, "The Religious Dimension: The Black Sacred Cosmos," p. 33–34.
[30]Albert J. Raboteau, "African Americans, Exodus, and the American Israel," in *Down by the Riverside*, pp. 20–23.
[31]Lincoln and Mamiya, *The Black Church*, pp. 3–4.
[32]James H. Cone, "Black Theology as Liberation Theology," in *Down by the Riverside*, p. 397.

The traditional artistic portrayals of Jesus as a European simply are not true to the biblical account of who Jesus was. Moreover, on a symbolic level, Jesus's blackness demonstrates Jesus's solidarity with all oppressed blacks.

God is a God of justice who does not support the ruling class and the status quo but instead supports the attempt to bring about a more just and equal society. This, too, reflects the importance of the prophetic books of the Christian Old Testament in black religious thought. In a similar vein, the Kingdom of God is seen in terms of justice and equality in this world. People, with God's help and guidance, are responsible for bringing it about. While it may not come in its fullness until God intervenes decisively in human history, it can be greatly advanced. Black religious thought translates religion into political action; concepts such as the Kingdom of God are politicized and translated into concrete changes in how people live.

A recent study of African-American religion notes that religion gives African-Americans a voice, indeed multiple and variegated voices, to speak not only of their spiritual quest and fulfillment but of their earthly trials and social yearnings as well. In this interplay of worldly and otherworldly images and attributes, African-Americans constructed their identity as a people. Consequently, African-American politics has always had and continues to have a decidedly religious slant, while African-American religion is deeply political.[33]

The interaction of Christianity with the diverse experiences of African-Americans have given rise to a number of distinct types of African-American churches.[34] There are the mainstream churches, the large black denominations. The eight largest are the pentecostal Church of God in Christ (COGIC, which is the largest pentecostal denomination in the United States), the African Methodist Episcopal Church, the African Methodist Episcopal Zion Church, the Christian Methodist Episcopal Church, the National Baptist Convention, U.S.A., the National Baptist Convention of America, the National Missionary Baptist Convention of America, and the Progressive National Baptist Convention, U.S.A. This category also includes predominantly black congregations within "white" denominations such as those described in Chapter 4, and Black Catholic congregations. The mainstream churches support a program of social reforms intended to integrate African-Americans into American society and culture. While protesting racism, they do not usually challenge the underlying racist and classist structures of the culture, but rather focus on enabling African-Americans to participate in the existing culture on parity with their white counterparts.

The **Congress of National Black Churches** was founded to promote unity, charity, and fellowship among member denominations. The Congress is a coalition of six major historic black denominations: African Methodist Episcopal; Church of God in Christ; National Baptist Convention of America, Inc.; National Missionary Baptist Convention of America; and the Progressive

---

[33]Baer and Singer, *African American Christianity*, p. xvii.
[34]Baer and Singer, *African American Christianity*, Chapters 3–6.

National Baptist Convention, Inc. It sponsors a number of programs, including programs for theological education, economic development, a black family program, and an anti-drug program, as well as facilitating unity among the nation's black churches.

Separatism and an overtly militaristic and nationalistic stance characterizes the messianic-nationalist groups. They launch a "fundamental critique of the place and treatment of people of African heritage in American society." Their founders are often "charismatic individuals who are regarded as Messiahs who will deliver black people from white oppression."[35] They often are quite critical of the more integrationist stance of the mainstream black churches.

Conversionist groups, as their name suggests, emphasize the experience of conversion. Most are holiness and/or pentecostal. They emphasize strict personal morality and are often not deeply involved with either social action or politics. As with members of many other African-American religious communities, members of conversionist or "sanctified" churches dedicate much of their Sunday to church activities:

> Sundays are extremely busy for Sanctified churches, beginning with Sunday school in the early morning and evolving into the Sunday worship service in the later morning and early afternoon. A special program . . . may occur in the afternoon. Finally, an evening service of two hours or longer often brings to a close the most sacred day of the week. This round of religious activities may be punctuated by more profane affairs, such as a midday dinner or a picnic. Many Sanctified churches also conduct services on Friday nights as a way of making the transition between the profanity of life in the larger society and the sacredness of the Lord's Day.[36]

Finally, thaumaturgical [miracle-working] groups use religious ritual and esoteric knowledge to seek worldly prosperity, good health, and other benefits. Otherworldly dimensions take second place to their emphasis on improving life in their world. Thus, they promise benefits that their adherents have been denied or found difficult to obtain in the racist white culture. They offer a sharp contrast with the other types described above. They emphasize the individual over the group, embrace health and prosperity as an indicator of spiritual position, and do not seek to reform the larger culture.

### Black Church Worship

The black church's worship is distinctive, with links back to the African and slave experiences of its members' ancestors. It is worship in which the Holy Spirit is encountered by the worshipers as an experiential reality, in which they

---

[35]Swatos, William H., Jr., ed., *Encyclopedia of Religion and Society* (Walnut Creek, CA: AltaMira Press, 1998), p. 9.
[36]Baer and Singer, *African-American Religion*, p. 170.

**Figure 7-3**    Easter Sunday service at Ebenezer Baptist Church, Poughkeepsie, NY.
*(Kathy McLaughlin/The Image Works)*

are transformed by the presence of their God. Theologian James Cone has noted the **six main elements in black worship**, wherever it takes place.[37]

**Preaching** is the most important, because in the sermon, the preacher speaks the word of God to the people. The people in the congregation participate by their shouts or more subdued responses of "Yes, Jesus," "Say it, Brother," "Amen!" and the like. This congregational responsiveness pulls preacher and listeners together in a common act of worship (Figure 7–3).

**Singing** prepares for, and then intensifies, the experience of the Spirit. It sets the mood, although it cannot force the Spirit to come. Both choral and congregational singing take place, with the emphasis on the congregation's participation in hymns. For white Christians accustomed to two or at most three hymns during a worship service, the sheer number of hymns and religious songs in a black church service, as well as the hand-clapping, hand-waving enthusiasm with which they are sung, may come as a surprise.

**Shouting** and **conversion** are closely related. Shouting, sometimes referred to as "getting happy," is understood in the black church as a response to the action of the Holy Spirit, a form of religious ecstasy. It is not the same as similar phenomena in white pentecostal churches, because it grows out of an altogether different sociopolitical background and set of life experiences. The white pentecostal is a member of the dominant race, whereas the black is oppressed. As black theologian James Cone writes very pointedly, it is

[37]James H. Cone, *Speaking the Truth* (Grand Rapids, MI: William B. Eerdmans Publishing Company, 1986), p. 22.

"absurd . . . to contend that the Ku Klux Klansman and the black person who escaped him are shouting for the same or similar reasons."[38] Blacks shout in joy over the authentic personhood given by Jesus and participation in his life and liberation, experienced as a present, here-and-now alternative to oppression and depersonalization. Shouting usually accompanies and is evidence of conversion and recurs when that experience is renewed. Conversion is, on the one hand, a one-time event, but on the other hand, it is an ongoing experience and process, and both events are signaled by shouting.

Prayer, free and spontaneous rather than formal and read from a book, is understood as communication with Jesus. Like so much else in black worship, it is rhythmic, with rhythms that echo the African past.

During **testimony**, people speak in front of the congregation about their determination to stay with their lives in Christ and in the church in spite of difficulties. They believe that they are called by God and testify to their intention to be worthy of that call. It is an encouragement both to the person testifying and to those who hear it. The congregational responses of "Yes, Sister" or "Tell it, Brother" let the speakers know that the rest of the congregation is with them against the temptations that arise.

People approach worship in black churches expecting to be changed. "There is an expectation that individuals will be different when they leave the worship experience. They will have received hope, healing, care, and empowerment to negotiate their daily lives."[39] In a social situation in which hope and empowerment are hard to come by, this is a great gift to the participants.

### Women in the Black Church

Like their predominantly white counterparts, black Christian churches have historically had a majority of female members and an almost exclusively male pastorate. This pattern continues in many black churches today. Women do have many other leadership roles in the black churches, such as evangelists, deaconesses, lay readers, Sunday School teachers, counselors, and the like.

The black Methodist denominations were the first to ordain women as pastors. Congregational polity among the Baptist groups has limited the development of consistent policies on the ordination of women, but the tendency is for fewer women to be ordained there. While policy usually does not explicitly prohibit it, tradition does. Pentecostals remain firmly against it. Overall, the reluctance to grant full ordination to women has come under increasing criticism, and changes are coming about slowly.

There are at least two unique positions of honor for women in many black Christian churches. Women may be *Mothers of the church*, a position that derives from African-based kinship networks that carry over into the

---

[38]Cone, *Speaking the Truth*, p. 27.
[39]Richards and Bergin, *Handbook of Psychotherapy and Religious Diversity*, p. 381.

African-American community. They are often given the honorific title "Lady." There is no parallel in white churches.[40]

Frances Kostarelos describes the role of church mothers in her ethnographic account of an inner city storefront church in Chicago:

> The Mothers Board . . . is . . . separated into junior and senior groups; the former includes women between fifty-five and sixty-five; the latter is for women who are over sixty-five. These women are also called church mothers. As church women approach their mid-fifties, they are expected to take their place on the Mothers Board. . . . Members of the Mothers Board say that through the good and evil they have known and a lifetime of serving God and their families, they have developed the personal qualities and habit of mind required for service on the Mothers Board. Church mothers are expected to be soberminded, temperate at all times, and emotionally balanced. They are to avoid calling attention to themselves through their clothing and manners. They are to dress and comport themselves in a reserved and discreet manner. On Sundays they wear white dresses or suits, hats, stockings, and dress shoes. Their outfits represent their spiritual elevation and humility before God. At all times they avoid wearing striking outfits such as those worn by younger women in the church.

> It is the duty of the church mothers to be moral and spiritual guides to others in the congregation, especially to young women seeking to live in the Spirit. . . . Church mothers have the responsibility of counseling younger women. They are women who have been wife to one husband, good mothers and housekeepers, and in the church working for the Lord. The hardships they have endured as wives, mothers, and servants of God are believed to have strengthened them and brought them closer to the Spirit. The church mothers are highly respected and enjoy a great deal of deference from younger women. Church mothers have a significant spiritual role in worship services.[41]

*Women may also serve as nurses in the church.* Usually, the nurses are women younger than those on the Mothers Board. Dressed in a recognizable white uniform for church services and funerals, they are responsible for helping anyone in the congregation who needs assistance. They particularly help members overcome with emotion during services, and women with children who need to be taken out because they are fussing. Women on the Nurses Board achieve respect by consistently demonstrating their excellence in traditionally "female" qualities, such as compassion, helpfulness, and being good with children.[42]

---

[40]Lincoln and Mamiya, *The Black Church*, p. 275.

[41]Frances Kostarelos, *Feeling the Spirit: Faith and Hope in an Evangelical Black Storefront Church* (Columbia, SC: University of South Carolina Press, 1995), p. 51.

[42]Kostarelos, *Feeling the Spirit*, p. 49.

It is clear that Mothers of the Church and Nurses have positions of great power within their congregations. Equally clear is the fact that their respect and position comes from their manifestation of traditionally feminine qualities and upholding traditional female role models. It is also important to note that black culture has not always encouraged males to respect females. The black church has been a key element in encouraging black men to respect all black women as mothers, wives, and sisters. Some women, barred from ordination, also founded their own churches, becoming powerful preachers and leaders in their own right.

Black feminist theologians have articulated a bleak picture of the position of black women in American culture and in African-American churches. They face "multiple jeopardy."[43] They are female, black, disproportionately in poverty and single mothers, and more often than their white counterparts the victims of physical, emotional, and sexual abuse. The *feminist* movement, including feminism in religion, has been largely white, middle to upper class, and educated. Black *theology* has been overwhelmingly male. Therefore, feminist theology has not usually addressed the concerns of *black* women (nor those of Latinas and other marginalized women), and black theology has usually failed to speak to the concerns of black *women*. Only recently has black feminist religious thought begun to find its own unique voice.

Womanist thought has grown out of the failure of white middle class feminism and black male theology to address the particular concerns of women of color:

> The term *womanist* was coined by Alice Walker in her work *In Search of Our Mothers' Garden: Womanist Prose* (San Diego: Harcourt Brace Jovanovich, 1983), xi–xii. The term is derived from the word *womanish* and refers to African American women as "courageous, audacious, concerned about family, community, and relationship with God." Walker calls the womanist "a black feminist, a feminist of color." Womanists are concerned about the multiple oppression . . . of African American women and women of color in general.[44]

### QUESTIONS AND ACTIVITIES FOR REVIEW, DISCUSSION, AND WRITING

1. If there is an Eastern Orthodox church where you live or where you go to school, try to make an appointment to visit the church during the week. Notice particularly the architecture of the building, the icons, and the iconostasis. Most priests will be glad to have you visit and will be quite willing to answer your questions. You might also want to consider attending the divine liturgy on Sunday morning.

---

[43]Cheryl Townsend Gilkes, "*If It Wasn't for the Women . . .*": *Black Women's Experience and Womanist Culture in Church and Community* (Maryknoll, NY: Orbis Books, 2001), p. 2.

[44]A. Elaine Brown Crawford, *Hope in the Holler: A Womanist Theology* (Louisville: Westminster John Knox Press, 2002), p. xi.

2. If you are accustomed to worshiping in a white congregation, attend a worship service at one of the historically black churches. If you worship in a mostly black congregation, attend a service in a mostly white congregation. Reflect on the differences you observe.

3. Get your class together in integrated groups of black and white students, and discuss your perceptions of each other's worship.

4. In your opinion, what are the advantages and disadvantages of the nonviolent methods of Martin Luther King, Jr.?

5. Read and report on James Baldwin's autobiographical novel, *Go Tell It on the Mountain*.

6. If you can get a videotape of the movie *The Long Road Home*, with Whoopi Goldberg, view it and write a brief essay on the roles that the black church played in the civil rights movement, as depicted in the film.

7. In what ways do the roles of church mother and church nurse allow women honor and position within the black church while remaining within traditional gender roles?

8. What is *Womanist* theology and why did it develop?

## FOR FURTHER READING

BAER, HANS A. and MERRILL SINGER, *African American Religion: Varieties of Protest and Accommodation, Second Edition*. Knoxville, TN: University of Tennessee Press, 2002. This revision of an earlier work is an excellent analysis of African American religion in the context of the dominant white American culture.

CLENDENIN, DANIEL B., ed., *Eastern Orthodox Theology: A Contemporary Reader*. Grand Rapids, MI: Baker Book House, 1995. Thirteen essays are included on major themes of Orthodox theology by Orthodox scholars/practitioners.

CONE, JAMES H., *Martin and Malcolm and America: A Dream or a Nightmare*. Maryknoll, NY: Orbis Books, 1995. Cone explores the role and influence of Martin Luther King, Jr., and Malcolm X, undoubtedly the two most influential black religious leaders in the history of the United States.

CRAWFORD, A. ELAINE BROWN: *Hope in the Holler: A Womanist Theology*. Louisville, KY: Westminster John Knox Press, 2002. It is in hope, embodied in the "holler," a cry to God, that has enabled black women to survive despite being "permissible victims." This is an excellent introduction to womanist thought.

HARAKAS, STANLEY S., *Living the Faith: The Praxis of Eastern Orthodox Ethics*. Minneapolis, MN: Light and Life Publishing Company, 1993. This book presents major themes in Orthodox ethical practice.

HARAKAS, STANLEY S., *The Orthodox Church: 455 Questions and Answers*. Brookline, MA: Holy Cross Orthodox Press, 1988. This older but concise and comprehensive handbook emphasizes Greek Orthodoxy but includes more general entries as well.

LITSAS, FOTIOS K., ed., *A Companion to the Greek Orthodox Church*. New York: Department of Communication, Greek Orthodox Archdiocese of North and South America, 1984. This is a good basic introduction to Eastern Orthodoxy in general.

MURPHY, LARRY G., ed. *Down By the Riverside: Readings in African American Religion*. New York: New York University Press, 2000. This is an outstanding collection of essays on a wide range of topics central to African American Christianity.

## RELEVANT WORLD WIDE WEB SITES

Greek Orthodox Archdiocese of North America: www.goarch.org

The Orthodox Church in America: www.oca.org

The Orthodox Theological Society in America: www.otsamerica.org

The Orthodox Page in America: www.ocf.org/OrthodoxPage

The Standing Conference of Canonical Orthodox Bishops in the Americas:
    www.oca.org/pages/orth_chri/Orthodox-Churches/SCOBA.html

National Baptist Convention, USA, Incorporated: www.nationalbaptist.com

Progressive National Baptist Convention: www.pnbc.org

African Methodist Episcopal Church: www.amecnet.org

Church of God in Christ: www.cogic.org

# AMERICAN-BORN CHRISTIANITIES

---

Days later, I found out that Aaron died. . . . We were all part of a community of devout Christian Scientists, a faith that shuns doctors and medicine and relies on prayer alone to cure the sick. . . . I thought of other deaths and suffering I'd witnessed over the years in the name of Christian Science. Most painful of all, I thought of the time seven years before when I'd almost let my own daughter die.[1]

I would like to thank God for a healing that occurred just after my husband and I got engaged. . . . And immediately all of the pain vanished—my understanding of the unreality of the accident was so powerful that it wiped out all illusion of pain. . . . I witnessed a complete and permanent healing of the skin, and there was no trace of scarring. I was in rehearsals for a musical two weeks later, dancing and singing without any hindrance. This healing has been an inspiration to me ever since.[2]

---

The first of the accounts above is by a former Christian Scientist, the other by a college student who is a follower of that faith. They typify the controversy that has characterized people's opinions of Christian Science, one of the American-born forms of Christianity to be discussed in this chapter.

The religious groups that are the spiritual home of the majority of America's population came to the United States from Europe. By contrast, the four religious groups discussed in this chapter began in the United States, and the nature of each bears the marks of that beginning. The four communities of faith described here include slightly less than 5 percent of Christians in the United States.

The communities of faith to which you were introduced in the first part of this book fit in with the culture of which they are a part, so much so that they have tended to disappear into that culture. More important, their way of seeing the world has come to be regarded as the normal view in the culture. It is necessary to distinguish **majority view** from **normal view**, even though the two are often believed to coincide. The *majority view* is simply the opinions

---

[1]Suzanne Shepard, as told to Marti Attoun, "Suffer the Little Children," *Redbook*, October, 1994, p. 66.
[2]Heidi Dittmar-Biever, in "Reports of Healing," *The Christian Science Journal*, August, 1994, pp. 54–55.

held by the majority of those in a given population. It takes on a different status when it comes to be thought of as the *normal*, correct, proper, or appropriate view. Then, it is the only one given full respect in a society. When this happens, it becomes a handicap for those whose views do not happen to be those of the majority. The indigenous American Christianities have much in common with traditional Christianity. In this, they are aligned with the majority culture. However, they interpret the tradition differently than do most Christians. The ways in which indigenous Christianities depart from more traditional teachings and practices usually result from the views of the founder of each group. They are the result of Christianity being passed through the lens of the unique vision of one person or a small group of people. It is changed in the process, although it retains clear and obvious links with more traditional groups. Participants in these communities of faith are Christians whose lives are centered in a faith that is different yet similar, clearly other and yet alike. The uniqueness of their insights and practices adds to the richness of religion in the United States. All of them, without exception, have been persecuted and looked down upon as a result of their nonconformity. Sometimes, they still are. They are living proof that the community of neighbors and not strangers has not been fully realized among us, because they are still looked upon as outsiders.

Have young Latter-day Saint (Mormon) missionaries ever come by your home asking to speak with you about their church? Have you perhaps seen them on your college campus? Have you seen a building in your community that is identified as a Kingdom Hall? It is the gathering place of Jehovah's Witnesses. Are you aware that Seventh-day Adventists worship on Saturday, or that followers of Christian Science do not rely on doctors and hospitals for medical care? All these people are representatives of the religions that you will learn about in this chapter. Ask yourself how you feel about people whose religion makes them stand out from the rest of the culture. Are you interested in why they behave the way they do?

These communities of faith contrast with mainstream religion in several respects. Their members often have a sense of separation from the world. Although they may work very hard at making converts, their expectations for their members are high. The Mormons and the Jehovah's Witnesses are good examples of this. Members must be willing to accept more stringent rules and standards than those that apply outside the group. It is in this sense that they are somewhat exclusive. Their standards lead to a sense of separateness from the rest of the world, and members usually believe that they are following the one true way in religion while the rest of the world goes astray.

In addition to the Bible, other writings are often considered authoritative. They may be thought of as part of a group's scriptures or as interpretations of the Bible. These additional writings, usually those of the founder, may be regarded as new revelations or as interpretations inspired by God.

The material contained in the founder's writings gives rise to beliefs and practices that are different from those of more traditional Christianity. New revelations or new interpretations give rise to these new beliefs, rituals, and lifestyles and at the same time provide support for them.

A corollary of the sense of being set apart from the larger society is that these groups tend to be very close knit. Separation from those outside is complemented by closeness and community among those on the inside. They socialize together much more than they do with outsiders, and members of the group can count on strong support from other members in time of need. They often provide their members with a complete lifestyle and a full round of activities, not necessarily all of a religious nature. This reinforces the closeness of the community and limits contacts with outsiders.

Their lifestyles are frequently distinctive, making their separation from the culture somewhat obvious. There may be restrictions on dancing, gambling, and the use of alcohol and tobacco. There may be food regulations, and sometimes there are dress codes, especially for female members.

Authority in these religions is usually strictly enforced from the top down, with little room for innovation at the local or individual level. It would, however, be incorrect to conclude that members of these religious groups are blindly following their leader. For most, the acceptance of a strong religious authority and submission to that authority is in itself an important belief, one that has been consented to and taken as one's own.

## LATTER-DAY SAINTS

When most of us think of the Mormons, we probably think of neatly dressed, clean-cut young men, most likely on bicycles or walking, going from house to house talking about their faith with all who will listen and hoping to make converts. Some may think of well-known U.S. citizens who are Mormon. Examples include the Osmonds; Ezra Taft Benson, former Secretary of Agriculture; and George Romney, former Governor of Michigan. Others might well think of the world-famous Mormon Tabernacle Choir or Brigham Young University. Mormons have grown from a group whose numbers could be counted on the fingers of one's two hands to one of the larger and better-known communities of faith in this country. Yet many people still feel that the Mormons are not a part of mainstream America. In some ways, they *are* different and choose to stand outside the mainstream. In other ways, such as their involvement in public life, they have moved into the center. In this section, some of the misconceptions that still surround this religious group will be dispelled. At the same time, some of the differences between their understanding of Christianity and that of their neighbors will be described. Some important ways in which their lives are different because of their faith will also be discussed.

The word Mormon itself is not the official name of the group. It is a nickname for members of **The Church of Jesus Christ of Latter-day Saints**. Mormon is believed by the church to have been a prophet in the area that would become the United States. In the concluding years of the fourth century C.E., Mormon compiled a book containing the records of the people of Lehi, a Hebrew who had led a colony of people from Jerusalem to America in about 600 B.C.E. Mormon's son Moroni added some information of his own, including a brief account of the people called Jaredites, who had come to North America at the time that the Tower of Babel was built. This record is preserved as the **Book of Mormon**.

The official name, Church of Jesus Christ of Latter-day Saints, tells us how this community of faith understands itself. They consider themselves to be Christians, members of the one true church that follows all the teachings of Jesus Christ. Although some more traditional Christian groups do not consider the Mormons to be fellow Christians, there is no doubt about their self-identification as Christians. They are neither Protestant nor Catholic nor Orthodox, however. The word *saints* is used in the Christian New Testament to mean "church members." *Latter-day* distinguishes this church from the church in the former days, which, according to Mormon teaching, fell away from the truth of Jesus Christ shortly after it was founded. About 2 percent of the population of the United States is Mormon.

The Latter-day Saints began in the first half of the nineteenth century in an area of New York State that scholars call the burned-over district. It has been given this colorful name because a large number of revivals swept the area with great fires of religious enthusiasm. **Joseph Smith** (1805–1844), who would become the group's founder, grew up in this climate of religious tumult. Confused, he earnestly tried to discover which of the many religious groups in the area was correct, so that he might join it. One day in his reading of the Bible, he read, "If any of you lacks wisdom, let him ask God, who gives to all men generously and without reproaching, and it will be given to him" (James 1:5, Revised Standard Version). Taking these instructions to heart, the young man went and knelt in an isolated grove of trees to seek God's guidance. God spoke to Joseph Smith, according to Mormon belief, telling him that none of the available religious groups was the true church, and that all had fallen away from the truth. Smith was to join none of them. Then, in 1823, the angelic messenger Moroni appeared to him and told him that he would be God's chosen servant to restore the church to the fullness of the Gospel. The restoration of the true church is an important Mormon belief. Mormons believe that the true church has been restored through the prophecy to Joseph Smith. This includes the restoration of true priestly authority so that sacred ordinances may again be rightly performed.[3]

Moroni appeared to Joseph Smith again in 1827 and revealed to him the location of golden plates upon which was written what would eventually become the *Book of Mormon*. Because they were written in an unknown script,

---

[3]Elder M. Russell Ballard, "Building Bridges of Understanding," (February 17, 1998), Latter-day Saints Web site (www.lds.org).

Smith was also provided with something to assist in the translation (identified as the Urim and Thummim mentioned in Exodus 28:30). The *Book of Mormon* was subsequently published in 1830. According to Mormon history, the golden plates were taken up into heaven after Smith had completed the translation. The Latter-day Saints believe that their church is founded, not upon the human words and work of Joseph Smith, but on the direct revelation of God, as surely as the earlier Christian Church had been founded upon God's revelation in Jesus Christ.

The church was established in the spring of 1830, shortly after the publication of the *Book of Mormon*. It began with only five people. They were persecuted almost immediately. Persecution led to the long westward trek that would eventually take them to Salt Lake City. They first moved from New York to Kirtland, Ohio, and then to a place near Independence, Missouri. From there, their travels took them to Nauvoo, Illinois. Trouble again broke out, and several of their number were jailed at Carthage, Illinois. Among those imprisoned were Joseph Smith and his brother Hyrum, both of whom were murdered by a local mob while in jail. Some of Smith's followers, led by Brigham Young, then began the journey to what would become Salt Lake City, in the Utah Territory. Salt Lake City became the world headquarters for the Church of Jesus Christ of Latter-day Saints in 1847. Some, including Smith's widow and young son, disputed Young's leadership and stayed in Illinois, forming the nucleus of what would become the second-largest Mormon group, the **Reorganized Church of Jesus Christ of Latter Day Saints** (now, the **Community of Christ**). The headquarters of this group is in Independence, Missouri.

One of the best-known and least-understood chapters of Latter-day Saints history is their practice of polygamy. For a time, men, although not women, were permitted to have more than one spouse. Some of the church's leaders believed that they had received a revelation from God in which God commanded this practice, which they began in 1843. It became public knowledge in 1852. It was met with public outrage, and the U.S. government moved quickly to undercut the power of the church in Utah and made the abandonment of multiple marriage a condition of statehood. In 1890, Mormon leaders announced that the practice was no longer approved. At any given time, probably less than 20 percent of the Church's leaders were actually involved in plural marriage. The only remaining polygynists are isolated in very small groups that are not recognized by the church. The era of plural marriage ended almost as quickly as it had begun.

## Beliefs

Modern-day Mormons have beliefs that are similar to those of other Christians yet are in many ways distinctive. **The *Book of Mormon* is considered to be scripture, alongside the Bible.** In addition, new revelations were received at various times for specific purposes, and these were collected as the *Doctrine* *and Covenants.* A third book, *The Pearl of Great Price,* also contains revelations believed to have been received by Smith.

A recent statement on the Latter-day Saints Web site identifies four cornerstones of Mormon faith. First among these is **Jesus Christ** himself. The **revelation to Joseph Smith** is the second. It is recorded in the **Book of Mormon**, which is the third cornerstone. The *Book of Mormon* is regarded as an additional Gospel. The fourth cornerstone is the **Mormon priesthood** that allows men to act with authority in the name of God.[4]

Mormons believe in God the Father, Jesus Christ the Son, and the Holy Spirit, as do most Christians. They are, however, believed to be separate individuals, united in purpose. Thus, their understanding of God as Father, Son, and Spirit differs from the traditional Christian view that the Trinity is but one God. Mormons do not hold people accountable for the sin of Adam and Eve, as do some Christians. Being held responsible for a sin in which one had no part is repugnant to Mormon sensibilities. The concept of **free agency** is a central aspect of Mormon belief. Human beings have free will and therefore will be punished for their own sins, not those of Adam. People have come to this earth from a pre-earth existence, and the freedom to choose between right and wrong is the most important thing people bring to Earth with them. Jesus' sacrificial death makes salvation available to all humankind, but may be lost through lack of human effort. There are also degrees of exaltation. Heaven is divided into various realms or states of being. Mormons teach that the highest of these is available only to those who have followed all the laws and ordinances of the church. Those who attain this exalted status become gods, to whom all other things are subject, even the angels.[5]

A distinctive Latter-day Saints belief is that people have a premortal existence in the heavenly realm before birth. Being given a human body is a unique opportunity to carry out the actions necessary to return to God and higher degrees of exaltation. Mormons, along with other Christians, believe that people are created in God's image. People come to earth from existence in the premortal realm. Earthly life as lived by devout Mormons, including observance of the sacred ordinances, enables people to return to the kingdom of the Father upon earthly death. Individuals can return to the presence of God from whence they came, and families can remain together eternally.[6]

Latter-day Saints believe God's will is revealed not only in the Bible, but to Joseph Smith, and, following Smith, to the leaders of the church throughout all the years of its existence. Revelation continues even now. The concept of **continuous revelation** allows the church's leadership to be flexible in responding to issues and questions that are not dealt with directly in the Bible

---

[4]Statement by Church President Gordon Hinckley, at www.lds.org.
[5]*The Doctrine and Covenants of the Church of Jesus Christ of Latter-day Saints* (Salt Lake City, UT: Church of Jesus Christ of Latter-day Saints, 1982), 132:20.
[6]Latter-day Saints President Gordon B. Hinckley, "The Family: A Proclamation to the World," (September 23, 1995), Latter-day Saints Web site (www.lds.org).

or the other Mormon scriptures. At the same time, the authority of divine revelation is maintained.

This is a distinctively American church. The Book of Mormon gives America a scriptural past. Many religious groups in this country have believed fervently that America has a special role to play in God's plans for the world, but none has expressed that belief as concretely as do the Latter-day Saints. They look forward to a literal regathering of Israel, restoration of the Ten Lost Tribes, and the building of the New Jerusalem, to which they refer as Zion, on the North American continent. Mormons affirm freedom of worship as a privilege for themselves and all other people and in obedience to the laws of the land and its leaders.

## Lifestyle

If you are acquainted with many Latter-day Saints, you probably know them as people with an upbeat and healthful lifestyle. They participate wholeheartedly in the programs of their church. Saints strive to practice honesty and truthfulness, chastity, benevolence, and doing good to all. The body is given by God and is sacred, and taking good care of it is a religious act. This is the reason behind the **Word of Wisdom**, a health code that Mormons teach was revealed to Smith in 1833. The code forbids smoking tobacco, drinking alcohol, drinking beverages with caffeine in them (such as coffee, tea, and many soft drinks), and taking drugs other than those prescribed by a physician for medical reasons. Meat is to be used sparingly, with the emphasis in the diet on grains, fruits, and vegetables. Physical exercise is encouraged, as is good grooming. They teach that following the Word of Wisdom will lead to great wisdom and knowledge, as well as to good health that includes moral, emotional, and spiritual dimensions along with the physical aspects of health.[7]

As many of you probably know, **the family is absolutely central in Latter-day Saints' thought and practice**. It is the basic unit of church and society and is held to be sacred. Local churches provide many family-oriented activities throughout the week, of both a religious and a nonreligious nature. In addition, families have "family home evening" once a week, using materials provided by their church. This is a time for families to be together for study and for worship and discussion of religious matters. They also simply enjoy being together and benefit from the interaction of parents and children. Church members called home teachers visit members' homes frequently to bring messages of hope and goodwill. They are the representatives of the church leaders in helping the family to solve problems.

Marriage is valued very highly by the Latter-day Saints. Everyone is enjoined to marry, and requiring anyone to remain celibate is specifically forbidden. Adultery is grounds for dismissal from the Church, and premarital sex calls for severe repentance. Children are valued, and, however great a man's

---

[7] *Doctrine and Covenants*, 89:19–20.

achievements, his highest goal and achievement is fathering children. The husband and father presides over the family. As a male member of the church, he holds a position within the priesthood. The family unit functions as a small church in and of itself. Traditional roles for men, women, and children are encouraged. The husband is the provider and leader for his family. His wife is the primary caregiver in the home and is the emotional heart of the family. Parents expect children to contribute as much as they possibly can by helping with chores and participating in family home evening programs. Through a special sealing ceremony that takes place in temples, husbands and wives, along with their children, may be joined for eternity.

The Mormon emphasis on the family involves the extended family through many generations, as well as the nuclear family of those presently living. The Church sponsors one of the largest genealogical libraries in the world and assists millions of people with research into their family backgrounds. Faithful Mormons engage in Temple work on behalf of ancestors who died without being able to follow the ordinances for themselves. This is believed to be a great benefit to those who have died and confers a blessing on the living as well. The Latter-day Saints' extensive genealogical archives are available free of charge for anyone, Mormon or not, to use.

Latter-day Saints emphasize education for both men and women. Mormon children attend public and private schools but also participate in church educational programs that emphasize religious education. Home-study courses are available for those in isolated areas. A basic goal of the church is that every member will be able to read, write, do basic arithmetic, and study the scriptures and other uplifting books. The Church sponsors several institutions of higher education, the best known of which is **Brigham Young University** (BYU) in Provo, Utah. A publicity brochure for BYU describes the university this way:

> The uniqueness of Brigham Young University lies in its special role—education for eternity—which it must carry in addition to the usual tasks of a university. This means concern—curricular and behavioral—not only for the "whole man" but for the "eternal man." Where all universities seek to preserve the heritage of knowledge that history has washed to their feet, this faculty has a double heritage—the preserving of knowledge of men and the revealed truths sent from heaven.[8]

In addition to studying a full range of course work, students are trained to become the type of people the Mormon tradition expects them to be. It may be of interest to many of you, because you are taking a religious studies class, to know that BYU students take at least one religious studies class every semester, ranging from world religions to Mormon theology.

Self-sufficiency is another trait encouraged by the Latter-day Saints. A detailed program of personal and family preparedness for self-sufficiency is

---

[8]*B.Y.U.: The Mormon University* (Provo, UT: Brigham Young University, University Relations, n.d.).

spelled out, including education, career development, financial management, and home production and storage of necessities (sewing, gardening, food preservation, and the manufacture of some household items). These preparations will help individual families through hard times. The emphasis on self-sufficiency is balanced by readiness to help others who cannot help themselves. The church maintains storehouses, administered by local bishops, that are used to help those who have exhausted their own resources. The church also sponsors an employment clearinghouse, social services, and other assistance programs that weave together into a comprehensive program of assistance for both members and nonmembers. Mormons who receive assistance through these services are expected to work to help earn what they need and to help others who are in need.

As with all religions, Mormons vary widely in their adherence to Mormon beliefs and their practice of the lifestyle that their church advocates. Some take it very seriously, while others pay little if any attention to it. Most come somewhere in between the two extremes.

## Ritual

When Mormons gather for worship on Sunday morning in local churches or chapels, they do many of the same things that are done in Protestant Christian services. People sing hymns, pray, hear a sermon, and may have the opportunity to tell how God has been especially active in their lives during the past week. Concerns of the church family are shared. Men and women, boys and girls participate in their own study classes. In the weekly sacrament meeting, communion is observed, using bread and water, because the Mormons do not use alcohol. Other religious services take place during the week, and other activities at the church abound.

The Latter-day Saints distinguish between these local churches and their activities and temples (Figure 8–1). The **temples** and the rituals that take place in them are the most distinctive feature of Mormon ritual life. The first of these special buildings was built in Kirtland, Ohio, and dedicated in 1836. It was built following a pattern that Mormons believe God revealed to Joseph Smith. It was a temporary structure only, without all the features found in modern-day temples. Temples are reserved for the performance of special ordinances of the church. Many have been open to the public for tours for a time after they were completed, but after they are dedicated they are considered sacred space, and only worthy Mormons may enter.

Before Latter-day Saints can enter the temple, they must receive a **Temple Recommend** from the bishop. The bishop and the stake president, who is a local officer, conduct interviews to determine worthiness to enter the sacred place and to participate in its ordinances. Among other requirements, people must have "a testimony of the gospel," support the church and follow its programs and teachings, keep the Word of Wisdom, be morally pure, be members in good standing of the church, and be free of legal entanglements.

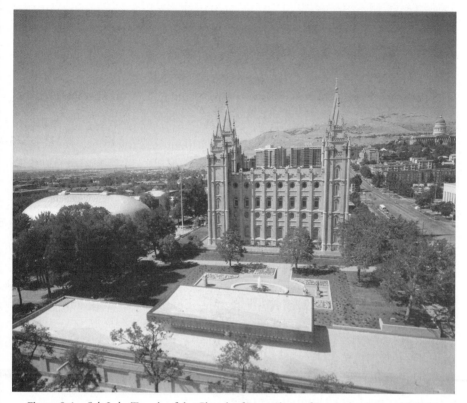

**Figure 8-1**    Salt Lake Temple of the Church of Jesus Christ of Latter-day Saints, Salt Lake City, Utah. Mormon Temples are used only for special Temple Ordinances. Because they are regarded as sacred spaces, they are not open to the public. *(Photograph copyright LDS Church. Used by permission)*

Mormons who are judged worthy and go to the Temple change from street clothing to clean, white clothing provided at the Temple as a sign and symbol of purity. My descriptions of Temple ceremonies are of necessity rather brief and very general. The details are not made available to non-Mormons, and those who participate in the ceremonies promise not to reveal the details of their experience. This reticence to discuss details stems in part from the long history of misunderstanding that has marked the career of the Latter-day Saints. It also reflects the sacredness that Mormons attribute to these special observances.

The first temple ceremony is the **endowment**. This is a prerequisite for any of the other ceremonies. The endowment is said to confer the knowledge necessary for a person to return to God after death. The history of the human race as the Latter-day Saints understand it is retraced, emphasizing the importance of the present time. Covenants or promises are made and obligations conferred, along with their accompanying blessings.

Another very important Temple ceremony is **eternal marriage**. Marriage according to the laws of the world, even if the wedding is performed in a Mormon church, ends with the death of one of the spouses. Marriage and family ties can continue into eternity, according to Mormon belief. The marriage of husband and wife, and the relationship of parents and children, can be made eternal by participation in temple ceremonies. Temple marriage is also required for entrance into the highest degree of exaltation following death.[9]

**Temple baptism** is another temple ordinance. Temple baptismal fonts rest on the backs of twelve sculptured oxen that represent the twelve tribes of Israel. Mormons are baptized in fonts in their local churches or chapels in a service very similar to that of other Christian churches. Baptism is by immersion and is restricted to those who are old enough to understand its meaning for themselves. Temple baptism is performed by the living on behalf of the dead. Many people die without hearing the teachings that Mormons believe are necessary for exaltation. Mormons believe that the opportunity to do so can be made available to them in the spirit world by a living member of their family who undergoes temple baptism on their behalf. Only these baptisms on behalf of another are performed in the temple. Part of the significance of tracing one's genealogy as far back as possible is to find those ancestors for whom temple work needs to be performed. Sealing ceremonies that join spouses, parents, and children for eternity can also be performed vicariously. In any case, the performance of a vicarious ceremony provides only the opportunity. The soul in the spirit world must give its voluntary consent. The concept of free agency applies even there.

### Organization

There are several distinctive things about the institutional or organizational life of the Latter-day Saints. In many ways, the Church is a theocracy believed to be under the direct rule of God, because Mormons believe that the highest leaders of the Church continually receive revelations from God. No officer, however, serves without a sustaining vote from the people he serves, so that there are also democratic elements. There are no professional clergy, and lay members who serve as officers do so without pay. Now, however, both major branches of the church pay a living allowance to those people in the central administration. The Church has a president, considered to be a prophet of God. He is advised by two counselors who, along with the president, make up the First Presidency. There is a Quorum of Twelve Apostles that advises the First Presidency. The Church is highly organized along geographic lines, with no congregation being so large as to become impersonal.

---

[9]*Doctrine and Covenants*, 132:15–19 and 131:2–4.

Priesthood in the Mormon church means the authority to act in the name of God. The priesthood is open to all worthy males, twelve years of age or older. There are two divisions, the Melchizedek (the higher order) and the Aaronic (the lower order). Each is further divided into three subdivisions. Specific responsibilities and privileges come with each designation, and a man moves through the designations in order as he studies and carries out the duties of his present designation. Women are not priests. They share in the blessings that are conferred by the priesthood through their husbands. The primary organization for women in the Church is the Relief Society. Women are eligible to serve on the governing councils of the Church. Mormons believe that the pattern of organization that they have is the same as that found in the primitive church before it fell away from the true Church of Jesus Christ.

Restricting the priesthood to men is only one of the ways the Latter-day Saints emphasize the importance of traditional roles for women. Although married women are not expected to work outside the home, many Mormon women do so, either out of choice or economic necessity. The role of women as wives and mothers is very highly respected. What distresses some Mormon women and angers the more militant among them is that this is the only approved role. Stepping outside it frequently leads to disapproval. Women who do so may be made to feel that they are endangering their eternal life with God. Speaking out publicly on feminist issues has occasionally resulted in dismissal from the Church. Mormons have also joined Catholics and conservative Protestants in their support of antiabortion legislation.

Another unique feature of the Latter-day Saints is their **emphasis on missionary work**. The rapid growth of this community of faith can be attributed largely to this energetic program. Thousands of young men and women and retired couples accept missionary assignments for up to two years, normally serving at their own expense, often receiving financial assistance from family and friends. The main work of these missionaries is going from house to house seeking converts to their way of life.

Music is an important part of Latter-day Saints culture. The **Mormon Tabernacle Choir** is a 325-voice group that began in the mid-1800s. Its "Music and the Spoken Word" program has been carried by many radio stations since 1929, making it the longest-running religious broadcast in the U.S. The choir's recording of "The Battle Hymn of the Republic" won a Grammy Award. There are also a Mormon youth symphony and a chorus, with 100 and 350 members, respectively. They, too, perform regularly.

The Saints' Conference Center, on the beautifully landscaped grounds of Temple Square in Salt Lake City, seats 21,000 people and can translate speakers' remarks into 100-plus languages simultaneously. It also houses an extensive collection of Latter-day Saints artwork.

The two major branches of the Mormon church grew out of a disagreement about who should be Joseph Smith's successor. The **Church of Jesus Christ of Latter-day Saints** (LDS) began with those who thought that

Smith's successor should be a member of the Council of Twelve Apostles that advises the church president. This group chose Brigham Young as their leader. This branch is now based in Salt Lake City, Utah. The Reorganized Church of Jesus Christ of Latter Day Saints was founded by those who believed that Smith's successor should be his biological descendant. The RLDS changed their name to the **Community of Christ** in 2002. The two groups are bound together by their shared commitment to the Christian Old and New Testaments, the *Book of Mormon,* and the *Doctrine and Covenants* as revealed scripture and the prophethood of Smith. They differ on several points. The Community of Christ has a core of salaried local ministers. Both women and men have been ordained to both orders of the priesthood since 1984. Two women were recently appointed to the Council of Twelve Apostles, a governing group second only to the three-member First Presidency in the church hierarchy. There is no baptism nor marriage of the dead by proxy, although those who die without hearing the Mormon gospel are believed to have the opportunity to do so after death. The single Community of Christ temple in Independence, Missouri, "is a house of public worship, and entrance to the temple or participation in its ministries is open to all."[10] There are numerous smaller points of difference, as well.

These churches offer their members a stirring vision of how life can be. They provide firm guidelines for life and a set of ritual ordinances that members believe will lead to a greatly enhanced quality of life now and eternal life in the future, with the promise of becoming gods. They offer a strong community and a full program of activities with other like-minded persons. Their emphasis on the family and on traditional morality offer a clear-cut alternative to the problems many people see besetting modern society.

### CHRISTIAN SCIENTISTS

Christian Scientists (members of the Church of Christ, Scientist) maintain a low public profile. They do not seek converts by missionary activity, but they do maintain Christian Science **Reading Rooms** where people can go and read the Bible as well as Christian Science literature. Christian Science is directly linked to the experiences of **Mary Baker Eddy**, its founder. In 1866, Mrs. Eddy reported a nearly instantaneous cure from a severe back injury after reading the account of one of Jesus' healings (Matthew 9:1–8). Along with the Bible, Eddy's Science and Health with Key to the Scriptures (first published in 1875) is the source of Christian Science teaching.

Christian Scientists believe that all that God creates is good, because a good God would not create that which was not good. Therefore, the only reality that the evils of sin, sickness, and death have is that which we give them,

---

[10]Community of Christ, www.cofchrist.org.

when our erring human thought attributes to them a reality they do not have. Christian Scientists rely on the power of God for healing rather than on medical treatment, although this is always an individual choice. Reliance on Christian Science healing is a choice, just as relying on conventional medicine is a choice. A Christian Scientist who utilizes traditional medical care is not condemned or required to leave the church.[11] They are however, strongly discouraged from mixing the two types of care. Christian Science is based on the belief that the cause and the cure of illness are spiritual. Medicine looks at both cause and cure as primarily material. Trying to use these incompatible systems together could compromise the healing process.[12]

Christian Science practitioners are specially trained by the church to assist those who seek Christian Science healing through prayer, and Christian Science in-patient facilities can provide supportive care to the seriously ill while treatment is given. Healing by prayer is divinely natural, an integral part of the harmonious order of the created world as God means it to be. Christian Science is not limited to physical healing but extends to psychological, emotional, and other problems.

Christian Scientists describe **God as divine Principle**, **Love**, **Mind**, **Spirit**, **Soul**, **Life**, **and Truth**, which are the seven synonyms for God.[13] God is understood to be wholly spiritual and not personalized. God includes qualities associated with both genders, and there is a tradition of gender equality throughout the church's organization. There are no ordained ministers. Readers elected from the congregation serve for a period of three years, often without pay. It is preferred that one reader be female and the other male. Practitioners are more often female than male, and all church organizational offices are open to women.

The words *Christian* and *Science* in this church's name tell us something important about it. It is a church *focused on Jesus the Christ*. Christian Scientists believe people are saved through Jesus's atonement.

Christian Scientists also believe that theirs is a *scientific religion. Science* is used to describe this religion because

> . . . it can be demonstrated. We see God as the universal, divine Principle underlying the life and healing work of Christ Jesus. God by His very nature must be unchanging Truth, invariable Love, operating through timeless spiritual laws rather than special miraculous acts. To understand these laws of absolute good is to find that Christianity can be scientifically applied to every human ill.[14]

The church meets for Sunday services that consist largely of readings from the Bible and *Science and Health*. Most of what takes place is determined

---

[11]The First Church of Christ, Scientist, www.tfccs.com.
[12]The First Church of Christ, Scientist, www.tfccs.com.
[13]Mary Baker Eddy, *Science and Health with Key to the Scriptures* (Boston: The First Church of Christ, Scientist, 1906), p. 465.
[14]*Questions and Answers on Christian Science.* (Boston: The Christian Science Publishing Society, 1974), p. 2.

by the Mother Church in Boston and is the same in all Christian Science churches. There is also music—organ music, hymns, and perhaps a vocal solo. Wednesday midweek meetings include readings from the Bible and from *Science and Health* and provide an opportunity for members and visitors to give and hear testimonies of healing. The First Reader chooses the subject and passages for the Wednesday evening meeting. One writer describes the two services this way:

> The Sunday service at a Christian Science church mingles something of the bare simplicity of the New England church services that Mrs. Eddy knew as a girl with a touch of the Quaker quietism and the Unitarian rationalism with which she came in friendly contact later. The midweek meeting . . . is chiefly known for the spontaneous "testimonies of healing" given by members of the congregation.[15]

The Board of Lectureship is authorized to give public lectures explaining Christian Science and inviting further inquiry, but this is the extent of this group's missionary activity.

The Church of Christ, Scientist, has faced a number of challenges to its practices over the years. Currently, Christian Science healing is an accepted alternative to traditional medical treatment. Major insurance companies will usually reimburse those who receive Christian Science treatment. The Internal Revenue Service recognizes the cost of treatment as an income tax deduction, as it does medical fees. Christian Scientists do not claim that they have found the only way to God. They claim to have found a way that brings them peace and joy as well as physical healing, a way that they can recommend to others on that basis but that they do not ever attempt to force upon someone who is not interested.

Christian Science is also known to the public through its publication of the *Christian Science Monitor* newspaper, widely recognized as one of the best in the nation. There are also Monitor radio and television networks. A religious magazine, the *Herald of Christian Science*, is published in a dozen languages plus Braille. Religious periodicals and the *Monitor* are a part of the church's missionary activity.

## SEVENTH-DAY ADVENTISTS

The Seventh-day Adventists are by far the largest single church within the group of churches that make up the adventist believers, a family that also includes the Latter-day Saints and the Jehovah's Witnesses. Adventism emphasizes the Christian teaching, found especially in the biblical books of Daniel and Revelation, that the return of Christ to the world will be a literal, physical

---

[15]*Christian Science: A Sourcebook of Contemporary Materials* (Boston: The Christian Science Publishing Society, 1990), p. 51.

event. Most adventists believe that this will happen in the near future. Those who rebel against God will be destroyed, while true believers will be saved. The return of Christ is said to be the "grand climax of the gospel." The righteous, both living and dead, will be saved and taken into heaven, while the unrighteous will die. This will happen in fulfillment of prophecy, according to the Adventists. Since no one can know when this will occur, people must always be ready.[16]

Adventism began early in the nineteenth century. Soon the United States was the location where its tenets and practices were best defined. Like many other movements that eventually became separate organizations, most adventists had no intention of breaking off from the churches of which they were a part. They set out to be an emphasis within a church, not a separate body. The emphasis created conflict, however, and many did break away. Adventism is sometimes linked with holiness (see Chapter 5), as believers seek to be prepared on a daily basis for the return of Christ.

Most of the divisions within adventism occurred when people set dates for the second coming. These dates passed, and nothing happened. In the sharp disappointment that followed such events, differences of opinion led to separations. A second major point of disagreement concerned whether the Lord's Day or Sabbath was properly celebrated on Saturday or Sunday. This difference contributed to the formation of the Seventh-day Adventist Church.

Some adventists predicted that Christ would return on October 22, 1844. When this prediction proved incorrect (sometimes known as the Great Disappointment), some of the people whose hopes had been dashed began meeting together. Among them were **Ellen G. White** and her husband. Mrs. White began entering into trance states in which she claimed to receive revelations, and she was soon accepted as a prophet by the group. Among the group's keystones was the **celebration of the Sabbath on Saturday rather than Sunday**. Mrs. White also confirmed the correctness of the 1844 date but redefined what happened on that date. Christ had not returned to the earth on that date, as was originally predicted, but had initiated the cleansing of the true, heavenly sanctuary described in Hebrews 8:1–2. This interpretation of the King James version of the text restored the adventist hope, and the effects of the Great Disappointment were overcome.

Seventh-day Adventists continue to celebrate the Sabbath on Saturday. "Seventh-day" in the group's name refers to this practice. Sometimes people who keep a Saturday Sabbath are called **Sabbatarians**. As they read the Bible, Seventh-day Adventists find nothing to warrant changing the Sabbath from the way it was commanded to be observed in the Hebrew Scriptures (Christian Old Testament). Proper observance remains from sundown Friday to sunset on Saturday. It is to be a day of rest and religious pursuits.[17]

---

[16]Seventh-day Adventist Web site (www.adventist.org.).
[17]Seventh-day Adventist Web site (www.adventist.org.).

Seventh-day Adventists believe that they are the "remnant church," a people called out in the last days to be the true church. Ellen G. White's gift of prophecy is recognized as a mark of such a remnant. Most of the church has fallen away from the truth, but this small remnant has been given the gift of true prophecy through the work of Ellen White in order to preserve the gospel and announce the second coming of Christ. Her words are regarded as authoritative and a source of truth, with the Bible being the standard by which all human words are judged.[18]

Like the Latter-day Saints, Seventh-day Adventists are known for their support of sound health practices, because they believe that the body is the temple of the Holy Spirit. Good health practices are a religious obligation. They abstain from the use of alcohol and tobacco as well as illicit drugs, and they advocate healthy habits such as exercise and proper nutrition. They encourage a positive mental outlook. Many are vegetarians. Seventh-day Adventists concentrate much of their missionary work, both in the United States and overseas, on hospitals and other medical missions.

Men's and women's roles emphasize the traditional over the innovative. Both genders are encouraged to dress modestly and to manifest a "gentle and quiet spirit." Church and church-sponsored activities play a large role in most of their lives. Especially in some areas of the country, Seventh-day Adventist children may attend schools sponsored by their church.

## JEHOVAH'S WITNESSES

Many Americans have become acquainted with the Jehovah's Witnesses through their extensive program of **door-to-door evangelism**. All members are expected to participate in witnessing to people in this way. In addition, members may become Pioneers, full time preachers who donate at least ninety hours monthly, or special pioneers or missionaries who commit to spending 140 hours monthly evangelizing in remote locations with the intent to form new congregations.

The Witnesses believe that we are in a time of transition that precedes the reign of Christ on the Earth. Jesus predicted that there would be wars, disease, famine, and natural disasters, as well as false prophets and false religious, that would precede his return to earth. We now live in such a time, say the Witnesses, and the second coming of Christ is near.[19]

Although most of us know them best as Jehovah's Witnesses, their official name is the **Watchtower Bible and Tract Society**. The name Jehovah's Witnesses comes from Isaiah 43:12, which, in some translations, has God saying to the people that God is named Jehovah and they are God's witnesses. Jehovah's Witnesses do not consider themselves to be a church, but rather a

[18]Seventh-day Adventist Web site, www.adventist.org.
[19]Watchtower Bible and Tract Society, www.watchtower.org.

group of Bible students and publishers of God's Word. *Publishing* here has two meanings. They translate and publish Bibles and religious tracts, and they publish (in the sense of making public) their understanding of God's message for modern-day people by every means at their disposal.

The group was originally organized by Pastor Charles Taze Russell (1852–1916), who is thought of as an organizer and not the founder, because God alone is considered to be the founder. Unlike Joseph Smith and Ellen G. White, Russell disclaimed and condemned contemporary revelation, asserting that God's whole revelation was contained in the Bible. The Witnesses believe that theirs is the one true faith mentioned by Paul in Ephesians 4:5 (there is "one Lord, one faith, one baptism").

The group has never wavered from its focus on Bible study, and its teachings are supported by an elaborate system of references to scripture. When they meet, usually more than once a week, in Kingdom Halls (their meeting sites are not called churches), most of their time is spent in Bible study and discussion. They believe that the Bible was written by individuals who recorded God's message accurately. However, they hold that modern translations contain errors, and, in 1961, they published their own *New World Translation* of the Bible. Witnesses believe that their translation corrects the errors of earlier translations.

God is presently gathering the righteous together, in order to spare them from the disaster that will take place in the universal battle of Armageddon described in the book of Revelation in the Christian New Testament. This cataclysmic battle will inaugurate the reign of Jehovah God on the earth. The Witnesses understand themselves as the forerunners of this new kingdom.

Witnesses believe that only a limited number of people—the 144,000 mentioned in the Book of Revelation 7 and 10—will live and reign with God in Heaven. The rest of the righteous will live in peace and harmony on an earth that has been restored to a paradisal state. Those saved to live on a restored earth vastly outnumber those whose eternal life will be in heaven. The Kingdom of God will come both on earth and in heaven, and saved human beings will be responsible for caring for the earthly Kingdom. This is one of the Witnesses' most distinctive beliefs.[20]

Those who are gathered out are called to separate themselves from the world and form a **theocracy**, a community under the rule of God. To maintain this separation insofar as possible, the Witnesses avoid involvement in the political process by neither voting nor running for public office. They do not serve in the military. Technically, they are not pacifists; they claim that they would fight in God's war. They do not salute the flag nor sing the national anthem. They believe that to do so is to worship the nation and make an idol of it. Oaths of any sort are forbidden. In an extension of the Christian Old Testament prohibition against drinking blood, they do not accept blood transfusions. Jehovah's Witness children do not participate in school celebrations of

---

[20]Watchtower Bible and Tract Society, www.watchtower.org.

holidays such as Easter and Christmas, nor do their families celebrate these holidays. They also do not celebrate birthdays:

> Jesus never commanded Christians to celebrate his birth. Rather, he told his disciples to memorialize, or remember, his death. . . . Christmas and its customs come from ancient false religions. The same is true of Easter customs, such as the use of eggs and rabbits. The early Christians did not celebrate Christmas or Easter, nor do true Christians today. . . . The early Christians did not celebrate birthdays. The custom of celebrating birthdays comes from ancient false religions. True Christians give gifts and have good times together at other times during the year.[21]

Jehovah's Witnesses are particularly critical of what they regard as the three strongest allies of Satan in his plan to destroy the world. These three Satanic allies are the government, big business, and churches that teach false doctrines (i.e., all those except the Witnesses). They must be destroyed in the coming battle before God can recreate the world. Although their aggressive missionary tactics anger and put off many people, Witnesses have earned a reputation for being honest, courteous, and industrious. Their conservative lifestyle stresses traditional roles for men and women. However, women participate fully in the evangelistic efforts of this group, and many times children are taken along. By the time they are ten years old or so, many children are accomplished Witnesses.

### REFLECTION: COMMUNITY AND REASSURANCE

What is it that motivates the members of these communities of faith to live a life that distinguishes them sharply from the culture of which they are a part? To be sure, there are many reasons. Many followers of these ways of life live with a keen sense that the world is a wicked and evil place and that only by separating themselves from it can they have any hope of salvation. They take the idea of God's last judgment literally and seriously. Many believe firmly that the time is near when Christ will return to earth to judge all persons and make a final separation of the saved from the condemned. Therefore, it is necessary to be ready at all times. They believe that they have increasing evidence of the work of the Holy Spirit in their lives and in the lives of their associates, and this helps to assure them that they will indeed be among the saved when that time comes.

Others have other reasons. For many, becoming a Mormon means joy and community in this life and the assurance that important family ties will remain intact on the other side of death. Christian Science offers not only an alternative to traditional medical care but an alternative way of understanding

---

[21]Watchtower Bible and Tract Society, www.watchtower.org.

God and human nature. For many Scientists, their faith simply makes more sense out of their experience than do other alternatives.

These communities of faith offer their followers two very important things. They offer a strong sense of community that can be a refuge for those who are lonely and without other ties to the culture. It is a community of sharing among like-minded people whose goals and values are very similar. More important, many believe that they are called out of the world and into a small select community of faith. They believe that they are people who have heard and follow the message of the one true faith. The guidelines for life in this spiritual elite are clearly spelled out. The moral ambiguity that characterizes so much of contemporary society is absent.

Second, those who keep the faith and follow the guidelines are assured of salvation. Faith in justifying grace came as a great relief to Martin Luther, as it has to millions of other Protestants. It is nonetheless difficult to pin down. How does one know one is justified? How can one be absolutely certain of a place in heaven? These forms of Christianity emphasize true faith and an upright life. How to live an upright life is described in clear behavioral terms. This leads to a greater sense of security. Thus, these American-born religions offer their followers answers to some of the deepest and most pressing problems of human life, answers with fewer ambiguities and uncertainties than those proposed by the religions of their neighbors in the religious consensus.

### QUESTIONS AND ACTIVITIES FOR REVIEW, DISCUSSION, AND WRITING

1. Think about how you would feel if you were a part of a religion that set very different standards for you than those followed by your classmates. Don't make this exercise too simple by concentrating solely on being different. Remember that such religions also offer security and the assurance that one is on the right path.
2. Most Latter-day Saints are very willing to discuss their faith with non-Mormons, and Mormon churches welcome visitors eagerly. If possible, arrange to attend a service. You might also want to ask the missionaries to describe their experiences to you.
3. Visit a Christian Science Reading Room, and look over the literature. Report on what you find.
4. If you are not a member of one of the religions discussed in this chapter, write an essay about how your life would be different if you were a member. If you are a member, write about how your life would differ if you were not.
5. With a group, construct a chart that outlines the distinctive features of the communities of faith described in this chapter.
6. This chapter has touched on only the most central aspect of each of these groups. Visit the official Web site of each of these organizations to learn something that you did not learn from reading and discussing the chapter.

### FOR FURTHER READING

KEPHART, WILLIAM M., and WILLIAM W. ZELLNER, *Extraordinary Groups: The Sociology of Unconventional Lifestyles*, 7th ed. Belmont, CA: Wadsworth Press, 2000. This book has chapters on several major alternative communities of faith. Kephart and Zellner's book is written from an objective, sociological point of view, yet it reads almost like a novel. Fascinating and very accessible.

KNOTT, RONALD ALAN., *College Faith: 150 Adventist Leaders Share Faith Stories from Their College Days*. Nampa, Idaho: Pacific Press Pub. Assn., 1995. Valuable because it shows how non-mainstream faith plays out among college students.

MAUSS, ARMAND L., *The Angel and the Beehive: The Mormon Struggle with Assimilation*. Champaign, IL: University of Illinois Press, 1994. Mauss analyzes the last forty years of Mormon history to focus on their transition from "outsider" status in the United states and their struggle with the resulting loss of distinctiveness.

PENTON, JAMES M., *Apocalypse Delayed: The Story of Jehovah's Witnesses*. Toronto: University of Toronto Press, 1998. Penton grew up a Witness, became a professional historian, and was later disfellowshiped from the church. He offers a critical but not polemic view that nicely blends personal insight with professional distance.

SHIPPS, JAN, *Sojourner in the Promised Land: Forty Years Among the Mormons*. Champaign, IL: University of Illinois Press, 2000. Jan Shipps is without doubt the most highly regarded non-Mormon scholar of the LDS tradition. In this collection of essays, she explores the Mormon experience from the perspective of an "insider-outsider."

WILLIAMS, JEAN KINNEY, *The Christian Scientists (The American Religious Experience)*. Danbury, CT: Franklin Watts, 1997. Williams includes history, beliefs, and practices, plus a review of Mary Baker Eddy's work, changes in belief and practice, and their location in American culture.

### RELEVANT WORLD WIDE WEB SITES

Latter-day Saints: www.lds.org

Community of Christ: www.cofchrist.org

Christian Science: www.tfccs.com

On line edition of the *Christian Science Monitor*: www.csmonitor.com

Seventh-day Adventists: www.adventist.org

Jehovah's Witnesses: www.watchtower.org

# LIVING A JEWISH LIFE
# IN THE UNITED STATES

Are you aware of any stereotypes about Jewish people? Many of us grow up with such stereotypes. What might cause people to believe them?

## WHO IS A JEW?
### American Jewish Voices[1]

*Dr. Ruth Westheimer*, the grandmotherly and outspoken sex educator, looks into her grandchildren's faces and knows that Hitler did everything he could to prevent their generation of Jews from ever being born. There is, she says, a lesson for the world in the Jewish experience. Despite having been the victims of unspeakable horror, they held fast to their conviction that their mission was to help repair the world by responding to hatred with a commitment to justice, peace, and the repair of the world.

One of the blessings used in the synagogue in which *Leonard Nimoy* grew up was to divide the four fingers of one's hand into a "V," which created the Hebrew letter shin, symbolizing Shah-dai, one of the names of God. "When we were creating the television program *Star Trek*," Nimoy says, "we needed a salute. I thought back to that hand symbol and proposed it. The rest, as they say, is history."

### Who Is A Jew? An American Jew?

To a greater extent than any other religion in the United States, the term *Judaism* encompasses many different things, not all of them religious. Different aspects vary in their importance to individual Jews. One can, of course, be a Jew *religiously*. In this sense, which will be the primary one for our purposes,

[1]From the American Jewish Committee Web site, www.ajc.org/JewishLife/BeingJewish.asp.

a "Jew is one who seeks a spiritual base in the modern world by living the life of study, prayer, and daily routine dedicated to the proposition that Jewish wisdom through the ages will answer the big questions in life—questions like Why do people suffer? What is life's purpose? Is there a God?"[2]

The Jewish faith has given rise to literature, music, foods, folkways, and a rich and complex cultural heritage. To be a Jew *culturally* is to identify with this cultural heritage of Judaism with or without claiming formal religious affiliation.

Judaism can also be *ethnicity*, people who have biological ties to Israel. Ethnicity and religion have in the past been closely tied together. Jewish ethnicity meant Jewish religion. Not all Jews share this ethnic link, because Judaism accepts Gentiles who want to convert to Judaism. About 10,000 Gentiles annually become "Jews by choice," which is the preferred term for those who choose Judaism rather than being born into the faith.[3] Once a person becomes a Jew, no distinction is made between Jews who are born Jewish and those who are not. In a sense, "all Jews are Jews by choice today, since even born Jews have to make the conscious decision that they will remain Jewish, rather than join another religion or become nothing in particular."[4]

Jews are not a race, because there are Jews of many races. Nor are they a nation, although early in their history they were identified with the nation of Israel.

Jews immigrated to the United States from many different Jewish cultures in Europe. This led to wide variations in Jewish practice and culture within the United States. This set the stage for the development of the varied styles of Judaism that have remained important into the present.

Today, Jews continue to lead the nation in education, professionalization, and income and are a noteworthy presence in politics and culture. Most American Jews live in major cities, and in the suburbs associated with them. Except for beliefs and practices specific to their religion, they are very much like their Gentile (non-Jewish) counterparts.

Studies of the Jewish population indicate that their number in the United States is decreasing, and the predictions are that this decline will continue. This is the result of three factors: There are few new Jewish immigrants, their birth rate is very low (less than two children per couple, so the previous generation is not being replaced), and their rate of intermarriage is quite high, with the result that fewer children are being raised Jewish.

One recent study notes that Jews in this country struggle to define what it means to be Jewish.[5] Synagogues must define who is a Jew as they decide whom to admit to membership. If their admission policy is very open, they must then decide who is eligible to read Torah in worship or to serve the congregation as an officer. Is the child of one Jewish and one Gentile parent

[2]Rabbi Morris N. Kertzer (revised by Rabbi Lawrence A. Hoffman), *What Is a Jew? New and Completely Revised Edition* (New York: Macmillan Publishing Company, 1993), p. 7.

[3]David C. Gross, *1,201 Questions and Answers about Judaism* (New York: Hippocrene Books, 1992), p. 277.

[4]Rabbi Morris N. Kertzer (revised by Rabbi Lawrence A. Hoffman), *What Is a Jew*, p. 8.

[5]Marc Lee Raphael, *Judaism in America, The Columbia Contemporary American Religion Series* (Irvington, NY: Columbia University Press, 2003), p. 2.

**Figure 9-1**    *The Magen David* (Star of David): The origin of the Star of David is lost in the mists of early history. It appears on synagogues as early as the second or third century C.E. In the early fourteenth century, it was used as a protective amulet or magical symbol. Apparently, it came into widespread usage as a symbol of Judaism (in the nineteenth century) because there was a desire to have a sign that would symbolize Judaism in the same way that the cross symbolizes Christianity.

Jewish? Questions like these bring up the issue of boundaries. In the face of declining numbers, it may be tempting to draw the boundaries very widely. This, however, raises the possibility of the loss of distinctive identity. American Jews are challenged by the need to find their way between clear identity and inclusiveness.

This is complicated by another factor. "No more than half the Jews in the United States consider themselves 'religious,' and less than half the Jews in American are affiliated with a synagogue."[6] Because Judaism comprises much more than the Judaic religion, many persons who consider themselves Jewish do not participate in the institutional dimensions of the religion of Judaism:

> [Some] Jews affirm their Jewishness but not Judaism. They do not consider themselves Judaic. Born of Jewish parents and thus (even if only the mother is Jewish) considered Jewish according to those who observe Jewish law, they have abandoned anything connected to the synagogue or to religious ceremonies, customs, observances and rituals.[7]

### JEWS AND CHRISTIANS

As many of you know already, Christianity began as a small sect within Judaism, as a variation on the teaching and practice of that ancient religion. The two share a common history, up to a point, and a common geography.

---

[6]Marc Lee Raphael, *Judaism in America*, p. 3.
[7]Marc Lee Raphael, *Judaism in America*, p. 10.

The cultural conditions out of which Christianity was born were those of the Judaism of its time. It is not surprising, therefore, that Jewish and Christian members of the religious consensus have many things in common.

To begin with, they have some of the Scriptures in common. The Jewish Bible[8] and the Christian Old Testament are nearly the same in content, although the books are not in the same order. The history that is recounted and the religious teachings that are contained in both are quite similar. In most Christian churches today, the Christian Old Testament is used for one of the regular Bible readings during worship.

These common scriptures tell of one God who commands that people worship no other gods. Judaism originated in an area in which it was most common for people to worship many gods and goddesses. The Jewish, and later the Christian, view held that there was but one God. This God is believed to be the creator of all that was, is, or ever will be. God is righteous and holy and acts in a just, upright, moral manner. God is personal; it is appropriate to talk of God's will, wrath, love, mercy, and judgment. God hears and responds to peoples' prayers, according to both Judaism and Christianity. Above all, God's character and will for people are shown to them by God's self-revelation.

History is important, because it is believed to be the record of God's continuing involvement with people. God is intimately involved in history, primarily through *covenants* with people. There are covenants with Noah and with Abraham, for example, described in Tanakh, and Jesus is referred to in the Christian New Testament as the bearer of a new covenant. These covenants define a people by their relationship with God. Judaism teaches that Israel was called into being as a people by God. Christianity teaches that the entire church is the Body of Christ, called into being by God.

The people who live in covenant with God are to live holy and righteous lives. Their special relationship with God is to be embodied in all that they do. The well-known Ten Commandments are revered in both Judaism and Christianity. Some of these commandments deal with people's actions with respect to God: having no other gods, keeping the Sabbath day holy, and not taking God's name in vain. Others have to do with relations between persons and groups of people: not murdering or stealing, not lying, and not wanting what is not one's own, for example. In both Judaism and Christianity, the way people relate with God and the way they relate with each other cannot be separated.

Both Jews and Christians emphasize the importance of personal and congregational worship. Worship in each community of faith is both individual and corporate. Individual worship usually takes the form of prayer and devotional reading. Corporate worship provides time for the entire community of faith to focus on God. Prayers are said and praises given. Instruction is given to the faithful in a sermon. It is usually based on one or more readings

---

[8]The preferred name among Jews themselves for the Jewish scriptures is **Tanakh**, an acronym for the Hebrew names of its three major divisions: the Law (*Torah*), the Prophets (*Nevi'im*), and the Writings (*Ketubim*).

from the Bible. The importance placed on history creates many holidays and festivals that recall and celebrate God's actions. Corporate worship also includes rites of passage. These are religious ceremonies that mark transitions from one stage of human life to another. Both faiths mark birth, coming of age, marriage, and death, for example.

There are many smaller points of agreement that could be discussed. These major points, however, clearly demonstrate that these two major religions found in the United States—Judaism and Christianity—have a great deal in common. Their common heritage and devotion to the same God means that they are neighbors and not strangers.

## PRINCIPAL BELIEFS AND PRACTICES OF JEWISH PEOPLE

Judaism in the United States has many variations in belief and practice. However, there are certain features that nearly all Jews share, in one way or another. Interpretations vary, but the basics are the same. Lists of what these basics are will be different from one author to another; what is included here is a minimal listing of fundamental points.

It should first be said that Judaism is primarily a religion of action; characteristically, it has emphasized proper *obedience* to the God of the covenant over proper beliefs *about* God. Samuel Belkin, President of Yeshiva University, the principal Orthodox Jewish educational institution in the United States, notes that "attempts . . . to formulate a coherent and systematic approach to Jewish theology" have not succeeded. Judaism is much more concerned with religious practice than it is with correct doctrine. Correct religious living takes precedence over doctrinally correct religious thinking.[9] Nevertheless, there are beliefs that can be identified as core in the Jewish way of thinking. Jewish theological thinking does not vary as much by Jewish subgroup as it does broadly between a traditional and a nontraditional interpretation. The discussion of beliefs below follows this distinction as delineated by Marc Lee Raphael.[10]

### Beliefs

There are both similarities and differences between the Jewish and Christian Bibles. The Hebrew Bible is very similar to the Old Testament in the Christian Bible, containing the same books, although in a different order. However, it is inappropriate to refer to the Hebrew Bible as the "Old Testament." That collection of writings is called the Old Testament by Christians because, for them, the New Testament is a part of the Bible. The Christian New Testament is not a part of the Jewish Bible. It has no authority and does not contain the revelation of

---

[9]Samuel Belkin, *In His Image* (New York: Abelard-Schuman, 1960), pp. 15–16.
[10]Marc Lee Raphael, *Judaism in America*, Chapter 2.

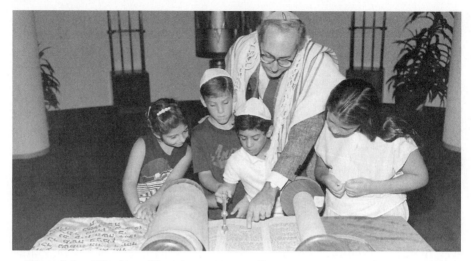

**Figure 9-2** A Torah scroll is an important part of any synagogue or temple. *(Bill Aron/Photo Researchers, Inc.)*

the God of Abraham, Isaac, and Jacob. To refer to the Torah as the "Old Testament" is offensive to persons of Jewish faith, for whom the revelation of God recorded in the Hebrew Bible can never be superseded by another revelation such as Christians believe is contained in their New Testament. The word **Tanakh** is often used for the Hebrew Bible. Tanakh is an acronym taken from the Hebrew first letters of its three divisions.

The first five books of the Bible—Genesis, Exodus, Leviticus, Numbers, and Deuteronomy—are considered by Jews to be the most important (Figure 9–2). These five books, which for Jews are the core of God's revelation, are believed by some Jews to have been revealed to Moses and are known as the **five Books of Moses**. They are also known as the **Pentateuch**, a Greek word that means "five books."

After the five Books of Moses are the Books of the Prophets. The rest of Tanakh is made up of the Writings and includes such well-known books as Psalms, Proverbs, Job, and Ecclesiastes, along with several others. In addition to the Tanakh itself, there is the **Talmud**, which is the written record of several centuries of discussion, interpretation, and commentary on Torah by the earliest rabbis, who were primarily scholars and teachers of Torah.

The cornerstone of the Torah is the **commandments** that Jews believe God gave to Moses at Mount Sinai. They are found in the Book of the Exodus, Chapter 20 (paraphrased in Figure 9–3). The core commandments can be divided into two groups: The first four deal with how one ought to relate to God, and the latter six with how one is to relate with other persons. These commandments are the heart of the Torah and of Jewish life and living.

Jews are *monotheists*—persons who believe in one God, as are Christians and Muslims. This central point is learned by Jewish children early in life and

**Figure 9-3**

---

### THE TEN COMMANDMENTS

1. You shall not worship any other gods.
2. Do not make images of God.
3. Do not take God's holy name in vain.
4. Remember to keep the Sabbath holy; in particular, you are not to work on this day.
5. Honor your parents.
6. Do not murder.
7. Do not commit adultery.
8. Do not steal.
9. Do not bear false witness against anyone.
10. Do not covet [i.e., be envious of] that which is your neighbor's.

---

repeated daily by many Jews as the **Shema**: "Hear, O Israel! The Lord is our God, the Lord alone" (Deuteronomy 6:4, Tanakh). The passage goes on to prescribe that this God is to be loved with one's entire self, holding nothing back. Monotheism has been a part of Judaism from its beginning.

In his recent study of American Judaism, Marc Lee Raphael notes that American Jews can be divided into two very broad categories, those who are traditional and those who are better described as nontraditional. These distinctions cut across, rather than correlate with the various Jewish denominations in the United States. Many Jews embrace elements of both.[11]

Traditional Jews hold to the attributes of God derived from Tanakh: omniscience, goodness, eternality, creatorship of the earth and of human beings, omnipotence. Those who are not traditional typically affirm belief in God, but leave it up to the individual to ascertain the characteristics of God. In particular, since the Holocaust, many modify the traditional pairing of God's omnipotence and all-goodness.

While traditionalists hold that the most important thing about Tanakh is that God revealed it, nontraditionalists have as their most basic characteristic a radical reinterpretation of the origin of their scriptures. Rather than a single event in which God revealed the Tanakh, nontraditionalists see revelation as the record of the ongoing process of human beings discovering the Holy.

Traditionalists take the concept of the Jews as God's "chosen people" to refer to the special responsibility placed on the Jews as the elected servants of the Almighty. Their less traditional counterparts are more likely to interpret it in nonliteral ways, more focused on Israel's choosing of God.

In worship, traditionalists use the full liturgy with little or no modification, while nontraditionalists feel free to modify and change it. As a result, there are widespread variations in worship among nontraditional Jews.

---

[11]Marc Lee Raphael, *Judaism in America*, pp. 17–27.

Traditional Jews retain the Jewish belief in the coming of a Messiah, an individual person who will lead Israel and the world into a time of peace and prosperity and will restore the monarchy of the House of David. Those who are less traditional shift their focus from the coming of the Messiah to the attainment of a messianic age by human effort in cooperation with God.

Traditional Jews struggle with the problem of evil in the world in the face of their belief in an all-powerful and all-good God. Nontraditionalists usually reject the ideas of God's omniscience, omnipotence, and unqualified goodness. The God of nontraditional Jews is often a God who is limited in some ways, not a God who is in complete control of the world.

Because the Jews are ever watchful to guard the uniqueness of God, they will not represent God in any material form; to do so would be to make an idol. Nor is there any way, in the Jewish understanding of God, that any human being could ever be God. This is one reason that people of Jewish faith do not accept the Christian teaching that Jesus is the Messiah whose coming is foretold in Isaiah. The idea of a person who is at once divine and human is utterly repugnant to Jewish sensibility. We must remember that the link between the verses in Isaiah that speak of the coming of the Messiah and the person Jesus is found in the Christian New Testament and is not a part of Hebrew scripture. The Messiah as understood by those of Jewish faith will be a leader who will bring freedom and restoration to the entire people of Israel in more political than individual terms. Jesus as described by the early Christian church—the savior of individual persons from sin and separation from God—is a different sort of savior than that expected in Judaism. According to most Jews, Jesus was a religious leader and teacher, perhaps a prophet, but not God.

Jews do not believe that God became human, nor that God had a son. They do not regard Jesus as a savior. These central Christian teachings are simply not a part of Judaism. The continued presence of suffering in the world leads Jews to believe that the Messiah has not yet come.[12]

The character of God has definite implications for how people treat each other. God is a just, loving, holy, and righteous God, according to the Hebrew Bible, and God's people must reflect these qualities in their lives and in their dealings with others. People's actions with other people must be characterized by an attitude reflective of God's own nature. Under the terms of the covenant, people are responsible to and for one another. One's fellow human being is God's son or daughter and hence is one's brother or sister. Righteousness, love, and tolerance must be the rule, not only among Jews but with all persons. It extends to strangers, servants, and animals. Special concern is to be given to the less fortunate, such as widows, orphans, the poor, and the ill. Fair treatment is to be given even to one's enemies.

Jews are united in their understanding of themselves as a people. In spite of being scattered around the world, and, in spite of speaking many languages and following different practices and beliefs, **the people of Israel are**

---

[12]Rabbi Morris N. Kertzer (revised by Rabbi Lawrence A. Hoffman), *What Is a Jew*, pp. 275–276.

**one people**. They are linked by the love they have for each other, by their common tradition and history, and by their shared past and present experience.

The unity of the Jewish people takes on concrete form in widespread support for the state of Israel. Since the destruction of the Temple in Jerusalem in 70 C.E., the Jews have been a wandering people. But they have maintained the conviction of belonging to the land into which the Bible records they wandered under God's leading. For centuries, Jews have prayed for the restoration and rebuilding of Jerusalem. "Next year in Jerusalem!" is spoken at the end of the Seder meal every Passover. Land and covenant are linked; the people of the covenant are the people of the land. This linking of land and people took political form in the Zionist movement. The founding of the state of Israel in 1948 is numbered among the most significant events of Jewish history.

### Practices

What can we say about Jewish lifestyles? Especially in the United States, Jews' lifestyles vary as much as do those of their non-Jewish neighbors. Overall, survey data tell us two factors that are important in understanding what it means to be a person of Jewish faith in modern day America. Of all the religious preference groups, Jews lead the nation in both education and income. Judaism has always fostered a love of learning, and Jews believe that there is no conflict between faith and reason. The second outstanding feature of the American Jewish population is that, across the board, Jews are more tolerant and broad-minded about moral issues, civil liberties, and nonbelievers than are their Christian neighbors. Yet another general feature than can be mentioned is the extensive involvement of Jews in social reform and assistance programs and in occupations such as social work and professional psychology and psychiatry. Their belief in God's covenant with them and their responsibility for their neighbors translates into vocational terms, for both religious and nonreligious Jews.

**Judaism in its traditional form has a very rich ritual life**. A set of rituals pace individual Jews through their lifetimes, and another set paces the community through its collective life. Differences in observance abound, but Judaism is united by these individual and collective religious practices. They are the people whose life, both corporate and private, is demarcated by these ritual observances. Here, I will note the principal ones.

I will first turn to those rituals that pace the individual through the life cycle. The circumcision of male babies and the Bar or Bat Mitzvah are two of the best-known. As is the case with every religion, birth is the first step of the life cycle to be ritually marked. After the birth of a girl, it is the father's responsibility and honor to read the Torah at the next synagogue service. He recites the usual benedictions before and after reading and officially announces his daughter's name. For a boy, it is more elaborate; **circumcision** is a major

Jewish ceremony. Although other peoples circumcise infant boys, Judaism understands this as a visible sign of the covenant between Abraham and God, made again in each generation (Genesis 17:9–14). It takes place on the eighth day after birth. The ceremony involves both religious and surgical elements and may be performed by a physician or by a specially trained *Mohel* who has both the necessary surgical and religious knowledge. A festive meal follows.

The next life-cycle rite in the life of a Jewish youngster is the **Bar Mitzvah**. Some Jews, although not all, celebrate the **Bat Mitzvah** for girls also. The words mean "son (daughter) of the commandment" and mark the religious coming of age of the child. The child is then considered to be an adult, responsible for observing the commandments and able to fill adult roles in the congregation, although the ceremony traditionally occurs on the Sabbath following the child's thirteenth birthday. The highlight of Jewish life for many, it is preceded by intensive study. The young person is called up to read Torah before the congregation for the first time. This is a great honor. The young person may also make a speech in which parents and teachers are thanked. Especially in the United States, this ceremony has grown in importance and is frequently the occasion for a lavish party with family and friends to recognize the person's new status. In some congregations that practice the Bat Mitzvah, the ceremony parallels that for boys, while other congregations have developed distinctive practices for it.

Some Jewish congregations have an additional ceremony of **confirmation** at about age fifteen or sixteen. Although originally intended as a replacement for the Bar or Bat Mitzvah, it is now a separate ceremony for Reform and Conservative Jews, in which the now somewhat older youths reaffirm their intention to live as Jews in the household of Israel.

Marriage is the next life-cycle ritual in the lives of most Jewish women and men. Judaism places a very high value on marriage and family, and celebrating the beginning of a new family unit in marriage is very important. The **Ketubah**, or marriage contract, which spells out the responsibilities of both spouses, is signed during the ceremony. It is a legally valid document as well as a religious one. The wedding ceremony itself is complex and reflects the sacred nature of marriage and family life. A celebration with family and friends follows. Although divorce is permitted by Jewish law, it is strongly discouraged. In practice, actual divorce statistics among Reform Jews differ little from those among their gentile neighbors; for Conservative and, especially, Orthodox Jews, the rate is somewhat lower. To be recognized as valid among traditional Jews, there must be a religious divorce as well as a legal one.

At the end of life, many Jews follow distinctive customs associated with death and burial. Jews differ in the extent to which they follow tradition, but certain customs are very common. The body is carefully washed in preparation for burial, with men washing men and women, women. Specific prayers accompany this sacred act. People are buried in a simple white shroud symbolizing the equality of all before God. Men are buried with their prayer shawls. Fancy caskets are not used; a simple wooden box suffices. The body is typically guarded by a family member, a member of a sacred burial society, or someone else, from the moment of death until burial. The person watching over the deceased recites Psalms during this time.[13] Jews believe that burial as quickly as possible is most respectful of the deceased, and a "viewing" is not held. Both cremation and embalming are forbidden by Jewish law as disrespectful of the body.

Jews tend to focus more on life in the here and now, leaving what happens afterward in the hands of God. However, one common belief is that all Jews have a place in the **World to Come**. However, this will not be the same for each person. The World to Come can be compared with a theater. Each soul has a reserved seat in that theater. But, as in earthly theaters, some seats are better than others. Some are on the main floor, and some in the balcony. Some have a clear view of center stage, while others may need to peer around obstructions. The moral choices made during life determine the seat.[14]

Jewish mourning customs are carefully structured in three stages that facilitate the grieving process and then encourage the mourner's return to the fulness of life. The first stage is a seven-day period of intense mourning and seclusion from public life. This is observed only by those who have lost a parent, spouse, sibling, or child. Ideally it is observed in the home of the deceased and all the mourners' needs are cared for by others. Thus, mourners do not have to put on a "public face," but may focus entirely on the needs of grieving. The second stage lasts for thirty days after the death and includes the first stage if observed. It is a time when people are still mourning but begin to return to normal life. Official mourning ends after this time except for the death of a parent. Mourning for the death of a parent lasts a full year after the death, including the first two stages. The longer time reflects a parent's formative influence on our lives.

As well as marking the stages in the individual's life with celebration and consolation, Judaism hallows time through a yearly cycle. This cycle lifts time out of the realm of a merely mechanical tracking of days and hours and uses it to keep history and tradition alive in the present.

The **Sabbath** is a high point in every week. In line with the accounts of creation in Genesis, the Jewish Sabbath is observed from sundown on Friday until nightfall on Saturday. The Sabbath is considered one sign of the covenant between God and Israel. God is said to have rested after the creation, and people, too, are to devote one day per week to rest. The Sabbath meal is prepared in advance. The Sabbath begins when the mother lights special Sabbath candles and recites the appointed blessings. There may be a synagogue service to welcome the Sabbath. The following morning, the family may attend the synagogue together, although in some congregations it is customary for the women to remain at home with the children.

---

[13]Plaza Jewish Community Chapel Web site, www.plazajewishcommunitychapel.org.
[14]Jewish Literacy Web site, www.aish.com/literacy.

A quiet day follows. Perhaps the best-known feature of the Jewish Sabbath is that any kind of work is strictly forbidden. To understand what it means to "keep the Sabbath," however, we must see beyond the prohibition of work. The Sabbath is intended as a way of separating oneself from the cares and toils of everyday living to make time for what is truly important. It is a time to be with one's God, with one's family, and with oneself, and, for that to be possible in our busy world, a special effort must be made to make it so. Torah study is an important part of what may be done on the Sabbath. Prayer and meditation are encouraged. Taking moderate walks with the family, doing quiet family things together, and visiting friends who live close by are often done.

Like the individual life, the year is marked throughout with festivals and days of great significance. I describe some of the more important festivals, although there are many others as well. Although each of the festivals leads naturally into the one that follows it, the most reasonable place to begin is where the Jewish religious calendar (which differs from the one we use to follow secular time) itself begins, with the Jewish New Year.

**Rosh Hashanah** (literally, the "head of the year") takes place in early autumn (September or October). Preparation for it begins the month before, which is used as a time of contemplation and spiritual self-searching. The Jewish New Year is not a time of partying and rowdiness, as the secular New Year often is. Rather, it is a time for looking back over the past year, for reflecting on deeds done and left undone. Judaism emphasizes human beings' free choice in whether we will do good or evil and our responsibility for that choice. With responsibility comes accountability, and God is known as the judge of human actions. It is this sense of judgment that pervades the Jewish New Year and the period that follows it. The oldest and probably best-known of the rituals connected with this festival is the sounding of the **shofar**, an instrument made from the horn of a ram, which makes a sound some have likened to the wailing of the heart of the human race.

Rosh Hashanah is the beginning of a time of intense reflection. Taking stock of one's life and behavior over the preceding year is accompanied by the resolve to do better. Two types of sin must be dealt with: those against God and those against other people. People can be forgiven for those against God by the rituals of **Yom Kippur**, the Day of Atonement, which follows the days of penitence. For those sins in which one has wronged another person as well, forgiveness must be sought not only from God but from the person wronged, and one must seek to make amends if at all possible. There is no savior in Judaism except God, and no mediator between God and people. Jews stand before God as individuals and as members of the household of Israel with their prayers for forgiveness and their resolve to live a better life. Given these factors, Judaism teaches, God will forgive the sincere penitent. The entire day of Yom Kippur is spent in fasting, prayer, and contemplation. Thus cleansed of previous sin and strengthened to live the Torah more fully, the Jew begins another year.

**Figure 9-4**   The Hanukkah Menorah

The next holiday is one that has come to be celebrated much more in the United States than it is elsewhere: **Hanukkah**, the Festival of Lights. It comes in November or December, and the increased emphasis it has received in the United States has come about in part because it is close to the time that the Christian majority and the culture in general celebrate Christmas. The word *Hanukkah* means "rededication" and refers to the rededication of the Temple after the Maccabean revolutionaries successfully recaptured it from the Greco-Syrians in approximately 160 B.C.E. Legend has it that only enough oil could be found to keep the Temple lamp burning for one day. Miraculously, the oil lasted for eight days, the time required to prepare and consecrate new oil. Thus, the Hanukkah candle holder, or **menorah**, has eight branches plus a ninth that holds the lighting candle, whereas the regular menorah holds seven candles (Figure 9–4). Another candle is lit every night of the eight-day celebration. There is another very beautiful Hanukkah story that the rabbis tell. When the Maccabees entered the Temple, they found that the menorah was not usable, having been destroyed by the raiding pagans. The Maccabees took their spears and used them to make a new menorah, turning the weapons of war into a symbol of peace.[15]

The Jewish holiday that gentiles probably know best is **Passover**, which comes in the spring. It has both associations remaining from the early times when the Israelites were an agricultural people and the historical significance

---

[15]Leo Trepp, *Judaism: Development and Life*, 3rd ed. (Belmont, CA: Wadsworth Publishing Company, 1982), p. 303.

that was given to it later. It exemplifies the way that religious rituals keep the important stories of the faith alive and assist in transmitting them to each new generation. As an agricultural festival, it recalls the spring harvest. Its primary significance is now the historical one, however, in that it commemorates the exodus of the Hebrews out of slavery in Egypt. This is one of the two foundational events of Jewish history. It is sometimes called the Feast of Unleavened Bread, and **matzoh**, a crackerlike bread, is eaten. Unleavened bread is eaten because the hurried flight of the Hebrews left no time for bread to rise (Exodus 12:37–39, 13:3, 6–8, Deuteronomy 16:1–4). The name Passover comes from the biblical promise that the angel of death would pass over those houses marked on the doorpost with the blood of a sacrificial lamb (Exodus 12:12–14). The central ritual of Passover is the **Seder** meal, in which the story of the Exodus is retold. Special foods are eaten that help to bring the story alive. This ritual involves everyone present and uses virtually all the human senses, mixing food, fun, and serious intention to serve as an outstanding educational and community-reinforcing tool. Jews who must be away from home at this special time may count on being taken into the home of another Jewish family wherever they may be for the Seder.

Following Passover is another ritual calling to mind a founding event. The **Feast of Weeks (Shavuot)** has roots as a harvest festival, but its contemporary meaning is as a celebration of the giving of the Ten Commandments to Moses on Mount Sinai. Thus, the two interwoven themes of Jewish life, God-given freedom from slavery and the giving of the Torah, are celebrated and remembered. Either one without the other is incomplete and does not do justice to the fullness of Jewish understanding.

**Yom Ha Shoah** is a Jewish observance of more recent origin. It is also called Holocaust Remembrance Day and takes place in the spring. The activities on this solemn day focus on two things: It is a time to remember those people—both Jewish and Gentile—who died in the Holocaust, and is also a time for rededication to the principle that such a thing can never be allowed to happen again. In many communities, Jews and Christians sponsor joint Yom Ha Shoah observances.

## JEWISH WOMEN

According to Tanakh, it was God's intention that men and women be equal. In the first account of creation, both are created in God's image. Woman is created from man in the second account, not as his subordinate but as one who is capable of fulfilling him. When Adam and Eve together violated God's commandments, however, their equality and mutuality was lost.[16] The Jewish

---

[16]William A. Young, *The World's Religions: Worldviews and Contemporary Issues* (Englewood Cliffs, NJ: Prentice Hall, 1995), p. 296.

tradition is characterized by a dialectical view of women. They are equal to men in essence, yet derivative in power and position.

The current status of women in Judaism, like women's status in Christianity, is complex. Women's roles and status have changed dramatically in the twentieth century. Jewish women have responded to these changes in the same ways that Christian women have. Some have left Judaism as they have come to feel that the changes did not occur fast enough or go far enough. Some have remained within their synagogues to work for change. And some have chosen to fight against changes that threaten to make their familiar traditions less meaningful to them.

As you might expect, women's roles in Orthodox Judaism have changed the least. Even here, however, the situation is complex. On the one hand, Orthodox women's roles center on home and family, and the role of wife and mother is highly respected. Women are required to perform three religious duties. One is to visit the ritual bath after her menstrual period. The other two, baking the Sabbath bread, or **challah**, and lighting the candles that officially begin the Sabbath observance are among the most important rituals in Judaism. Children are very important in Judaism and especially so in Orthodoxy. Women's role as the bearers and nurturers of children earn them great honor.

Women also play the central role in maintaining a kosher home. Following all the kosher observances is complicated and time consuming. It is also considered one of the most important Orthodox observances because it serves to set the Orthodox apart from other people and reminds them on a daily basis of their life as the covenant people. The contribution of the wife and mother in the family is indispensable.

On the other hand, women cannot be ordained as Orthodox rabbis, nor can they serve as cantors.[17] Nonetheless, they can and do teach in Orthodox Jewish schools. Groups for women's study of both Tanakh and Talmud have increased rapidly. Women may lead prayer services for women's groups, services that differ little from those for men.

The principle used by modern Orthodox Jews to decide what can and cannot be done illustrates well the difference between their approach and that of the more "modernized" branches. Motivation is central, and the entire body of Jewish law—Halakah—is the ultimate authority. Liberalization of women's roles cannot be justified on the basis of appeal to feminist ideology or modern culture. As one Jewish author notes:

> We are committed to the basic halakhic structure of distinctiveness of obligation. . . . This may go against the contemporary sensibility that regards . . . egalitarianism as a fundamental religious value; but it is a cornerstone of halakhic reasoning.[18]

---

[17]Cantors assist the rabbi by chanting some of the prayers.

[18]Joel B. Wolowelsky, *Women, Jewish Law and Modernity: New Opportunities in a Post-Feminist Age* (Hoboken, NJ: KTAV Publishing House, 1997), pp. 15–16.

On the other hand, no exclusion can be justified if inclusion is appropriate in light of Halakah. If the motivation is religious growth, and it increasingly is, then inclusion, within the bounds of Halakah, should be the norm.

There is also in Orthodoxy the phenomenon of the newly Orthodox Jewish woman, the *ba'alat teshuvah*, women who have returned to strict Orthodoxy. Most are of middle-class background, well educated, and had assimilated into the secular culture. For them, Orthodoxy provides meanings that they had been unable to find in the secular culture: a way of making moral sense of their lives, a hedge against relativism, boundaries where there had been none, valuation of the feminine virtues of nurturing, family, and motherhood, a sense of dignity and control.[19]

The attitude toward women in Reform and Reconstructionist Judaism is much more liberal by present-day standards. A significant number of women have been ordained as rabbis and as cantors. Women apply to non-Orthodox rabbinical schools in numbers equal to those of men. Reform and Reconstructionism have eliminated the distinctions between men and women in synagogue seating and in the performance of religious ritual. Reform and Reconstructionist women have led in developing new forms of traditional rituals, such as the Passover ritual. The newer rituals include women's contributions to the story of Judaism in explicit ways. These branches of Judaism also pioneered the development and celebration of the Bat Mitzvah to mark a young girl's attainment of religious responsibility. The old ideas and practices concerning ritual impurity have been discarded. Women in these two branches of Judaism have been among the leaders of the women's rights movement in the United States. While motherhood remains important in the more modernized forms of Judaism, there is no bias against women holding jobs outside their homes.

Conservative Judaism has tried to maintain a middle-of-the-road position where women are concerned. Actual observance varies a good bit from family to family and from woman to woman. Men and women sit together in worship. Although the Conservative rabbis voted officially some time ago to ordain women to the rabbinate and as cantors, the actual practice varies from congregation to congregation, and the degree of acceptance of female rabbis is uneven. While many Conservative Jews welcomed the ordination of women as a needed step forward, a significant number refuse to recognize those women who have been ordained.

Observance of the kosher laws and the laws concerning ritual uncleanness varies considerably. While not required, it is strongly supported by many Conservative congregations. Freedom from compulsion makes it possible for some women to observe the tradition without experiencing it as an oppressive

---

[19]Debra Renee Kaufman, *Rachel's Daughters: Newly Orthodox Jewish Women* (New Brunswick, NJ: Rutgers University Press, 1991).

burden. For many, Conservatism has been a way to uphold aspects of the tradition that are meaningful while moving toward greater male-female equality.

## ONE JUDAISM WITH SEVERAL EXPRESSIONS

Judaism in America is a single religious tradition that is spread across a wide range of practices and to a lesser extent beliefs. It remains, however, a "unified and unitary structure," and its varieties are "sectors of one tradition."[20] Due regard must be given to both the differences and the commonalities. Previous sections have described many of the commonalities, along with relevant differences. We will look at the differences in this section. As one author notes:

> Both the continuities and the distinctiveness are important among Jews themselves. . . . While Orthodox Jews believe that their form of Judaism is the only valid and correct one, people who are active in Reform, Conservative, or Reconstructionist groups look upon their forms of Judaism as being best for them personally and for the community in which they participate. . . . Viewed from a strictly logical perspective, there is probably more that divides the non-Orthodox Jew from the Orthodox than the teachings they share in common. From an emotional standpoint, however—and from the perspective of history—most Jews place an emphasis on what they share in common.[21]

For Jews, expressing a preference for one or another of the sectors of Judaism is one way to identify how they wish to live a Jewish life in the United States. In part, it involves what balance they choose to seek between the ways of the secular culture and the traditional religious ways. Jewish Orthodoxy is the smallest group, with under 10 percent of Jews in the United States. Roughly 35 percent of American Jews are Reform and between 40 and 45 percent are Conservative. About 2 percent are Reconstructionists.[22]

### Orthodoxy

We will begin with Jewish **Orthodoxy**. Orthodox Jews believe that their way of being Jewish embodies the authentic Jewish tradition that has existed since Judaism began. Prior to the nineteenth century, all Jews were in essence "premodern." While there were variations among them, there was no "Orthodox"

---

[20]Jacob Neusner, ed., *Understanding American Judaism: Toward a Description of a Modern Religion, Vol. II, Sectors of American Judaism: Reform, Orthodoxy, Conservatism, and Reconstructionism* (New York: KTAV Publishing House, 1975), p. xiii.

[21]Rabbi Roy A. Rosenberg, *The Concise Guide to Judaism: History, Practice, Faith* (New York: Penguin, 1994), pp. 144–145.

[22]Jacob Neusner, *World Religions in America, an Introduction, Revised and Expanded* (Louisville, KY: Westminster John Knox Press, 2000), p. 119.

designation. "Orthodox" as a designation for a particular approach to being Jewish came about only after some Jews set out to modernize their religion to make it compatible with the European Enlightenment. Jews who disagreed with this modernization were referred to as Orthodox.[23]

Orthodox Jews emphasize very close observance of the commandments or mitzvot of God.[24] Orthodoxy, despite what the name and basic outlook might suggest, is not a monolith. There are vast variations in what Orthodox Jews actually believe and do. There are, however, factors that we can identify as clearly distinctive. The Bible is regarded as divinely revealed and altogether accurate, at least in the Books of Moses. (The Books of Moses are those called the *Torah*, including Genesis, Exodus, Leviticus, Numbers, and Deuteronomy.) It has absolute divine authority. The ceremonial law is as binding as the ethical commandments, because both come from the same source and it is not for human beings to make distinctions among them. They are to be observed simply because they are commandments and because they were given to the people of Israel by God with the directive, "Do this." **Halakah**[25] is as authoritative as Torah itself, having sprung from the same source and having divine authority behind it. For most non-Jews, the two most distinctive things about Orthodoxy are the strict Sabbath observance (discussed below) and the keeping of the **kosher dietary laws**. Work of any kind is strictly forbidden on the Sabbath.

The kosher dietary laws are a collection of instructions regarding food, its preparation, and consumption. These regulations divide everything edible into three categories: edible or "kosher," things unfit for consumption, and neutral foods. The laws of *kashrut* or ritual purity are very complex, but they may be summarized this way: All fruits, vegetables, and nuts are kosher and may be eaten with anything else. Fish that have both fins and scales may be eaten. Meat from animals that have a split hoof and chew their cud may be used for food. Permitted animals must be ritually slaughtered and treated to remove as much of the blood as possible. Domesticated fowl may be eaten; wild birds and birds of prey may not. Fowl must be slaughtered and prepared ritually in the same ways as meat animals. All dairy products are permitted but may not be mixed with meat. This goes back to three different places in the Torah in which it is forbidden to cook a baby goat in its mother's milk (Exodus 23:19 and 34:25 and Deuteronomy 14:2). For example, cheeseburgers may not be eaten, and milk may not be drunk at a meal containing meat. In a fully kosher kitchen, the same set of cookware, utensils, and dishes would not be used for meat and dairy. Furthermore, a separate set of dishes is kept for Passover, necessitating a total of four completely different sets of dishes. Although they frown on drunkenness, Jews usually do not abstain from alcohol. Foods that are kosher have been prepared under close rabbinic supervision

---

[23]Rabbi Morris N. Kertzer (revised by Rabbi Lawrence A. Hoffman), *What Is a Jew?*, p. 9.

[24]Orthodox Jewish Congregations of America, www.ou.org.

[25]*Halakah* is the rabbinic record of the application of Torah law to specific circumstances through history.

throughout. Foods so certified are marked, often with a "U" (for the Union of Orthodox Rabbis) or a "K" (for Kosher) on the container.

The overall effect of the kosher commandments, of which I have named only a few, is to keep the following of God's commandments uppermost in the minds of faithful Jews in matters as common as cooking and eating. In Judaism, the body is as holy as the soul and must be treated as such; keeping kosher is one way of doing so. The meaning of keeping kosher can be summarized by saying that Jews keep the commandments because they *are* commandments, because God commands them, and that is reason enough to keep them. Over time, other interpretations have been added, amplifying its meaning. It is a way of hallowing everyday life in the very basic act of nourishing oneself and one's family. It helps teach reverence for life, particularly for animal life. It is a way of expressing connection to countless generations of Jews and of passing that connection on to one's children. It is part of the religious discipline that goes along with being Jewish.[26]

The other outstanding effect is to strengthen community among observant Jews and distinguish them from outsiders. Much of the time, they live close together because it is necessary to have ready access to a kosher butcher shop, bakery, and grocery. They socialize together, because full observance prohibits eating at the table of one who does not keep kosher.

Other features also are common among Orthodox Jews. In synagogue, women and men sit separately, and in some communities it is not common for the women to attend. The separation varies from simply being seated on separate sides of a center aisle to being separated by a high partition. All of the service is in Hebrew, and the holidays and festivals are observed to their fullest. Men wear the **kippah**, or skullcap, at all times, out of respect for their always being under the watchful eye of God. They wear prayer shawls and **tefillin**[27] for formal daily prayer. Marriage to a non-Orthodox Jew is regarded as invalid even if performed by a rabbi. Orthodox rabbis do not perform interfaith marriages.

Organizationally, Orthodoxy in the United States is represented by the Orthodox Jewish Congregations of America (commonly, "Orthodox Union").

## Reform Judaism

Reform is the most modernized and liberal of the main three Jewish groups. According to Reform teaching, Judaism is a fully modern religion that must change to keep pace with changes in the rest of the culture. Monotheism and the moral law are constant. Everything else is conditioned by circumstances and therefore changes as circumstances change.

---

[26]Anita Diamant and Howard Cooper. *Living a Jewish Life: Jewish Traditions, Customs, and Values for Today's Families* (New York: HarperCollins Publishers, 1996), pp. 98–100.

[27] *Tefillin* are small leather boxes containing Bible verses. Orthodox Jewish men wear them on their foreheads and left arms during prayer.

Reform Jews affirm the validity of Judaism and believe that Jews must study and know their tradition. They do, however, emphasize the importance of individual conscience in the interpretation and living out of that tradition. That interpretation may entail questioning practices and beliefs that seem inconsistent with modern life. Teachings that run counter to the individual's conscience may be rejected.[28]

Hebrew Union College and seminary in Cincinnati, Ohio, is Reform's major educational institution. Its U.S. organization is the Union for Reform Judaism. Rabbi Eric H. Yoffie, writing as President of the Union, lists five principles that distinguish Reform Judaism:

1. Reform Jews are committed to a Judaism that changes and adapts to the needs of the day. Thoughtful change keeps Judaism a living religion rather than a historical artifact.
2. Reform Jews are committed to the absolute equality of women in all areas of Jewish life.
3. Reform Jews are committed to social justice, regarded as the highest contribution of Reform Judaism.
4. Reform Jews are committed to the principle of inclusion, not exclusion, while understanding the need for boundaries to define Judaism.
5. Reform Jews are committed to a true partnership between the rabbinate and the laity. In the rest of Judaism, decisions are made by highly regarded rabbis or seminaries. Reform Jews support a more democratic approach to understanding.[29]

## Conservatism

**Conservative** Judaism follows a middle road between Orthodoxy and Reform Judaism. Unlike Reform Judaism, it supports religious tradition. But unlike Orthodox Judaism, it also supports the evolution and change of interpretation over time. Conservatives are passionate about Jewish law and at the same time willing to change it carefully and thoughtfully. Conservative Judaism supports both the extensive use of Hebrew in worship and English language sermons, as well as respect for traditional rites, rituals, and customs, including Sabbath and dietary observance, along with scientific training in biblical research for rabbis. Conservatism thus seeks to meld sensitivity to the evolution of human understanding and culture with genuine respect for Jewish tradition.[30]

The dietary laws illustrate the types of accommodation that Conservative Jews may make. Most do keep kosher at home. However, when eating with friends or in restaurants, they do not insist on full observance. Thus, they can dine at the homes of nonkosher friends, and any Jew, even the most observant, can dine at their table.

---

[28]Rabbi Morris N. Kertzer (revised by Rabbi Lawrence A. Hoffman), *What Is a Jew*, p. 10.
[29]Rabbi Eric H. Yoffie, "Why Be Reform?" (www.uahc.org/yoffie/whyref.shtml).
[30]Marc Lee Raphael, *Judaism in America*, pp. 83–84.

The United Synagogue of Conservative Judaism is a primary organizational embodiment. Its Executive Vice-President, Rabbi Jerome M. Epstein, has recently noted that large numbers of Conservative Jews do not live out their Jewish Conservatism very well. A relatively open membership policy has led to both growth and non-observance. He calls on Conservative Jews to restore meaningful observance to Jewish life through following his proposed "Conservative Compact of Jewish Commitment." Although he does not propose this as a definition of Conservatism, but as a beginning point for authentic Conservative Jewish life, it gives an outline of the current situation of Conservatism in the United States. It has six points:[31]

1. As congregations and as individuals, Jews must contribute to the betterment of the world, to make the world more as God wishes it to be. While financial giving is essential, personal action is also necessary, because responding to the needs of the world is a commandment.
2. Jews should live out the Jewish calendar of holidays and observances to help bring about a rebirth of Jewish observance.
3. Jews should eat as Jews, if not following the whole of the kosher law, at least avoiding those foods that are forbidden and by beginning each meal with prayer.
4. Jews must learn as Jews, committing themselves to study and to learn what is necessary to live in the image of God as Jews understand that.
5. Jews must commit themselves to Jewish family life. Conservative Jews must seek to encourage those who intermarry to create a rich and meaningful Jewish home life, while continuing to hold marriage within the faith as a strong norm.
6. Commit to Israel. Travel there. Give money to help someone else who wishes to visit or live in Israel.

### Reconstructionism

Conservatism did not unify American Judaism as much as its proponents had hoped. The **Reconstructionist** movement was another attempt at unification. Reconstructionism's founder, Rabbi Mordecai Kaplan, was a teacher at the Jewish Theological Seminary. When he looked out over the whole of American Judaism, he saw two things. The House of Israel was in fact rather fragmented. More seriously, by 1920, those Jews not affiliated with any synagogue at all far outnumbered the total of Orthodox, Conservative, and Reform Jews combined. In 1934, Kaplan wrote a book entitled *Judaism as a Civilization*. In it, he said that Judaism should be thought of as a civilization that has evolved through the ages, based on the continuous life of the Jewish people themselves. While Reconstructionists regard religion as central, they also affirm that Jewish culture includes art and music, literature and drama, as well as the

---

[31] Rabbi Jerome M. Epstein, "A Conservative Compact of Jewish Commitment," www.uscj.org/Conservative_Compact780.html.

tionship with the historical land of Israel. Unlike Reform Jews, who emphasize the role of the individual, Reconstructionists emphasize the importance of community. They seek to develop living communities in which people can participate in all of Jewish life with heartfelt commitment. Freedom of choice in practice and observance is a hallmark of these groups, with group custom an important guideline.[32]

Reconstructionism is the only expression of Judaism that has been produced solely in America. It was a response to the situation of Jewish people in this country. Despite its small numbers, it has had a large impact on Judaism in the United States.

## Zionism

The last sector of American Judaism we will consider here is Zionism. Zionism is based upon the importance of the Jewish people as a nation. Theodor Herzl was a Viennese reporter who wrote an emotional pamphlet titled *The Jewish State* (1896), in which he said that the only hope for the Jews was the establishment of a national homeland, preferably in Palestine itself. In 1897, the First World Zionist Congress met in Basel, Switzerland.

Although the leadership of the Zionist movement tended to be mainly nonreligious, Orthodox Jews supported it because it correlated with the Orthodox belief in the eventual restoration and rebuilding of Israel and the Holy City of Jerusalem. The Conservatives also were in favor of most points in the Zionist program. Reform Jews at first found little in it that was attractive, because it conflicted with their desire to be at home in whatever culture they found themselves and with their teaching that Judaism was a religion that could be at home anywhere.

After the Holocaust, virtually all American Jews supported Zionism wholeheartedly. When the state of Israel was founded in 1948, American Jews raised huge sums of money via United Jewish Appeal to help resettle refugees. This focus on Israel remains a powerful unifying force for American Judaism. The Six Day War of 1967, with Israel seeming to be threatened with annihilation from its Arab neighbors, further mobilized Zionist sentiment and action, virtually eliminating any remaining questions about the necessity and appropriateness of Zionism's program.[33]

## Hillel International

The primary organization of Jewish students on United States college campuses is Hillel International. It is named after Rabbi Hillel, a noted Jewish rabbi who lived at about the same time as did Jesus. Founded at the University

---

[32]Jewish Reconstructionist Federation, "Is Reconstructionist Judaism for You?" www.jrf.org/recon.
[33]Gerald Sorin, *Tradition Transformed: The Jewish Experience in America* (Baltimore, MD: The Johns Hopkins University Press, 1997), pp. 213–214.

of Illinois in 1923, it has become the largest Jewish campus organization in the world. It reaches out to all Jewish students, those who are religious and those who are not:

> The Hillel network brings to the college world all the richness and diversity of Judaism and Jewishness. Its historical commitment to a pluralistic community encourages intellectual challenge and growth. Hillel maintains a presence on over 400 campuses, and is in the vanguard of those who are determined to build a fuller and stronger Jewish people in the twenty-first century.[34]

## HOLOCAUST, MEMORY, AND RELIGIOUSNESS

The **Holocaust**, as many of you know, refers to the German killing of over six million Jews during the Third Reich. Many other people whom the Nazis deemed "undesirable" were killed by mass extermination methods as well. Contemporary Jews often refer to this almost unspeakable event by its Hebrew name, *Sho'ah*. Both Holocaust and Sho'ah mean the same thing—burnt sacrifice. Gentiles sometimes criticize Jews for what they regard as an unnecessary preoccupation with what Gentiles regard as a past event. Why set apart a day every year to remember? Why establish courses and centers and museums? Why keep references to Sho'ah in the words of the liturgy?

There are religious, practical, and moral reasons to remember. Religiously, it is important that the dead be remembered. By remembering the victims, they are dignified. Practically, human beings tend to repress and conveniently "forget" that which is so horrible or to generalize it to make it easier to think about. Very specific remembrances counteract these tendencies. If Jews fail to remember the worst of what Hitler and those in agreement with him did, it increases the risk that it will happen again. Anti-Semitism still exists, and keeping its worst effects in mind may hasten the day when it will no longer do so.[35]

In many communities, Christians join with Jews in remembering in formal ceremonies and services on Holocaust Remembrance Day. While they would deny that Hitler's motives were in any way Christian, Christians nonetheless recognize the complicity of some Christian ways of thinking about Jews in the events that led to Sho'ah.

## ANTI-SEMITISM

The Holocaust came about because of an especially intense form of anti-Semitism. Anti-Semitism—dislike or hatred of and aggressive acts toward Jews simply because they are Jews—still exists in the United States. It seems unlikely that anti-Semitism will ever disappear completely. However, the situation of Judaism as a religion and most Jews as individuals has been and is

---

[34]Hillel International, www.hillel.org.
[35]Rabbi Morris N. Kertzer (revised by Rabbi Lawrence A. Hoffman), *What Is a Jew*, pp. 159–162.

better in the United States than it was and is elsewhere. While there have never been pogroms nor respected anti-Semitic political parties, Jews are still sometimes thought of as outsiders in a predominantly Christian land.

One of the factors that led, and still leads, to anti-Semitism is the erroneous belief held by some Christians that Jews were responsible for Jesus' death. It is quite clear that Jesus was put to death by the Romans, not the Jews. Indeed, Jesus died because his intense Jewish patriotism made the Romans think he was disloyal. Nonetheless, this idea persists. Many Christians also find it very difficult to understand why Jews do not accept Jesus as the savior of humankind. This leads to both anti-Semitism and efforts to convert Jews to Christianity.

A second historical facet of Jewish-Christian relations is that the Christian church in medieval times did not permit charging interest on money loaned. European Jews thus became associated with money and banking, and many people came to feel that the Jews were prospering at the expense of the Christians. This historical fact gave rise to a distrust of Jews in financial matters and to the stereotypes that "all Jews are rich" and "all Jews are stingy."

The Sephardic Jews who settled in what was to become New York found in Peter Stuyvesant a governor who referred to them as a "deceitful race" who would "infest and trouble" his colony. Civil liberties and the vote were denied to any except Christians in many of the colonies and in some states for a time after the Revolution. In 1861, when Congress established a chaplain corps for the Union army, it was restricted to ministers of any Christian denomination. President Lincoln succeeded in securing an amendment to that action that allowed for Jewish chaplains, but some damage had been done, nonetheless. The immigration bill adopted by Congress in 1924 was shamefully xenophobic, and that attitude was not eliminated until this bill was replaced by Lyndon Johnson's Immigration Measure. The Ku Klux Klan has been quite active throughout American history in anti-Semitic activities and diatribes. Henry Ford supported the publication of *The Protocols of Zion*. This classic piece of hate literature embodied an idea that also had currency elsewhere—that the Jews were engaged in a conspiracy to take over the world by overthrowing Christianity.

More general patterns of discrimination also occurred, such as quota systems that barred all but a few Jews from prestigious eastern colleges and restricted Jews to a handful of the professions. There are still private clubs that either restrict the number of Jewish members or do not admit them at all. Discrimination in housing has also been fairly commonplace. Synagogues have been defaced, frequently being spray-painted with Nazi swastikas, and crosses have been burned in the yards of synagogues and Jewish homes. Often, the attacks are verbal in nature, but there is also a pattern of physical attacks on Jewish property and Jewish people.

The Christian Identity Movement is staunchly anti-Semitic in its thinking, as well as advocating prejudice against Catholics, blacks, homosexuals, and various other people. People in the movement often describe the current situation as one in which a battle for the world is being fought under the direction of God, a battle between the whites whom God intends to inherit the earth and the Jews (and others) from whom they must wrest control of it. The close identification of some groups within this movement with the neo-Nazi movement is especially troublesome to Jews, as well as to other people.

Survey data demonstrate that a low level of general anti-Semitism continues. In the years 1990 through 1996, about 6 percent of people in the United States thought of Jews as "lazy," and 12 percent felt that Jews were "violent." Nine percent thought of them as "unintelligent" and 10 percent as "unpatriotic." Fourteen percent were opposed to living in a neighborhood in which half their neighbors were Jews, and 24 percent felt that Jews have too much influence in the United States.[36]

That there is less anti-Semitism now than at some other times in our history must not lull us into indifference. Remaining anti-Semitism, as well as other forms of discrimination, prejudice, and bigotry, whether religious or otherwise, must be addressed, and to whatever extent possible, eliminated.

Acceptance must not and cannot be contingent on differences being reduced to some sort of lowest common denominator or to minorities conforming to the majority opinion of how the minority ought to be. To do so dehumanizes the individuals in the minority and impoverishes the entire community, which is denied the richness of variety that healthy, culturally conscious minorities provide.

Community is in large part a dialogue, and for a lively dialogue to occur, there must be lively differences. To insist upon conformity as a condition of acceptance and as a criterion of membership in the community will ultimately destroy the dialogue upon which genuine community is based and which is its lifeblood. It will create strangers where there might have been neighbors, because they will have nothing to discuss.

## AMERICAN JUDAISM: INTO THE FUTURE

We turn again to Jewish practitioner and scholar Marc Lee Raphael, who looks into the future of Judaism in the United States.[37] As the new century begins, people in the United States continue to seek *new spiritualities* that transcend, and sometimes ignore, institutional religion. This trend affects Judaism, too. As Jews look for new meaning in their Jewishness, both personal and internal as well as institutional, they also seek new institutional forms to support the new spiritualities.

There is greater interest in persons becoming "Jews by choice," converts to this ancient faith. Raphael records an increase in Judaism on the part of

---

[36]National Opinion Research Center General Social Surveys for 1990–1996.
[37]Marc Lee Raphael, *Judaism in America*, Chapter 6.

non-Jews and a corresponding effort by Jews to reach out to people with no religious affiliation.[38] There has been a rise in conversions as Jews and Gentiles intermarry. All of this has made and continues to make American Judaism more multicultural and ethically diverse.

There has also been an increase in gay and lesbian congregations and support groups within congregations, as well as in commitment ceremonies for same-sex partners. While Orthodox and Conservatives officially disallow homosexual behavior, Reform and Reconstructionist Jews accept gay and lesbian rabbinical students and perform commitment ceremonies. Dialogues were held, including some in Orthodox congregations, around the film *Trembling Before G-d*, in which gay Orthodox Jews try to reconcile these two aspects of their identity.

Twenty-first century Judaism has also seen a surge in Jewish day schools and supplemental education, with most programs serving students from all denominations of Judaism. Jewish education has become a family matter, with children and parents both involved in study, often studying ages-old truths with the benefit of the latest in technology. Judaism also has a strong Internet presence, with all denominations represented.

Not only has Judaism been influenced by America, but it has influenced America, as well. The prophetic ideal of caring for those less able to care for themselves meant that Jews have strongly supported liberal social legislation. Jews have been in the forefront of support for individual civil liberties. The non-Orthodox have frequently led the women's movement. Avant-garde tendencies in the arts have benefitted from Jewish support. Popular culture has been receptive to Jewish popular culture, with its distinctive foods and language ("that isn't kosher" applied to actions that aren't right or the advice to "be a mensch!").[39]

### QUESTIONS AND ACTIVITIES FOR REVIEW, DISCUSSION, AND WRITING

1. In what different ways may someone be Jewish?
2. What are the key similarities and differences between Jews and Christians?
3. Be sure that you know the basic beliefs and practices shared by most religious Jews.
4. If possible, attend a service at a temple or synagogue. This might be done by the entire class together. Write an essay in which you describe what you observed.
5. If possible, arrange to interview an Orthodox Jew about her or his Sabbath and kosher practices. Do the same with a Reform or a Conservative Jew.
6. If there is a kosher restaurant nearby, arrange a visit there. Talk with the owner(s)/employees about kosher dietary practices and what they mean to Jews in the United States.
7. In your own words, describe each of the expressions of Judaism. Of these, which seems the most attractive to you, and why?

---

[38]Marc Lee Raphael, *Judaism in America*, pp. 120–21.
[39]Robert M. Seltzer and Norman J. Cohen, eds., *The Americanization of the Jews*, p. 9.

8. Describe the attitude toward women in each of the major denominations of Judaism.
9. If possible, interview a Jewish woman about what being Jewish and female means to her.
10. Why is it important to Jews to remember the Holocaust?
11. What trends seem important as Judaism moves into the future in the United States?
12. Visit the Web site of Jews for Jesus, a Messianic Jewish organization (www.jews-for-jesus.org). What is this group about? Visit the site of Jews for Judaism (www.jews-forjudaism.org). What is this group about? What is the issue between them?

### FOR FURTHER READING

BRODY, LESLIE, ed., *Daughters of Kings: Growing Up as a Jewish Woman in America*. Boston: Faber and Faber, 1997. This is a collection of primarily first-person accounts from a variety of perspectives.

COHN-SHERBOK, DAN, and LAVINA COHN-SHERBOK, *The American Jew: Voices from an American Jewish Community*. Grand Rapids, MI: William B. Eerdmans Publishing Company, 1995. Like the previous book, this contains primarily first-person accounts. Both are highly recommended for this reason.

HERTZBERG, ARTHUR, *A Jew in America: My Life and a People's Struggle for Identity* (San Francisco: HarperSanFrancisco, 2003). This is an engaging account of the interwoven identity of Jews as a people in the United States with one man's search for his own Judaic identity.

RAPHAEL, MARC LEE, *Judaism in America*, The Columbia Contemporary American Religion Series (Irvington, NY: Columbia University Press, 2003). This is a careful and thorough study of the development of Judaism in the United States in the last quarter century, emphasizing the distinctiveness of American Judaism.

WERTHEIMER, JACK, ed., *Jews in the Center: Conservative Synagogues and Their Members* (Piscataway, NJ: Rutgers University Press, 2000). Wertheimer brings together scholars from a variety of disciplines to provide a multifaceted portrait of this most numerous Jewish denomination.

### RELEVANT WORLD WIDE WEB SITES

Judaism and Jewish Resources: www.shamash.org/trb/judaism.html

Judaism 101: www.jewfaq.org

Jewish Feminist Resources: www.jew-feminist-resources.com

United States Holocaust Memorial Museum: www.ushmm.org

Orthodox Jewish Congregations of America (Orthodox Union): www.ou.org

United Synagogue of Conservative Judaism: www.uscj.org

Union for Reform Judaism: www.uahc.org

Zionist Organization of America: www.zoa.org

Women's Zionist Organization of America: www.hadassah.org

Hillel International: www.hillel.org

# HUMANISM AND THE UNITARIAN

# UNIVERSALISTS

The history of Western civilization shows us that most social and moral progress has been brought about by persons free from religion. In modern times the first to speak out for prison reform, for humane treatment of the mentally ill, for abolition of capital punishment, for women's right to vote, for death with dignity for the terminally ill, and for the right to choose contraception, sterilization, and abortion have been freethinkers, just as they were the first to call for an end to slavery.[1]

What associations, if any, does the word *humanism* brings to your mind? Does it have positive or negative connotations? What do you think about people who say that they are humanists? Do you think humanism necessarily excludes belief in God? Does your school have a college or department of humanities? Do you think these two words might be related? How?

There are many varieties of humanism. The group whose quotation appears above represents a thoroughly secular humanism, one that has no room for religion. Other forms of humanism are religious, as we will see.

## WHAT IS HUMANISM?

**Humanism** can be defined briefly as a worldview or philosophy that derives its values from the experience of human life in this world, without reference to God as Jews and Christians understand God or to anything else supernatural. In order to fill in this brief definition, we will look at some recent statements of the meaning of humanism. The American Humanist Association defines humanism as a "progressive lifestance that, without supernaturalism, affirms our ability and responsibility to lead meaningful, ethical lives capable of

---

[1]Freedom from Religion Foundation, www.ffrf.org.

adding to the greater good of humanity."[2] Another humanist notes that "humanists believe in what Robert Ingersoll called the trinity of science: reason, experience, and observation."[3] A somewhat longer description focused strongly on the ethical dimension of humanism describes humanism as rational, scientific, and compassionate. It promotes the self-determination of each individual while affirming both individual and planetary responsibility. It affirms the democratic process, human rights, and social justice. It requires no reference to nor support from anything supernatural. Values derive from human experience in this world rather than from theological beliefs.[4]

A review of these and other descriptions of humanism reveals several common themes:

- Humanism affirms human reason, compassion, responsibility, and the trustworthiness of human experience.
- Humanism affirms human life in this world, as a part of nature.
- It affirms the worth and dignity of each individual woman, man, and child, and the fundamental equality of all persons.
- It is possible for human beings to find meaning and fulfillment in life without recourse to the supernatural; people have the responsibility to engage in a search for meaning.
- Humanism supports the fullest development of democracy in all areas of life, human rights, social justice, and the expansion of individual rights to the fullest extent consonant with responsibility.
- Ethical and moral life is to be based on human experience, reason, and valuing.

Humanism, in other words, is based on the faith that people can live truly good lives in the here and now, that we have the capacity to cooperate to build a good society that balances out the needs of the individual and the larger group, and that we can find meaning and fulfillment without recourse to anything supernatural. Or, as one humanist puts it, humanism is "the use of reason in human affairs, applied in the service of compassion."[5]

Not all humanists are secularists, although many are. Jewish and Christian humanism also has a significant place in the story of American humanism. The humanist belief in the dignity and worth of every person, the emphasis on ethical conduct and human responsibility, and compassion in the context of human community are all shared by most religions. Liberal religion shares with humanism a belief in the basic goodness of human nature, its insistence that the context must be taken into account in making moral decisions, and its support for the use of reason and opposition to authoritarianism. Much of liberal religion agrees with humanism that supernaturalism in religion is outdated and that scientific inquiry can and should be used to evaluate claims to

[2]American Humanist Association, www.americanhumanist.org.
[3]African Americans for Humanism, www.secularhumanism.org/aah.
[4]The American Humanist Association, www.americanhumanist.org.
[5]H. J. Eysenck, "Reason with Compassion," in *The Humanist Alternative*, ed. Paul Kurtz (Buffalo, NY: Prometheus Books, 1973), p. 91.

religious truth. Humanism and liberal religion also share the belief that the sacred and secular worlds cannot, in the final analysis, be separated. Social justice, opposition to prejudice in all forms, and an interest in peacemaking also characterize both.

"The adventure of religion," writes one advocate of religious humanism, "is not in the discovery of Eternal Truth or Absolute Meaning—arenas in which human beings do not and cannot deal—but in our individual and communal search for and creation of meanings and values that dignify and enhance life."[6] Another explains how humanism seeks to modify religion: "Humanism attempts to rid religious institutions, myths, creeds, prayers, and sacraments of superstitious beliefs, while enhancing their significance as expressions of human needs, hopes, and values."[7]

## HUMANISM IN THE UNITED STATES

The recent history of humanism in the United States is built on the foundation of centuries of earlier history, both in the United States and throughout the world. Rather than tracing this early history, however, we will look briefly at the more recent course of humanism in the United States. Humanism as a self-conscious movement began in the United States in 1933, when *Humanist Manifesto I* was written. There had been humanists and humanist philosophers in America as far back as the Declaration of Independence and even farther. Conscious attempts to articulate the principles of American humanism date from the first manifesto, however.

### Four Humanist Statements

The first of these four statements is the *Humanist Manifesto I*, written in 1933 by a group of humanists in the United States who set out to draft what they understood to be the basic principles of the movement. It is an optimistic and upbeat document that expresses great confidence in humanism as the wave of the future. "In every field of human activity," they wrote, "the vital movement is now in the direction of a candid and explicit humanism." The humanism of this document is explicitly religious humanism. Its authors wanted to separate religion from doctrines and from methods that they believed were "outmoded" and not workable in the twentieth century. They intended it to be a "new statement of the means and purposes of religion." It is written in the form of a series of fifteen brief statements with an introduction and conclusion and deals with those themes that we have already seen in connection with humanism.[8] While the authors of the first major humanist

---

[6]Kenneth W. Pfifer, *The Faith of a Humanist* (Boston, MA: Unitarian Universalist Association, n.d.).
[7]Herbert W. Schneider, "Religious Humanism," in *The Humanist Alternative*, ed. Paul Kurtz, p. 65.
[8]Paul J. Kurtz, *Humanist Manifesto I* (Buffalo, NY: Prometheus Books, 1973).

statement were critical of the religious institutions of their day and regarded many religious beliefs and practices as unsuitable for life in the twentieth century, they were not, on the whole, hostile to religion.

The authors of *Humanist Manifesto II* (1973) also expressed great confidence in people's ability to solve the problems that existed. It calls for people to "fuse reason with compassion in order to build constructive moral values." A major change from the first document is that this manifesto states that religion cannot be reinterpreted sufficiently to be made viable; something radically new is needed. It also has a much more clearly political tone than did its predecessor. Political and economic arrangements between nations receive more explicit attention.

*A Secular Humanist Declaration*, written in 1980, is a very different sort of document. It outlines an explicitly secular humanism that clearly believes itself to be under attack and on the defensive. It names a variety of points of view and groups such as Christian fundamentalism, the Catholic papal hierarchy, Muslim clericalism, nationalistic Judaism, and many New Age beliefs and practices. It accuses them of promoting unthinking reliance on authority, restricting human freedom, and bypassing the use of reason and the scientific method to solve problems. It then moves on to a series of positive affirmations and calls for action that reflects the humanist values we have seen before.[9]

This document reflects a situation that had become more and more polarized. As Christian fundamentalism has named secular humanism as the main focus of its attack, religious fundamentalism has become the focus of secular humanism's attack. There can be no doubt that the views of fundamentalists and humanists are sharply different at almost every point. Fundamentalists tend to oppose both secular and religious humanism, believing that both are examples of human rebellion against God's authority. The kind of society envisioned by the one would have no room for the other. Each provides a framework within which significant numbers of Americans live and attempt to construct a meaningful life. If we really are to become neighbors and not strangers, there must be room in the neighborhood for both points of view. The tendency of each to view the other as an obnoxious enemy must give way to an appreciation of what each provides for those who live their lives by it.

Humanists wrote a fourth official statement of their position in 2003, one which in many ways echoes the documents that preceded *A Secular Humanist Declaration*. *Humanism and Its Aspirations* is subtitled *Humanist Manifesto III, a successor to the Humanist Manifesto of 1933*. It is noteworthy that its list of affirmations does not mention religion at all.

- Knowledge of the world is derived by observation, experimentation, and rational analysis.
- Life's fulfillment emerges from individual participation in the service of humane ideals.

---

[9]Paul J. Kurtz, "A Secular Humanist Declaration," *Free Inquiry*, 1, no. 1 (Winter, 1980).

- Humans are social by nature and find meaning in relationships.
- Working to benefit society maximizes individual happiness.
- Humans are an integral part of nature, the result of unguided evolutionary change.
- Ethical values are derived from human need and interest as tested by experience.[10]

### HUMANIST ORGANIZATIONS IN THE UNITED STATES

Humanist organizations are not nearly as well known as more traditional religious organizations, but there are several such groups in the United States. They are more common in major urban areas than in smaller communities and along the coasts than in the heartland.

Felix Adler founded the **Ethical Culture Society** in 1876. He was trained as a rabbi but left Judaism in favor of ethical humanism based on the dignity and worth of every individual. The member societies of the Ethical Culture Society hold Sunday meetings that are of an educational and morally uplifting nature. The group is also characterized by intense social activism in the areas of education, war and peace, and racism, among others. *The Statement of Purpose of the American Ethical Union* describes the Ethical Culture movement as "a humanistic religious and educational movement inspired by the ideal that the supreme aim of human life is working to create a more humane society."[11]

The **American Humanist Association** was formed in 1941 as an effort to link the various humanist interests in the United States. Like the Ethical Culture Society, it supports an active program of social involvement that is based on the principles in the *Humanist Manifestos*. It publishes a periodical, *The Humanist*, and supports Prometheus Books, the largest American publisher of humanist literature.

**HUUmanists**, formerly Friends of Religious Humanism, publishes the journal *Religious Humanism*. It was founded in 1962 as the Fellowship of Religious Humanists. It is an affiliate of the Unitarian Universalist Association. It regards humanism as a religious way of approaching life, a philosophy that makes sense in religious terms. It emphasizes the interconnection of all life. It speaks of "a haunting sense of wonder which never leaves one for whom life itself is a mystery and miracle." For religious humanists, this is the heart of religion.[12]

The **Society for Humanistic Judaism** is the major Jewish humanist organization. It was founded by Rabbi Sherwin T. Wine in 1963 as a "nontheistic alternative in contemporary Jewish life." Several of the affirmations of the Society significantly reinterpret traditional Jewish teaching along humanistic lines. For example:

---

[10]The American Humanist Association, www.americanhumanist.org/3/HumandItsAspirations.htm.
[11]The American Ethical Union, www.aeu.org.
[12]Peter Samson, Friends of Religious Humanism, www.americanhumanist.org/hsfamily/huumanist.html.

- Judaism is defined in terms of Jewish history and culture, with no reference to *religious* Judaism.
- Jewish history is solely human history, not in terms of divine intervention. Jewish history is more traditionally interpreted as the saga of God's power working in and with the House of Israel.
- Humanistic Judaism centers on human power and human responsibility to shape life in beneficial ways. Traditional Judaism is theocentric (God-centered) from beginning to end.[13]

The role of the black church has been central to the life of the African-American community in the United States (see Chapter 7). However, there is also an association of **African Americans for Humanism**. Although many of its goals are similar to those of the black Christian churches, its rationales and methods are those of humanism. The association believes that religion is responsible for many of the problems that have affected the African-American community. Its members apply the basic tenets of humanism to their lives as members of the African-American community.[14]

The **Campus Freethought Alliance** began in 1996 with "representatives of various student skeptical, secular humanist, atheist, agnostic, and freethought campus organizations." The students who joined to form the Alliance were in search of a community for freethinkers among the college population. The group provides support for secular students and when necessary helps to defend their rights.[15]

These and other similar groups provide some organizational cohesiveness to the humanist movement in America and provide a means by which people in agreement with this point of view can find fellowship and engage in social action. They also provide a means by which humanists can voice their concerns. Humanist organizations work to get legislation passed that reflects their viewpoint, just as do other political interest groups, including religious interest groups.

There can be no doubt that humanism serves many of the same functions for its adherents that traditional religions do for theirs. It has many of the same emotional dynamics. Like the religions, humanism deserves a place among the myriad ways that Americans organize their lives in a meaningful fashion. It is a continuing element in the American landscape, one that will interact with religion for a long time to come.

### ATHEISM AND AGNOSTICISM

Before you read further, stop and ask yourself what might lead someone to be an atheist or agnostic. Do those views seem to you to be reasonable ones for someone to hold, whether or not you, yourself, do?

---

[13]Quoted material is from the Society for Humanistic Judaism, www.shj.org.
[14]African Americans for Humanism, www.secularhumanism.org/aah.
[15]Campus Freethought Alliance, www.campusfreethought.org.

Atheism, agnosticism, and various other types of "free thought" that are not in accord with the Judeo-Christian perspective have been a part of the religious and cultural perspective ever since Europeans came to the New World. Atheism and agnosticism were included in the plurality of religious views held by the early colonists and by the framers of the Constitution. Most people in the United States do believe in the existence of God as commonly understood. However, current survey data indicate that around 15 percent of the population does not believe in some higher power. The American Survey of Religious Identification notes that "the greatest increase [between 1990 and 2001] in absolute as well as in percentage terms has been among those adults who do not subscribe to any religious identification; their number has more than doubled from 14.3 million in 1990 to 29.4 million in 2001; their proportion has grown from just eight percent of the total in 1990 to over fourteen percent in 2001."[16]

We'll begin with a brief definition of each word. In the United States, **atheism** usually means not believing in God as God is thought of in the Judeo-Christian-Islamic tradition. However, many atheists think that this definition is inadequate. While acknowledging that the word **atheist** is used to mean a person who *denies* the existence of God, they press for a distinction:

> [M]ost atheists . . . would hold that an atheist is a person *without* belief in God. The distinction is small but important. Denying something means that you have knowledge of what it is that you are being asked to affirm, but that you have rejected that particular concept. To be *without* belief in God merely means the term "God" has no importance or possibly no meaning to you.[17]

**Agnosticism** has a number of meanings. Some agnostics hold that they themselves simply do not know if God exists. Others believe that it is impossible for anyone to know if God exists. Some would put it in terms of the evidence being inconclusive. Others believe that, even if we can say with some degree of certainty that some sort of higher being or power does exist, we can have absolutely no knowledge of the nature or character of that being.

### Reasons for Disbelief

There are a number of different themes that appear repeatedly in people's reasons for disavowing belief in a supreme being or higher power. Some believe that people simply project their need for an eternal father figure onto the being whom believers call God. Following psychiatrist Sigmund Freud, for

---

[16]American Survey of Religious Identification, The Graduate School of The City University of New York, www.gc.cuny.edu/studies/key_findings.htm.

[17]Gordon Stein, "Introduction," in *An Anthology of Atheism and Rationalism*, ed. Gordon Stein (Buffalo, NY: Prometheus Books, 1980), p. 3.

example, some atheists say that we as human beings want a father figure to protect us, to punish us when we deserve to be punished, and to reward us when we have been good. We want, in other words, to remain in a childlike relationship with a powerful father. Because our earthly fathers inevitably die—and also fail to meet our expectations while they are alive—we create a God who is an omnipotent, all-knowing father. Alternatively, following Marx, people who are oppressed and mistreated project a God who will reward them in the future for present suffering and deprivation. This, then, invites abuse by the privileged and ruling classes, who can promise those they oppress future rewards in heaven for compliance and punishments in hell for disobedience. This dynamic was at work in some of the uses made of Christianity by slaveholders.

Another alternative of this type is more sociological. Following sociologist Emile Durkheim, this view holds that a society (rather than individuals) projects a God as the source of its dearest values and social norms. The social norms and cultural values gain authority and sanction by being attributed to the deity. A very similar dynamic can be seen when proponents of various (and often opposing!) social positions claim that "God is on their side," as has been done by both sides in the abortion rights debate and the homosexual rights debate.

Some atheists believe faith in God is simply not consistent with a scientific view of reality and the methods that such a view entails. In other words, "God" cannot be proven by the methods of science, especially as refined and practiced by the natural sciences. Furthermore, the concept of God may be used to fill in where knowledge does not exist, as a substitute for knowledge, thus hindering the development of knowledge. This is sometimes called a "God of the gaps" theology. "God" is brought in to explain that for which there is no other explanation. Thus, as human knowledge grows, God must necessarily shrink. Although most theologians do not support the "God of the gaps" view, it is fairly common among believers generally.

Some people think that the word God simply does not have a clear, unambiguous meaning. Statements about God cannot be verified or falsified in the usual ways and thus are an unacceptable use of language.

A particularly troublesome problem for many people is that they cannot reconcile the existence of an all-powerful and loving God with the presence of so much human suffering. Catastrophic disasters, terror attacks, pain and suffering endured by innocent populations, and horrifying illnesses that afflict apparently "good" people all have led to questions about God's existence. Even if they do not question God's existence, people may question God's simultaneous goodness and power (cornerstones of the Judeo-Christian-Islamic view). If God is both all-good and all-powerful, the argument runs, why does God allow things like this to happen? These questions run the gamut from individuals asking "Why?" after the death of a parent, child, or spouse, to those of Jewish faith who asked and continue to ask "Why?" after the Holocaust.

Other atheists argue that God's existence is incompatible with the recognition of the autonomy and worth of humankind. The Christian insistence that people need a savior or the Jewish and Muslim avowal that people need the guidance of God to live truly good lives seems to some people to contradict human autonomy, freedom, and worth.

Some people feel that belief in God takes away from people's proper focus, which is to work actively for positive change in the social order. In some instances, this is a response to the perceived social conservatism of religion, religion's tendency to maintain the status quo rather than support change. As you have seen, some women feel very strongly that their churches and synagogues have been on the side of female oppression rather than on the side of women's rights. In other cases, this view stems from the shift in focus that sometimes goes along with belief in God and life after death. For some, although certainly not for most, believers, life in this present world is greatly devalued compared with eternal life with God. This devaluation then undercuts any attempt to better this life.

Finally, some people simply point to the fact that, the world around, many people, including many who espouse very high ideals, do not believe. If the whole experience of humankind is taken into account, there are just too many people for whom God is not a fact of their experience.

While several of these views are most likely to lead a person to atheism, at least three of them might also lead to agnosticism. Many agnostics simply feel that there is not enough evidence either for or against God's existence to warrant certainty. Some are disturbed by the ambiguity and lack of clarity that surrounds our use of the word *God*. And certainly some do wonder about how well people get along without such belief. Fewer agnostics than atheists tend to be militant about their position. For the most part, their "unknowing" makes them reluctant to try to make converts.

There are few atheist organizations in the United States, and, for most people, atheism is a matter of private belief and conviction. Probably the best-known American atheist was **Madalyn Murray O'Hair**, the twentieth-century atheist whose name became for a time nearly synonymous with atheism itself. She founded **American Atheists, Incorporated**. The following list of principles comes from that organization. Although it begins with an emphatic denial of the existence of any deity, its basic tone is a positive consideration of human responsibility in light of that denial:

1. There is no heavenly father. Man must protect the orphans and foundlings, or they will not be protected.
2. There is no god to answer prayer. Man must hear and help man.
3. There is no hell. We have no vindictive god or devil to fear or imitate.
4. There is no atonement or salvation by faith. We must face the consequences of our acts.
5. There is no beneficent or malevolent intent in nature. Life is a struggle against preventable and unpreventable evils. The cooperation of man is the only hope of the world.
6. There is no chance after death to "do our bit." We must do it now or never.

7. There is no divine guardian of truth, goodness, beauty and liberty. These are attributes of man. Man must defend them or they will perish from the earth.[18]

Most atheists do not try to persuade other people to join them in their
denial of God, although they do encourage this type of positive, humanisti-
cally based ethic alongside their denial of the God of the believers. While they
do not share the belief in God that most Americans have, they do share many
of the same moral commitments.

Humanism, agnosticism, and atheism are some of the alternatives or
supplements to participation in an organized community of faith. Woven into
the tapestry of American religious life along with the mainstream alternatives,
they help to make it a rich blend of colors and textures unrivaled anywhere
else in the world.

## UNITARIAN UNIVERSALISM

**Unitarian Universalism** is an organizational embodiment of the very liberal
religious tradition in the United States. The present Unitarian Universalist Association is the result of a merger between the Universalists and the Unitarians. We will first consider the two separately and then look at the Unitarian
Universalist Association today.

### The Universalists

Simply put, universalism is the belief that all persons will eventually be saved
by God; in other words, salvation is universal, not limited to an elect number.
This belief is suggested by certain Biblical passages. For example, Acts 3:21
speaks of a time of restoration or restitution of all things. John 1:29 refers to
Jesus as the Lamb of God who takes away the sins of the [whole] world, and
Romans 5:18 speaks of the righteousness of Jesus being imparted to all people. In Revelation 21:5 God is said to say, "I make all things new." Clearly, traditional Christian teaching has not taken these and other similar passages in
this light, but this interpretation was seized upon by those who could not
reconcile the concept of a God of love with the idea that such a God would
condemn anyone to everlasting punishment. Nonetheless, universalism usually has been regarded as a heresy (unacceptable belief) throughout Christian
history.

By the time of the American colonies, universalism was already present
on the American religious scene and would remain there. English-born John
Murray (1741–1815) is sometimes considered the father of American Universalism. In 1770, he preached what may well have been the first Universalist
sermon in America, in New England. The first covenant for a Universalist

---

[18]J. Gordon Melton, ed., *The Encyclopedia of American Religions: Religious Creeds* (Detroit: Gale Research
Company, 1988), p. 636. The gender-exclusive language is in the original.

church was drawn up in Murray's church in Gloucester, Massachusetts, in 1779, and in 1780 he met with a group in Philadelphia to help draft a Universalist declaration of faith.

Elhanan Winchester (1751–1797) was another early leader, an intellectual and writer whose writing ability helped to spread the Universalist message and give it credibility. Both Murray and Winchester remained within the framework of trinitarian Christianity.

Hosea Ballou (1771–1852) was not a trinitarian, however, but a unitarian, who believed that God was one instead of three persons. Ballou's universalism was blended with his unitarianism in ways that prefigured the eventual merger of the two groups. Ballou's *Treatise on the Atonement* was the first American attempt to develop a coherent theology along Universalist lines. He became the pastor of the Second Universalist Church in Boston and held that post for over thirty years, becoming the chief spokesperson for Universalism in the new world. During part of his pastorate in Boston, he worked closely with William Ellery Channing, who would become known as the father of American Unitarianism.

The denomination spread slowly in the nineteenth and twentieth centuries. It was especially successful in the rural and frontier areas, while the Unitarians were more concentrated in urban areas. By the mid-1900s, Universalism had become known as a liberalized and universalized form of Christianity, which it remained until its union with Unitarianism.

## The Unitarians

While the universalists were teaching universal salvation as a clearer expression of the will of an all-loving God, the Unitarians reacted to other elements in traditional Christian teaching. First among these was the doctrine that God is a trinity, formalized at Nicaea in 325 C.E. This doctrine, you will recall from the discussion of basic Christian beliefs, holds that God is three distinct persons with but one substance. The **Unitarians** taught the oneness of God, against the trinitarians. Although their name derives from this one teaching, there were other Christian doctrines to which they objected. Among these were the infallibility of the Bible, human depravity and the inheritance of original sin, and the doctrine that some will be damned eternally. This last point aligned them with the Universalists. The Unitarians also encouraged the use of reason as a way of determining religious truth, a theme that we saw in our discussion of humanism and one that remains a hallmark of modern-day Unitarianism.

The first church in the United States that took an explicitly Unitarian view of God did so in the late 1700s. In 1785, King's Chapel in Boston (Episcopal) appointed a young minister with Unitarian views, James Freeman. Freeman led his congregation in changing the Anglican Prayer Book to eliminate all references to the Trinity. The Episcopal Church refused to recognize the church as Episcopalian, and, in 1787, Freeman became the first American-ordained Unitarian minister. What had been the first Episcopal Church in Boston became the first Unitarian Church.

William Ellery Channing (1780–1842) is often said to be father of American Unitarianism. American religious historian Sydney Ahlstrom compares Channing's role in the Unitarian reformation in America to that of Martin Luther in the German reformation.[19] In 1819, Channing preached his famous sermon, "Unitarian Christianity," in which he defined the new movement. Channing's Unitarianism remained firmly Christian. In his interpretation, God the Father sent the Son and gives the Holy Spirit to those who seek it. These three are not to be considered three persons in one God, however. Six years later, Channing founded the American Unitarian Association. **Transcendentalism** played a large role in the early Unitarian movement. An American adaptation of English romanticism and German idealism, transcendentalism sought to refine Unitarianism and bring in into conformity with what it believed was the common substance of all the world's religions. Ralph Waldo Emerson (1803–1882) was the best-known leader of the Transcendentalist movement. Emerson preferred to be called a theist rather than a Christian, because the term was more general.

Harvard Divinity School and College (later, Harvard University) became the intellectual stronghold of Unitarianism. Most faculty and students were consciously Unitarian in their outlook, and, especially in the decade between 1811 and 1820, Harvard became the leading Unitarian training center in the United States. Unitarianism remained strongest in New England and in the more urban areas of the growing nation. In rural areas and along the frontier, where Universalism was stronger, Unitarianism was looked upon as an elitist religion. It was that aspect of Unitarianism that led someone to remark that Unitarians believed in "the fatherhood of God, the brotherhood of man and the neighborhood of Boston."

Unitarianism gradually transformed itself from the distinctly Christian Unitarianism of Channing's sermon into an ethically oriented, pragmatic, humanistic, and sometimes theistic, religion. Along the way, and indicative of the changes that were taking place, American Unitarians played a dominant role in organizing and supporting the Parliament of Religions in Chicago in 1893. It was this transformed Unitarianism that carried over into the present-day Unitarian Universalist Association.

### The Unitarian Universalist Association

As we have seen, the Universalists and the Unitarians shared both a dissatisfaction with the prevailing religious orthodoxies of their times and a substantial body of common beliefs and religious sensibilities. Nonetheless, despite

---

[19]Sydney E. Ahlstrom, *A Religious History of the American People* (New Haven, CT: Yale University Press, 1973), p. 398.

Hosea Ballou's repeated calls for unity, there was almost no cooperation between them in the early years. They came from different social backgrounds, and, while many of their quarrels with traditional Christianity were similar, they arrived at their positions by different routes. The Universalists began with the conflict between the doctrine of God's love and the idea of eternal damnation. This gave their protest a different emotional quality than that of the more rational and intellectual Unitarian objection to what they saw as the illogic of belief in a trinitarian God.

However, as both groups changed, in many ways moving even closer together, interest in cooperative efforts grew, spurred by the fact that neither group was large. Their small size meant that they needed each other. Finally, in 1947, a commission was set up to determine what kind of cooperation was actually possible. By 1951, this commission had drawn up a plan, which was accepted by both its constituencies, for cooperative work in several key areas, such as religious education, public relations, and publications. They also recommended moving gradually toward a full merger. The merger was completed in the spring of 1961, bringing into being the Unitarian Universalist Association, the national organization for the church today.

### Unitarian Universalism Today

Many of us, when we encounter a community of faith with which we are unfamiliar, want to know, "What, exactly, do you believe?" Unitarian Universalism has no official creed. There is no statement of beliefs to which members must give assent. There is no confession of faith that is repeated regularly in Sunday services. Rather than having a set of firm beliefs worked out and handed to people, the Unitarian Universalists support a set of very broad operating principles that serve as guidelines for individual and community decision making.

**Individual freedom of religious belief** is perhaps the most fundamental of all these guidelines. All people, following the guidance of their own best understanding and informed by the community of faith as a whole, are responsible for working out their own beliefs. Unitarian Universalists believe that people are capable of doing this without divine revelation. This understanding of how religious beliefs come about leads Unitarian Universalists to a large measure of tolerance for differences within their ranks, as well as appreciation for religious views other than Unitarian Universalism. The emphasis, in other words, is not on having a correct set of beliefs handed down from church authorities or from a sacred book, but on responsibly working out one's own beliefs, subject to change as one's understanding grows.

Unitarian Universalists believe that religious beliefs should change as people change throughout the course of their lives, rather than saying that there are beliefs that should be clung to "through thick and thin." The process of arriving at religious beliefs is of central importance. For most, if not all, ethical action in the world, with and on behalf of other people, is of greater importance than belief.

A bookmark-sized pamphlet lists "Ten Good Reasons for Joining a Unitarian Universalist Congregation." Among the reasons given are that it's a place where people worship "with open hearts and minds, seeking what is sacred among us." Other reasons refer to the denomination's long tradition of tolerance and reasonableness, its honoring its Jewish and Christian roots while affirming truth in other religions as well, and Unitarian Universalists' belief that revelation is never finished and people are empowered to search for new truths. The denomination also encourages children's questions, welcomes diversity, work to bring about a more just society, respects the whole self, mind, body, and spirit, encourages its members and friends to be true to themselves and offers people a supportive community.[20]

These principles of belief lead most Unitarian Universalists to a lifestyle that includes engagement in social action. One notable characteristic of the members of this church is that they are, compared with their relatively small numbers in most areas, vastly overrepresented in those organizations that are identified with liberal social concerns. Organizations that work to make life better for all citizens can usually count on support from Unitarian Universalists. Groups that work on increasing civil liberties also attract Unitarian Universalists' interest. For most, political involvement, in the widest sense of that term, is a central way of working out their religious commitments in day-to-day life.

The freedom to work out one's own religious beliefs without pressure from any external authorities attracts the highly educated into Unitarian Universalism. They are the most highly educated, on the average, of any American church. This also means that this church includes many professional people among its members, both men and women. The freedom of religious belief that characterizes Unitarian Universalist churches also draws couples of mixed religious faith, because they can attend services at the same place without either of them compromising their own faith. People may also become part of a Unitarian Universalist congregation if they live too far from their own community of faith to participate in its activities.

Unitarian Universalists are also among the most culture-affirming people. They raise hard questions about the culture in which they live, especially when that culture seems less humane than it might be. Nonetheless, Unitarian Universalists believe in full participation in the life of the society of which they are a part. Restrictions on individual decision making about things like drinking alcohol, dress, and sexual arrangements between consenting adults are simply not a part of the Unitarian Universalist philosophy.

Unitarian Universalist congregations provide corporate ritual activity, but describing a "typical" service is difficult. The freedom that we have noted

[20]Bill and Barbara Hamilton-Holway and Mark Harris, "Ten Good Reasons for Joining a Unitarian Universalist Congregation" (Boston, MA: Unitarian Universalist Association, 1995).

**Figure 10-1**    Unitarian Universalist services attract people seeking freedom of religious thought. *(Joe Traver/Liaison)*

in belief translates into freedom in deciding what format religious meetings will take. Regular services usually occur on Sunday morning (Figure 10–1). It is not unheard of, however, for a church to hold services at some other time that suits the needs of the congregation better. In some churches, the service may be hard to distinguish from any other very liberal Protestant service. In others, greater experimentation and innovation are the rule. There is a *hymnal*, or hymn book, that includes traditional hymns that are modified to eliminate gender-exclusive language. Other hymns specifically reflect the church's own teachings. Readings in a typical service might be taken from many sources. The Jewish and Christian scriptures, the sacred writings of other world religions, contemporary poetry, and novels are only a few possibilities. It is not unusual to find a reading from the Christian New Testament and a reading from a recent novel side by side. The minister or a guest speaker gives a sermon, talk, meditation, or commentary (some churches do not use the more distinctly religious word *sermon*). It may concern a matter of ethical importance, social involvement, self-development, or human relationships, to name but a few examples. An offering is usually received. A person expecting prayers might be surprised; Unitarian Universalist church services sometimes do not include them.

I have avoided using the word *worship* to describe the church services. *Worship* usually carries with it the idea that there is a god or supreme being that is being worshiped, an idea upon which not all Unitarian Universalists agree. There are no sacraments. Children are welcomed into the congregation and dedicated, at which time their parents and the congregation affirm their commitment to the child and celebrate the new life that has come into being.

Other ceremonies, such as marriages and funerals, echo the liberal and humanistic perspective that is so much a part of the life of these communities of faith. Nearly all services include time for fellowship and refreshments before or after.

**Fellowship** is very important for the members of Unitarian Universalist congregations. One Unitarian Universalist church in the Midwest, where midweek worship services are the order of the day for the Christian majority, sponsors a weekly Wednesday Revival Hour at which those who want to do so can get together for discussion and fellowship. The group meets at various local restaurants or cocktail lounges or may have a carry-in dinner at someone's home. Larger churches support a full range of activities from which members and friends can choose. Discussion, education, and debate characterize the life of these communities of faith. Education for adults, young people, and children is built into the Sunday morning activities, and other activities may occur during the week. Often their churches provide meeting space for groups too small to have their own space, such as Buddhist meditation classes. Unitarian Universalist ministers often participate in interfaith groups.

Organizationally, each local church is fully autonomous. The Unitarian Universalist Association, with headquarters in Boston, takes care of many operational details and serves as the central offices for the group. Its statements have only an advisory function where local congregations are concerned. There is a national conference annually. Beacon Press is the church's publishing house. The Association also supports a unique outreach program. Called the **Church of the Larger Fellowship**, this program was designed especially for religious liberals who live too far from a Unitarian Universalist church to attend. It makes available a news bulletin that contains sermons and inspirational writings, as well as reports on activities. A *Handbook of Services* for the major celebrations of life is provided for each member. A minister is available by mail or telephone. A religious education director provides parents with assistance in developing a religious education program for their children. There is also a lending library.

On some college campuses, there are organizations for Unitarian Universalist and other religiously liberal students, sponsored by a local Unitarian Universalist congregation.

Humanism and liberal religion provide meaningful alternatives to traditional religion for significant numbers of Americans. They have influenced more traditional religion in the direction of increased social concern. Humanism and humanitarianism have been and continue to be very closely linked in the United States, and the presence of humanism has encouraged the society to be more humanitarian. Atheists and agnostics, too, have contributed to the American cultural landscape. Like their sparring partners, the fundamentalists, humanists and freethinkers deserve a place in the community of neighbors, not strangers.

### QUESTIONS AND ACTIVITIES FOR REVIEW, DISCUSSION, AND WRITING

1. Take a current ethical or moral problem of which you are aware. Think it through (1) beginning with the assumptions of Judaism or Christianity and (2) again from a humanistic viewpoint. What differences in the process and in the conclusions do you notice? You might want to organize this as a debate with a friend, each of you taking one point of view.

2. Humanism opposes all forms of authoritarianism. Do you agree, or do you feel that authoritarianism has a place in certain situations? Is it important to distinguish between authority and authoritarianism? For what reasons and in what circumstances might one person or group exercise authority over others?

3. In your opinion, is humanism a religion? Why or why not?

4. Which of the reasons given for atheism is most persuasive to you? Least convincing? Why?

5. Visit a Unitarian Universalist Church or Fellowship if there is one in your community or close by. In what ways is the Sunday service similar to others with which you may be familiar? How is it different? Many members of these churches became Unitarian Universalists after having been part of other religious groups. If possible, make arrangements to speak with the minister about how some of the people in the congregation came to their present religious outlook.

6. What might be the advantages and disadvantages of being a part of a community of faith that expects that religious beliefs will change throughout people's lives, rather than offering a set of beliefs that are expected to remain constant?

7. Visit the Web sites of two of the organizations listed under "Relevant World Wide Web Sites" in order to learn something about each organization that goes beyond what is in this chapter.

### FOR FURTHER READING

ALLEN, NORM R., JR., *The Black Humanist Experience: An Alternative to Religion*. Amherst, NY: Prometheus Books, 2002. Allen, Executive Director of African Americans for Humanism, has compiled a thoughtful collection of essays that emphasizes what humanists embrace rather than what they reject.

GAYLOR, ANNIE LAURIE, ed., *Women without Superstition: The Collected Writings of Women Free-thinkers of the Nineteenth and Twentieth Centuries*. Madison, WI: Freedom from Religion Foundation, 1997. Gaylor includes fifty mainly United States nonliterary figures whose writings are arranged chronologically by their year of birth.

GRAYLING, A.C., *Life, Sex, and Ideas: The Good Life without God*. New York: Oxford University Press, 2003. Grayling writes short, informal essays on ethics, ideas, and culture from the standpoint of one who describes religion as "no greater social evil."

PETERSON, MICHAEL and RAYMOND VANARRAGON (Eds.), *Contemporary Debates in the Philosophy of Religion*. Malden, MA: Blackwell Publishers, 2003. This book gives an overview of the key debates in the modern philosophy of religion and covers most of the key issues in the debate between theists and atheists.

SOLOMON, ROBERT C., *Spirituality for the Skeptic: The Thoughtful Love of Life*. New York: Oxford University Press, 2002. Solomon's book is born of his own quest to reconcile religion and philosophy. The central question is how one can be spiritual without belief in the supernatural, and he answers it by setting out a paradigm for spirituality based on passionate engagement with the here-and-now.

## *RELEVANT WORLD WIDE WEB SITES*

Unitarian Universalist Association: www.uua.org
American Humanist Association: www.americanhumanist.org
Campus Freethought Alliance: www.campusfreethought.org
HUUmanists (religious humanism): www.americanhumanist.org/hsfamily/huumanist.html
American Ethical Union: www.aeu.org
Society for Humanistic Judaism: www.shj.org
African Americans for Humanism: www.secularhumanism.org/aah
American Atheists: www.atheists.org
The Secular Web: www.infidels.org
Freedom from Religion Foundation: www.ffrf.org

# MUSLIMS IN THE UNITED STATES:
# AN INCREASING MINORITY

Imagine six million people who are Americans. Imagine that they believe in paying taxes and building community. Imagine that this group doesn't drink alcohol or consume drugs because of their beliefs in self-control. Imagine that they have to keep a schedule allotting time to pray five times in the day as well as time for work, family, and enjoying themselves. Imagine a group of six million who believe in respecting women, specifically their rights to education, to consent to marriage, to divorce, to vote, to hold political office, among other things. Too good to be true? You don't have to imagine—this group is real. They are the Muslims of America.[1]

Adherents of all the major religions of the world live in the United States. In the next two chapters, we will look at three of the larger and better-known world religions whose members live in this country. The first, Islam, began in the same general geographic area as did Judaism and Christianity and has much in common with them. The second and third, Hinduism and Buddhism, began in India and are in many ways very different from the Abrahamic religions. I have kept the use of unfamiliar words to a minimum, instead using more familiar equivalents that convey the sense of what is meant. I have used less familiar terms when doing so seemed warranted because (1) they are used often in discussing a particular religion, (2) you would be likely to encounter them in your other reading or experience, or (3) they are often used and/or greatly preferred by followers of the religions.

### ISLAM, AND ISLAM IN THE UNITED STATES

Islam is the third of the major Abrahamic monotheistic religions, along with Judaism and Christianity. Abrahamic is a general term that refers to practitioners of religions who hold that Abraham is their common ancestor, and so

---

[1]Asma Gull Hasan, *American Muslims: The New Generation* (New York: Continuum, 2001), p. 3.

includes Judaism, Christianity, and Islam, as well as others. People who practice Islam are properly called **Muslims**. The word **Islam** means the peace of one who submits wholly to God (or **Allah**, an Arabic name for God used by Arabic speaking Jews and Christians as well). A *Muslim* is one who submits to Allah. You may have heard Muslims referred to as "Muhammadans" or a similar term. This is incorrect and offensive to Muslims, because they are followers of Allah, not of Muhammad.

Before you read further, think about what your own opinion of Muslims and of Islam is. Do you know any Muslims personally? What kinds of things have you heard about Muslims, or about Islam as a religion?

Muslims are still regarded by many people in the United States as outside the religious mainstream. However, consider the following: Muslims outnumber Episcopalians, Lutherans, Presbyterians, and members of the United Church of Christ in the United States. The percentage of Muslims here is expected to exceed that of Jews soon, if it hasn't already done so. There are at least 3000 mosques, Islamic centers, and other prayer locations in the United States, along with perhaps 300 Muslim schools and six Muslim colleges. Americans are becoming Muslim in significant numbers.[2] Over 22 percent of American Muslims were born here. Nearly three-quarters of American Muslims believe strongly that they should participate fully in American institutional and political life, and they vote in greater numbers than does the non-Muslim population. Over 60 percent are college graduates. And the United States Postal Service issued its first Eid Al-Fitr stamp in 2001.[3] By contrast, a Hanukkah stamp has been available since at least 1996.

## MUHAMMAD

The story of Islam begins with Muhammad, whom Muslims believe is the "Seal of the Prophets," the last and final prophet in a long line of prophets sent by Allah to bring God's truth to humankind. He was born about 570 C.E. Forty years later, Muhammad had an experience in which he believed that the angel Gabriel spoke to him, conveying the actual words of Allah himself. He was told that he had been chosen as a prophet and that he must repeat the words that he would be given to all who would listen. The revelations continued until shortly before Muhammad's death in 632. Islam thus began as an oral tradition passed from Muhammad to a few close associates and, finally, to the world.

Muhammad, the Prophet, was a human being like all other human beings. The Christian identification of the person Jesus of Nazareth with God is blasphemous to Muslims because making a human being God's equal does not recognize the incomparable greatness and oneness of Allah. Muhammad is, however, regarded as the model for what an ideal person is, and the stories

[2]"Muslims in America: Profile 2001," www.soundvision.com/info/yearinreview/2002/profile.asp.
[3]"Facts About Muslims in America," www.opendialogue.com/english/facts.html.

about his life are a source of inspiration for his followers. What Muhammad said and did, as recorded by his companions in the tradition (**Hadith**), provides a blueprint for the interpretation and application of the Qur'an to the various situations of life. Poetry in praise of the Prophet and his life exists in virtually every language spoken by Muslims, and love for him and for his family marks Muslim devotion. Standards for Muslim belief and action come not only from the Qur'an but from its application exemplified in the life and sayings of Muhammad.

## THE QUR'AN

The sacred scripture of Islam is called the **Qur'an**, or the **Holy Qur'an**. It was originally written in Arabic, and most Muslims believe that it is fully authentic only in that language. Because Islam is a missionary religion, however, the Qur'an has been translated into many languages, including English.

The first chapter is recited at the beginning of prayers. It summarizes many of the principal themes of Islam:

> All praise is due to Allah, the Lord of the Worlds.
> The Beneficent, the Merciful.
> Master of the Day of Judgment.
> Thee do we serve and Thee do we beseech for help.
> Keep us on the right path.
> The path of those upon whom Thou hast bestowed favors.
> Not (the path) of those upon whom Thy wrath is brought down, nor of those who go astray.[4]

Allah commanded that Muhammad **recite** the Qur'an, and reciting still plays an important part in Muslim devotion:

> Recitation of the Qur'an is thought to have a healing, soothing effect, but can also bring protection, miraculous signs, knowledge, and destruction, according to Muslim tradition. It is critical that one recite the Qur'an only in a purified state, for the words are so powerful that the one who recites it takes on a great responsibility. Ideally, one learns the Qur'an as a child, when memorization is easiest and when the power of the words will help to shape one's life.[5]

## BELIEFS

The core beliefs of Islam, from which all others arise, are the oneness and unity of Allah and the prophethood of Muhammad. There are two primary subgroups within Islam, the **Sunni** Muslims (by far the larger subgroup) and

---

[4]The *Holy Qur'an*, trans. M. H. Shakir (Tahrike Tarsile Qur'an, 1983), www.hti.umich.edu/relig/koran/.
[5]Mary Pat Fisher and Robert Luyster, *Living Religions* (Englewood Cliffs, NJ: Prentice Hall, 1991), p. 275.

the **Shia Muslims**. There is a nucleus of beliefs that is widely shared among Muslims in North America, and these form the basis for our discussion here.

Muslims, as stated above, believe in **the oneness of Allah**. "Oneness" here is not primarily a matter of arithmetic, of there being numerically only one God. Rather the emphasis is on the utter incomparability of Allah, there being nothing as great as Allah. It is also not simply an intellectual matter but requires trust in Allah, submission to the will of Allah, and reliance upon Allah for everything in life. These attitudes follow logically from Muslims' belief in the incomparable greatness of Allah.

They also believe in the **angels of Allah**. Angels are spiritual beings whose entire role is to serve Allah. Each has a specific duty to perform. This belief arises from the prior belief that knowledge cannot be limited to what can be perceived with the senses, that there are in fact things that exist that we cannot know through the senses (Qur'an 16:49–50 and 21:19–20).

Muslims also believe in **all the books of Allah**, including the sacred writings of Judaism and Christianity, culminating in the Qur'an. There are specific references in the Qur'an to God's having given Torah to the House of Israel and the New Testament to Christians. The Qur'an is the standard by which the others are judged. Insofar as they agree with it, they are true and are to be accepted. When they differ from the Qur'an, it has precedence.

As a result of this, Muslims also believe in **all the prophets of Allah**. There are approving references to many of the Hebrew prophets (Abraham, Moses, and David among them) as well as to John the Baptist and Jesus. Each age and each nation is believed to have had its messenger from Allah. **Muhammad**, as stated before, **is the last and final Prophet** in this long succession. Allah entrusted him with the prophecy that completes and corrects those that have gone before.

Those of Islamic faith also affirm **life after death**. The Qur'an paints vivid pictures of both paradise and hell, as well as of a day of judgment in which all people will be called to account for their lives. Muslims believe that Allah keeps an accurate account of everything people do and think. Good deeds will be rewarded and evil ones punished.

Muslim morality is very similar to that of Christianity and Judaism. Marriage and family are very important; marriage is considered a duty and is based on a legal contract to which both husband and wife agree. Sexual relations outside marriage are strictly forbidden. Divorce is permitted but strongly discouraged. Anything injurious to oneself or to others—mentally, physically, or morally—is forbidden. Respect and care for the elderly is considered very important, and people are expected to care for their parents in their later years. The equality of all persons and dealing with others with respect and total honesty is a fundamental moral value.

## THE FIVE PILLARS OF ISLAM

Islam is second only to Christianity in its number of worldwide followers. Wherever they live, Muslims share five core practices, called the **Five Pillars of Islam**. The Five Pillars are **five specific acts required of all faithful Muslims**. Although they are classified as "required," their actual observance varies from one person to another, even in traditionally Muslim countries. There is tension between those who support strict observance as the only way to be a "good Muslim" and those who accept a wider range of observance. This tension is not unique to Islam but exists in all religions. The first pillar is **faith**, shown in the **repetition of the creed** (*Shahadah*): "There is no God but Allah, and Muhammad is the Prophet of Allah." Devout Muslims repeat this affirmation of faith daily. Doing so helps keep the major principles of their faith at the center of their lives. These are often the first words spoken to a newborn Muslim baby, and the last words spoken or heard by one who is dying. While saying the Shahadah is important, the faith which it expresses is the central concern.

The second pillar is **prayer five times daily**. Muslim life is based on consciousness of God at all times, and frequent prayer facilitates this. Ritual cleansing precedes the prayers, and each prayer is accompanied by specific ritual actions, such as sitting, standing, and prostrating oneself with the forehead touching the floor or ground. Muslims pray facing Mecca, the holy city of Islam, located in what is now Saudi Arabia. These are set, formal prayers. In addition, Muslims are encouraged to repeat these prayers more times than is required and to add their own personal prayers to the required ones. Prayers are said at dawn, at midday, midafternoon, dusk, and at night. There is some flexibility in the exact times; the idea is to have the prayers paced throughout the day. Doing so helps keep Muslims continually aware of Allah and of the need for submission to him. Those who can are encouraged to attend the **mosque (masjid)**, the Islamic place of worship (Figure 11–1) for the midday prayers on Fridays.

Islam does not have a weekly Sabbath, but the community of faith gathers to pray these prayers together and usually to hear the Qur'an read and explained in a talk by the *imam* or prayer leader. While the Jewish Sabbath is a day of rest, and Christians have traditionally interpreted Sunday (the Lord's Day) similarly, Muslims are explicitly enjoined to attend to their work before and after Friday midday prayer. Whether individually or with others, Muslims pray as members of the community of faith and use "we" rather than "I" as they pray.

As you can imagine, the required prayers can be difficult for Muslims in the United States. Prayer times may conflict with work times, and there may not always be an appropriate place to pray in the workplace. Employers may not always want to make the slight accommodation necessary to allow time for prayers, and the curiosity of fellow workers can be embarrassing. On the other side, many Muslims appreciate the opportunity it gives for them to express their faith to non-Muslims.

**Figure 11-1**    The *Masjid*, or mosque, Islamic Center of Toledo, Ohio. The presence of Muslims, Hindus, Buddhists, and others of the less familiar religions in the United States expands the range of religious architecture, as well as of religious beliefs and practices. *(Photo courtesy of Richard J. Fears)*

The third pillar is the **giving of alms** to help those in need. This is not simply charity. It is more like a religious tax in that it is required. It amounts to about 2 1/2 percent, based on a person's net worth. Muslims in the United States select a Muslim organization to which they will pay the alms; for many, it is the Muslim Student Association. They are encouraged to make other charitable contributions, as they are able. Muslims do not look down on wealth, as long as it is gotten honestly; the honest earning of money and wise management of it is a tribute to Allah. But Allah must also be worshiped through one's wealth, and this is the point of almsgiving.

Fourth is **fasting during the month of Ramadan**. The Islamic religious calendar differs from the civil calendar, so Ramadan occurs at different times in different years. Ramadan is the month in which tradition holds that the revelation to Muhammad began. Fasting, in this instance, means complete abstention from eating, drinking, smoking, the use of tobacco, and sexual activity during daylight hours. A meal is eaten immediately before and immediately following the hours of fasting. This activity helps unite Muslims around the world, encourages empathy for those who are hungry or otherwise lacking, and reinforces submission to the will of Allah. Ramadan is also a time of increased spiritual awareness, when Muslims often spend extra time in reading and studying the Qur'an and in prayer. Many Muslims read the entire Qur'an during the month. Fasting is not required of young children, women who are pregnant or menstruating, travelers, the elderly, and those who are ill or frail, as well as others on whom it would impose an unreasonable burden.

The fast is followed by Eid Al-Fitr, the Festival of Fast-Breaking. This is a joyous time in which families and friends gather together to rejoice in the end of this strenuous time and to celebrate the spiritual benefits gained from it. For many Muslim families in the United States, it is a time to invite non-Muslim friends to join in the celebration and share special foods from their religious and national cultures. My own graduate school days were punctuated by Eids spent with the family of my daughter's Muslim elementary school classmate.

The last of the Pillars is the **hajj**, or **pilgrimage to Mecca**, a journey that Muslims are required to make at least once in their lives, as long as they are mentally, physically, and financially capable of doing so. Hajj brings Muslims from around the world together for a series of religious rituals in and around Mecca. Its center is the Grand Mosque and the Kabah, a large stone building that Muslims believe was built by Abraham and Ishmael for the worship of Allah. Most pilgrims also visit Medina, the city in which Muhammad found shelter after he was forced to flee Mecca because people there would not accept his teaching. After the Meccan tribes were defeated, Muhammad made a pilgrimage back to Mecca in 629. The rites that he performed then are the prototype for those carried out by Muslims today.

The pilgrimage is very demanding, both physically and emotionally. Huge numbers of people converge and emotions run very high. Nonetheless, Muslims regard it as a joyful occasion, not simply a duty. People stand before Allah as individuals in community, in the places where their spiritual history took root. Those who make hajj do not forget it, and they are privileged to use the title, *hajji*, designating one who has made hajj.[6]

## MUSLIMS IN THE UNITED STATES

Estimates of the number of Muslims in the United States vary considerably. It is not necessary to be a member of a mosque to be a Muslim. Too, some Muslims remain hesitant to identify themselves as Muslims because prejudice still exists. Another possible source of inaccuracy in the data is that there may be Christians from Arab countries who identify culturally but not religiously with the Muslim community. Most nonimmigrant Muslims in the United States are black,

---

[6]"Stoning the Devil," *The Wall Street Journal*, February 6, 2004, p. W 23.

although this accounts for only about 2 percent of the black population in the United States. Contrary to what you might expect, most Arab Americans are Christians, perhaps because Christians tend to emigrate to the United States from Muslim countries in greater numbers than do non-Christians.[7]

Muslims have come to the United States from virtually all of the Middle Eastern countries in which Islam is common, as well as from India, Pakistan, China, the former Soviet Union, and elsewhere. There have been Muslims in the United States for many generations, as well as a steady influx of recent immigrants. There are also American converts to Islam. Thus, on the one hand, there is an Islamic *community* here: a group of people united by a common religion. On the other hand, there are several *communities* of Muslims here: American-born, descendants of immigrants, and recent immigrants, as well as Muslims of various national and ethnic backgrounds.

As the Muslim community becomes more thoroughly integrated into the larger culture of the United States, distinctions such as "immigrant" and "indigenous" are becoming less useful to describe Islam in America as sociological changes occur over time:

> "Immigrant" communities are becoming "establishment," children are growing and intermarrying, foreign-born Muslims are becoming American citizens, demarcation between the "older" immigrants and the new African and Asian immigrants taking on racist overtones.[8]

Recent analyses of the Muslim experience in the United States indicate that the two key problems facing both immigrant and native-born Muslims are deciding how they will live an Islamic life in America and dealing with prejudice. Work schedules do not make daily prayers convenient and it can be very difficult to follow Muslim dietary practices (which include a detailed list of permissible and forbidden foods) in institutions such as colleges, the military, and prisons. Many Muslims regard the pervasive use of alcohol, sexual permissiveness, and less than modest dress in the United States as problematic. American Muslims strive to be faithful to Muslim ideals in spite of these and other adverse circumstances.[9]

There is a growing subculture of young Islamic Americans, children of immigrant Muslims in the 1960s and 1970s, who are determined to forge an integrated identity that is both Muslim and American. Their doing so calls into question the usual stereotype of Islam as a "foreign" faith. They are also finding new ways to formulate that faith, ways that might well be unimaginable in the Muslim nations from which their parents came:

> American Muslims are experiencing both exhilaration at the opportunity to increase their numbers and develop their institutions and frustration and dismay

---

[7] *New York Times National*, April 10, 1991, p. 1.
[8] Gisela Webb, "Expressions of Islam in America," in *America's Alternative Religions*, ed. Timothy Miller (Albany, NY: State University of New York Press, 1995), pp. 240–241, n. 2.
[9] Webb, "Expressions of Islam in America," in *America's Alternative Religions*, p. 237.

as they continue to experience prejudice, intimidation, discrimination, misunderstanding, and even hatred. . . . [Muslims in the United States] have unprecedented freedom to experiment with forms and structures for the separation of religion and state away from the watchful eyes of wary governments and the criticism of traditionalists. At the same time, this freedom is fraught with the danger of innovation and deviance; the great range of options available in the American context carries the threat of sectarian division and fragmentation.[10]

Like members of most other religious groups, Muslims in the United States range from liberals who seek accommodation with the surrounding culture to the very conservative who seek to preserve the inherited tradition and advocate separation from those who do not agree. There are also differences of opinion between Muslims who want to convert non-Muslims and those who do not.

The Muslim mosque (*masjid* is being used increasingly) has changed character in the United States. In most traditionally Muslim countries, the mosque is simply a place in which the community of the faithful gathers for the Friday midday prayers. The *imam*, or prayer leader, is a member of the community who is skilled in Qur'anic recitation and perhaps exposition. There is no professional clergy in Islam, and usually the imam holds another job. In the United States, the mosque has become much more like a church or synagogue, and the imam has become a professional clergyman, in most instances. Mosques offer a full range of activities, both religious and cultural, for the Muslim community. Besides the traditional prayer service, there will often be women's groups, classes for all ages and both genders, social activities, and day care. The imam is expected to function as the leader of the congregation, a counselor, an administrator, and the representative of the Muslim community to the surrounding culture.[11]

As traditionally interpreted, Islamic law covers every aspect of life for Muslims: religious and secular (a distinction that is itself alien to Islam), private and public, extraordinary and mundane. Muslims who live in a non-Muslim culture must decide the extent to which full adherence to Islamic law is possible or desirable. As you might expect, individual Muslims vary in how carefully they keep all the details of Islamic law. There are two sources of variation: (1) different aspects of observance receive different attention, and (2) different Muslim subpopulations vary in their observance.

In the first place, some regulations are kept much more fully than others. For example, Muslim law forbids the payment or receiving of interest on money. Using the American banking system makes this extremely difficult. Most Muslims in the United States do have bank accounts and do use credit

[10]Yvonne Yazbeck Haddad, "Introduction: The Muslims of America," in *The Muslims of America*, ed. Yvonne Yazbeck Haddad (New York: Oxford University Press, 1991), pp. 3 and 5.

[11]For an ethnographic study of the changes that have occurred in one immigrant Muslim congregation, see Rogaia Mustafa Abusharaf, "Structural Adaptations in an Immigrant Muslim Congregation in New York," in *Gatherings in Diaspora: Religious Communities and the New Immigration*, ed. R. Stephen Warner and Judith G. Wittner (Philadelphia: Temple University Press, 1998), pp. 235–261.

when necessary. Muslim law also forbids the consumption of pork, pork products, and alcohol. The great majority of Muslims do not knowingly consume pork or pork products, and most Muslims make a conscientious effort to find out if prepared foods contain them. Fewer adhere absolutely to the alcohol prohibition, although a majority do. Whether or not Muslims themselves choose to use alcohol, they must decide whether to offer it to non-Muslim guests in their homes. Some do and some do not.

There is no consensus among Muslims in the United States about the application of Muslim laws and values. There is no doubt that observance declines with a number of factors. Less strict observance is associated with being in the United States for a longer time, with interacting with non-Muslim Americans, and "apparently as a general result of living in American culture."[12] Age is also a factor. While 70 percent of adults aged 18 and older surveyed in the Los Angeles area believe that Islamic values should be observed "strictly," among those under 18, only about half agreed.[13]

Muslims are discouraged or forbidden from dating as it is practiced in the United States. Youth meet prospective mates through their families and at activities at the mosque. Social interaction takes place only in well-chaperoned group settings. Marriages are usually arranged. Women especially, but men also, are discouraged from marrying outside the faith. If they do, they may marry only a Jew or a Christian (other "people of the Book"). This makes finding a suitable partner within such a small population difficult. Muslim magazines often carry matrimonial ads in which families invite correspondence from potential partners for a daughter, sister, son, or brother.

An Islamic popular religion is also developing in the United States as more and more items become available as the market for them increases. There are Muslim Scout troops and compact disc Qur'ans and Islamic art screen savers for personal computers. An "I [heart] Allah" mug has been spotted, as well as a "Praise Allah" bumper sticker. Several companies cater to the clothing needs of Islamic women who wish to maintain traditional dress.[14]

## MUSLIM COLLEGE STUDENTS

Muslim college students have come to study in the United States from nearly every country in the world where Muslims live. **The Muslim Student Association** was founded in 1963 to provide for the needs of Islamic students on American campuses and to help non-Muslim students come to know Islam and its followers better. It remains one of the largest and most active among

[12]Yvonne Yazbeck Haddad and Adair T. Lummis, *Islamic Values in the United States: A Comparative Study* (New York: Oxford University Press, 1987), Chapters 3, 4, and 5.

[13]Kambiz GhaneaBassiri, *Competing Visions of Islam in the United States: A Study of Los Angeles* (Westport, CT: Greenwood Press, 1997), p. 49. This book provides considerable data on varying attitudes and degrees of observance among Muslims in the greater Los Angeles area.

[14]Using "Islamic clothing" or "Muslim clothing" as your search term will bring up several Internet sites offering such clothing.

Islamic organizations, appealing to both immigrant and American-born Muslims.[15] It is an active and multi-faceted organization

> that serves Muslim students during their college and university careers by facilitating their efforts to establish, maintain, and develop chapters of Muslim Student Associations, Unions, Organizations, and Islamic Societies. Emphasis is placed on the learning and well-being of the individual Muslim student, as well as networking and growth of the chapter through sponsorship of educational programs, camps, zonal and annual conferences, and worker training programs. . . . MSA National strives to inform and mobilize students to respond to crises around North America and the world.[16]

There are very few specifically Muslim colleges or universities in the United States. The American Islamic College in Chicago was founded in 1983, and is the first school of its kind in the U.S. It is "a bachelor of arts–granting institution approved by the Illinois Board of Higher Education and offers a range of studies in the social and physical sciences, computer science, economics, history, and other areas, as well as a number of courses in Arabic and Islamic studies."[17] The first Muslim graduate school was begun in 1996, the School of Islamic and Social Sciences in Virginia. It offers two programs of study, a Master's program in Islamic studies and a program for training imams.[18]

A Web site offers "Top Ten Tips for Muslim College Students." Some of the tips are similar to those you might find on any similar site, such as advice to not skip classes and keep up with your reading assignments, remaining in contact with professors and fellow students, and taking classes in which you're genuinely interested. Others, however, focus specifically on being a *Muslim* college student: College is an excellent opportunity to introduce others to Islam. Hang out with others who help you to be a better Muslim rather than pulling you down. Stay away from situations that you think will compromise your faith and practice, such as social events at which alcohol is served. Be active in the Muslim Student Association. Balance college studies with Islamic studies.[19]

### MUSLIM ORGANIZATIONS

There are a number of Muslim organizations in the United States. I will mention only a few of them. Most of you who are reading this book are college students. Some of you are members of or active in campus religious organiza-

---

[15] A Web search using "Muslim Student Association" as your search string will return a list of MSA groups at specific colleges and universities; many of these are informative and very well done.

[16] MSA of the U.S. and Canada, www.msa-national.org/about/faq.html.

[17] Jane I. Smith, *Islam in America, Columbia Contemporary American Religion Series* (New York: Columbia University Press, 1999), p. 132.

[18] The URLs for these two institutions' Web sites are American Islamic College (www.aicusa.edu), and the School of Islamic and Social Sciences (www.siss.edu).

[19] University of Oklahoma Neislein Students Association Web site www.ou.edu/student/oumsa/tips.doc.

tions sponsored by your community of faith. The Muslim Student Association, described above, is one of the constituent groups of **The Islamic Society of North America**, an umbrella organization of several groups. It is generally considered to be the primary national Muslim organization, especially by immigrant Muslims. It publishes a journal, *Islamic Horizons*. The American **Muslim Mission** is the largest organization of American-born Muslims. It publishes *The Muslim Journal*.

Recall that in the discussion of Muslim beliefs, we distinguished between Sunni and Shia Muslims. There is a third group of Muslims in the United States, the **Sufi Muslims**, or simply, Sufis. Sufism is the mystical branch of Islam, comparable in that respect to Hasidic Judaism and Christian mysticism. Sufism first came to the United States in 1910 with an Indian musician named Pir Hazrat Inayat Khan. There are now organizations throughout the United States. Their beliefs focus on the essential unity of all religions. They affirm that there is one God, one holy book, "the sacred manuscript of nature," one religion, one law, one human brotherhood, one moral principle, one truth, and one path.[20] Meditation and ecstatic dancing facilitate communion with God. The Order accepts individual students as initiates, sponsors worship as the Universal Worship of the Church of All, and also has a Healing Order that works with group healing rituals.

## MUSLIM WOMEN IN AMERICA

Under Qur'anic law, women received more equal treatment than was otherwise common in Muhammad's lifetime. Religiously and legally, women and men were equals. It is also the case that, while having equal standing before Allah and before the law, women and men were thought to be different from each other, with different primary spheres of responsibility. Current research indicates that American Muslim women support equal rights and opportunities for women and men, while understanding their roles as complementary rather than identical.[21]

Many American Muslim women seek a path that allows for both fulfilling traditional Islamic expectations and exploring the new options and opportunities presented by life in American culture. What is distinctive in the U. S. is the individual choice that each woman can make, without interference, as she follows her own conscience in these matters.

Several issues are at the forefront of the discussion as women find their way in these new circumstances. While there is general agreement that working outside the home is acceptable and, for some, commendable, there is less disagreement on which occupations are preferable and how much interference

[20]"Sufi Thoughts," Sufi Order, Lebanon Springs, NY, n.d.
[21]Jane I. Smith, *Islam in America, Columbia Contemporary American Religion Series* (New York: Columbia University Press, 1999), p. 105.

with family life is allowable. There is agreement, too, that modesty in dress, especially by American standards, should be the norm, but what this means is less clear. In particular, whether it means covering the hair or not, and if so, to what extent, is debated. What it means to raise Muslim children, and the best ways to do this, are also matters that are discussed. Other things pertaining to running a Muslim home in the United States are also interpreted differently. For example, even though most Muslims abstain from alcohol themselves, should they offer it to non-Muslim visitors, and should they attend social functions where it is served? Some women feel caught between the demands of their own increasingly complicated lives and the strong Muslim expectation that aging parents are to be cared for in the homes of their children.

Even as they are excited about new opportunities to study and interpret the Qur'an for themselves, some Muslim women are frustrated by the limits placed on the roles they can play in their masjids. Although leadership roles in education and fund-raising are open to women, especially as American mosques become centers of religious and social life for the entire family, the key role of the imam is not. For some, not being allowed to sit with their husbands and older sons in prayer is frustrating, as well.

## Islam and Black Americans

Black Americans were attracted to Islam by its message of complete racial equality. Muslim tradition holds that a daughter of Muhammad married a black man. Islam also offered belief in one God and a strong ethical code, as did Christianity, but it was not identified with the white oppressors. The story of Islam as it relates to the struggle for black freedom and self-definition is complex, as is the history of black Muslims in the United States. What is clear is that Islam offered American blacks an opportunity for a more positive self-identification:

> Although very few references explain how ideas about Islam became available in the black community, it is clear that this religion promised a new identity, a feeling of "somebodiness" denied by the dominant culture, a liberation from . . . relegation to insignificance. The new adherents shed Christianity, which they perceived as the root of their oppression in its glorification of suffering and promise of redemption in the hereafter.[22]

Islam was initially linked with the black power movement. Elijah Muhammad emerged in 1934 as the leader of what was then known as the Nation of Islam.

In the 1960s, a group arose within the Nation of Islam who did not fully agree with Muhammad. This group was led by Malcolm X (born Malcolm

---

[22]Beverly Thomas McCloud, "African-American Muslim Women," in *The Muslims of America*, ed. Haddad, p. 178.

Little in 1925). Malcolm X had earlier accepted Muhammad as a "divine leader." Especially later in his life, however, Malcolm X and his followers wanted to move the Nation closer to traditional Islam and away from complete separation from whites. They founded the Muslim Mosque, Incorporated, in 1964.

In 1975, Elijah Muhammad died and his son, W. D. Muhammad (b. 1933) assumed control of the Nation of Islam. Under his leadership, the Nation moved closer to the viewpoint of the Muslim Mosque. Followers of Warith Muhammad are now accepted by Muslims worldwide as followers of traditional Sunni Islam.

It is Malcolm X who has retained, even after his death, a hold on the imagination of American blacks, Muslim and non-Muslim alike. A poll done at the time that Spike Lee's controversial movie *Malcolm X* came out indicated that although only about half of American blacks really understood what Malcolm X stood for, a majority consider him a hero. Most rank him second only to Martin Luther King, Jr., in importance to contemporary blacks.[23]

Although the themes of black power and separatism have been muted among most black Muslims, Islam remains a viable alternative for American blacks. It has important similarities with both Christianity and Judaism while not being identified with slavery and oppression.

People who were dissatisfied with the emphasis on racial equality in mainstream Islam came together around Louis Farrakhan in a movement to return to the separatist views and policies of the old Nation. Minister Farrakhan's followers have remained an outspoken minority among American Muslims. A list of their demands includes:

- Complete freedom, justice, and equality of opportunity, particularly equal opportunity in employment
- The provision of land for the descendants of slaves to establish their own homeland
- The freeing of Islamic and other black prisoners, particularly those on death rows
- An end to police brutality
- Freedom from all taxation until equal justice is a reality
- Separate but equal education under all black teachers
- No intermarriage[24]

The Nation of Islam also links black separatism with traditional Muslim beliefs. For example, they affirm:

- A "mental resurrection" that will begin with "the so-called Negroes," who are identified as God's chosen people.

---

[23]*Newsweek*, November 16, 1992, p. 68.
[24]The Nation of Islam World Wide Web site, www.noi.org. The same material often appears in *The Final Call*, the Nation's newspaper.

- The final judgment will take place in America.
- Master W. Fard Muhammad [an early leader of the black Muslim movement] was himself the incarnation of God, the "Messiah of the Christians and the 'Mahdi' [a savior figure] of the Muslims."[25]

The Nation of Islam under Minister Farrakhan's leadership continues the themes of separatism and retribution that the Muslim Mosque, Incorporated, has muted or eliminated entirely. As such, the Nation of Islam gives expression to the anger, bitterness, and resentment of a group of people so damaged in body, mind, and spirit by centuries of oppression that all talk of cooperation and "friendship" with the oppressors must ring hollow and hypocritical.

## INTO THE FUTURE

Muslims see several issues as especially relevant to Islam in America in the next decade. The degree of compromise and accommodation is a pervasive one, as Muslims seek to balance adherence to tradition with relevance to contemporary American life:

> Those who up to now have tried to lead lives of relative isolation, fearful that too much contact with America will compromise their own faith and culture, may have to question whether generations to come will find it necessary to be more open, more receptive to the culture of which they find themselves a part. Those who have opted for complete identification with America, abandoning many of the elements of Muslim observance, may find that they have lost some of the clarity and distinctiveness of what it means to be Muslim.[26]

Other nonmainstream religious groups (Orthodox Jews, for example, holiness Christians, Buddhists, and Hindus) face a similar necessity to balance tradition and modernization.

There are several additional matters of concern. Who has the authority to determine what or who is a "good Muslim" when there are so many options and no central authority? What, if anything, unifies all American Muslims? Recruiting and training American-born imams and other leaders is crucial. In order to have their voices heard in the political arena, Muslims must learn ways to be effective in the political process. Political action committees (PACs) have been formed, and Muslim lobbyists work at the federal and state levels.[27]

---

[25]The Nation of Islam World Wide Web site, www.noi.org. The same material often appears in *The Neap Final Call*, the Nation's newspaper. The site has the full text of the demands and beliefs.

[26]Smith, *Islam in America*, p. 175.

[27]Smith, *Islam in America*, Chapter 8.

### QUESTIONS AND ACTIVITIES FOR REVIEW, DISCUSSION, AND WRITING

1. If you live or attend school close to an Islamic mosque (look in the yellow pages under "Religious Organizations," or perhaps "Churches"), make arrangements to attend the Friday midday prayer. Non-Muslims are welcome at mosques. There likely will be some dress restrictions; inquire before you attend.
2. Especially if visiting a mosque is not possible, try to arrange for a Muslim student who attends your college or university to come and speak to your class.
3. If you are not a Muslim, pick one of the Five Pillars of Islam and discuss what it might mean to you if you were. You may want to do some additional reading on the Pillar that you choose. If you are a Muslim, discuss what one of the Pillars means to you.
4. If your library subscribes to any periodicals published by United States Muslims, read through two or three issues, and write about what impression you form of Islam.

### FOR FURTHER READING

HADDAD, YVONNE YAZBECK and JOHN L. ESPOSITO, Eds., *Muslims on the Americanization Path?* New York: Oxford University Press, 2000. This collection of essays focuses on the ways in which Muslims deal with balancing tradition and accommodation.

HASAN, ASMA GULL, *American Muslims: The New Generation.* New York: The Continuum International Publishing Group, 2001. Hasan, a "self-proclaimed Muslim feminist cowgirl" (p. 3) writes about Muslims in the United States with warmth and humor, covering such issues as women, Jesus, jihad, militant black Islam, and Muslims in the media.

McCLOUD, AMINAH BEVERLY, *African American Islam.* New York: Routledge, 1995. McCloud covers the history and contemporary functions of Islam in the African-American community. Chapters 3 ("The Family Structure and Domestic Life") and 5 ("Women in Islam") especially have a wealth of ethnographic detail that makes African-American Islam come alive for the reader.

SMITH, JANE I., *Islam in America, Columbia Contemporary American Religion Series.* New York: Columbia University Press, 1999. An accessible and well-written book that covers all the basic issues of what it means to be Muslim in America.

### RELEVANT WORLD WIDE WEB SITES

Resources for Studying Islam: www.arches.uga.edu/~godlas

The Islam Page: www.islamworld.net

Islam 101: www.islam101.com

Muslim Public Affairs Council: www.mpac.org

Muslim Student Association: www.msa-natl.org

Nation of Islam: www.noi.org

Islamic Center of North America: www.isna.org

# HINDUS AND BUDDHISTS:
# ASIA COMES TO AMERICA

As Dr. Ravindra Marri left his home in Bangalore, India, to enter a medical residency program at a hospital in New York City, his mother carefully handed him cloth-wrapped religious objects from their home shrine. . . . In his New York apartment, Marri placed these objects on a shelf beside his bed. Later he went back to India to get married and returned to New York with his wife. She brought sacred objects from her home and set up a small shrine in the kitchen. They consolidated the sacred objects in a home shrine in the family room of their first house.[1]

Despite its gentle mein, Buddhism is a profoundly subversive force in postmodern consumer society. The structure of our economy, our psychology, our whole social reality is built around the unquestioned assumption that we are each of us separate, autonomous selves. Selves with endless appetites for consumer goods to set us off from the crowd, make us feel good about who we are, and give us a sense of identity. Selves identify with a particular ethnic group, political party, or ideology. Selves driven by a sense of inadequacy, driven by the desire to be better, richer, or wiser people, driven by the need to prove their worth, driven by dark fears about the future and the fate that awaits us. What would happen if enough people saw through all that?[2]

Hinduism and Buddhism both began in India, a far different world than that which gave rise to Judaism, Christianity, and Islam. What we now call Hinduism began in India, sometime between 2,000 and 1,500 years before the lifetime of Jesus. Buddhism began later, in the fifth century B.C.E. Hinduism and Buddhism each account for less than 1 percent of the U.S. population, but are religious minorities whose visibility is increasing.

---

[1]Gurinder Singh Mann, Paul David Numrich, and Raymond B. Williams, *Buddhists, Hindus, and Sikhs in America* (New York: Oxford University Press, 2001), p. 81.
[2]James William Coleman, *The New Buddhism: The Western Transformation of an Ancient Tradition* (New York: Oxford University Press, 2001), p. 230.

The Hart-Celler Immigration Law of 1965 helped enable the growth of Asian religions in America. Prior to 1965, Asians had been restrained from entering the U.S. through a series of restrictive laws, such as an immigration act in 1917 that created an "Asiatic Barred Zone" and a ruling in 1923 that immigrants from India were not eligible for American citizenship. Coupled with anti-Asian sentiment following World War I, such laws meant that prior to 1960, fewer than 15,000 Asian Indians came to the United States, for example. The Hart-Celler legislation opened the door to immigrants from south and east Asian nations, and with them, to religions of Asian origin.[3]

We will concentrate on Hinduism and Buddhism, the two Asian religions with the largest numbers and highest public profiles in this country. Although, as we will see, there are substantial differences between them, each exists here in three broad forms: Their **ethnic** forms have come to this country with Asian immigrants and are largely confined to immigrant communities. Their **export** forms have come to the United States with missionaries from Asia who have actively sought converts among non-Asians. Finally, their **elite** forms have appealed to well-educated, largely upper middle class and upper class Americans seeking alternatives to the more predominant religions in the United States.[4]

## HINDUISM AND HINDUS IN THE UNITED STATES

Unlike the religions you have studied so far, Hinduism has no single founder. The word **Hinduism** is an umbrella term for a vast collection of religious beliefs and practices that nonetheless have enough in common to warrant grouping them together. Indians themselves often use the term **Sanatana Dharma** for their religion. It means "original religion," because Indians believe that theirs is one form of the religion that has existed since the dawn of humanity. This religion is not Hindu, nor Buddhist, nor Muslim, nor any particular religion. It is simply *human* religion, and Hinduism is but one embodiment of it. Hinduism differs dramatically in many respects from the religions you have learned about thus far. Religion in the United States tends to be about belief, or doctrine. Hinduism, on the other hand, is much more concerned with practice. Hindus, as one author points out, have basic obligations and responsibilities that extend to such things as bathing, the preparation and consumption of meals, marriage, and interaction with others.

There is no one worldview or set of beliefs that is required of Hindus, nor any to which all hold without exception. However, the Himalayan Academy, an American Hindu organization headquartered in Hawaii, cites nine

[3]Peter W. Williams, *America's Religions: From Their Origins to the Twenty-First Century* (Urbana, IL: University of Illinois Press, 2002), p. 457.
[4]Williams, *America's Religions: From Their Origins to the Twenty-First Century*, pp. 458–459.

"bedrock concepts on which most Hindus concur." They're paraphrased below, along with interpretive comments.[5]

1.    The **Vedas** and the **Agamas** are revered. The Vedas are the oldest of the sacred writings and have influenced the entire development of Hinduism. Loyalty to the Vedas is regarded by many Hindus as the litmus test of authentic Hinduism. In addition, Hindus regard the Agamas as revealed scripture. While the Vedas help to define what Hinduism as a whole is, the various Agamas are important to specific groups within it. The **Bhagavad-Gita** is an important devotional classic and is the best known and best loved sacred writing among Hindus. It is a section of a much longer epic work, the **Mahabharata**.

2.    The sacred, while One, is known in many forms and by many names. Whereas the Semitic religions distinguish clearly between God as Crea*tor* and everything else as crea*tion*, Hindus do not make this distinction. Rather, **every living thing is a manifestation of the sacred**. The divine can be seen and known in everything that is, and everything that is can be seen as a part of the divine. Everything else exists only insofar as it participates in the sacred; nothing has independent existence. This also means that, fundamentally, there can be no sharp separation between things—between the divine and the human, or between people and all other beings. In the innermost core of our being, myself, my cat, and the fly my cat is chasing are one.

3.    The "universe undergoes endless cycles of creation, preservation and dissolution." Rather than a creation from nothing by the will of God, Hindus believe that the **universe goes through endless cycles** that have neither a beginning nor an end.

4.    **Karma** is the moral law of cause and effect through which our actions create our destiny. The principle of karma states that every action has a reaction. In our own culture, even if we ourselves are not a part of the Judeo-Christian-Islamic tradition, most of us are accustomed to thinking in terms of rewards and punishments: Good deeds will be rewarded and evil ones punished. Karma, by contrast, is a moral law that operates analogously to natural laws such as gravity. Certain results inevitably follow certain actions.

According to a contemporary analysis, the Hindu belief in karma provides answers to three major questions:[6]

- Why am I "me" rather than someone else?
- Why does what happens to me happen to me, rather than something else happening?
- And why does it happen to me, instead of happening to someone else?

This analysis, which attempts to reinterpret central Hindu beliefs for the present time and for a context that transcends their Indian origins, offers a

---

[5]"Hindu Basics," www.himalayanacademy.com.
[6]Arvind Sharma, *Hinduism for Our Times* (Bombay: Oxford University Press, 1996), p. 25.

twofold reinterpretation of the doctrine of karma. The results of our actions affect not just ourselves, but the community of which we are a part. Karma has a social dimension as well as an individual one. The person who chooses to smoke turns other people into passive smokers. Second, karma can be reinterpreted to address the question of *why* people act as they do. Not only do the results of our actions affect us, but they become extended in the way that we treat other people, including people who had nothing to do with how we were treated. Both functional and dysfunctional family patterns, for example, tend to persist throughout generations.[7]

   **5.   Reincarnation** is widely believed throughout India. Reincarnation means (1) that a person's present life was preceded by other lives and will likewise be followed by other lives. It also means (2) that these lifetimes do not happen randomly but are connected. The way that life is lived in one lifetime determines the quality of the next incarnation.

   Belief in reincarnation brings up the question of what it means to be a person, according to Hindus. First, we must distinguish between our empirical self and our real self. Our empirical self is what we think we are, what ordinary experience tells us we are. Most of us think about it as including our physical body, our mind and personality, and our subconscious. All these aspects of us are individual and personal: They pertain to us as individuals and as personal beings. The **Real Self**, on the other hand, is that of the divine within each and every person. It is not personal, nor is it individual. This real self moves from lifetime to lifetime throughout successive incarnations.

A contemporary Hindu catechism, written specifically for Hindu young people in the United States, describes it this way:

> Our individual soul is the immortal and spiritual body of light that animates life and reincarnates again and again. . . . We are not the physical body, mind, or emotions. We are the immortal soul, *atman*.[8]

   **The human problem,** as it is expressed by Hindus, is not sin and disobedience (as in Judaism, Christianity, and Islam), but **ignorance and illusion.** We fail to understand the real nature of reality and of ourselves, and, in that misunderstanding, act in ways that reinforce the illusion of separateness. As long as we think and act as though we *are* our empirical selves, as long as we think and act as though we are separate from other beings and from the universe itself, we remain trapped in the cycle of death and rebirth.

   **The ultimate goal of human life is escape from the cycle of death and rebirth**. Throughout however many lifetimes it requires, a person comes increasingly closer to grasping the unity of all things, including the real self, in the divine. Eventually, when that unity is fully grasped, incarnation ceases and

---

[7]Sharma, *Hinduism for Our Times*, pp. 27–29.
[8]Satguru Sivaya Subramuniyaswami, *Dancing with Shiva: Hinduism's Contemporary Catechism* (Kapaa, Hawaii: Himalayan Academy Press, 1997), p. 79.

the real self is reunited with the divine, which, of course, it never really left. Most Hindus describe this as an uninterrupted communion between the real self and the divine, in which the distinction between the two is preserved while the separation is overcome. Others, however, prefer to picture it as a complete merger between the real self and the divine, in which both separation and distinction are overcome. For the majority of Hindus, this is a far-distant goal. Most look forward to living better lives throughout successive reincarnations. Hindus believe that all persons, without exception, will eventually reach a state of liberation.

6.    Hindus recognize **many divine beings**, gods and goddesses as well as other spiritual beings. Worship and ritual, both personal and corporate, can bring people into communion with these beings. Hindu worship life revolves around the home altar that is an important part of most Hindus' homes. The altar will probably have a statue or statues of the chosen deity or deities. After ceremonial cleansing, people make offerings of fruit, incense, or flowers to their deities. They see the deity in the image and in return are seen by the deity. The food offered to the deity may then be eaten by the worshiper as a part of the deity's blessing. Some people perform this ritual, or *puja*, twice daily, while some perform it only in the mornings. While approximately 75 percent of Hindu women perform daily devotions for the benefit of their families, only about half of Hindu men do so. Puja is also performed in *temples*, where it is more elaborate.

Each god and goddess has a festival day, and these are celebrated with worship at the temple. Other religious holidays are celebrated as well. Often, weekly worship is also held, usually fitted into the common Sunday morning time period. This is a distinctive feature of Hinduism in America, a key aspect of its accommodation to the non-Hindu culture. It resembles worship at the home altar, with the addition of readings from sacred texts, a sermon or lecture, and devotional songs. Many temples in the United States have become social centers for the Indian community, as well, and sponsor a number of social events, in addition to holding classes for children and adults.

Priests associated with the temple—who may hold another job as well—also perform life-cycle rites such as birth rituals, weddings, and funerals for Hindu families. Hindus who do not live close enough to attend a temple regularly can request that puja or other services be performed at a distant temple in return for a financial contribution. While most temples in India are dedicated to one primary deity, those in the United States are often dedicated to several.

Hindus accommodate to United States religious culture in other ways, as well. Some Hindus celebrate the five-day festival of Pancha Ganapati on December 21–25. Ganesha is a deity who is revered as a remover of obstacles. Families may build a shrine to Ganesha in their homes and decorate it with pine boughs, ornaments, tinsel, and lights. Christmas trees, Santa Claus, and other religious and secular symbols are not supposed to be used. Gifts are placed before the shrine daily and worship is offered to Ganesha. After the final puja on December 25th, the gifts are opened with great festivity and celebration. Gifts are also given to employees and employers, as well as friends.[9]

7.   Many Hindus believe **a reliable, personal teacher** or **guru** is necessary, especially for those dedicated to the more rigorous forms of spiritual development. **Good conduct** is also required if one is to progress spiritually.

The moral life is one that coincides with the natural order of the universe, the **dharma**. What it means to live by the dharma differs, depending on a person's place in the society, stage in life, and gender. There are also ethical prescriptions and proscriptions that are constant.

*Dancing with Shiva* offers this summary portrait of good conduct:

> We should be uplifting to our fellow man, not critical or injurious. We should be loving and kind, not hateful or mean. We should express the soul's beautiful qualities of self-control, modesty, and honesty. We should be a good example to others and a joy to be around, not a person to be avoided. Good conduct is the sum of spiritual living and comes through keeping good company. . . . The Hindu fosters humility and shuns arrogance, seeks to assist, never to hinder, finds good in others and forgets their faults.[10]

Hinduism recognizes four goals of human life, all consistent with the living of an ethical life. These goals pull together diverse elements of life into a unified whole. Each is appropriate in its place, as long as we recognize that only the last one can provide ultimate satisfaction.

> The *joy* cluster (sensual, sexual, artistic, aesthetic joys, compatible with ethics), the *economic and social fulfillment* cluster, the *morality* cluster (duties, obligations, right action, law, righteousness, general virtues and supreme ethical virtues. . .), and the *spiritual goal of salvation/liberation* (union and oneness with God).[11]

8.   **All life is sacred**, and thus noninjury or nonharming, *ahimsa*, is a central moral virtue. Noninjury and gentleness in thought, emotions, and actions are described as "the first and foremost ethical principle of every Hindu." This is why most Hindus refrain from eating meat or eat it very sparingly. Noninjury is practiced because there is the divine in everything and also because harm done to another returns to oneself by the law of karma.[12]

[9]*Hinduism Today*, 14, no. 12 (December 1992), p. 16.
[10]Subramuniyaswami, *Dancing with Shiva*, p. 181.
[11]Dr. T. K. Venkateswaran, "A Portrait of Hinduism," in Joel Beversluis, ed. *A Sourcebook for the Community of Religions* (Chicago: The Council for a Parliament of the World's Religions, 1993), pp. 62–66.
[12]Subramuniyaswami, *Dancing with Shiva*, p. 181.

**9.** No one religion embodies the only way to salvation or liberation. **All genuine religious paths are valid.** As there are any number of ways to climb a mountain, say most Hindus, so there are many paths to reunion with the divine. Differences of belief and practice are external only, in this view, and the inner essence of all humankind's religions is identical. Such a view does not rule out having personal preferences among these "externals," nor does it necessitate approval of them all. It does entail the belief that all sincere seekers, by whatever path or paths they choose, will in time arrive at their destination:

> The soul, in its intelligence, searches for its Self, slowly ascending the path that leads to enlightenment and liberation. It is an arduous, delightful journey through the cycles of birth, death and rebirth culminating in Self Realization, the direct and personal spiritual experience of God, of the Self, of Truth.[13]

### Hindu Ways of Liberation

Within itself as well, Hinduism offers people more than one way to seek release and liberation. These ways are not exclusive; people usually follow more than one, accenting one over the others and perhaps changing emphases during a lifetime. People differ in their personalities, in their stage and station in life, and one method will not be best for all. Finding the *appropriate* path is more important than locating the right one.

One very popular way is **devotion to a god or goddess.** By increasingly identifying with their chosen god or goddess, people increase their intuitive grasp of the oneness of themselves and the divine. Many Hindus worship **Shiva**, and many others are devotees of **Krishna** or **Vishnu**, gods whose concern for human beings is paramount. Others are devotees of the **Great Goddess**, who takes many forms. Deities are worshiped by prayer and offerings to their images at home altars and in temples. Deity worship personalizes the divine, giving the devotee the opportunity for a warmly emotional relationship with the sacred. It satisfies the human longing for knowing and being known by the sacred in a way analogous to that shared with a lover, close friend, or family member.

Hindu religious art abounds with images of deities, both pictures and statues. Statues are especially important. It may be difficult for you to understand the role that images of gods and goddesses play in Hinduism. For Hindus, *seeing the divine* is a basic way of experiencing communion with the sacred. The divine is present precisely *as* the image, giving itself for worship. These are not idols. The clay or the brass of the statue is not worshiped, but the deity whom it portrays and makes present to the devotee is worshiped.

A second popular way to seek liberation is through **duty**, **work**, or **action**. To follow this way means to do what is called for by one's position in

---

[13]Subramuniyaswami, *Dancing with Shiva*, p. xxiv.

life, without allowing oneself to become attached to the results of the action. Neither hope of reward nor fear of punishment is the motivation here, but simply the presence of a duty to be done. Scripture says that people have a right to their actions but not to the fruits of those actions. Attachment to the results of what we do binds us in the cycle of reincarnation. To whatever extent our working is selfless, without thought of "what's in it for me?" we can lessen the grip of karma, according to Hindu belief. This path makes the ongoing flow of daily life the way to liberation.

For countless generations of Indian Hindus, for whom survival in the face of extreme poverty and climatic conditions is problematic, this allows for religious fulfillment without having to do something additional. For contemporary Hindus caught up in the realities of professional and business life combined with family and community responsibilities, it offers the same hope. Beyond that, it affords the opportunity to transform the dailyness of life into something sacred and meaningful.

For students, this would mean, for example, studying, attending class, and doing homework simply because they are students, rather than in order to get a good grade on the test and succeed in the class. For professors, it would mean carrying out the tasks expected of us without having an eye on the next promotion or other professional recognition. Making daily life the focus of spiritual liberation calls for acting rightly *because* it is right, not because it will produce beneficial results.

Other, less widely practiced, ways of liberation include intense study and **contemplation** of sacred writings, the physical disciplines of **yoga**, and the intensive practice of **meditation**.

### Women in Hinduism

Hinduism's attitude toward women has always been highly ambivalent. On the one hand, the Great Goddess is worshiped and adored in all her manifestations. The major gods have their female consorts. Female energy is important in the attainment of liberation in certain approaches to meditation. In Vedic times, women were educated, participated in religious rituals, and were recognized as scholars, poets, and teachers.

On the other hand, women have been relegated to second-class citizenship throughout most of the Hindu world. Arranged marriages often took place when a girl was very young, and submission to one's husband has often been considered a woman's paramount virtue. The practice of a widow's burning herself on her husband's funeral pyre (now outlawed in India) highlights the dreadful situation of a woman without a man.

Hindu women in the United States are primarily cosmopolitan and educated. They move in social circles that include professionals, administrators, and managers. Their lives are less determined by the Hindu tradition regarding women than by their position in American society. However, temple leadership is usually limited to male priests, with women having a role to play as teachers of children. Typically, women are the ones who maintain the tradition of worship at a home altar for the benefit of their families.

## Hindus in the United States

There has been much less detailed research done on Hindus in the United States than there has been on Muslims. The number of Hindus remains quite small—less than 0.5 percent of the population. Nearly all Hindus are either immigrants or descendants of immigrants from Hindu countries; fewer Westerners have become Hindus than have embraced either Islam or Buddhism. As you saw with Arab Americans, most Asian Americans are Christians. With a few exceptions, Hindus have not sought converts. Most live in urban areas. The largest concentrations are in the Los Angeles, San Francisco, New York City, and Chicago metropolitan areas. Many Hindus now living in the United States are professionals, intellectuals, and upper-level management personnel.

There are a number of Hindu groups in the United States, many of which are quite small. Some offer Indian Hindus the opportunity to maintain community and culture. Others are primarily ways for non-Indians to become involved with Hinduism. A recent analysis describes **five broad categories of Hindu groups in the United States**. Many Asian Indians are **secular Hindus** who do not identify with religious Hinduism in any sense yet are not affiliated with any other religion. **Nonsectarian Hindus** practice a broad, inclusive form of Hinduism. **Devotional Hindus** choose to worship a particular deity. Most are devotees of Shiva, Vishnu, Krishna, or Shakti, as noted above. **Reformist-Nationalist Neo-Hindus** link interest in their homeland of India with religion and do not seek to make converts. Finally, **Guru-Internationalist-Missionizing Neo-Hindus** are loyal to a particular guru and actively try to convert non-Hindus to Hinduism.[14]

The **Vedanta Society** was founded in 1894 by Swami Vivekananda. It was the first Hindu organization in the United States and is arguably the most influential on an intellectual level, although it is neither the largest nor the best known. Each Vedanta Center in the United States is a branch of the Ramakrishna Order, the monastic organization that Vivekananda founded in India.

Vedanta seeks to incorporate the methods and ideals of all Hindu movements. It describes itself as "a federation of faiths and a commonwealth of spiritual concepts." It supports all the pathways to liberation that were described earlier:

> Vedanta teaches that man's real nature is divine, and that the aim of human life is to realize that divinity through selfless work, devotion to God, control of the inner forces, and discrimination between the real and the unreal. It recognizes that Truth is one and accepts all religions, properly understood, as valid means of realizing the truth.

[14]Gerald James Larson, "Hinduism in India and in America," in *World Religions in America, Third Edition*, ed. Jacob Neusner (Louisville: Westminster John Knox Press, 2003), p. 138.

Religion is a way of life rather than a set of dogmas, and Vedanta places great importance on actually experiencing the truth for ourselves. Through spiritual practice we try to establish contact with the divine reality and then manifest that divinity in all our actions.[15]

Vedanta centers usually offer weekly worship that is similar to that already described for Hindu temples. They usually offer classes in various aspects of Hinduism as well. The leader, or **swami**, who is invited by a local Board of Trustees to come from the Ramakrishna Order in India, also gives private instruction to students. The organization also operates Vedanta Press, a source for Hindu religious literature and other relevant books.

The primary embodiment of Hindu devotionalism in the United States is the daily and weekly worship that Hindus perform in their homes and in temples. The **International Society for Krishna Consciousness** (also known as ISKCON or the **Hare Krishna Movement**) is an organizational embodiment of Hindu devotionalism. It was founded in the United States by His Divine Grace A. C. Bhaktivedanta Swami Prabhupada (1896–1977) in 1965. The Krishna Consciousness movement emphasizes union with the divine attained through ecstatic devotion to Krishna. The Movement describes its mission as

> to promote the well being of society by teaching the science of Krishna consciousness according to the *Bhagavad-Gita* and other ancient Vedic scriptures of India.[16]

Members follow five rules of conduct: (1) No meat, fish, or eggs may be eaten. (2) No intoxicating drinks or plants may be used, including tobacco, alcohol, coffee, and tea. (3) There must be no gambling. (4) Illicit sexual activity (defined as any sexual activity between people who are not married to each other or marital sex except for procreation) is also prohibited. Finally, (5) the name of Krishna is to be chanted daily in a prescribed ritual.

Devotees who choose to devote full time to the movement and live in the temples follow a rigid schedule of devotion and work. There are also opportunities for those who cannot or do not wish to enter this fully into the community. Devotees, whether living in the temple or not, give very high priority to *sankirtan*, daily chanting of the **mantra**. Mantra chanting has been a part of Hindu religious practice since its earliest times. Mantras—spiritual phrases—help to focus the mind and are believed to have power in and of themselves to align the devotee's consciousness with the deity.

Krishna Consciousness members practice chanting the Hare Krishna mantra, a song of praise to the Lord Krishna, as the best way to find union with the divine:

> Hare Krishna, Hare Krishna (Praise to Krishna, Praise to Krishna)
> Krishna Krishna, Hare Hare (Krishna, Krishna, Praise, Praise)

---

[15]Vedanta Society of Chicago, www.vedantasociety-chicago.org.
[16]"International Society for Krishna Consciousness Fact Sheet," (Alachua, FL: ISKCON Foundation, 1990).

**Figure 12-1**    Congregational members of the International Society for Krishna Consciousness live and work in the general community, practicing Krishna consciousness in their own homes and attending the temple on a regular basis. *(Photo courtesy of the International Society for Krishna Consciousness)*

> Hare Rama, Hare Rama (Praise to Rama, Praise to Rama)
> Rama Rama, Hare Hare! (Rama, Rama, Praise, Praise!)

The *a* in Rama is soft, as *ah*, and *hare* is pronounced *ha-ray*. Rama is one of Vishnu's incarnations, the hero of the epic poem the *Ramayana*. The Krishna Consciousness Movement teaches that this one mantra is the mantra for everyone in this present age, rather than following the more traditional practice that requires that mantras be given individually by gurus and kept secret.[17]

Temples are always open to visitors, who are welcomed into a world that may make them feel as if they have been magically transported to India itself (Figure 12–1). There are about fifty ISKCON temples in the United States, as well as six farm communities and six vegetarian restaurants. The organization claims about 3000 fully initiated members and an additional 500,000 lay members who participate in temple activities at least monthly.

Besides the temples, farm communities, and restaurants, the Society operates the Bhaktivedanta Book Trust for the publication of literature on Indian philosophy and religion. It also publishes *Back to Godhead: The Magazine*

[17]An audio of this mantra can be heard on the Krishna Consciousness Web site, www.iskcon.com.

*of the Hare Krishna Movement*. Its "Food for Life" program distributes meals at no cost to those who need food. This program is an outgrowth of the custom of sponsoring a free meal every Sunday at the temples, which began in the very early days of the movement.

The rigorous monastic life and the sometimes aggressive solicitation of Krishna's American devotees have marked them off as distinctive and unusual. Their way of life is a small slice of India in a very non-Indian culture. There can be little doubt, however, about the sincerity and devotion of these followers of an Indian deity whose main attribute is his desire to help struggling human beings attain release from spiritual suffering.

There are many different Hindu groups in the United States that are based on some form of yoga. The **Self-Realization Fellowship** is typical of these. It was founded by a Bengali Indian, Paramahansa Yogananda, in 1925. Yogananda (1893–1952) taught in this country for more than thirty years.

Yogananda taught the classical form of yogic meditation outlined in the *Yoga Sutras* of Patanjali. His teaching and the practices that he developed are based on the traditional Hindu belief that the divine is within each person and can be experienced directly through meditation. Having experienced it in meditation, people can come to manifest it increasingly in everyday life. According to the Self-Realization Fellowship:

> The science of Yoga offers a direct means of stilling the natural turbulence of thoughts and restlessness of body which prevent us from knowing what we really are. By practicing the step-by-step methods of Yoga . . . we come to know our oneness with the Infinite Intelligence, Power, and Joy which gives life to all and which is the essence of our own Self. . . . [The] inner fulfillment we seek *does* exist and *can* be attained. In actuality, all the knowledge, creativity, love, joy, and peace we are looking for are right within us, the very essence of our beings. All we have to do is realize this.[18]

The Self-Realization Fellowship emphasizes that the techniques they teach and practice do not have to be accepted on authority or faith but can be tested in the life of each person. It is a scientific method for self-discovery and realization. Awareness and consciousness, energy, are withdrawn from outward concerns and redirected inward toward the goal of self-realization. There are eight temples and about 150 smaller centers in the United States, as well as a program of correspondence study. The centers offer classes, workshops, and weekly devotional experiences. Besides laypeople who participate in the centers' activities, there are renunciants who have chosen to pursue liberation more arduously and remain celibate, spending quite a lot of time in meditation and study.

---

[18]*Undreamed-of Possibilities: An Introduction to Self-Realization: The Teachings of Paramahansa Yogananda* (Los Angeles: Self-Realization Fellowship, 1982), pp. 5 and 3.

## Why American Converts?

As previously noted, most Hindus are Indian immigrants or their descendants. There are, however, a small number of Americans who become "Hindu by choice." What attracts them? The answer to this question helps to reveal the complexity of how new religions come to fit into the predominant Judeo-Christian culture of the United States. Hinduism attracts American converts due to its similarities to what Americans already know and due to the genuine alternatives it presents.

First the similarities: Many forms of Hinduism emphasize the necessity of self-effort, a common theme throughout American culture. Many are compatible with science, and some, such as the Self-Realization Fellowship, emphasize this compatibility. Most teach that theirs is a method to be tried and tested in each individual's experience, not accepted "on faith." This practical empiricism also runs throughout the culture. Some, such as the Vedanta Societies, offer a somewhat "Protestant" style of worship, often on Sundays. Those that focus on devotion to a deity are similar in their approach to Christian devotion to Jesus; the Vedanta Society even encourages the worship of Jesus along with other deities.

On the other hand, they attract by their differences. Hindu tolerance and universalism offer an alternative for people for whom exclusivist claims have become problematic in a religiously plural world. Hinduism's very positive view of human nature, "we *are* the divine," can be a relief to those accustomed to talk about sin and depravity. Reincarnation and karma appeal to some more than either the Judeo-Christian concept of life after death or the secular alternative. Most Hindu groups offer practical *techniques* for spiritual transformation, an approach that has characteristically been lacking in Judaism and Christianity. Often these techniques facilitate the attainment of calmness and inner peace despite life's busyness and frustrations. Finally, many Hindu approaches to personal spiritual life emphasize a close relationship with one's guru or religious teacher, who becomes a guide on the path of self-realization.

## Hindu Ideas in U.S. Culture

As we will see in the next section, Buddhism's effect on the larger culture of the United States is greater than that of Hinduism. A recent study, however, notes that Hindu ideas, too, have seeped into non-Hindu Americans' awareness. (1) Hinduism rejects the dichotomy between body and spirit, and sees the body as a means for spiritual realization. Increasingly, non-Hindu Americans are coming to share this view. (2) Religious experience is regarded as more important than dogma. The focus is on understanding and developing our own spiritual reality rather than conforming to a preset idea of what it should be. (3) God or the sacred is best imaged as a Higher Power, beyond human comprehension and description. (4) Feminist theology has heightened

**Figure 12-2**    Statues of the Buddha show him in serene meditation.

awareness of the feminine aspects of divinity in a way that has long been a part of Hindu religious experience. (5) There are many ways to liberation or salvation and something valuable can be learned from all of humankind's religious and spiritual traditions.[19]

## AMERICAN BUDDHISM AND BUDDHISTS

As a young man, the Hindu prince Siddhartha Gautama became very distressed over the inevitable suffering of human life—aging, sickness, and death, among other things. Although born to a noble life, he renounced his life of privilege and set out in search of a resolution to the spiritual unrest that plagued him. According to Buddhist tradition, he found what he sought during meditation, discovering the way to release from the burden of suffering (Figure 12–2). He then went about teaching what he had learned to other people and founded an organization based on his teachings. His followers called him "**the Buddha**," which means "**the awakened** (or **enlightened**) **one**."

Like Hinduism, Buddhism has a number of different sacred writings. The **Pali Canon** records what Buddhists take to be the teachings of the Buddha himself after his Enlightenment. Its importance is agreed upon by the great majority of Buddhists. Beyond that, various Buddhist subgroups accept other scriptures as valid.

---

[19]Polly Trout, *Eastern Seeds, Western Soil: Three Gurus in America* (Mountain View, CA: Mayfield Publishing Company, 2001), pp. 218–224.

## Basic Buddhist Teachings

The Buddhist worldview is different than that of Hinduism in some important respects, although there are similarities as well. As do Hindus, Buddhists affirm that the principles of **rebirth** and **karma** operate in every human life. Where Buddhists and Hindus differ is that Buddhists do not believe that there is a real self that reincarnates. Rather than seeing the universe as myriad manifestations of an eternal, unchanging spiritual reality, Buddhists see it as a vast, interconnected process. Buddhists also believe that **there is an intrinsic, moral order of the universe**, akin to the Hindu concept of dharma.

Interbeing and impermanence are central attributes of everything that is. **Interbeing** means that nothing exists in and of itself. Everything that exists does so with endless connections to all other things. **Impermanence** points to the Buddhist belief that everything changes. Everything in the universe, including ourselves, is part of this vast, interconnected process. What underlies the universe as we observe it is not the eternal, changeless absolute of Hinduism, but constant change, constant becoming.

This leads to a reinterpretation of rebirth, because there is no eternal Real Self that goes through the rebirth process. Buddhists simply say that each lifetime is connected to the ones before it and will be connected to those that come after it in a chain of causation. The analogy of lighting the wick of one candle from the flame on another is often used. Nothing is transmitted from candle to candle, but the flame of the second is unarguably connected to the flame of the first.

The **Four Noble Truths** is a basic statement of Buddhist belief, attributed to the Buddha himself. It is an application of the Buddhist vision of the world to human life and the human problem. We'll take the Truths one at a time. My interpretation loosely follows *The Heart of the Buddha's Teaching*,[20] a contemporary interpretation of basic Buddhist teachings by Thich Nhat Hanh, a Vietnamese Buddhist monk whose work is widely appreciated in the United States.

1. **All of life is marked by suffering.** The Buddha was not, and Buddhists today are not, long-faced pessimists without joy and happiness. Quite the contrary! What the Buddha had in mind here is that, no matter how good life is, there is always an element of dissatisfaction or suffering about it. Birth and death, he said, cause suffering on either end of the life cycle. In between, there is illness, having to deal with things we do not like, and being separated from things that we do like. There is wanting more than we have or wanting something different than what we have. However, suffering is not necessary. It is a feeling, not something basic to existence, and it can be transformed.

2. **We can know the causes of our suffering.** The traditional interpretation holds that all suffering comes from inappropriately holding onto

---

[20]Thich Nhat Hanh, *The Heart of the Buddha's Teaching: Transforming Suffering into Peace, Joy, and Liberation* (Berkeley, CA: Parallax Press, 1998), pp. 131–132, 21–22, and 11.

things that inevitably slip from our grasp. However, we can also see that there are other causes, such as anger, ignorance, suspicion, false pride, and various misunderstandings. The secret is to identify the cause of suffering clearly so that we can eliminate or at least modify it.

3. **We can end our suffering.** By eliminating the cause, the effect is eliminated. While we cannot avoid life's inevitable challenges and problems, we can limit their tendency to make us miserable. Healing is possible.

4. **The Buddha proposed a method for accomplishing this goal.** Buddhists call it the *Noble Eightfold Path*, sometimes called the Path of Eight Right Practices. It is a set of guidelines for living in a way that lessens suffering.

Because the Buddha became enlightened by his own efforts, traditional Buddhists teach that people are responsible for bringing about their own liberation from suffering. The first two steps on the path refer to **wisdom**: right understanding and right motivation. Right understanding is our ability to see things as they really are, changing and impermanent. Right motivation is sincere desire to work on bringing about change, steady effort, and determination. The next several steps have to do with **morality**. Right speech is to speak truthfully and compassionately, without exaggeration, harshness, or rudeness of speech. Right action is observing the basics of Buddhist morality. Beyond that, it means acting with a balance of wisdom and compassion, always seeking the good. Right occupation says that one's occupation (which takes up a significant part of one's time) should not involve violating the moral precepts and should be such that it encourages peace and harmony, again striving for the good of all beings. Right effort is steady attention to weeding out negative and unhelpful ways of thinking and acting and replacing them with positive and helpful ways. The emphasis here is on constancy; the Path is a map for minute-by-minute existence, not for occasional use. The last two steps have to do with **meditation**. Right mindfulness is being aware in every moment. Right meditation deals directly with meditation techniques. Buddhists do not practice meditation as a way of going inward to find a changeless Self (which, remember, does not exist, according to Buddhism). Different schools of thought teach different techniques. What unites them is that meditation is used as a way of being fully aware in every moment, then letting that moment go, as a way of calming and focusing the mind and bringing home the fleeting nature of everything.

Like Hindus, Buddhists believe that there can be an end to the cycle of death and rebirth. This is the ultimate goal of the Eightfold Path. The Buddhist word for that goal is **Nirvana**. The Buddha did not speak very much about Nirvana, believing that doing so was not useful in the search for liberation. It certainly means living without dissatisfaction and thus with complete peace. It means the elimination of anything that separates the individual from the interconnectedness of all that is, the end of the illusion of isolated existence. When someone who has reached this advanced state of spiritual awareness dies, he or she escapes from rebirth.

The **Three Treasures** (also, **Three Refuges**, or **Three Jewels**) is another way Buddhists summarize what is important in their faith. Although there is no affirmation of faith that is required to become a Buddhist nor any set formula that makes a person a Buddhist, the Refuges help to define what being a Buddhist means. Usually, when someone becomes a Buddhist by choice, they formally take the Three Refuges and the Five Precepts in the setting of a Buddhist community, or *Sangha*.

For Buddhists, *faith* is not faith in an unseen deity nor in something that cannot be known. It is not assent to propositions that cannot be demonstrated. It is an expression of what practitioners can know and verify through the effects of the practice in their own lives. Buddhist teacher Sharon Salzberg describes Buddhist faith as

> the capacity of the heart that allows us to draw close to the present and find there the underlying thread connecting the moment's experience with the fabric of all life. . . . [Faith] is the magnetic force of a bone-deep, lived understanding, one that draws us to realize our ideals, walk our talk, and act in accord with what we know to be true.[21]

**"I take refuge in the Buddha."** To take refuge in the Buddha means to place one's trust and confidence in the Buddha having become the Enlightened One. For traditional Buddhists, especially, the Buddha is a human being, nothing more. Thus, that he, through his own effort and determination, was able to achieve liberation means that *any* person can do so, provided they are willing to make the effort. The Buddha's humanity also means that the Buddha nature is to be found in all persons, as well as other beings. A contemporary American Buddhist nun describes the optimistic view of human nature that this entails:

> Each of us has within us the seeds of perfection, the natural and evolving Buddha potentials, and these seeds can be neither stolen or destroyed. There is no reason for us ever to feel hopeless and helpless. Because our Buddha potential is inseparably within us, there is always a basis for self-confidence and positive aspiration. . . .
>
> This is the beauty of our human life: we have the indestructible Buddha potentials which have been with us since beginningless time, and we have the perfect opportunity to realize and develop them in this lifetime.[22]

**"I take refuge in the Dharma."** Buddhists use the word **Dharma** to refer primarily to the Buddha's teaching. To take refuge in the Dharma, then,

---

[21]Sharon Salzberg, *Faith: Trusting Your Own Deepest Experience* (New York: Riverhead Books, 2002), pp. 80 and 153.

[22]Thubten Chodron, *Open Heart, Clear Mind* (Ithaca, NY: Snow Lion Publications, 1990), pp. 119 and 123.

means to have confidence in the Buddha's teachings as a true analysis of reality and as a way to accomplish what he accomplished. Many Buddhists also interpret it as a vote of confidence in our own capacity as human beings to comprehend reality as it truly is.

"I take refuge in the **Sangha**." Sangha has two levels of meaning. Narrowly, it is the community of Buddhist monks. For traditional Buddhists, liberation is possible only after one has become a monk. Monks work for liberation full time, and they symbolize the goal of Buddhists. On a broader level, the *sangha* means the entire community of people, living and dead, who have walked the path to enlightenment mapped out by Gautama. Buddhists live in the certainty that they are not alone in their quest for enlightenment. Others walk with them on their journey.

Lama Surya Das, an American whose affiliation is with the Tibetan Dzogchen lineage, translates the Three Refuges in a way that links the traditional understanding with the practitioner's vow to practice:

> I go for refuge in the Buddha, the enlightened teacher;
> I commit myself to enlightenment;
> I go for refuge in the Dharma, the spiritual teachings;
> I commit myself to the truth as it is;
> I go for refuge in the Sangha, the spiritual community;
> I commit myself to living the enlightened life.[23]

## Buddhist Morality and Ritual

Buddhist morality has already been mentioned as one of the steps on the Eightfold Path. One standard statement of Buddhist morality is the **Five Precepts.**

**1. Do not kill.** Buddhists expand this precept to include not harming any living being, insofar as it is possible to avoid such harm. Positively, it means doing all that one can for the good of all beings on the earth. Nonviolence and noninjury are central in any Buddhist system of ethics. Stated positively, the precept advocates compassion for all beings.

**2. Do not steal.** Again, Buddhists understand this as going beyond outright stealing. It also means not taking advantage, not appropriating anything that is not ours. Avoiding paying legitimate taxes is another example, as is borrowing and not returning an item. Positively, the precept urges an attitude of generosity with our time, resources, and talents.

**3. Refrain from wrongful sexual behavior.** Complete abstinence outside of marriage is the traditional rule. Buddhist monks and nuns are celibate. Sexual activity is regarded as appropriate only for committed couples. Wrongful sexual behavior includes any behavior that degrades another person,

---

[23]Lama Surya Das, *Awakening the Buddha Within: Eight Steps to Enlightenment: Tibetan Wisdom for the Western World* (New York: Broadway Books, 1997), p. 56.

as well as sexual behavior that might spread disease. This precept is about practicing loving, responsible relationships.

4.    **Do not lie.** Expanded, this includes refraining from saying anything that is hurtful, such as slander and gossip, rude and harsh speech, impolite language, running down other people, as well as idle chatter when silence would be better. Speak the truth with care, lovingly.

5.    Finally, Buddhists **avoid the use of intoxicants** of all kinds, such as alcohol and intoxicating drugs. Using them clouds a person's mind and also increases the likelihood that other ethical principles will be violated. Not all Buddhists take this as an absolute prohibition on an occasional drink, interpreting the precept as a ban on *intoxication* rather than on intoxicants. However one interprets this precept, its point is to keep a clear and sober mind.[24]

Buddhism presses home the importance of cultivating proper attitudes and a proper frame of mind, so that outward actions flow freely from internal dispositions. Four attitudes are especially valued. Buddhists strive to cultivate loving-kindness and friendliness, compassion and empathy, joy and rejoicing, and equanimity and peace of mind.[25]

Like Hindus, Buddhists often have a small altar or shrine in their homes. A Buddha statue represents the historical Buddha and helps devotees focus on the Buddha nature within themselves, as well. Flowers symbolize enlightenment and a candle or altar light symbolizes the light of wisdom. Incense is often offered in gratitude for the Three Refuges and other blessings. An offering of water represents cleansing and a food offering represents giving and the willingness to share what one has with other beings.

**Meditation** is central to Buddhist practice, and is a main focus of practice for most Buddhists in the United States. There are three aspects to meditation. The first is developing one-pointed *concentration*, the ability to truly do one thing at a time. To do this, people often practice by concentrating on their breathing. The second is the development of *insight* into the true nature of reality. This facilitates experiencing reality as it is, without getting caught up in conceptualizations of it. The third is the extension of these attitudes into daily living as *mindfulness* in everyday life. Put simply, although it is far from simple to attain, this means being fully present to whatever one is doing in the present moment.

Buddhists who live where they can go to a temple may participate in activities that center around the natural rhythms of the lunar calendar. The holy days occur at the new moon, the full moon, and eight days after each, making them about a week apart. Attendance at the temple is not required, and some Buddhists participate much more than others. There is a religious new year festival in the spring, and the Buddha's birthday is widely celebrat-

---

[24]For an interesting discussion of the precepts, see the KwanUm Zen World Wide Web site, www.kwanumzen.com.

[25]This particular translation of the "four noblest qualities of mind" comes from Das, *Awakening the Buddha Within*, p. 292.

ed. Temples also offer classes, special rituals for the passages of life, and serve as social centers.

## Women and Buddhism

Traditional ideas about women and women's capabilities persisted in Buddhism even as in Hinduism. At the same time, Buddhism allowed for the establishment of orders of nuns. The rules established for nuns, however, guaranteed submission of nuns to monks and ensured that their number would remain small. That they existed and continue to exist, however, is significant.

One of the ways that Buddhism has changed as it has come West has been that greater gender equality in the West has forced the issue within the Buddhist community. American women have been and continue to be interested in Buddhism, and their increased participation, especially in leadership positions, contributes distinctive accents to the practice of American Buddhism, while helping to ameliorate things that have been difficult for female practitioners of the Dharma in the West:

> Seduced by a fascination with orientalism or a taste for the exotic, or programmed by their female training and family background, some American women practicing Buddhist meditation have accepted situations inimical to their own good and insulting to their common sense and human dignity. But the honeymoon is over, and the actual dynamics of the marriage are becoming increasingly more apparent. We are Americans, with a heritage of egalitarianism and resistance to authority, as well as a history of women's effort to define ourselves and realize ourselves fully in religious as well as secular life. None of this is inconsistent with the essential teachings and practice of Buddhism.[26]

Specific changes that can be traced to the influence of women include greater egalitarianism and warmth in relationships between teachers and students, increased emphasis on working with the emotions and with the body, emphasis on sharing and openness, downplaying of traditional themes such as effort and striving in favor of themes of healing and openness, and a strongly activist orientation.[27]

The influence of women in American Buddhism leads to changes in Buddhist theology, as well. Over a decade ago, Buddhist theologian Rita Gross enumerated four changes that she foresaw in Buddhist thought as a result of the increasing presence of trained and respected female leaders and thinkers in the United States. Current research indicates these changes have indeed occurred. (1) In the United States, Buddhism is seen as a path to living with greater freedom, joy, and compassion within the world, rather than as a means of escape from the world. The constantly changing nature of existence

---

[26]Sandy Boucher, "Brave Beginnings," in *Turning the Wheel: American Women Creating the New Buddhism,* Updated and Expanded Edition, ed. Sandy Boucher (Boston: Beacon Press, 1993), pp. 21–22.

[27]Joseph B. Tamney, *American Society in the Buddhist Mirror* (New York: Garland Publishing, 1992), p. 95.

is not the problem; the difficulty is the attitude we have toward that change. (2) There is a deeper appreciation of the importance of the sangha or community, of the social dimension of religion. (3) The focus of practice is everyday life, not life as a nun or monk. The ordinary life of the householder is transformed and is just as valid as the life of a monastic. (4) While meditation is important and necessary, it is not the only important aspect of Buddhism.[28]

## Asian Buddhists in the United States

It is difficult to estimate the percentage of the American population that is Buddhist; it may be somewhere between 0.5 percent and 1.0 percent. Like Hindus, Buddhists are found primarily in major metropolitan areas. Buddhists have come to the United States from every Buddhist country in the world and have tended to remain clustered in national groups. This "ethnic" Buddhism is one aspect of Buddhism in the United States. Buddhists came from China as early as the 1800s to work in the mines during the Gold Rush. Japanese Buddhists arrived later, but their impact has been greater. Even later, Buddhists came from Vietnam, Cambodia, Thailand, and Laos. Buddhists also came here from Tibet when the Chinese Maoist regime overran that country.

Buddhists came to the United States in the wake of the Khmer Rouge regime's attack on Cambodian Buddhists in the 1970s, especially following the Vietnam War. There are a greater number of Vietnamese Buddhists in the United States than those from other Southeast Asian countries. They are spread more widely across the country, as well, due to efforts to resettle the large numbers of Vietnamese refugees. The majority of Vietnamese in the United States are Buddhists, although a significant minority are Christians. I will note representative Buddhist groups in each immigrant community to convey the scope of Asian "ethnic" Buddhism in the United States.

The **International Buddhist Meditation Center** in Los Angeles, California, although it now includes non-Asian Buddhists, is a primary locus for **Vietnamese Buddhism**. The center blends various Buddhist schools of thought and practice. Buddhist leaders and teachers from a variety of backgrounds teach there and many groups use the facilities. Ordination for monks borrows from a number of traditions as well. It was the first temple in the United States to ordain non-Asians. Worship services feature chanting of the scriptures in several languages, including English.

The largest **Japanese** Buddhist organization in the United States is the **Buddhist Churches of America**. It is considered to be a mission outpost of the Japanese church, which is the largest Japanese Buddhist group. BCA focuses on lay Buddhism, rather than the life of a nun or monk.

---

[28]Rita Gross, "Buddhism after Patriarchy?" in *After Patriarchy: Feminist Transformations of the World Religions*, ed. Paula M. Cooey, William R. Eakin, and Jay B. McDaniel (Maryknoll, NY: Orbis Books, 1991), pp. 65–86.

This form of Buddhism teaches that faith in **Amida Buddha**, the Buddha of Infinite Wisdom and Compassion, will bring liberation and rebirth in the Pure Land, a state close to complete enlightenment. Rebirth in the Pure Land means becoming a Bodhisattva, dedicated to returning to earthly existence to assist the liberation of all beings.

In its "church" type of organization and focus on the importance of regular participation in the activities of the church, BCA has adapted Buddhism to its American context. Because its teaching about the importance of reliance on Amida Buddha to bring about liberation is similar to Protestant Christians' reliance on the power of faith in Jesus as the Christ, it has not appeared completely alien to American religious sensibilities and has provided an important vehicle for the acculturation of Japanese Buddhists. It has also attracted some American converts and offers an outreach membership program for those who live far from any BCA church.

**Zen,** probably the form of Buddhism best known in the United States, also came here from Japan. One of the largest Zen centers is in Los Angeles, California. It has branched out into centers throughout the United States. Zen followers concentrate on meditation, practicing daily meditation and participating in periodic retreats in which many hours daily can be devoted to *zazen*, Zen "sitting meditation." The awareness developed during meditation is practiced in everyday life. ZCLA offers daily zazen for practitioners, classes, regular talks and discussions, weekend retreats, and longer retreats. It also offers *sesshin*, the opportunity for practitioners to discuss their practice with leading monks. It is also the form of Buddhism that has appealed most to non-Asian Americans.

**Shasta Abbey** is the headquarters of the **Order of Buddhist Contemplatives,** a Zen organization that consciously adapts traditional Zen practice to Western culture. It was founded in 1970 by a British-born Buddhist nun, the reverend Jiyu Kennett-Roshi. Its main focus is training women and men for the Zen Buddhist priesthood in the United States. The daily order of the monastery is a good example of life in a Zen monastery in the United States (Figure 12–3). The schedule is intended to provide variety while keeping the participants' attention focused on spiritual pursuits and ensuring a minimum of distractions. Meals are vegetarian. Participants are expected to conduct themselves mindfully, aware of the spiritual purpose of their being there and the need to respect that same purpose in others.

The largest organizational representation of Chinese Buddhism in the United States is the **Dharma Realm Buddhist Association,** founded in 1959. It teaches all five major schools of Chinese Buddhism. As well as attracting Chinese Americans, it also has a following among American Buddhists. Its emphasis on monastic Buddhism with strict discipline makes it unique among Buddhist organizations in the United States. Its Dharma Realm Buddhist University was the first Buddhist university established in the West. The moral principles that students are expected to follow reflect Buddhist values and make it dissimilar to most other United States colleges and universities:

**Figure 12-3**

---

### TYPICAL DAILY SCHEDULE OF THE MOUNT SHASTA ABBEY

| | |
|---|---|
| 5:55 | Rising |
| 6:15 | Meditation |
| 6:55 | Morning Service |
| 7:25 | Temple Cleanup |
| 8:40 | Breakfast |
| 9:15 | Work |
| 10:45 | Meditation (three periods) |
| 12:30 | Lunch |
| 1:40 | Rest |
| 2:45 | Work |
| 3:45 | Midday Service/Meditation |
| 4:30 | Class |
| 6:05 | Dinner |
| 6:35 | Rest |
| 7:30 | Meditation/Walking Meditation |
| 8:10 | Meditation/Evening Office |
| 10:00 | Lights Out |

---

There is a broad emphasis on students as members of communities, including the Buddhist religious community. The university encourages students to practice mindful awareness and to conduct themselves in accord with Buddhist morality. By doing so, they can become examples to others. Some of the virtues emphasized include "humaneness, integrity, [and] filial respect," as well as "not seeking for personal gratification, unselfishness, service, and honesty." Both faculty and students pledge to abstain from the use of alcohol and illicit drugs, smoking tobacco, social dancing and sexual promiscuity. Vegetarian food is the norm on campus.[29]

Tibetan Buddhists fleeing the Maoist regime's purge of Buddhism in Tibet brought **Vajrayana** Buddhism to the United States. **Vajradhatu**, headquartered in Boulder, Colorado, is the largest of several such organizations in the United States. It sponsors a full range of ritual and educational activities and serves as a focus for the Tibetan Buddhist community in the United States. It also sponsors the **Naropa Institute**, one of the better-known Buddhist educational facilities in the United States. Its **Shambhala Press** is one of the major publishers of Buddhist literature in the United States.

[29]Dharma Realm Buddhist University, www.drba.org/drbu.htm.

## Americans and Buddhism: The Dharma in the West

Non-Asians in the United States become Buddhists in far greater numbers than they become Hindus, and there may well be more non-Asian Buddhists than Asian Buddhists here now. Non-Asians who have become Buddhists are predominantly white, middle-class, and well-educated. They are also far more liberal religiously and politically, and more likely to be involved in ecological and peace and justice causes.

Non-Asian Americans have been interested in Buddhism for different reasons. One factor often cited by converts to the Buddha's path "is an existential longing for a road map for personal change." Although the forms of Buddhism vary greatly, "virtually all of them offer clear-cut instructions for daily religious practice." They promise that sincerely following the practice will in time bring about significant change in the spiritual quality of one's life.[30] A recent analysis of Buddhism's role is postmodern society points to the radical way in which Buddhism transforms spirituality. A key characteristic of postmodern society is that identity is not a given; in a fragmented society, individuals must actively work to construct their identities. This leads to anxiety. Part of Buddhism's appeal to many of its practitioners is that it offers resources for coping with this anxiety about selfhood, grounded in mediation practice. In this, it is similar to psychotherapy. Beyond that, however, lies something far more radical:

> Its most profound teachings do not offer a new identity or a new set of techniques for managing our problems but deconstruct the whole project of the self to bring us to see the pointlessness of our desperate efforts to construct, maintain, and protect our self-identity that consume so much of our lives.[31]

Our idea of a self is a social convenience only, and it is not necessary to expend time and energy defending it.

Buddhism has reached into the mainstream of American cultural life to a much greater extent than has Hinduism. Buddhist teachings about the human self and the nature of reality inform many in the fields of psychology and clinical social work. Stress-reduction techniques based on Buddhist meditation practices are widely used and are written about in the popular press. Movies such as *The Little Buddha*, *Kundun*, and *Seven Years in Tibet* have brought Tibetan forms of Buddhism into the public eye. Well-known sports figures have embraced Buddhist techniques as a way of maintaining the focused awareness necessary in competition. Performers such as Tina Turner have been quite public in their embrace of this Asian path. Musical groups have added to the public presence of Buddhism with songs such as the Beastie

---

[30] Jan Nattlier, "Why Buddhism, Why Now?" www.ambedkar.org.
[31] James William Coleman, *The New Buddhism: The Western Transformation of an Ancient Tradition* (New York: Oxford University Press, 2001), p. 213.
[32] Jeff Greenwald, "Big Mind, Small Screen: *Six Feet Under's* Alan Ball," *Tricycle: The Buddhist Review* (Summer, 2004), p. 43.

Boys' "Bodhisattva Vow." The new century saw the debut of the prime-time television series "Six Feet Under," described as a "quirky meditation on attachment, mortality, and . . . life, in the constant presence of death."[32]

In the process, Buddhism has changed as it has interacted with American culture. We have seen this (to a lesser extent) in Islam and Hinduism as well. Such change is inevitable when a religion comes from one culture and enters into the life of a very different culture.

New York–born Lama Surya Das points out that Buddhist adaption to life in the United States has happened in part through the evolution of Buddhist leadership here. American Buddhism is increasingly led by American teachers who have themselves trained in America with American-born Dharma teachers. He provides a portrait of American Buddhism.

- Americans typically look to Buddhism as a meditation practice with the goal of improving our quality of life. We "want personal transformation, direct religious experience, and we want to integrate wisdom, goodness, and compassion into our daily lives."
- Ours is a practice oriented to lay or householder practitioners much more than it is to nuns and monks.
- Gender equality remains an unrealized goal, but one that appears to be attainable.
- It is less institutional and hierarchical, and more democratic and personal, than its Asian predecessors.
- It tends to eliminate or minimize "complex, esoteric rites and arcane rituals designed for initiates only."
- It is ecumenical, with much less emphasis on specific schools of thought and practice and a willingness to combine old forms in new ways even as it invents new forms.
- American Buddhism is a "psychologically astute" Buddhism that focuses on individual spiritual growth and well-being.
- It encourages questioning and exploration. It is a Buddhist practice intent on "being. . . inquiring, skeptical, rational, and devoted to testing and finding out for ourselves."
- The Sangha, in the largest sense of a "community of spiritual friends," is important. Participation in it is of the essence of the holy life.
- Contemporary American Buddhism is a "Lobby for Wisdom and Compassion," as it develops a strong social and ecological consciousness.[33]

### QUESTIONS AND ACTIVITIES FOR REVIEW, DISCUSSION, AND WRITING

1. If you are fortunate enough to live or attend school close to a Hindu or Buddhist temple, arrange to visit, and write an essay on what you observe and your response to it.

---

[33]Das, *Awakening the Buddha Within*, pp. 376–387.

2. Especially if attending a temple is not possible, try to arrange for a Hindu or Buddhist student who attends your college or university to come and speak to your class.

3. If your library subscribes to any periodicals published by United States Hindus or Buddhists, read through two or three issues, and write about what impression you form of the religion.

4. Yoga as a form of physical exercise and relaxation is taught in many physical education departments. If your school has such a class, invite the instructor to demonstrate some of the basic postures with class participation.

5. Discuss with a group of your classmates the ways in which the Four Noble Truths might apply in (1) your own lives and (2) American culture in general.

6. What are some practical, concrete applications of the Hindu and Buddhist ideal of noninjury or nonviolence in our own culture? How could you as an individual put this ideal into practice?

7. How do you think you would respond to the daily routine of the Shasta Abbey?

8. How would your life as a college student be different than it now is if you attended Dharma Realm Buddhist University?

9. Visit the Web site of either the Association of American Buddhists or the American Buddhist Congress (or both). In what ways do they reflect a specifically American interpretation of Buddhism?

### FOR FURTHER READING

COLEMAN, JAMES WILLIAM, *The New Buddhism*: *The Western Transformation of an Ancient Tradition*. New York: Oxford University Press, 2001. Coleman, a sociologist of religion and Buddhist practitioner, uses survey data and his own interviews with American Buddhists to develop this review of the varieties of Buddhism in the United States.

LOUNDON, SUMI, *Blue Jean Buddha: Voices of Young Buddhists*. Somerville, MA: Wisdom Publications, 2001. This is a fresh look at Buddhism in America through the eyes of its younger practitioners. As such, it will be of particular interest to college students.

MANN, GURINDER SIKH, PAUL DAVID NUMRICH, and RAYMOND B. WILLIAMS, *Buddhists, Hindus, and Sikhs in America*. New York: Oxford University Press, *Religion in American Life* series, 2001. Although directed to somewhat younger readers, this introductory work provides an excellent overview of the basics without talking down to its readers.

NHAT HANH, THICH, *The Heart of the Buddha's Teaching: Transforming Suffering into Peace, Joy, and Liberation*. Berkeley, CA: Parallax Press, 1998. A presentation of basic Buddhism, this book covers all the major Buddhist teachings and practices in a way that reflects Thich Nhat Hanh's gentleness of spirit.

Trout, Polly, *Eastern Seeds, Western Soil: Three Gurus in America*. Mountain View, CA: Mayfield Publishing Company, 2001. Trout's book is a biography of three Hindu gurus in the United States, told in the joint context of Hinduism's Indian roots and American culture. She combines sociological and phenomenological insights well.

### RELEVANT WORLD WIDE WEB SITES

*Hinduism Today* (journal): www.hinduismtoday.com

The Hindu Universe: www.hindunet.org

Self-Realization Fellowship: www.yogananda-srf.org

International Society for Krishna Consciousness: www.harekrishna.com

Hindu Resources Online: www.hindu.org

Hindu Temple of Greater Chicago: www.ramatemple.org

Shasta Abbey/Order of Buddhist Contemplatives: www. obcon.org

*Tricycle: The Buddhist Review:* www.tricycle.com

Mountains and Rivers Order/Zen Mountain Monastery: www.mro.org

Zen Center of Los Angeles: www.zencenter.org

Dharma Realm Buddhist Association: www.drba.org

Dharma Realm Buddhist University: www.drba.org/drbu

Dzogchen Foundation: www.dzogchen.org

Insight Meditation Society/Barre Center for Buddhist Studies: www.dharma.org

Naropa Institute: www.naropa.edu

The Association of American Buddhists: www.americanbuddhist.info

The American Buddhist Congress: www.americanbuddhistcongress.org

*Shambhala Sun* (Journal): www.shambhalasun.com

# chapter 13

# OTHER RELIGIOUS
# AND SPIRITUAL MOVEMENTS:
# DIVERSITY AND DISSENSION

The Web site of the Freedom of Mind Center is published by a mental health counselor whose specialty is "rescuing" people who have become involved in unconventional religions. He uses the term "cult" to describe such groups. According to this perspective, participation in unconventional religions usually causes extensive psychological or emotional damage. Ex-members are said to be unusually vulnerable to symptoms of post-traumatic stress, such as panic attacks, anxiety, and sleep disorders. The site's author believes that unconventional religions in general are dangerous because they use a wide range of mind control techniques that can cause anyone to fall victim to the group's wishes.[1]

On the other hand, Ontario Consultants on Religious Tolerance states that "cult" is usually a "hateful snarl word" that people use to disparage an unconventional religious group. The use of the word cult greatly encourages religious intolerance. Their authors believe that only a "handful" of unconventional religions are dangerous and destructive. Usually, these groups simply have beliefs and practices that differ from the usual ones in North America.[2]

What do *you* think about "cults"?

This chapter draws together several diverse movements. They include the New Age Movement, the self-help movement and twelve-step programs, feminist spiritualities, the Fellowship of Metropolitan Community Churches, religion on the Internet, as well as others. The self-help movement and twelve-step programs have become an accepted feature of the American landscape. The rest are controversial.

[1]Freedom of Mind Center, www.freedomofmind.com.
[2]Ontario Consultants on Religious Tolerance, www.religioustolerence.org.

## THE NEW AGE MOVEMENT

The **New Age movement** is difficult to pin down, because it is not a specific group but a very loose network (a favorite New Age word) of groups, organizations, and individuals with a common set of concerns. At the same time, the New Age movement is probably one of the two most popularly recognized movements; the other is the twelve-step movement. There are authors, psychologists, teachers, leaders, body workers, and the like who are well known to most New Agers. There is, however, no single authority. There are well-known and widely accepted books but no single authoritative text. There are several common beliefs and practices yet no absolutely definitive belief or practice.

### Beliefs

The teachings and practices of the New Age movement are diverse. There are, however, several major themes that stand out because they recur frequently in New Age literature. We can begin with the major beliefs and attitudes that characterize New Age thinking.

One emphasis is the need to **overcome the dualism** that has characterized much of Western thought. Many of these dualistic ways of thinking have become part of how we view the world and ourselves: sacred or divine/profane or ordinary, religion/science, spirit/matter, mind/body, male/female, thinking/feeling. Virtually without exception, New Age thinkers believe that dualism must be replaced with a *holistic vision* of the world and ourselves that overcomes dualism while including legitimate differences.

An important corollary of this view is the belief in **the immanence of the divine within all things**. New Agers believe that there is a single life force that is inherent in all living things. The New Age philosophy is *monistic*. The same universal energy animates everything that is. This energy is usually thought of as psychic or mental in nature rather than physical.

This means that **all things are intimately interrelated**. The entire universe is a seamless web of life. Nothing happens in isolation, and anything that happens has an impact on the whole.

This leads directly to a concern for the earth and an interest in **ecology**. Because all things are interrelated, the fate of all hinges upon the fate of each. Everyone is responsible for the preservation of the Earth's resources and species. "Think globally, act locally" is an often-repeated phrase.

**Transformation of self will lead to a transformation of the culture and the planet**. Individuals have a responsibility to work to transform themselves in order to bring about planetary transformation. No one is exempt from this responsibility, and everyone can do something about the fate of the whole by working on themselves. Most of those who identify themselves as a part of the New Age movement share a nearly boundless optimism about the possibilities for both personal and communal transformation.

However, self-transformation is but one aspect of what the New Age calls upon individuals to do. **Compassionate service** to individual people, to one's community, and on wider levels is a prominent theme, although one that receives relatively little attention from outside the movement. Through such service, people can have a dramatic impact on universal transformation.

The underlying **unity of all religions** is also a central belief. Although religion takes many forms in different cultures, beneath the differences is a universal religion that will eventually be recognized by all people. This universal religion is grounded in the cycle of the changing seasons and the cycle of human lifetime. It understands life as a continual process of transformation through which people grow into greater consciousness. Inner exploration, psychic development, and self-awareness are valued highly.

This is one dimension of the **belief that the development of a planetary culture is both possible and desirable**. This worldwide (and some would say universe-wide) culture will *not* replace the distinctive cultures that now exist. It will complement them, both enhancing them and being enriched by them. Legitimate differences will remain. New Age believers look forward to a time when there will be one world government and a world language that is spoken and understood by all, facilitating communication and greater understanding among nations. Some favor the development of a worldwide monetary system to facilitate trade and a world court system as well.

**Cooperation is more important than competition** and much more desirable. If everything is indeed interconnected, competition is simply the various parts working against the whole. Cooperation benefits the whole by eliminating conflicting actions of the parts.

Most followers of the New Age believe in some form of the Asian teachings of **karma** and **reincarnation**. They often emphasize the karmic effects of actions in the present lifetime. Another way in which the New Age belief in reincarnation differs from most classical Indian teaching on the subject is that New Agers often believe that people can become aware of past lives through meditation, hypnosis, or past-life regression therapy. Doing so is held to be an important way of resolving present problems.

### Rituals and Lifestyle

Several key practices are shared by many within the New Age movement. **Intentional spirituality** is important to most New Age believers. For some, this means choosing one path and staying with it for a lifetime. For others, it means sampling a variety of spiritual disciplines and combining elements from many into a uniquely personal synthesis. Many draw on Hindu or Buddhist practice. For some Americans, the importance of finding a compatible spiritual path has led to the study and practice of Native American (Indian) spirituality. Whatever path or paths are chosen, the **goals are awareness of the life force and self-development**. The goal of union with the mysterious reality that is both within and beyond can be attained more quickly if an intentional path is taken, rather than leaving it to chance.

The most important religious act is getting in touch with this life force through **meditation** and ritual. People meditate for many reasons and by many specific means. Meditators seek to quiet and focus their minds. Doing so is said to bring a sense of peace and focus to all of life, a kind of heightened awareness and perspective that extends beyond the time spent in meditation, so that it infuses all activities and relationships. Many people believe that it also has significant health benefits. It is a primary way of being in touch with the sacred. It is a way to reenergize and replenish the energy spent in transformation.

There are nearly as many ways to meditate as there are people who meditate. Many people focus on their breathing, counting to a specific number and then starting over, being aware of how their breathing feels. This helps them stay focused on the present. Some may focus on other objects such as a statue of a deity, a candle flame, or a flower. Some use music for a focus. In mantra meditation, a word or phrase is used. By focusing on one thing with complete concentration, distractions are kept to a minimum.

Rituals of many kinds are also important elements of New Age practice. Meditation is itself a ritual. Rituals may be done to celebrate the changing seasons and the phases of the moon. The New Age movement offers the opportunity for people to construct their own rituals to mark events and occasions for which the larger culture does not have rituals or to develop creative, more personalized rituals to be used instead of more common ones. Many individuals develop private rituals for themselves. **Affirmations** seek to replace negative thoughts with positive ones. **Visualization** encourages people to "see" mentally and spiritually the goals they seek, believing that such seeing helps to bring them into being.

**Holistic health** and **alternative healing** are important aspects of the New Age movement. The underlying philosophical and religious assumptions of the movement lead people both to question standard medicine and to seek out alternatives to it. Chiropractic, herbal medicine, traditional systems of healing such as those of China and India, and nutritional approaches to healing are all part of the New Age healing repertoire. So are many kinds of body work and massage, done to benefit body, mind, and spirit. Aromatherapy makes use of the effects attributed to specific scents, and color therapy does the same with color. Healing through the use of crystals is popular with some. As with nearly everything in the New Age movement, there is a wide-ranging pragmatism in its approach to healing—"try it and see if it works." Different things work for different people and in different situations. Nontraditional health-care practitioners treat many New Age followers who are disillusioned by standard Western medicine and want therapies that attend to the entire person, not just the disease, and are usually less invasive. **Complementary medicine** is an approach that combines standard medical approaches with alternative ones.

Many advocates of the New Age try to follow what they describe as a **simple, natural lifestyle**. This means different things to different people but often includes a preference for clothing made from natural fibers such as cotton and wool over synthetics, natural cosmetics and household products, organic food and growing food at home, and limits on participation in America's consumer-based culture.

## Organization

There is **vast diversity** within the New Age movement. Beliefs and, especially, practices range from the serious and thoughtful to the frivolous and mercenary. Prominent New Age author David Spangler helps us distinguish the serious from the less serious. Merchants have discovered that New Age sells and do not hesitate to take advantage of that fact. Most of the publicity surrounding the New Age movement has focused on many highly publicized teachers and adepts, a renewed interest in angels, channelers, and popular self-help books and tapes. The requirement for inclusion at this level seems to be that some glitzy aspect of the movement catches public interest.

Other followers of the New Age movement are genuinely committed to dramatic change in themselves and in their culture. Economics, politics, social institutions, education, and technology are all involved and are all changed to support planetary goals. People with this perspective speak about becoming able to see everything that is as holy, a reintegration of the human with the sacred and with the earth conceived as a living being. In Spangler's words, it is "a deepening into the sacramental nature of everyday life, an awakening of the consciousness that can celebrate divinity within the ordinary and, in this celebration, bring to life a sacred civilization."[3]

A group of **journals and magazines** makes new information available and facilitates communication among New Age believers. Titles include *East/West Journal, Yoga Journal,* and *Body and Soul.*

New Age followers are a diverse group of people for whom an authentic spiritual search has led generally eastward and inward. Their affiliation with the movement varies from being at its center to barely touching its edges. They are among those whose religious needs have not been met in the more usual religions. New Age believers do not meet in church buildings or have an organized hierarchy of leadership. It is a religion, however, in that it provides for its followers the four elements of belief, lifestyle, ritual, and organizations in a way that helps to make life meaningful and good.

The New Age movement is not something wholly alien to American culture. It integrates themes and basic ways of approaching religion that have

---

[3]David Spangler, *Emergence: The Rebirth of the Sacred* (New York: Dell Publishing Company, 1984). Spangler's analysis still seems correct today.

been a part of our culture almost from the beginning. The viewpoints and methods it offers extend beyond the movement to the larger culture, as well.

## The Self-help Movement and Twelve-Step Programs

**Twelve-step programs** such as **Alcoholics Anonymous** are only part of a larger movement that we can call the self-help movement. However, the founding of Alcoholics Anonymous marked the beginning of a new era in self-help movements as well. Its twelve steps to recovery provide the blueprint for many such programs today.

A.A., as it is most commonly known, began in Akron, Ohio, in 1935. It was founded by a layman, William G. Wilson, and a doctor, Robert Smith (usually referred to as "Bill W." and "Dr. Bob," because anonymity is a cornerstone of group procedure). These two men, along with a third individual, began talking together about how to overcome their struggles with alcohol, and the organization was born out of their experience together.

The approach that A.A. takes to recovery from alcoholism is that it is a disease that has physical, mental, and spiritual dimensions. It can be best treated through its spiritual dimension. When alcoholics work on their spiritual lives, physical, and mental recovery will follow as well. This is best done, say A.A. members, in the context of supportive groups of fellow sufferers. The strategy is summarized in the famous Twelve Steps.[4]

> **1.**   *We admitted that we were powerless over alcohol, that our lives had become unmanageable.*
> **2.**   *We came to believe that a power greater than ourselves could restore us to sanity.*
> **3.**   *We made a decision to turn our will and lives over to the care of God as we understood him.*

A.A. regards the admission of one's inability to deal with the problem on one's own as the necessary starting point. It echoes the Christian belief in people's powerlessness apart from God. "As we understood him" is central to the spiritual view of A.A. People do not have to accept a particular belief in God or a Higher Power but are left free to conceptualize their Higher Power as they will. For some, however, this remains a stumbling block, and there have been a few groups formed that follow a similar approach to that of A.A. but without the overtly religious overtones. The largest of these self-consciously secular sobriety groups is S.O.S., or Secular Organizations for Sobriety (also, Save Our Selves).

---

[4]The Twelve Steps are listed in nearly every Alcoholics Anonymous publication. The steps are in italic type. I have added comments to some of them.

Women and black people, especially, have questioned this emphasis on reliance on a Higher Power, feeling that it can reinforce their sense of oppression and powerlessness, which is often part of the problem. They have also asked if it simply substitutes one kind of dependency—albeit perhaps a less destructive one—for another.

**4.**   *We made a searching and fearless moral inventory of ourselves.*
**5.**   *We admitted to God, to ourselves, and to another human being the exact nature of our wrongs.*

These two steps clearly reinforce the distinctive spiritual or religious nature of A.A.'s technique. Self-examination and confession to God and to another person are important dimensions in many religious groups.

**6.**   *We became entirely willing to have God remove our defects of character.*
**7.**   *We humbly asked him to remove our shortcomings.* Willingness to be helped is understood to be a necessary precondition of being helped. Again, this belief is a feature of many religions, as well.
**8.**   *We made a list of all persons we had harmed, and became willing to make amends to them all.*
**9.**   *We made direct amends to such persons whenever possible, except when to do so would injure them or others.* You may remember that the Jewish practice of repentance includes making amends to people who have been wronged. Buddhists, as well, believe that direct amends should be made whenever possible and whenever no further injury will result from doing so. The same is true of some other religions.
**10.**   *We continued to take a daily inventory, and when we were wrong promptly admitted it.* Commitment to consistency and regular, mindful self-examination is also a feature of many religions. It was practiced, for example, by the Puritans who were in the New World from the earliest days of the colonies.
**11.**   *We sought through prayer and meditation to improve our conscious contact with God, praying only for knowledge of his will for us and the power to carry that out.* The spiritual dimension of this step is obvious. It carries forward the theme of surrender of self-will to the will of a higher power.
**12.**   *Having had a spiritual awakening as the result of these steps, we tried to carry this message to alcoholics, and to practice these principles in all our affairs.* Three of the major religions of the world—Christianity, Islam, and Buddhism—are missionary religions, carrying the message of spiritual awakening to other people. "Spreading the Gospel" has been an important feature of Christianity in the United States, as well as elsewhere.

This analysis of the twelve steps clearly delineates the spiritual character of the movement. Like organized religions, twelve-step and other self-help programs offer their followers something from each of the four dimensions of religion. Perhaps the most important belief is that human beings *can* transform their lives. Even when the situation appears hopeless—or most of all *when* it appears hopeless—people have the capacity to make a better life for themselves. Some programs, like A.A., advocate reliance on a power outside oneself. Other programs focus on self-effort. Certainly the reliance on "other power" is more in tune with the predominance of Christianity in this country. Reliance on self-effort, however, echoes a theme as old as the beginning of the United States: the self-reliant frontiersman or frontierswoman setting out to conquer the wilderness. Self-effort and individualism, although not always highlighted in American religion, are significant parts of the larger American cultural story. The importance of "working on oneself" and bettering oneself goes back as far as the Puritans, for whom growth in personal character was a highly prized goal. Taking responsibility for one's actions and their results is also a theme that is written large in both religion and secular culture in the United States.

There is yet another presupposition of the self-help movement that draws on an important feature of American religion. In self-help groups, people are aided in their own efforts by their peers. While a few groups have a professional leader or counselor, many do not. Even in those that do, the professional is there primarily as a facilitator, not as the person whose responsibility it is to fix everything. Democracy in government in the United States has spilled over into many areas of life. We noted that even those communities of faith that are primarily hierarchical in their organization are usually less so in their American embodiments. There is a tendency to see the leaders as leading their congregations in ministry, rather than being the only ones involved in ministry. Many alternative popular spiritual groups are very democratic in their structure. Especially in recent years, trust in professionals has declined, and many people have sought to take a larger role in their religion, health care, education, or automobile repair. Many people no longer think that calling in a professional is the only or the best solution.

Alcoholics Anonymous teaches the importance of changing one's lifestyle if one is to stay sober. Lasting sobriety is not likely to be achieved if recovering alcoholics continue to go to bars, socialize with former drinking buddies, and engage in whatever other behaviors were associated with their drinking. Most self-help groups emphasize changes in lifestyle. The details of these changes depend upon the goal of the particular group, but lifestyle is a focus for nearly all. New habits must replace old, and new rewards must supplant old, negative ones. This reflects the importance that lifestyle and morality in general have for American religion.

The ritual dimension is there as well. Meeting together for mutual support and fellowship is central for the self-help movement. It is customarily believed that the best context for making important changes is a fairly small, supportive group of people who know what each other are going through because they're "all in the same boat." Some groups help people develop rituals to mark important changes of life, recognizing that rituals simply do not exist for many contemporary occasions that nonetheless need rituals. Alcoholics Anonymous groups celebrate the anniversaries of their members' sobriety, for example.

Certainly the organizational dimension is present. Alcoholics Anonymous itself spawned a number of other organizations such as Al-Anon (for families of alcoholics) and Alateen (specifically for teenagers), and, most recently, groups for adult children of alcoholics. Twelve-step groups have been formed to help people recover from other compulsive behaviors, including drug addiction, gambling, overeating, uncontrolled spending, and spouse and child abuse. These organizations have then developed groups for spouses and other family members of the recovering person.

A nearly limitless number of other kinds of support groups have formed, all based on the premise that the best support in a crisis comes from other people who have been through similar experiences. Some direct all their energies toward helping the people involved. Weight Watchers is one example. There are also support groups for people with cancer (and for their families and friends), and those who are divorcing, chronically ill, or in chronic pain. Your campus may have a variety of support groups for students, such as a group for students who suffer test anxiety.

Other support groups have also developed a "political" dimension that complements their supportive function. Mothers Against Drunk Driving (MADD) began as a support group for parents whose child had been killed or injured in an alcohol-related accident. They soon began working actively to reduce the number of such accidents. Support groups for people who are HIV-positive or who have AIDS (and their families and friends) often undertake political activity on behalf of affected people.

As we have seen, the self-help movement, exemplified by Alcoholics Anonymous and other similar groups, is clearly a spiritual movement. For some people, it is an adjunct to participation in a community of faith. For others, it is a substitute for such participation. The specific format, and certainly the proliferation of these groups, is relatively new on the American scene. On the other hand, as we have seen, some of the themes and presuppositions are as old as the United States itself.

## FEMINIST SPIRITUALITIES

Most—although not all—of the religious groups and organizations in the United States share at least some of the patriarchal viewpoints and practices that continue to mark American culture in general. This has created concern for many women in these communities of faith. We can describe the responses that women make to this situation in terms of a continuum. At one end are those many women for whom traditional structures, views, and rituals are meaningful and fulfilling. Survey data strongly indicate that women are more traditionally religious than are men. Many women, perhaps the majority, are not disturbed by references to God as "He" and to humanity as "man." These women can and do remain within their traditional communities of faith and find meaning there, without seeking or desiring change.

Most women choose to stay in their communities of faith, either accepting things as they are or working actively to change the things with which they disagree. But some women choose not to remain in their churches, temples, or synagogues and found or join groups specifically based on women's spirituality. This is the response that I will focus on in this section. More specifically, I want to look at **goddess worship** and the **Wiccan** tradition as it relates to feminist spirituality.

Women and men who consider themselves to be followers of the types of religion described in this section also do not agree completely on how the religion should be named. Some prefer *Wicca* (practitioners are *Wiccans*), a word meaning "Wise Ones." It has the same root as our word "wisdom." Some of its advocates believe that using this less familiar word helps overcome the negative connotations often associated with the word "witch." Others deliberately use *Witchcraft* and *Witch* in a bold move to reclaim the word from its detractors. Others prefer *the Craft*, with its emphasis on the ritual work that Wiccans do. For still others, *the old religion* signifies the ancient roots of this worldview. I will use these terms interchangeably.

Attempts to develop an agreed-upon statement of Wiccan belief have fallen far short of universal acceptance among actual Wiccans. Decentralization and the autonomy of individuals and groups is a primary organizing principle. However, it is possible to describe certain basic beliefs that are widely shared among Wiccans. In a similar fashion, I will describe common ritual practices.

Wicca is one form of a larger worldview, that of **magick**. When used this way, magick is spelled with a *k* to distinguish it from stage magic. Sybil Leek, a contemporary American witch, defines magick as "the art of producing a desired effect or result through the use of various techniques such as incantations and presumably assuring human control of supernatural agencies or the forces of nature."[5] Ritual is the primary tool for working with these forces. In a nation in love with technology (although perhaps less enamored of its promises than we once were), Witchcraft offers a "spiritual technology" with which to interact with unseen forces. At the same time, it runs against the primary grain of American thought about the divine. The Judeo-Christian tradition that has had the greatest influence on American religious ideas emphasizes that God cannot be manipulated nor controlled by human beings.

Most Wicca in the United States traces its roots back to British author and lecturer Gerald B. Gardner (1884–1964) and therefore it is called "Gardnerian Wicca." Although there are various accounts of exactly how Gardner developed his religious thought and practice, it blended together elements from Western occult and magickal traditions with various pieces of Eastern religions that he picked up while living in India and Southeast Asia. The Gardnerian tradition came to the United States with Raymond and Rosemary Buckland in the mid-1960s. The Bucklands formed a coven on Long Island, and Gardnerian thought and practice spread from there. Although there are

[5]Sybil Leek, *Diary of a Witch* (Englewood Cliffs, NJ: Prentice Hall, 1968), p. 4.

many variations within the American Wiccan community, most of them retain at least the outlines of Gardner's world view and ritual. Among the most closely related schools is the Alexandrian, formed by Alexander Sanders (1926–1988).

One indication of the evolution of the Wiccan movement in the United States is that the well-known Wiccan practitioner and author Starhawk (Miriam Samos) has written a book titled *Circle Round: Raising Children in Goddess Traditions.*[6] What this indicates is that Wicca in the United States is no longer just a movement of converts, of first-generation practitioners, but that a need has developed to address the issue of raising up the next generations.

## Beliefs

The way in which the sacred or holy is thought about and spoken about, addressed in prayer and celebration, is one of the most central beliefs in any religion. Instead of the traditional habit of thinking and speaking of God in the Judeo-Christian-Islamic tradition as if God were male, some women have turned to belief in and worship of the goddess instead. **Goddess worshipers believe in a female creator, often paired with a god as the male principle.** Followers of the goddess look back to religions that predate Judaism and Christianity, in which the goddess was very important. Worshiping both a god and a goddess, with the emphasis placed on the goddess, restores a balanced view of ultimate reality or the holy for her followers, in ways that simply altering traditional language cannot. Not all followers of the goddess are Wiccans, but virtually all Wiccans are worshipers of the goddess. For followers of the goddess, she provides a strong affirmation of the female in a way they do not find elsewhere.

One practicing Wiccan woman puts it this way: Images of deity as goddess "inspire us to see ourselves as divine, our bodies as healthy, the changing phases of our lives as holy, our anger as purifying, and our power to nurture and create, but also to limit and destroy when necessary, as the very force that sustains all life."[7]

For many goddess worshipers, **the goddess is a way to the recognition and celebration of the divinity within themselves.** They experience the entire world as one divine whole and see themselves as a part of it. To address and celebrate the goddess is but a step on the way to "reclaiming [their] own divinity as part of the vastness of the natural world."[8]

Wiccans usually worship the Goddess in her threefold form, sometimes referred to as the **Triple Goddess.** She is **maiden**, **mother**, and **crone**, signifying the various ages of woman. She is frequently symbolized by the phases of

[6]Starhawk, Anne Hill, and Diane Baker. *Circle Round: Raising Children in Goddess Traditions* (New York: Bantam Doubleday Dell, 1998).

[7]Starhawk (Miriam Samos), *The Spiral Dance: A Rebirth of the Ancient Religion of the Great Goddess* (San Francisco: Harper & Row, Publishers, 1979), p. 8.

[8]Hallie Inglehart, *Womanspirit: A Guide to Women's Wisdom* (San Francisco: Harper & Row, Publishers, 1983), p. 97.

the moon—the waxing or rising crescent, the full moon, and the waning or subsiding moon. Wiccans draw on the goddess traditions of many times and cultures, believing that all the names of the goddess are equally valid. Most also worship her consort, *Pan* or the *horned god* of the fields. He, likewise, has had many names in many times and places.

Wiccans also **affirm the divinity and holiness of all living beings and of the earth itself** (or, as many would put it, herself). They experience the sacred in the changing seasons and in the constant rhythms of life. All aspects of the cycle of life and death are sacred.

Witches believe that people, because we are conscious and have freedom of choice, have a unique responsibility toward the environment. It is up to people to live a lifestyle that reflects respect for earth and to live in harmony with nature. Often, earth is revered as a manifestation of the Goddess.

**Witches do not worship Satan or the Christian devil**. The beginnings of Wicca predate Christianity, while Satanism relies on the development of the idea of Satan within the Christian tradition. Although they are often carelessly lumped together, there is no relationship between them aside from the underlying magickal worldview they share.

Nor do witches try to put evil spells and curses or hexes on people. Such behavior is always considered unethical. **Self-determination, personal freedom**, and **autonomy** are central values in Wiccan ethics and morality. Most witches feel that it is unethical even to work a spell for someone's benefit without their knowledge and agreement. There are two basic principles that guide behavior. One is the "Wiccan Rede," *An ye harm none, do what ye will. An* is an ancient use of the word that means "as long as." The second is the principle that what people do returns to them. Many put this in terms of the *Threefold Law*: Whatever we do returns to us three times over, be it good or ill.

### Practices

Witches often organize into **covens or small groups** of three to twenty people to perform rituals and enjoy fellowship. There are also solitaries, witches who, through personal choice or circumstances, practice alone. Some covens are all female (and a few are all male), and some are mixed. Although there are traditional rituals that have been handed down, most feel very free to improvise and create new rituals as occasions call for them.

**Casting a circle** is a fundamental ritual. The circle thus marked off becomes a sacred space. Wherever it is, indoors or out, city or farm, it becomes a place in which the sacred can be contacted and interacted with. Ritual purification of the circle removes negative energy from it, protects those within it, and helps to concentrate their own spiritual energies on the task at hand. This is most often done using the traditional elements of air, earth, fire, and water. Often, gods and goddesses are called upon to be present alongside the human participants.

The circle having been cast and purified, participants often **raise a cone of power**. This is done by chanting or dancing (or both) or running around the circle. The cone of power represents and taps the power of the combined wills of the group, intensified and focused through ritual and meditative techniques.

The focus can be any of a number of things. **Healing**, both physical and emotional, is a common focus. Healing can be directed toward individuals (within the circle or outside it), groups, or the earth itself. Sometimes the focus is simply to raise positive energy. Coven work often centers around directing positive energy toward the goals of the members and others—be it finding a job, a love relationship, overcoming a crisis, or simply living with grace and joy in everyday life. This type of work is done in **esbats**, coven meetings that are held traditionally at the time of the full and new moons, although they may be held at other times as well. Some covens, for example, meet weekly. The ritual work is most often followed by sharing a meal or at least refreshments and a time of fellowship.

There is also a series of **seasonal festivals or Sabbats** that reflect the natural cycle of the seasons and the positions of the sun and earth relative to each other. There are **four Great Sabbats**: (1) *Samhain* or the Celtic New Year on October 31; (2) *Candlemas* on February 2, a winter festival that focuses on purification and the beginning of spring; (3) *Beltane*, May 1, the great spring festival of fertility and renewal symbolized by the marriage of the god and goddess; and (4) *Lughnasadh* (in some accounts, *Lammas*), the August 1 festival of the first fruits of harvest that also looks toward the seasonal decline of winter. Four Lesser Sabbats celebrate the summer and winter solstices (June and December) and the spring and fall equinoxes (March and September).

**Initiation** is an important ritual for individual witches. Although some witches believe that a person must be initiated by another witch, others support self-initiation, especially if the opportunity for initiation by a practicing witch is not available. However it is carried out, it is a rite of beginning, of accepting and celebrating one's status, and of becoming a part of the Wiccan community of faith and agreeing to live by its norms.

## Organizations

Most Wiccan covens are small, and there is no central organization. Those that I describe here are intended to be examples of some of the better-known ones. The **Church and School of Wicca** in New Bern, North Carolina, is one of the most accessible of the witchcraft groups. Its members have campaigned energetically to promote what they believe is a correct understanding of the meaning of the craft and to help overcome centuries of prejudice and misunderstanding. In 1972, it became the first Wiccan group to be granted federal tax-exempt status as a religious organization.

The **Church of Circle Wicca** is "a synthesis of Wiccan spirituality, nature mysticism, multicultural shamanism, and humanist and transpersonal psychology."[9] Like the Church and School of Wicca, it has maintained a much higher public profile than have most Wiccan groups. It is believed to be the largest network for such groups, and its Circle Sanctuary is the site of many intergroup conferences and celebrations.

The **Covenant of Unitarian Universalist Pagans** (CUUPS) is a network of pagan- and Wiccan-identified Unitarian Universalists. It is formally acknowledged and supported by the denomination, which also lists "earth-centered spirituality" among its sources of belief and practice. CUUPS is the first such recognition of the goddess tradition within a mainstream American denomination.

What are we to make of Wicca? What does it offer its adherents? It seems to me that there are several things. (1) As a part of the magickal tradition, it offers people techniques for dealing with the mystery of the divine in constructive ways that people believe allow them to benefit from sacred forces. (2) It offers an alternative to the patriarchalism of the prevailing Western and most Eastern religions. (3) It teaches the immanence of the divine in all things and thus seems to many to be more "earth-friendly" than the monotheistic religions. Its seasonally based ritual calendar gives people ways to celebrate their closeness to the natural world. (4) Similarly, its emphasis on the sacred within every person suggests new ways of understanding what it is to be a human being. (5) For many women, Wicca provides a way to affirm and celebrate being a woman in a culture that has not always valued women as highly as men.

### THE UNIVERSAL FELLOWSHIP OF METROPOLITAN COMMUNITY CHURCHES

The Universal Fellowship of Metropolitan Community Churches is a Christian community of faith for "lesbian, gay, bisexual, and transgendered" persons. Homosexuality has been and continues to be thought of as sinful by a significant proportion of Christian churches. As a result, gays, lesbians, and transgendered people have often felt unwelcome in these churches. They have been unable to find a welcoming community for their spirituality. The Universal Fellowship of Metropolitan Community Churches provides such a place, and gives people a way to openly affirm both their Christianity and their sexual orientation.[10] The founder and moderator of the Universal Fellowship of Metropolitan Community Churches is Troy Perry, author of *The Lord Is My Shepherd and He Knows I'm Gay*.[11]

Within the context of the mainstream Christian tradition as far as belief and worship are concerned, the Fellowship teaches that God's promises of

[9]J. Gordon Melton, Ed., *Encyclopedia of American Religions, 7th Edition* (Detroit: The Gale Group, Inc., 2003), p. 913.
[10]Fellowship of Metropolitan Community Churches World Wide Web site, www.ufmcc.com.
[11]Troy D. Perry, *The Lord Is My Shepherd and He Knows I'm Gay* (Kalamazoo, MI: Steven J. Nash Publishing, 1972).

salvation and fellowship are offered to all persons, without regard for sexual orientation. Homosexuality is regarded as neither a sin nor an illness, but as something natural and God-given that neither can nor should be changed. As God creates some people heterosexual, others are created homosexual. The Bible does not condemn "loving, responsible homosexual relationships," and therefore these relationships should be encouraged, affirmed, and celebrated.

The Fellowship is the largest and probably the most widely known religious organization for gays, lesbians, and transgendered persons. It is not the only one. There is also a Gay Buddhist Fellowship, an organization of Gay and Lesbian Atheists and Humanists (GALAH), and a National Gay Pentecostal Alliance.

## RELIGION ON THE INTERNET

We have already seen that many religious groups have pages or sites on the World Wide Web. Religious organizations have found the Web a useful place on which to present their views to others and to keep their own constituencies informed. Individuals motivated by religious concerns maintain sites and pages to present their views.

When I use the term *religion on the Internet* I have something else in mind. There are manifestations of religion that have developed specifically on and for the Internet or World Wide Web. This section provides a description of some of them, with URLs. To explore this dimension of religion further on your own, a good place to begin is Yahoo's category "Cyberculture Religion." [12]

In February, 1998, three Tibetan Buddhist monks at the Namgyal Monastery in New York State prayed for a half-hour, conducting a formal Buddhist blessing of cyberspace:

> In the monks' view, cyberspace resembles space in general, which Tibetan Buddhists characterize more as the absence of obstructions than as a distance between two points. . . . Where there is an absence of obstructions, there is the potential for something to arise, the nature of which depends on the motivation of those who use it. In blessing cyberspace, the monks reasoned, they could offer prayers that the motivation of Internet users become more positive and that the benefits of using the Internet become more positive. [13]

The monks chanted a traditional Buddhist prayer for the welfare of all, in the hope that the positive potentials of cyberspace would develop in such a way that they would outweigh the negative ones.

There are a number of "virtual congregations" on the Web, existing only in cyberspace. One example is **The First Church of Cyberspace**, founded by

[12]http://dir.yahoo.com/Society_and_Culture/Cultures_and_Groups/Cyberculture/Religion (Remember that URLs are often case-sensitive.)

[13]This rationale for the blessing, along with an audio clip of the blessing itself, came from the Web site of the Namgyal Monastery in New York, www.namgyal.org. It is no longer available on the site.

a Presbyterian minister.[14] It offers a sanctuary (sermons, music, prayers), movie reviews, bulletin boards, galleries, and discussions of contemporary issues, among other things. You can listen to Bach's "Jesu, Joy of Man's Desiring," a classical Christian composition, by clicking on an audio icon. The **First International Church of the Web**[15] is conservative, evangelical Christian. Its founder, Rev. Dr. David M. Ford, also founded the **International Alliance of Web-Based Churches**.[16]

Unlike "bricks and mortar" religion in the United States, which is increasingly diverse, Internet-based churches seem to have become predominantly Christian since the previous edition of this book. The Shin Buddhist White Path Temple and the Jewish Havienu L'Shalom, for example, no longer exist.

A serious attempt at creating an internet religion, although with an unlikely name, is the **Church of Virus**.

> It is an atheistic religion with a scientific emphasis. It intends to provide people with a "conceptual framework for leading a truly meaningful life and attaining immortality" without reference to anything supernatural. Its founders chose the name "Church of Virus" because the word "virus" has such a negative connotation, particularly among computer users acquainted with the havoc that computer viruses can cause. It was chosen to "deliberately antagonize" people and to warn people that it might "infect" them with the truth.[17]

Another manifestation of religion on the Internet is the inclusion of methods to ask questions on some religious organization sites. The Zen Mountain Monastery, for example, features CyberMonk, a means whereby visitors to the site can e-mail questions to the monastery.[18]

What are we to make of religion in cyberspace? It would seem to be very difficult to replicate some of the features of "real world" religion in virtual religion. There is communication, to be sure, some of it very personal, in cyberspace. However, it is not face-to-face. People and groups can easily deceive others about their identity when the only connection is through words on a computer monitor. Accountability is seriously lacking, or wholly absent. Despite the development of emoticons to indicate emotions, these fall far short of a real human hug or smile. A "virtual congregation" cannot come sit with you while your partner or child has surgery.

One of the things that is most often used as a marker for something being religious is the presence of ritual. In spite of some few attempts, ritual has shown itself to be hard to do in cyberspace. So much of ritual is about embodiment—about bread and wine as the body and blood of Jesus in the

---

[14]The First Church of Cyberspace, www.godweb.org.
[15]First International Church of the Web, http://ficotw.org.
[16]First International Church of the Web, http://ficotw.org/alliance.html.
[17]Church of Virus, http://virus.lucifer.com/about.html.
[18]The Mountains and Rivers Order of Zen Buddhism, www.zen-mtn.org.

Christian Eucharist, for example, or about offerings of flowers or fruit or rice. And virtual reality is very much *dis*embodied reality.

That having been said, if virtual religion seems to be a questionable matter at this time, the role of the Internet—the Web, bulletin boards, chat rooms, newsgroups—in providing a forum for people to share their religious views, to advocate for their particular community of faith, to learn about religions other than their own, to find support among those with similar views has become an important part of religion in the United States.

## SATANISM

Students are often curious about **Satanism**. We can distinguish between two types of Satanism. Anton LaVey (1930–1997) founded the Church of Satan in 1966. He collected standard occult and magickal teachings around the motif of the worship of Satan. Secrecy is part and parcel of this perspective. It is a defense against hostility and misunderstanding, as well as against curious people who might become involved for shallow reasons (e.g., the chance to participate in an orgy). More important, Satanists feel their rituals are very powerful tools that would be dangerous in the hands of most people.

The Church of Satan teaches that those things that Christianity has usually condemned as sins (such as pleasure seeking, vengeance, and pride) are actually virtues. Logically, the Church of Satan is dependent on Christianity; it is a reaction to it. LaVey's teachings are contained in three books: *The Satanic Bible* (1969), The Compleat Witch (1970), and *The Satanic Rituals* (1972). A list of Nine Satanic Statements at the beginning of *The Satanic Bible* summarizes LaVey's teachings:

1. Satan means indulgence, not abstinence.
2. Satan means living fully now, not vague spiritual aspirations for a future life.
3. Satan means self-knowledge, not hypocrisy and self-deceit.
4. Satan stands for kindness to those who deserve it, not love for the unworthy.
5. Satan stands for vengeance, not forgiveness.
6. Satan means responsibility for those who are responsible, not misplaced concern for "psychic vampires."
7. Satanism teaches that humans are simply animals, animals whose intellectual and spiritual development can make them more vicious than the other animals.
8. Satan encourages gratification of physical and mental desires.
9. "Satan has been the best friend the church has ever had, as he has kept it in business all these years!"[19]

The Church of Satan, in other words, encourages individuals to seek the greatest gratification of their desires and feel free to practice "selfish virtues." The followers of Satan developed a religious framework for a pleasure-seeking life, without violating laws. For the most part, they maintain a very low profile in society. The shock value of something that calls itself Satanism has

[19]Church of Satan Web site, www.churchofsatan.com/Pages/NineStatemts.html

made its members the target of persecution. At the same time, it has been an ideal vehicle for those who wish to rebel against the predominant culture. (Remember that one of the characteristics attributed to Satan is that he is the arch-rebel.) Although membership figures are not made public and members are often understandably reluctant to reveal their affiliation, membership in the Church of Satan is not widespread.

The individual's birthday is the most important holiday celebrated. Walpurgisnacht (April 30) marks the rebirth of nature in the spring, and Halloween is celebrated as well. Various other magickal and celebratory rituals round out the ritual calendar. In line with its orientation to magick, ritual is the central focus of Satanism in any of its forms.

The second form of Satanism consists of ritual magick groups. These small and loosely organized groups believe that people can use the power attributed to Satan to enhance their own power.

Participating in these groups is often a way that their members act out psychological and emotional disturbances. It is important to distinguish cause and effect here. One model depicts Satanism itself as leading to violent, criminal, and antisocial behavior. Another, more accurate model, posits a prior cause—anger and rage, alienation, social maladaptation—that leads both to membership in a Satanic group and to the violent, criminal, and antisocial behavior.

It is important to put concern about Satanism in perspective. The presence of Satanic symbols and motifs in the youth culture, especially in music, the fantasy game *Dungeons and Dragons* along with similar games, and the high-profile accounts of evangelical Christians describing their former involvement with Satanism may make it seem as if there are far more Satanists than can actually be documented. Mainstream author J. Gordon Melton notes that

> in spite of attempts to locate Satanist groups by law enforcement officials and widespread attention focused by anti-Satanist groups, direct evidence of any significant new growth of Satanism has yet to be produced and much counter evidence has surfaced. Many of the claims of ritual abuse of children and even the stories of some evangelical Christian converts have proved unfounded and/or based on hoax.[20]

## CHRISTIAN IDENTITY

The term **Christian Identity** has two meanings. (1) Its earlier meaning refers to Anglo-Israelism or British-Isrealism, the belief that white Anglo-Saxons, Germanic peoples, Scandinavians, Celts, and similar cultures are the true descendants of the biblical Israel. Americans and Canadians who are descendants of these groups are a part of this true Israel as well. (2) The meaning that is more commonly used in the United States refers to a number of faith groups whose members accept British-Isrealism and combine it with beliefs

[20]Melton, Encyclopedia of Religions in America, p. 179.

that are intensely homophobic, racist, sexist, and anti-Communist. These very conservative and fundamentalist Christians believe Jews are descended from Satan. They usually oppose equal rights for homosexuals, gun control and any control over militia movements.[21]

There is no national structure to the movement. It is more a collection of independent groups united by their loathing of all persons of non–northern European descent, homophobia, embrace of paramilitary activity, and their belief that the present age will soon end in a cataclysmic battle which will result in their victory as God's "elect."

Many Americans feel threatened by the problems that confront us all: inadequate health care funding, AIDS, terrorism at home and abroad, economic problems, unemployment and underemployment, homelessness, and discipline problems among youth, to name but a few. In this situation, it is easy to look for a scapegoat. Christian Identity focuses this scapegoating and gives it a violent edge, at the same time assuring its followers that they are the only ones who are truly doing God's will.

The movement has been criticized on several grounds. Biblical scholars point out that its theology cannot be supported from any evidence. More pointed criticism has been directed against the racial views and policies of its constituent groups. Because the movement's theology inherently contains the potential for violence, its activities are closely monitored in areas where groups exist. Some members have been indicted on charges ranging from murder to burglary and conspiracy, with some convictions resulting from the charges.

### THE WAY, FAITH ASSEMBLY, AND THE UNIFICATION CHURCH

The following three religions are important examples of less controversial non-mainstream religions. **The Way, International**, was founded in 1942 by a former Evangelical and Reformed Church (now a part of the United Church of Christ) minister, Victor Paul Wierwille (1916–1985). He gave the organization its present name in 1974. The Way is quite active on some college campuses. The group's beliefs are stated in the language of traditional Christianity. While these beliefs agree with those of more traditional Christians on many points, some are distinctively different.

1. The Old and New Testaments are held to be inspired by God and perfect as originally given. The various books are said to pertain to different periods in God's relationship with humankind. The Way uses its own translation of the Bible and emphasizes the books of Ephesians, Colossians, Philippians, and Galatians.
2. Belief in God, Jesus, and the Holy Spirit is affirmed, but Jesus is not believed to be God and is not considered divine. The Spirit is the power of God and is impersonal, rather than personal.

---

[21]Ontario Consultants on Religious Tolerance Web site, www.religioustolerance.org.

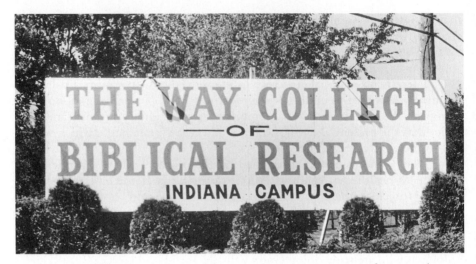

**Figure 13-1**    The Way, International, has an extensive training program for its members. *(Photo by the author)*

3. The Way is Pentecostal, believing in the gifts of the Holy Spirit, such as speaking in tongues, healing, and prophecy.
4. They believe in one baptism, that of the Holy Spirit, and reject water baptism.
5. The organization of The Way reflects the way in which they believe that the earliest Christian church was organized.

The Way has often been the target of deprogrammers when parents have charged that their daughters and sons were being held by the group against the children's will. It has also been criticized for its financial policies, and in 1985 its tax-exempt status was revoked by the Internal Revenue Service. The revocation was overturned by the Supreme Court in 1990.

**Faith Assembly** was founded near Warsaw, Indiana, by Hobart Freeman. Its headquarters are now in Wilmot, Indiana. There are now Faith Assembly branches in all forty-eight connecting states and at least six foreign countries. Freeman, a former professor at Grace Theological Seminary, had begun collecting a group of devoted followers around him even before he lost his teaching position because his views were no longer acceptable to his colleagues and his church. He then devoted all his time to developing the point of view that he had begun to believe while at Grace and to gathering an even larger band of followers.

The new church existed for some time without attracting much public attention. Then a public health nurse noticed that the infant mortality rate and the death rate for women in childbirth were much higher for Faith Assembly members than for the population at large. The investigation that followed thrust the Faith Assembly into the public eye. Controversy followed as newspapers, especially the Fort Wayne *News-Sentinel*, published reports of more deaths, along with rigid control over members by Freeman and a "Gestapo-like" mentality within the leadership ranks. The unsolved murders of an editor of the *News-Sentinel* and his family added to the controversy.

Freeman taught the complete avoidance of all conventional medical care and reliance upon prayer to Jesus for all healing. He told those who listened to him that if they died, or if their children died, it was because their faith was deficient. Adequate faith, coupled with the positive confession of that faith, guaranteed results. One of Freeman's own daughters and her husband left the group after their baby died. Freeman himself died in 1986, and leadership passed to the remaining son-in-law. Under his leadership, the group's views moderated somewhat. While they continue to teach and practice reliance on religious healing, they became less opposed to medical care, especially for children. In part, this came about because the deaths of children led to several court cases and a number of convictions on charges ranging from child neglect or abuse to manslaughter.

The charges and convictions arising from Faith Assembly cases raise the thorny question of the relationship between religious belief and practice in a nation that declares itself to be on the side of religious freedom. The courts have held that if an adult wishes to abstain from traditional medical care for religious reasons, that is not the concern of the government. It has become clear in the Faith Assembly cases that it *is* appropriately the government's concern when minor children are deprived of medical care that could have saved their lives. In these instances, the state has charged, and the courts have agreed, that the state does have a compelling interest in protecting the lives of helpless children, an interest that overrides the parents' freedom of religion.

The **Unification Church** is a Korean Christian church that has worked very hard at attaining greater acceptance in American culture. The Unification Church (also known as the Holy Spirit Association for the Unification of World Christianity) was organized in 1954 by the Korean Sun Myung Moon ("Shining Sun and Moon"). Its members are frequently called Moonies, a derogatory term. According to Unification Church teaching, Adam and Eve were created by God, sinless, and could therefore have been the parents of a perfect human race. However, as the story in Genesis portrays it, Eve was led astray by the devil (in the form of the snake) and then led Adam astray also. Thus, sin and death came into the world.

Seeking to restore humanity to fellowship with God, God sent Jesus as the Messiah, the savior. Jesus was not able to complete his mission and bring about salvation that was both physical and spiritual, however. According to the Christian Bible, Jesus did not marry and thus could not provide the foundation for the beginning of a new and perfected humanity. Another messiah was needed. This messiah must be male, to reflect God's masculine nature, and must marry a wife who reflects God's feminine nature; together they will produce the children that will be the beginning of the perfected race. The key role of perfected, sinless families in bringing about a restored world order is the reason for the mass weddings for which Moon became famous.

The key sacred text for Unification theology is *Divine Principle*. It is an interpretation of the Christian Bible that is said to clarify the divine principle that Unification followers believe the Bible contains. All of the group's teachings are drawn from this book and others that enlarge upon its principles.

The church carries out a complex program of activities in the United States. Many of its organizations take different names. Some of these are the International Cultural Foundation, the Conference on the Unity of the Sciences, Professors World Peace Academy, Washington Institute for Values in Public Policy, National Council for the Church and Social Action (CAUSA, an anti-communist group), Paragon Press, Rose of Sharon Press, and CARP (Collegiate Association for the Research of Principle, its college evangelism branch). National headquarters are now in New York City. There are about 5,000 members in the United States, with more in Japan and Korea.

Moon spent thirteen months in prison for tax evasion in 1984–1985. While this event hindered the group's quest for acceptance, it should be noted that many organizations and individuals within the framework of consensus religion came to Moon's defense, on the basis that the government's interference in the internal affairs of any religious group was a threat to all religious groups.

It is still too early to determine if the Unification Church's bid for greater acceptance will be successful. Its American followers have a clean-cut "all-American" quality about them that will certainly help their search for a place in the mainstream. The church's outspoken support for causes such as the antiabortion movement, anticommunism, and government noninterference in church-operated schools has lessened antagonism from conservative Christians, to whom these issues are very important. Many of their leaders have been trained in theology at some of our leading graduate schools of religion. (Two were my graduate school classmates at Vanderbilt.) Their conferences are instrumental in bringing together scholars from many areas. The church's beliefs differ considerably from the average, as do some of their practices. Yet they have had at least limited initial success in forging links with other religious groups. They may move into a position in society parallel to that occupied by the Latter-day Saints. They will be accepted or tolerated by the mainstream without actually being admitted as a part of it.

Religions outside the mainstream have been a part of the religious scene in the United States almost since its beginning. They will continue to be present, probably in increasing diversity. In this situation, it seems important to maintain a balance between naive, uncritical acceptance of everything that wears the label *religion*, and unreflective negative reaction to everything that appears to be *unconventional* religion.

### QUESTIONS AND ACTIVITIES FOR REVIEW, DISCUSSION, AND WRITING

1. If there is a New Age bookstore in your community, visit it and note the types of literature, music, and other items that are available. If you can, speak with the owner, manager, or someone who works there about their clientele and the purpose that they believe the store serves.
2. What might be some advantages of overcoming the dualistic ways in which we usually think about ourselves and the world? What might be the disadvantages?
3. If you have been a part of a twelve-step or self-help group, reflect on the extent to which it was based on spiritual presuppositions or had a spiritual impact on you.
4. If you can locate one in your community, attend a Wiccan ritual or meeting. Write an essay on what you observe and how you respond to it. If this is not possible, try to find a Wiccan who is willing to come and speak to your class.
5. What effect do you think that ritual observance of the changing seasons and phases of the moon would have on you?
6. Briefly identify in your own words each of the following faith groups discussed in this chapter: the New Age movement, self-help movement, twelve-step movement, Wicca, Universal Fellowship of Metropolitan Community Churches, Internet religion, Satanism, Christian Identity, the Way, Faith Assembly, the Unification Church.

### FOR FURTHER READING

ANDERSON, SHERRY RUTH, and PATRICIA HOPKINS, *The Feminine Face of God: The Unfolding of the Sacred in Women*. New York: Bantam Books, 1991. Based heavily on interviews with "spiritually mature women in our time and culture" who describe "the unfolding of the sacred in their lives in their own words, in the language of their own hearts," this book includes minimal commentary with a focus on the process rather than the result. It's a good read.

BRASHER, BRENDA. *Give Me That Online Religion*. San Francisco: Jossey-Bass, 2001. The author's explorations in cyberspace have revealed over a million online religion sites. The book introduces the phenomenon of online religion and locates it within modern culture.

HARDMAN, CHARLOTTE, and GRAHAM HARVEY, Eds., *Paganism Today: Wiccans, Druids, and the Goddess: Ancient Earth Traditions for the 21st Century*. San Francisco: HarperSanFrancisco, 1996. Hardman and Harvey describe the history of the pagan movement, including Wicca and explores its many facets.

LEWIS, JAMES R., and J. GORDON MELTON, eds. *Perspectives on the New Age*. Albany, NY: State University of New York Press, 1992. This book begins with a thorough historical overview that relates the present movement to its historical predecessors and covers various aspects of the movement. It includes essays on the New Age in several foreign countries.

*Nova Religio: The Journal of Alternative and Emergent Religions*. This journal, published by Seven Bridges Press, LLC, began publication in the fall of 1997. It is devoted solely to the examination of new religious movements from a variety of academic perspectives. Its cross-cultural and interdisciplinary approach makes it highly recommended.

### RELEVANT WORLD WIDE WEB SITES

*Body and Soul, the Natural Guide to Mindful Living* (magazine): www.bodyandsoulmag.com

*Yoga Journal*: www.yogajournal.com

Alcoholics Anonymous: www.alcoholics-anonymous.org

Covenant of the Goddess: www.cog.org

The Witches' Voice: www.witchvox.com

Pentacle: Pagans 12 Step CyberMeeting: http://members.aol.com/JehanaS/recovery.html

Universal Fellowship of Metropolitan Community Churches: www.ufmcc.com

Satanism 101: www.satanism101.com

Kingdom Identity Ministries: www.kingidentity.com

The Way: http://theway.com

Unification Church: www.unification.org

# NEIGHBORS, NOT STRANGERS

I hope that this book has left you with a continuing interest in religion in the United States. Knowing our neighbors, religiously speaking, does not guarantee our appreciation of them. However, living in ignorance may well guarantee, or at least substantially contribute to, intolerance and lack of acceptance. Ignorance allows prejudice, preconceptions, and misunderstanding free rein. Strangers may easily become enemies. *We must continue becoming a community of neighbors, not strangers.* In the kind of world we live in today, we simply cannot afford the corrosive poisons of hatred, fear, and suspicion.

*Neighbors* are people who are part of the same *community*. It is no accident that the words *community* and *communicate* stem from the same root. Neighbors are those who can and do communicate with each other. Communication in the community of neighbors must be based on several things. There must be the *willingness* to communicate—to share ideas, beliefs, and feelings openly. There must be *openness* to receive what is shared. This requires an open space, as it were, free of prejudice and preconceptions. There must be *accurate information*, in order for communication to be meaningful. And, there must be *difference*. The community of neighbors is not based on uniformity. It is based on respect for difference. It cannot be based on an attitude of weighing differences to see who is right and who is wrong. People in the community of neighbors, although committed to their own communities of faith and the values they uphold, are also committed to the larger endeavor of understanding and appreciation, not to judgment.

The idea of treating others as we ourselves wish to be treated (which is affirmed in all of the major religions of the world and by humanists as well), *if actually lived out*, would go a long way toward bringing about a climate in which strangers can become neighbors.